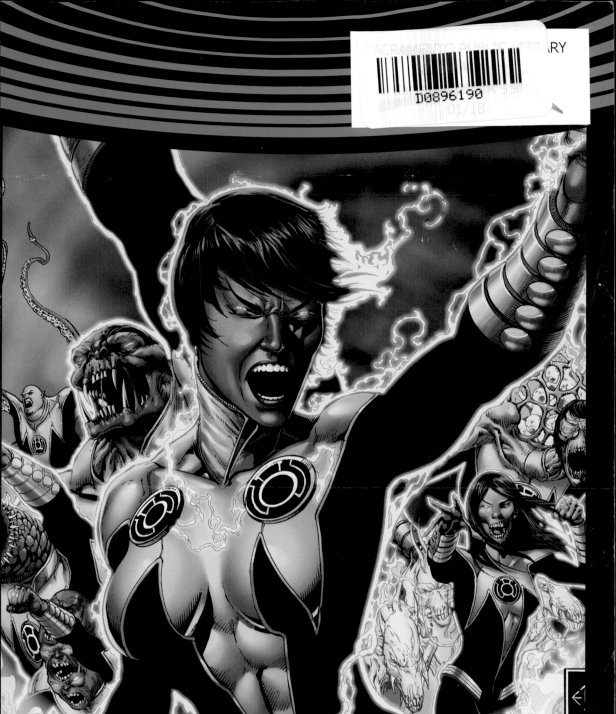

HAL JORDAN AND THE GREEN LANTERN CORPS
VOL.4 FRACTURE

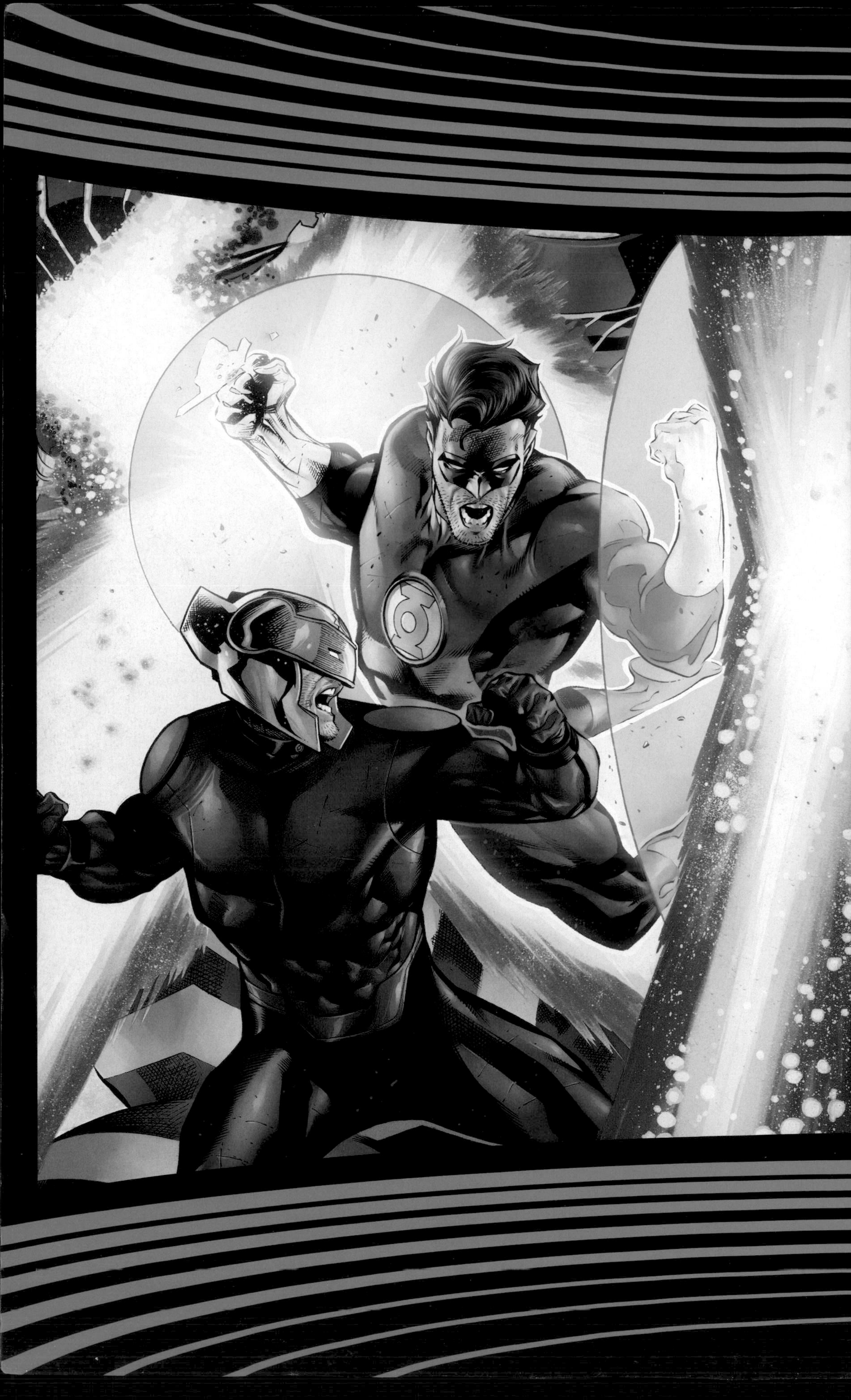

HAL JORDAN AND THE GREEN LANTERN CORPS
VOL.4 FRACTURE

ROBERT VENDITTI
writer

ETHAN VAN SCIVER * **RAFA SANDOVAL** * **JORDI TARRAGONA**
artists

JASON WRIGHT * **TOMEU MOREY**
colorists

DAVE SHARPE
letterer

ETHAN VAN SCIVER and JASON WRIGHT
collection cover artists

NEW GODS and **LIGHTRAY** created by **JACK KIRBY**

MIKE COTTON Editor - Original Series ⬥ **ANDREW MARINO** Assistant Editor - Original Series
JEB WOODARD Group Editor - Collected Editions ⬥ **PAUL SANTOS** Editor - Collected Edition
STEVE COOK Design Director - Books ⬥ **MONIQUE NARBONETA** Publication Design

BOB HARRAS Senior VP - Editor-in-Chief, DC Comics
PAT McCALLUM Executive Editor, DC Comics

DIANE NELSON President ⬥ **DAN DiDIO** Publisher ⬥ **JIM LEE** Publisher ⬥ **GEOFF JOHNS** President & Chief Creative Officer
AMIT DESAI Executive VP - Business & Marketing Strategy, Direct to Consumer & Global Franchise Management
SAM ADES Senior VP & General Manager, Digital Services ⬥ **BOBBIE CHASE** VP & Executive Editor, Young Reader & Talent Development
MARK CHIARELLO Senior VP - Art, Design & Collected Editions ⬥ **JOHN CUNNINGHAM** Senior VP - Sales & Trade Marketing
ANNE DePIES Senior VP - Business Strategy, Finance & Administration ⬥ **DON FALLETTI** VP - Manufacturing Operations
LAWRENCE GANEM VP - Editorial Administration & Talent Relations ⬥ **ALISON GILL** Senior VP - Manufacturing & Operations
HANK KANALZ Senior VP - Editorial Strategy & Administration ⬥ **JAY KOGAN** VP - Legal Affairs ⬥ **JACK MAHAN** VP - Business Affairs
NICK J. NAPOLITANO VP - Manufacturing Administration ⬥ **EDDIE SCANNELL** VP - Consumer Marketing
COURTNEY SIMMONS Senior VP - Publicity & Communications ⬥ **JIM (SKI) SOKOLOWSKI** VP - Comic Book Specialty Sales & Trade Marketing
NANCY SPEARS VP - Mass, Book, Digital Sales & Trade Marketing ⬥ **MICHELE R. WELLS** VP - Content Strategy

HAL JORDAN AND THE GREEN LANTERN CORPS VOL.4: FRACTURE

DC Comics, 2900 West Alameda Ave., Burbank, CA 91505
Printed by LSC Communications, Kendallville, IN, USA. 12/1/17. First Printing.
ISBN: 978-1-4012-7519-8

Library of Congress Cataloging-in-Publication Data is available.

PEFC Certified

Printed on paper from
sustainably managed
forests, controlled
sources

PEFC/29-31-337   www.pefc.org

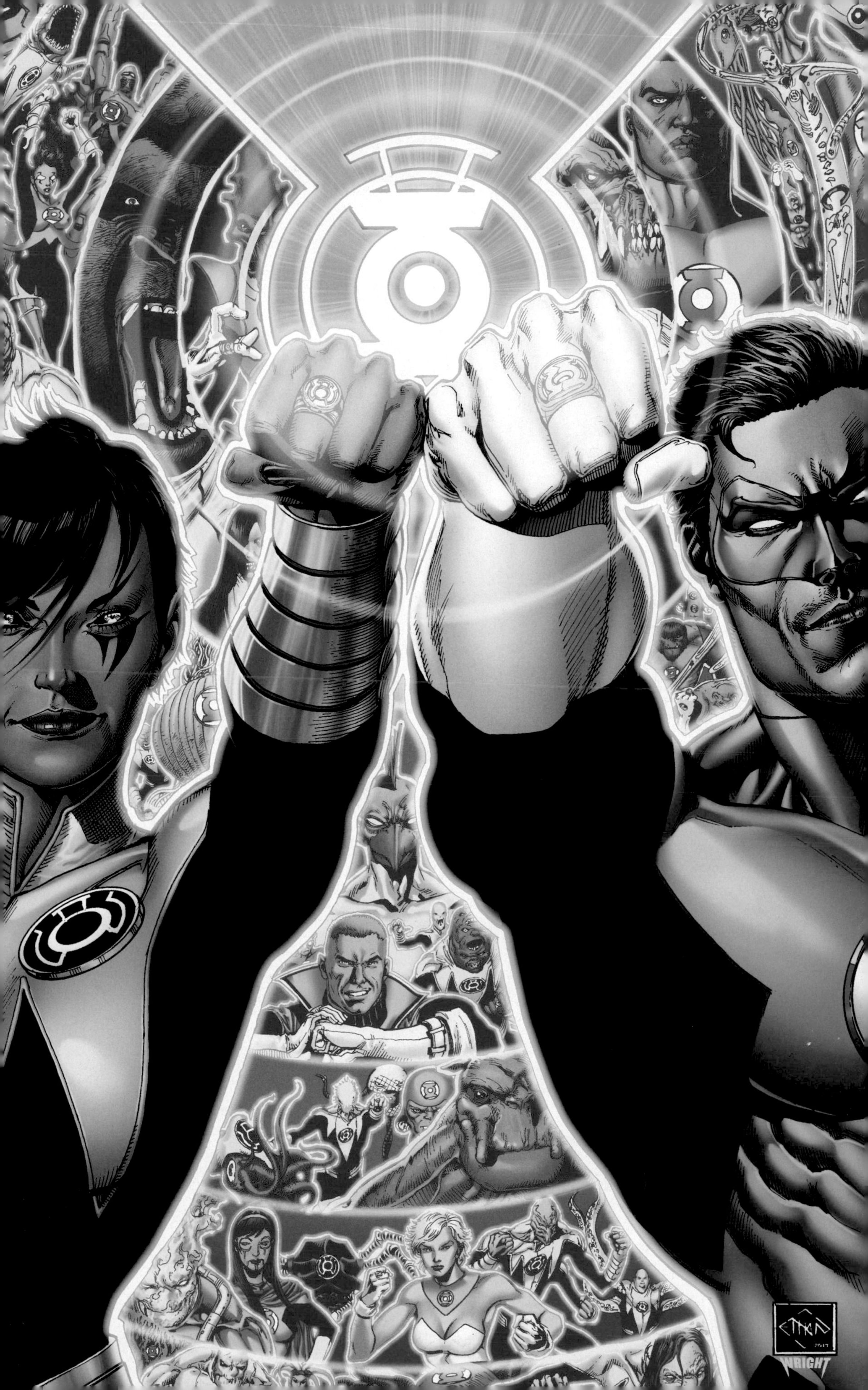

"FRACTURE PART 1: UNIFIED"

ETHAN VAN SCIVER artist * JASON WRIGHT colorist

cover art by ETHAN VAN SCIVER and JASON WRIGHT

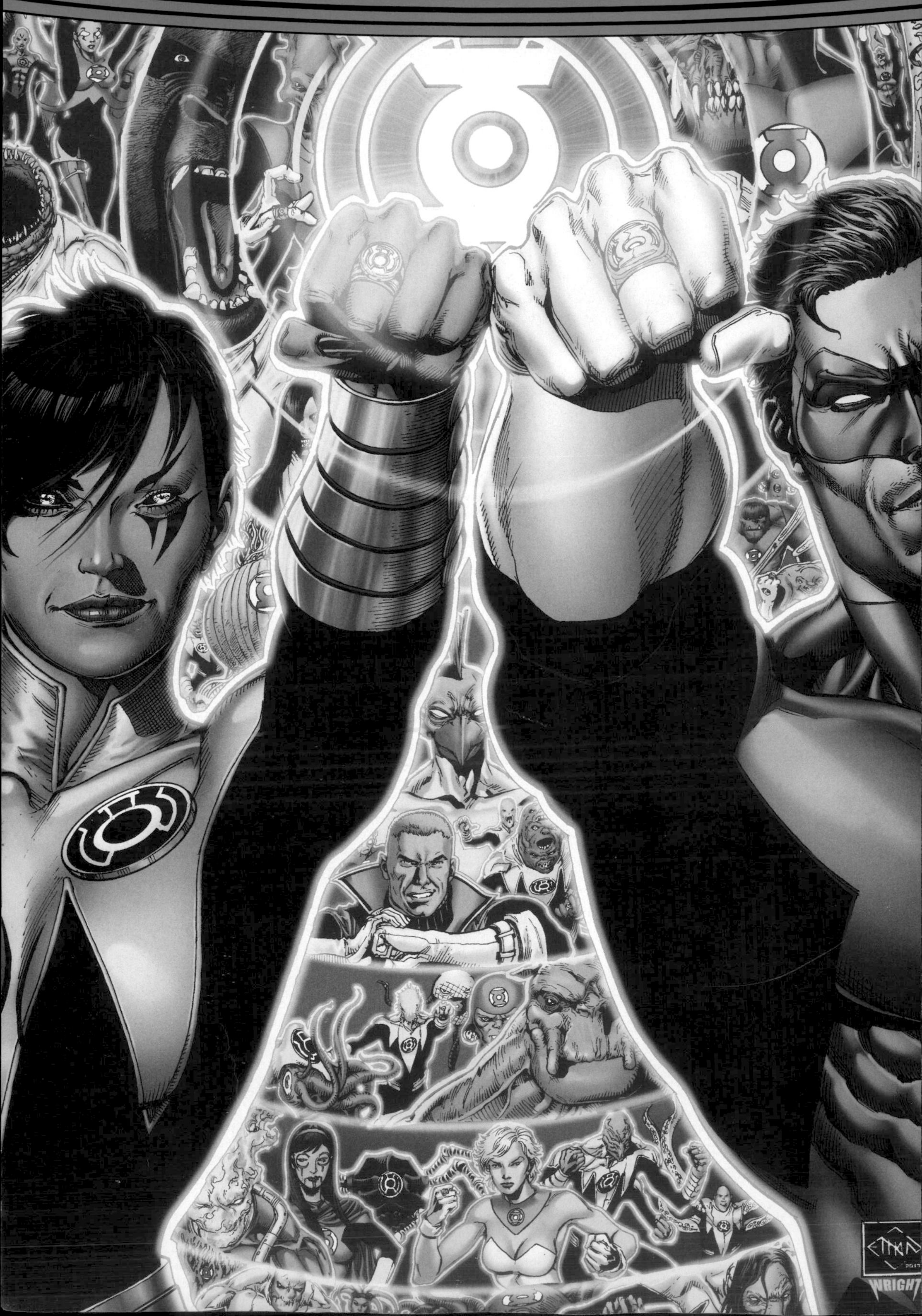
WRIGHT

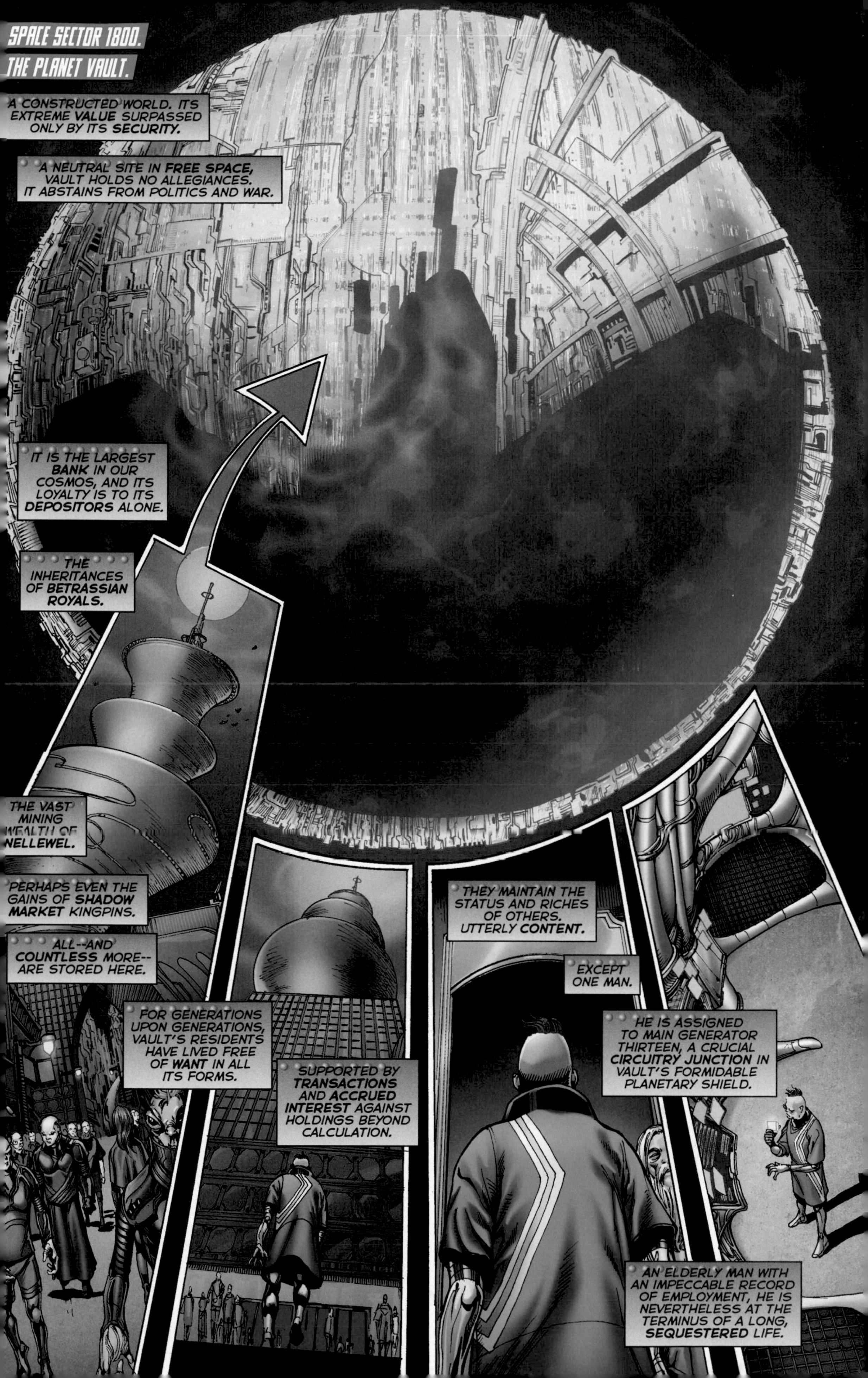
SPACE SECTOR 1800.
THE PLANET VAULT.
A CONSTRUCTED WORLD. ITS EXTREME VALUE SURPASSED ONLY BY ITS SECURITY.
A NEUTRAL SITE IN FREE SPACE, VAULT HOLDS NO ALLEGIANCES. IT ABSTAINS FROM POLITICS AND WAR.
IT IS THE LARGEST BANK IN OUR COSMOS, AND ITS LOYALTY IS TO ITS DEPOSITORS ALONE.
THE INHERITANCES OF BETRASSIAN ROYALS.
THE VAST MINING WEALTH OF NELLEWEL.
PERHAPS EVEN THE GAINS OF SHADOW MARKET KINGPINS.
ALL--AND COUNTLESS MORE--ARE STORED HERE.
FOR GENERATIONS UPON GENERATIONS, VAULT'S RESIDENTS HAVE LIVED FREE OF WANT IN ALL ITS FORMS.
SUPPORTED BY TRANSACTIONS AND ACCRUED INTEREST AGAINST HOLDINGS BEYOND CALCULATION.
THEY MAINTAIN THE STATUS AND RICHES OF OTHERS. UTTERLY CONTENT.
EXCEPT ONE MAN.
HE IS ASSIGNED TO MAIN GENERATOR THIRTEEN, A CRUCIAL CIRCUITRY JUNCTION IN VAULT'S FORMIDABLE PLANETARY SHIELD.
AN ELDERLY MAN WITH AN IMPECCABLE RECORD OF EMPLOYMENT, HE IS NEVERTHELESS AT THE TERMINUS OF A LONG, SEQUESTERED LIFE.

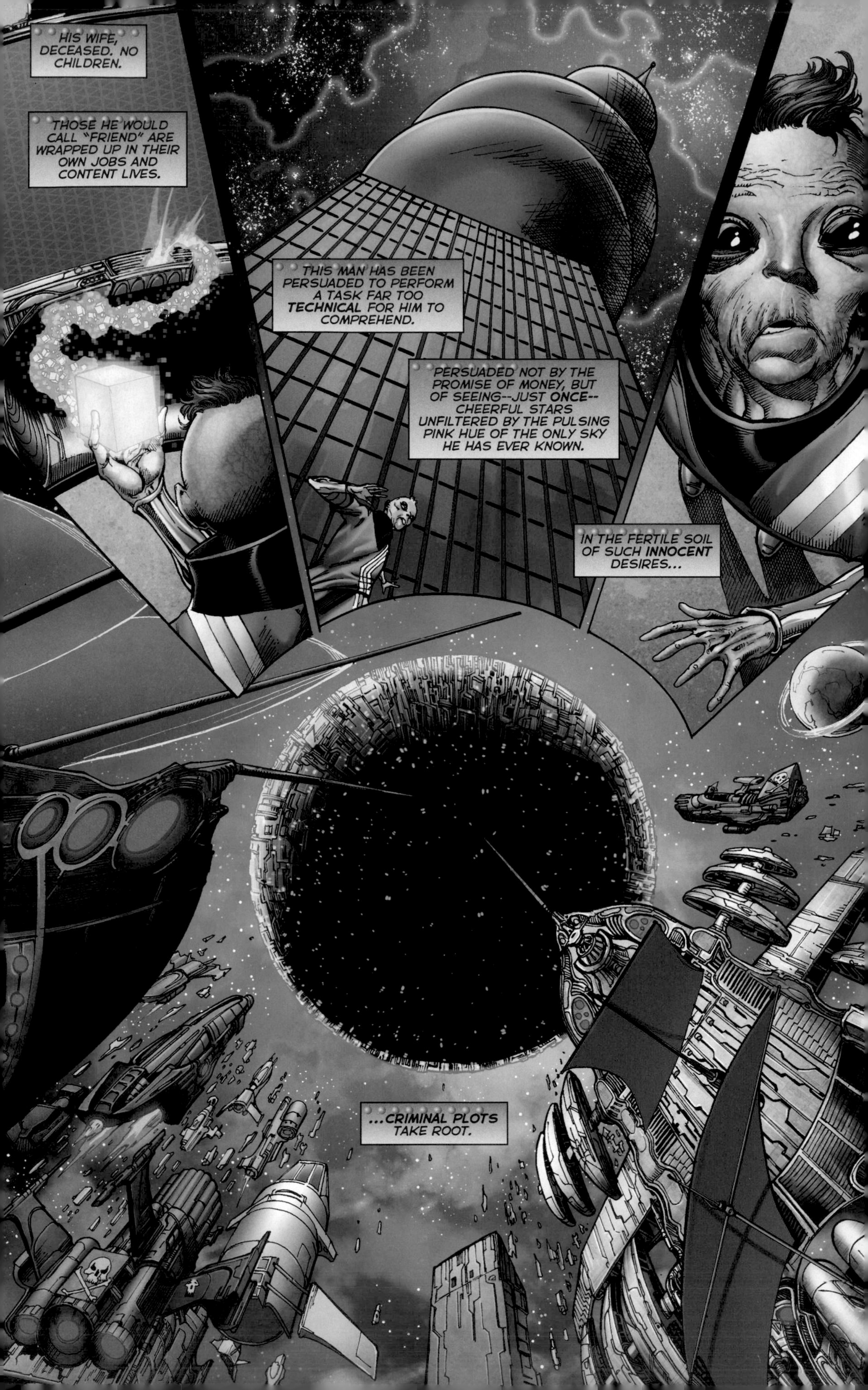
HIS WIFE, DECEASED. NO CHILDREN.
THOSE HE WOULD CALL "FRIEND" ARE WRAPPED UP IN THEIR OWN JOBS AND CONTENT LIVES.
THIS MAN HAS BEEN PERSUADED TO PERFORM A TASK FAR TOO TECHNICAL FOR HIM TO COMPREHEND.
PERSUADED NOT BY THE PROMISE OF MONEY, BUT OF SEEING--JUST ONCE--CHEERFUL STARS UNFILTERED BY THE PULSING PINK HUE OF THE ONLY SKY HE HAS EVER KNOWN.
IN THE FERTILE SOIL OF SUCH INNOCENT DESIRES...
...CRIMINAL PLOTS TAKE ROOT.

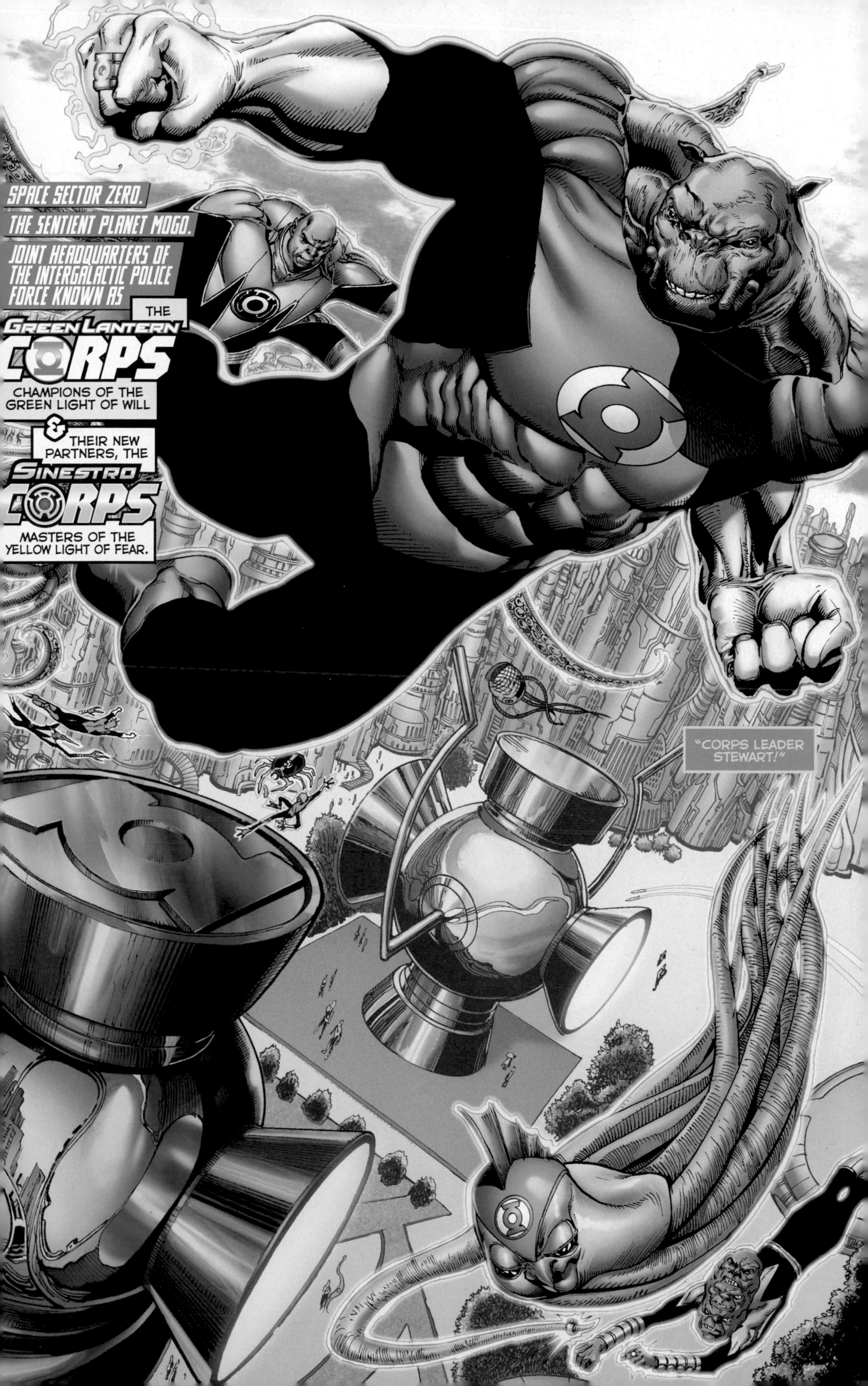
SPACE SECTOR ZERO.
THE SENTIENT PLANET MOGO.
JOINT HEADQUARTERS OF THE INTERGALACTIC POLICE FORCE KNOWN AS
THE GREEN LANTERN CORPS
CHAMPIONS OF THE GREEN LIGHT OF WILL
& THEIR NEW PARTNERS, THE SINESTRO CORPS
MASTERS OF THE YELLOW LIGHT OF FEAR.
"CORPS LEADER STEWART!"

DISTRESS CALL FROM PLANET VAULT!

ENHANCE AUDIO!

THIS IS THE CHIEF OF ACCOUNTS! WE'VE LOST OUR DEFENSE SHIELD!

A MALIGNANT DATA INCURSION HAS CRIPPLED OUR SYSTEMS!

WE'RE BEING LOOTED!

GET YOUR PEOPLE SOMEWHERE SAFE, CHIEF. HELP IS ON THE WAY.

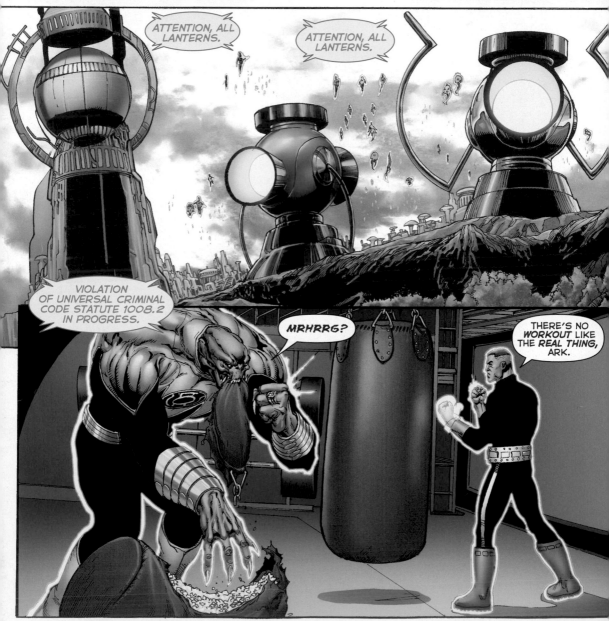

ATTENTION, ALL LANTERNS.

ATTENTION, ALL LANTERNS.

VIOLATION OF UNIVERSAL CRIMINAL CODE STATUTE 1008.2 IN PROGRESS.

MRHRRRG?

THERE'S NO WORKOUT LIKE THE REAL THING, ARK.

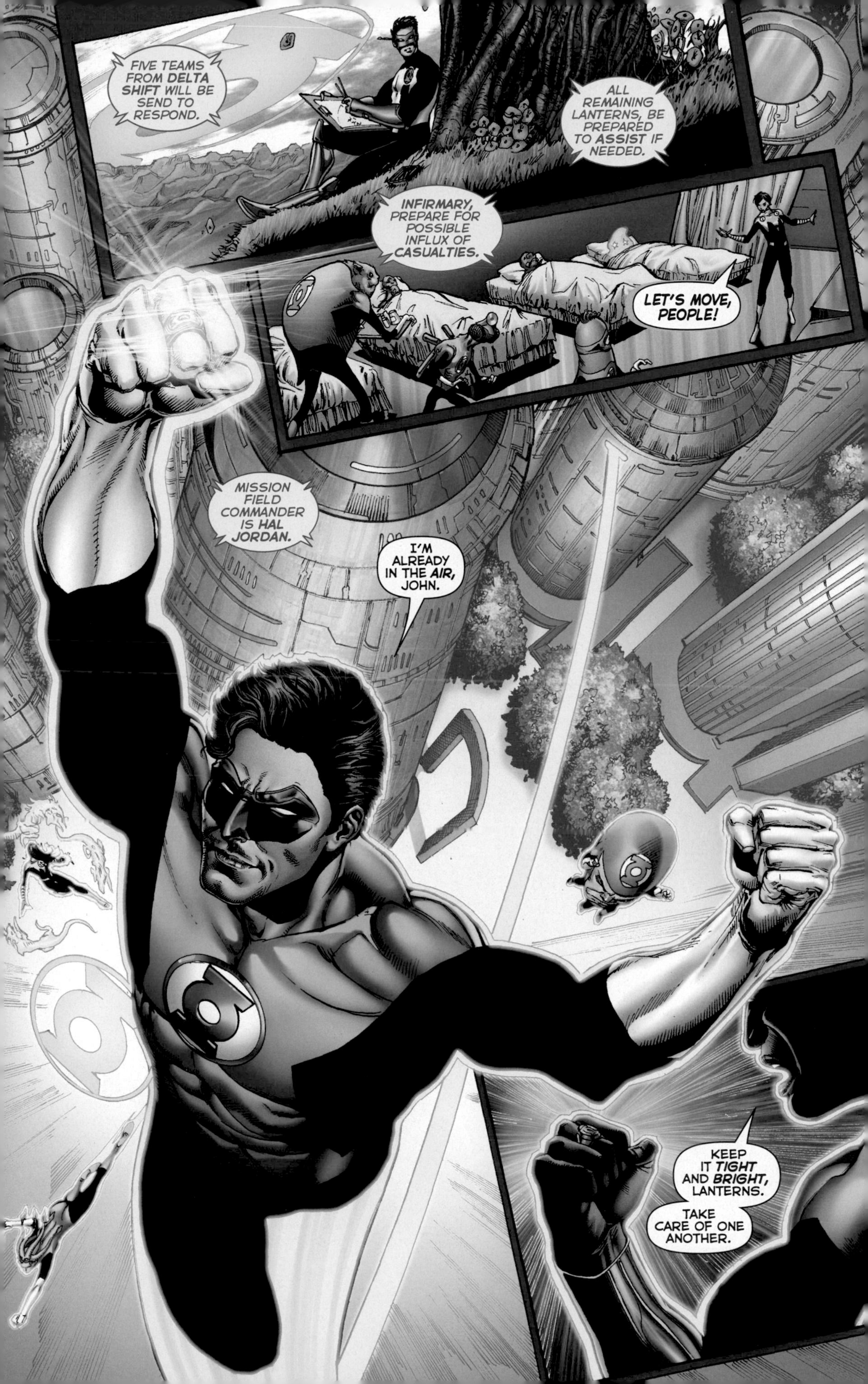
FIVE TEAMS FROM DELTA SHIFT WILL BE SEND TO RESPOND.
ALL REMAINING LANTERNS, BE PREPARED TO ASSIST IF NEEDED.
INFIRMARY, PREPARE FOR POSSIBLE INFLUX OF CASUALTIES.
LET'S MOVE, PEOPLE!
MISSION FIELD COMMANDER IS HAL JORDAN.
I'M ALREADY IN THE AIR, JOHN.
KEEP IT TIGHT AND BRIGHT, LANTERNS.
TAKE CARE OF ONE ANOTHER.

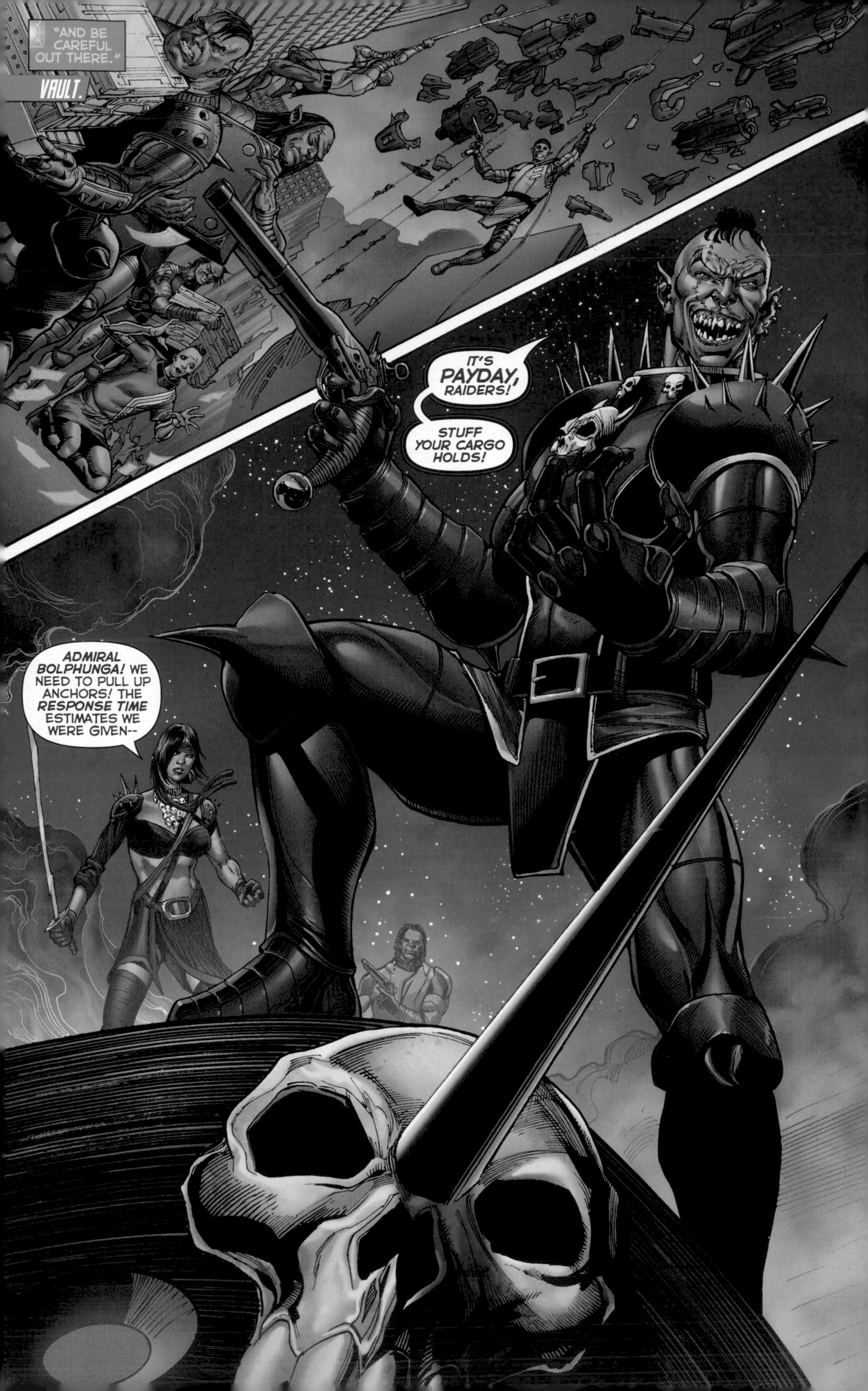
"AND BE CAREFUL OUT THERE."
VAULT.
IT'S PAYDAY, RAIDERS!
STUFF YOUR CARGO HOLDS!
ADMIRAL BOLPHUNGA! WE NEED TO PULL UP ANCHORS! THE RESPONSE TIME ESTIMATES WE WERE GIVEN--

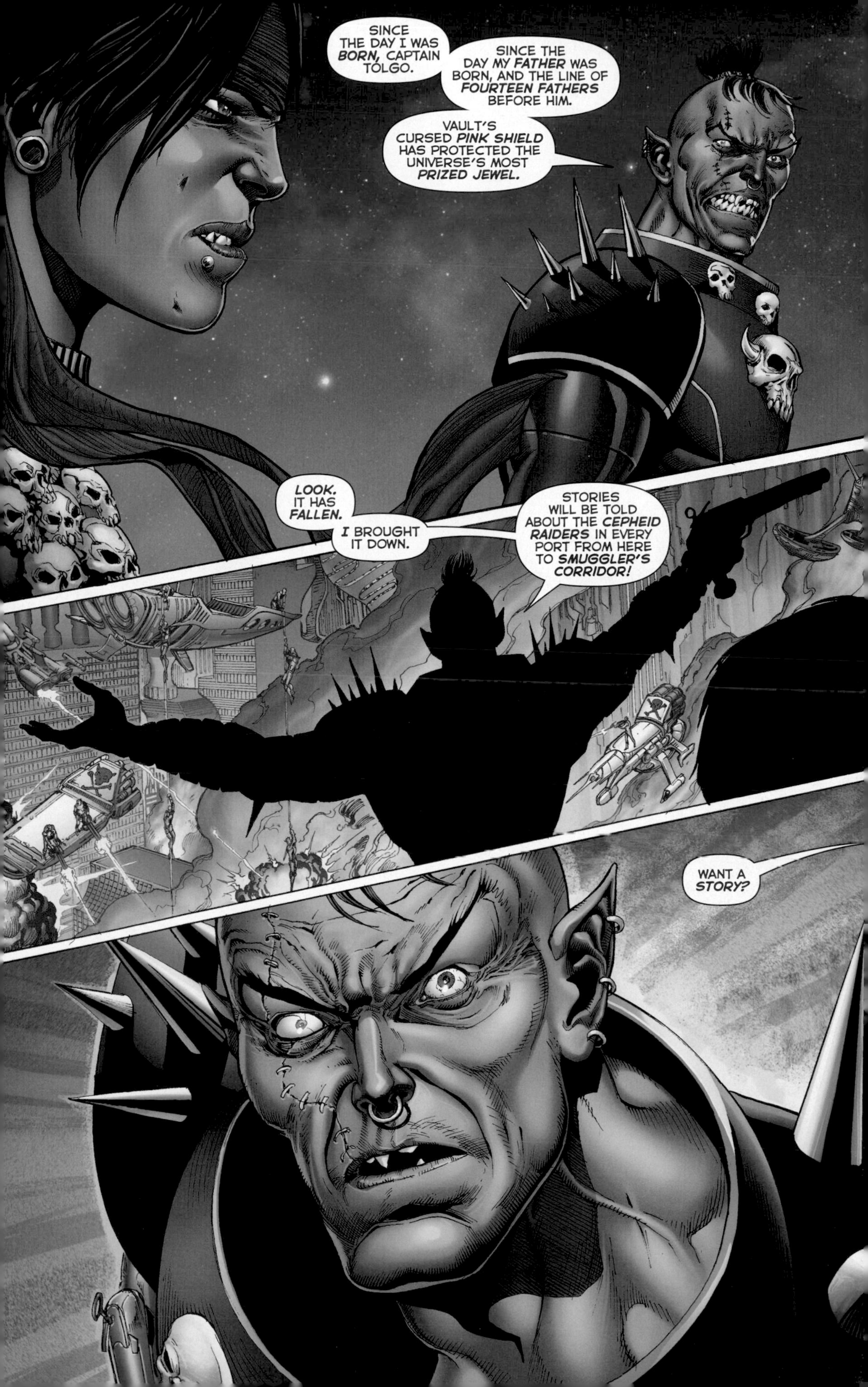
SINCE THE DAY I WAS BORN, CAPTAIN TOLGO.
SINCE THE DAY MY FATHER WAS BORN, AND THE LINE OF FOURTEEN FATHERS BEFORE HIM.
VAULT'S CURSED PINK SHIELD HAS PROTECTED THE UNIVERSE'S MOST PRIZED JEWEL.
LOOK. IT HAS FALLEN.
I BROUGHT IT DOWN.
STORIES WILL BE TOLD ABOUT THE CEPHEID RAIDERS IN EVERY PORT FROM HERE TO SMUGGLER'S CORRIDOR!
WANT A STORY?

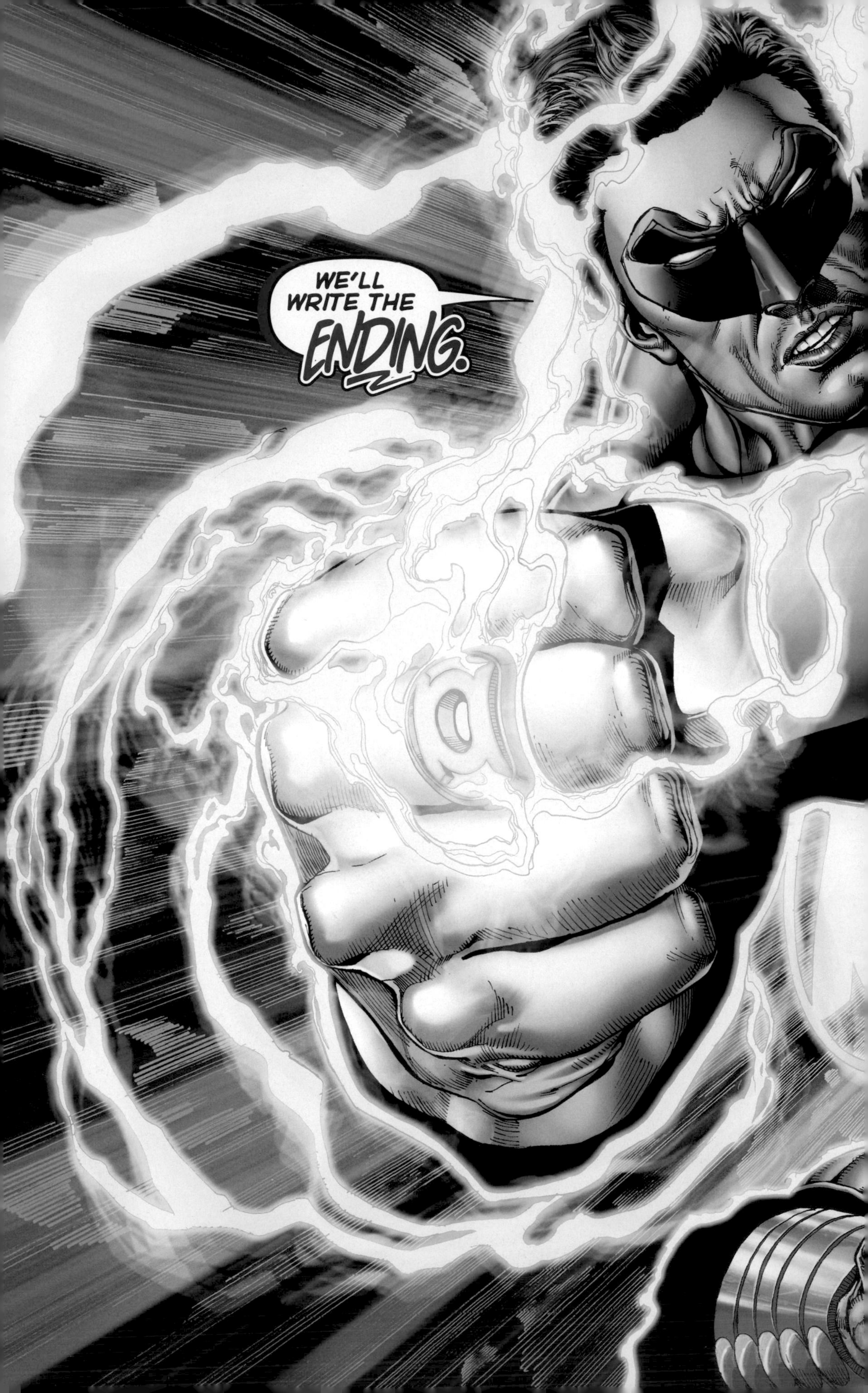
WE'LL WRITE THE ENDING.

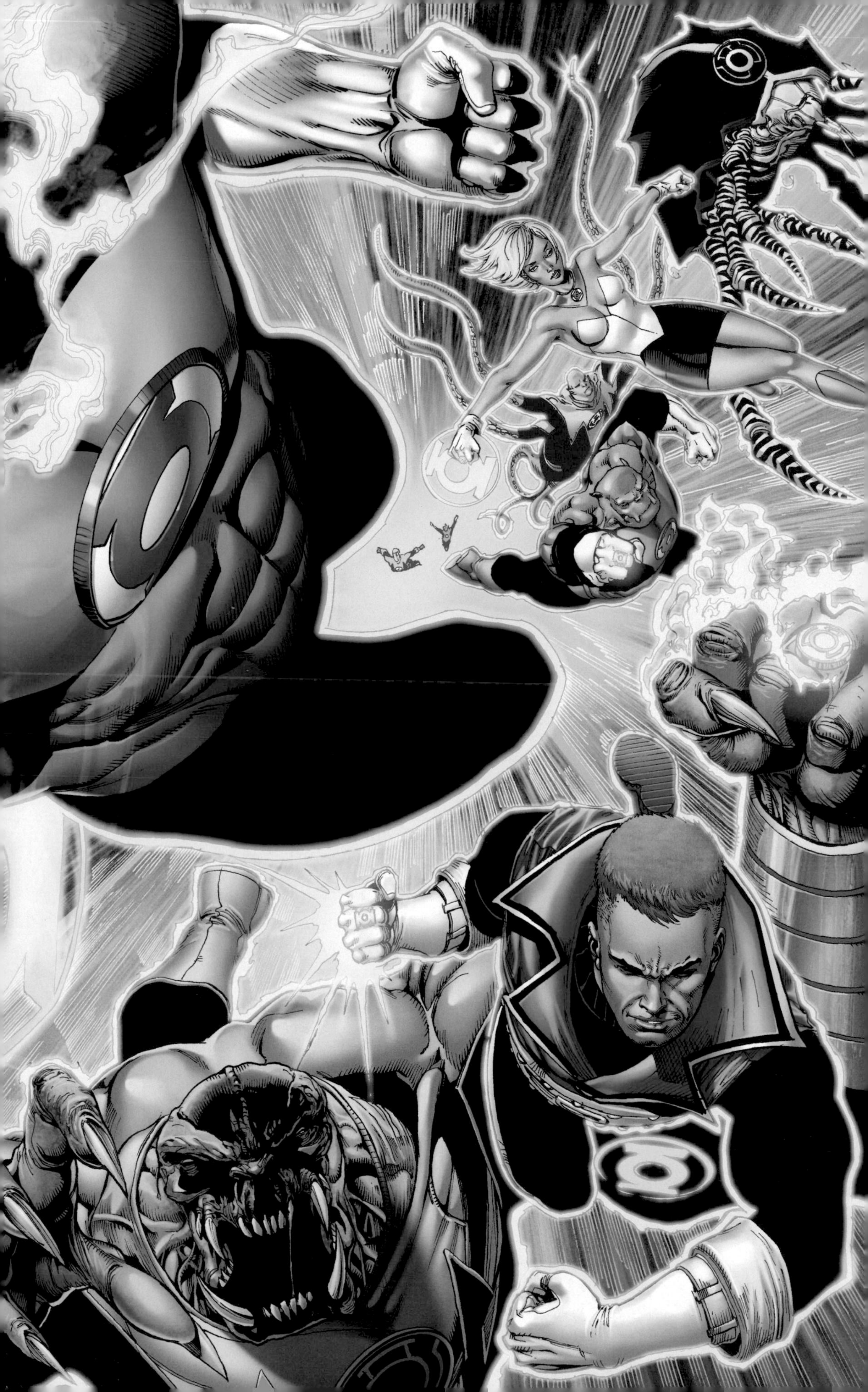

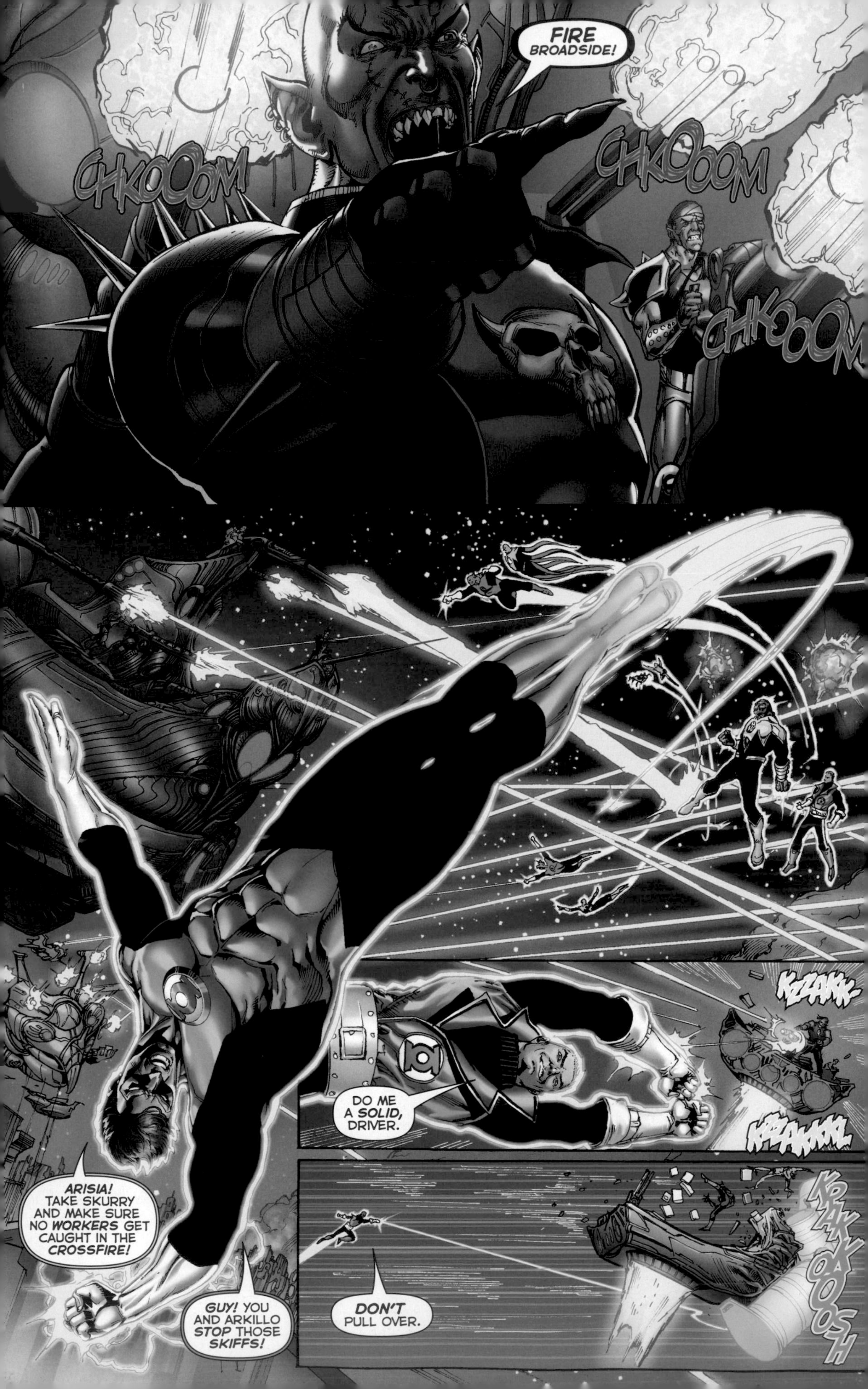
FIRE BROADSIDE!
CHKOOOM
CHKOOOOM
CHKOOOM
KZZAKK
DO ME A SOLID, DRIVER.
KZZAKKKL
ARISIA! TAKE SKURRY AND MAKE SURE NO WORKERS GET CAUGHT IN THE CROSSFIRE!
GUY! YOU AND ARKILLO STOP THOSE SKIFFS!
DON'T PULL OVER.
KRAKOOOOOSH

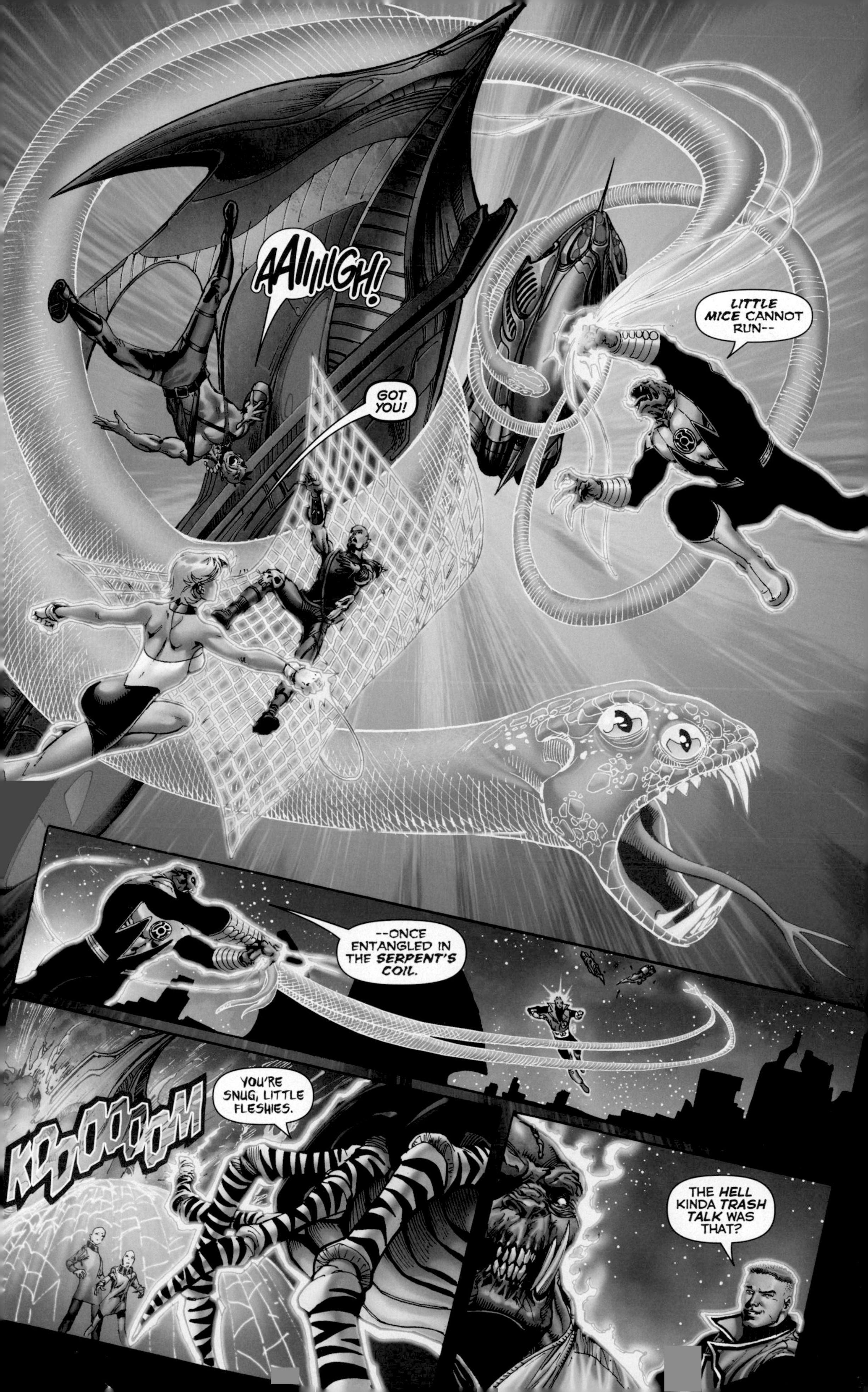
AAIIIIIGH!
LITTLE MICE CANNOT RUN--
GOT YOU!
--ONCE ENTANGLED IN THE SERPENT'S COIL.
KDOOOOOM
YOU'RE SNUG, LITTLE FLESHIES.
THE HELL KINDA TRASH TALK WAS THAT?

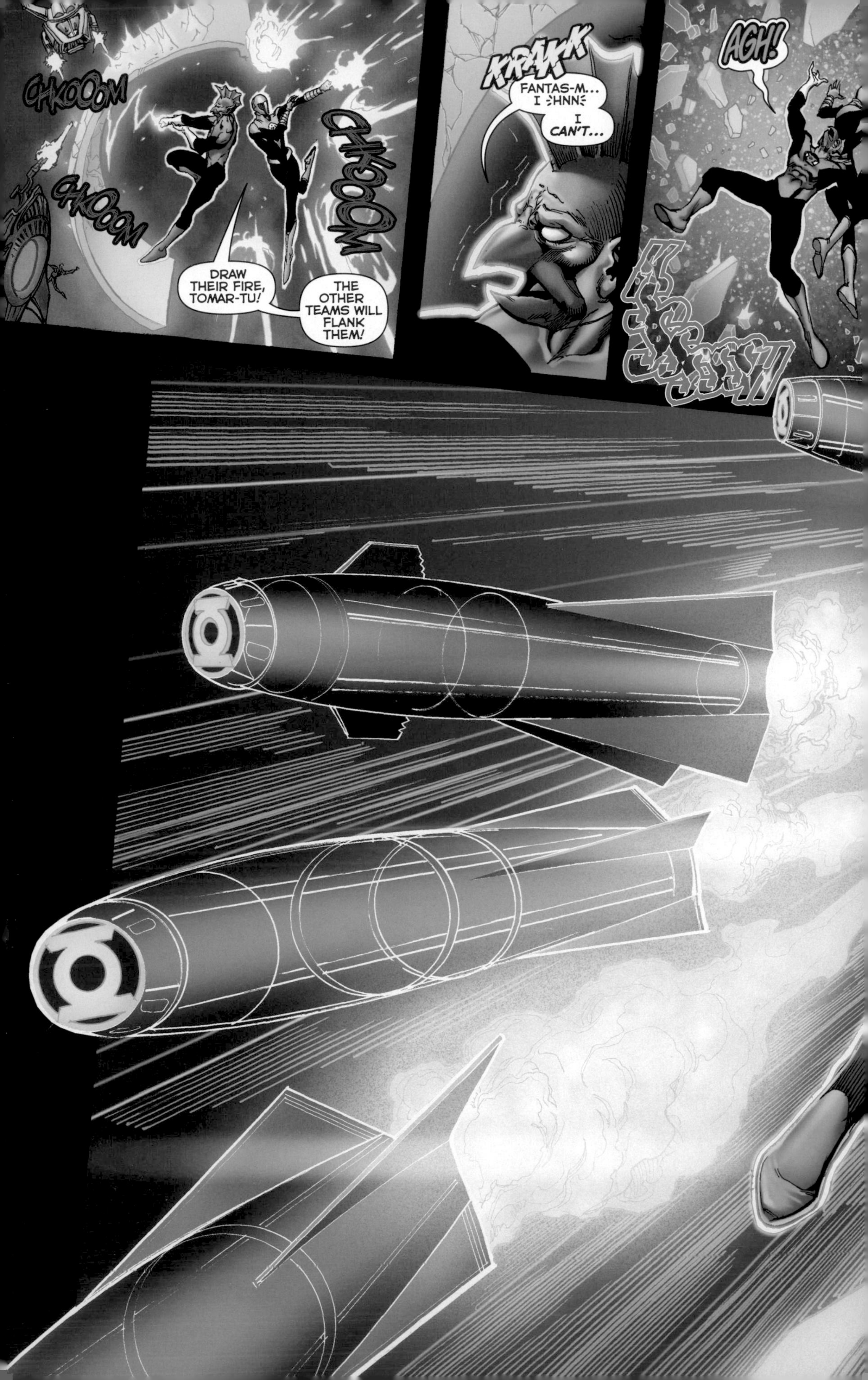
CHKOOOM
CHKOOOM
CHKOOOM
DRAW THEIR FIRE, TOMAR-TU!
THE OTHER TEAMS WILL FLANK THEM!
KRAKK
FANTAS-M... I HNN
I CAN'T...
AGH!

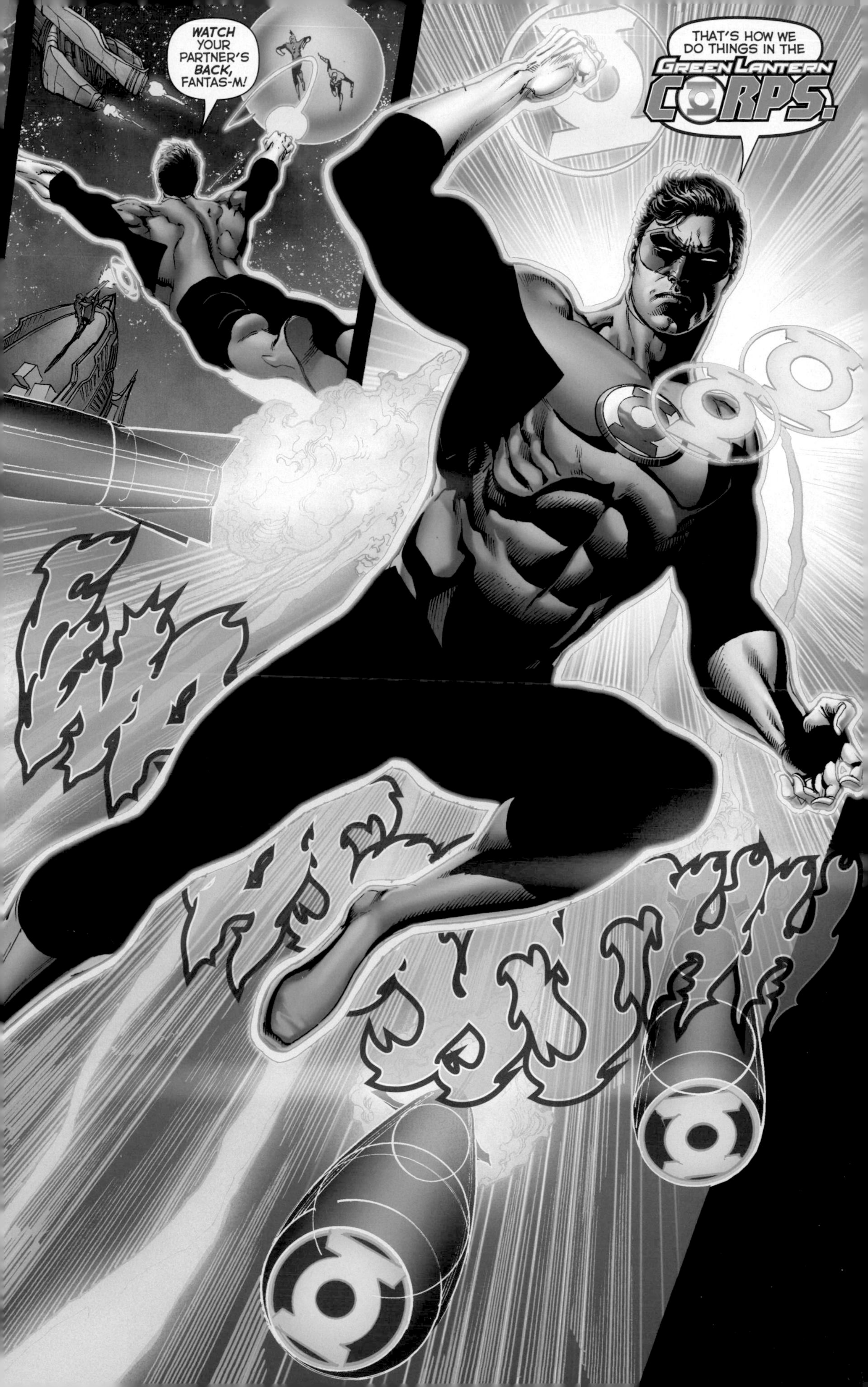
WATCH YOUR PARTNER'S BACK, FANTAS-M!
THAT'S HOW WE DO THINGS IN THE GREEN LANTERN CORPS.

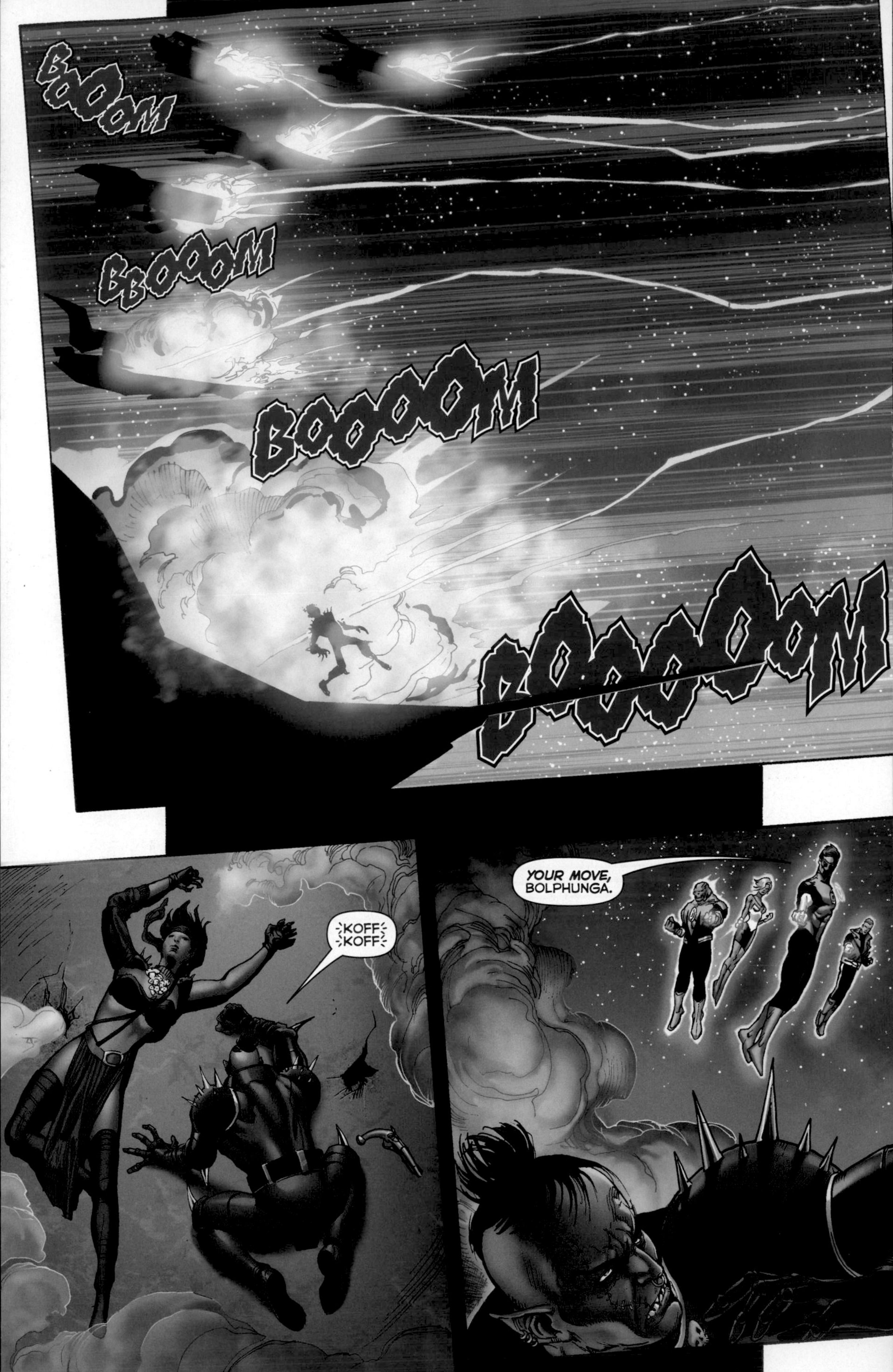
BOOOM
BBOOOOM
BOOOOM
BOOOOOM
KOFF KOFF
YOUR MOVE, BOLPHUNGA.

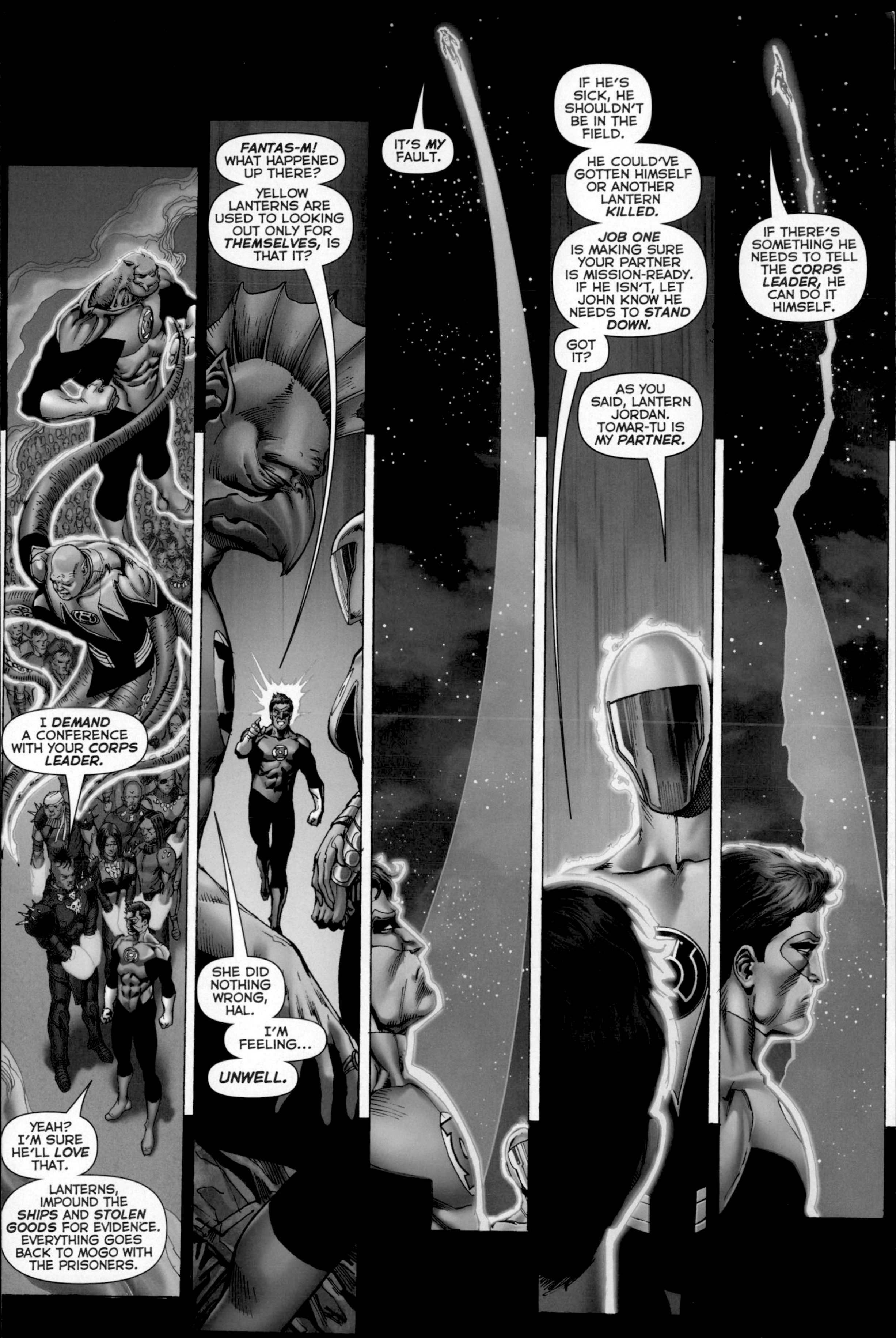
I DEMAND A CONFERENCE WITH YOUR CORPS LEADER.
YEAH? I'M SURE HE'LL LOVE THAT.
LANTERNS, IMPOUND THE SHIPS AND STOLEN GOODS FOR EVIDENCE. EVERYTHING GOES BACK TO MOGO WITH THE PRISONERS.
FANTAS-M! WHAT HAPPENED UP THERE?
YELLOW LANTERNS ARE USED TO LOOKING OUT ONLY FOR THEMSELVES, IS THAT IT?
SHE DID NOTHING WRONG, HAL.
I'M FEELING...
UNWELL.
IT'S MY FAULT.
IF HE'S SICK, HE SHOULDN'T BE IN THE FIELD.
HE COULD'VE GOTTEN HIMSELF OR ANOTHER LANTERN KILLED.
JOB ONE IS MAKING SURE YOUR PARTNER IS MISSION-READY. IF HE ISN'T, LET JOHN KNOW HE NEEDS TO STAND DOWN.
GOT IT?
AS YOU SAID, LANTERN JORDAN. TOMAR-TU IS MY PARTNER.
IF THERE'S SOMETHING HE NEEDS TO TELL THE CORPS LEADER, HE CAN DO IT HIMSELF.

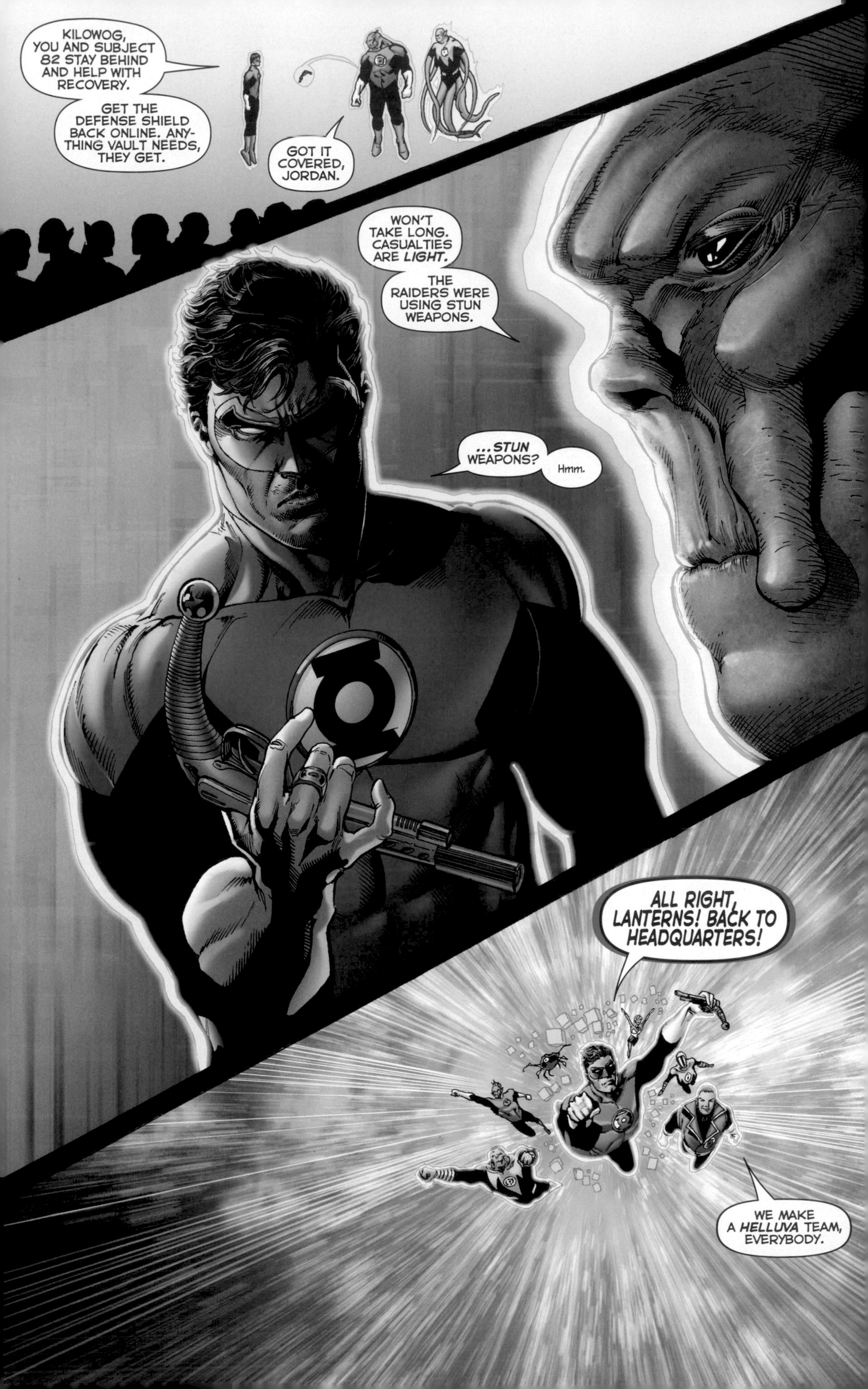
KILOWOG, YOU AND SUBJECT 82 STAY BEHIND AND HELP WITH RECOVERY.
GET THE DEFENSE SHIELD BACK ONLINE. ANY-THING VAULT NEEDS, THEY GET.
GOT IT COVERED, JORDAN.
WON'T TAKE LONG. CASUALTIES ARE *LIGHT.*
THE RAIDERS WERE USING STUN WEAPONS.
...*STUN* WEAPONS?
Hmm.
ALL RIGHT, LANTERNS! BACK TO HEADQUARTERS!
WE MAKE A *HELLUVA* TEAM, EVERYBODY.

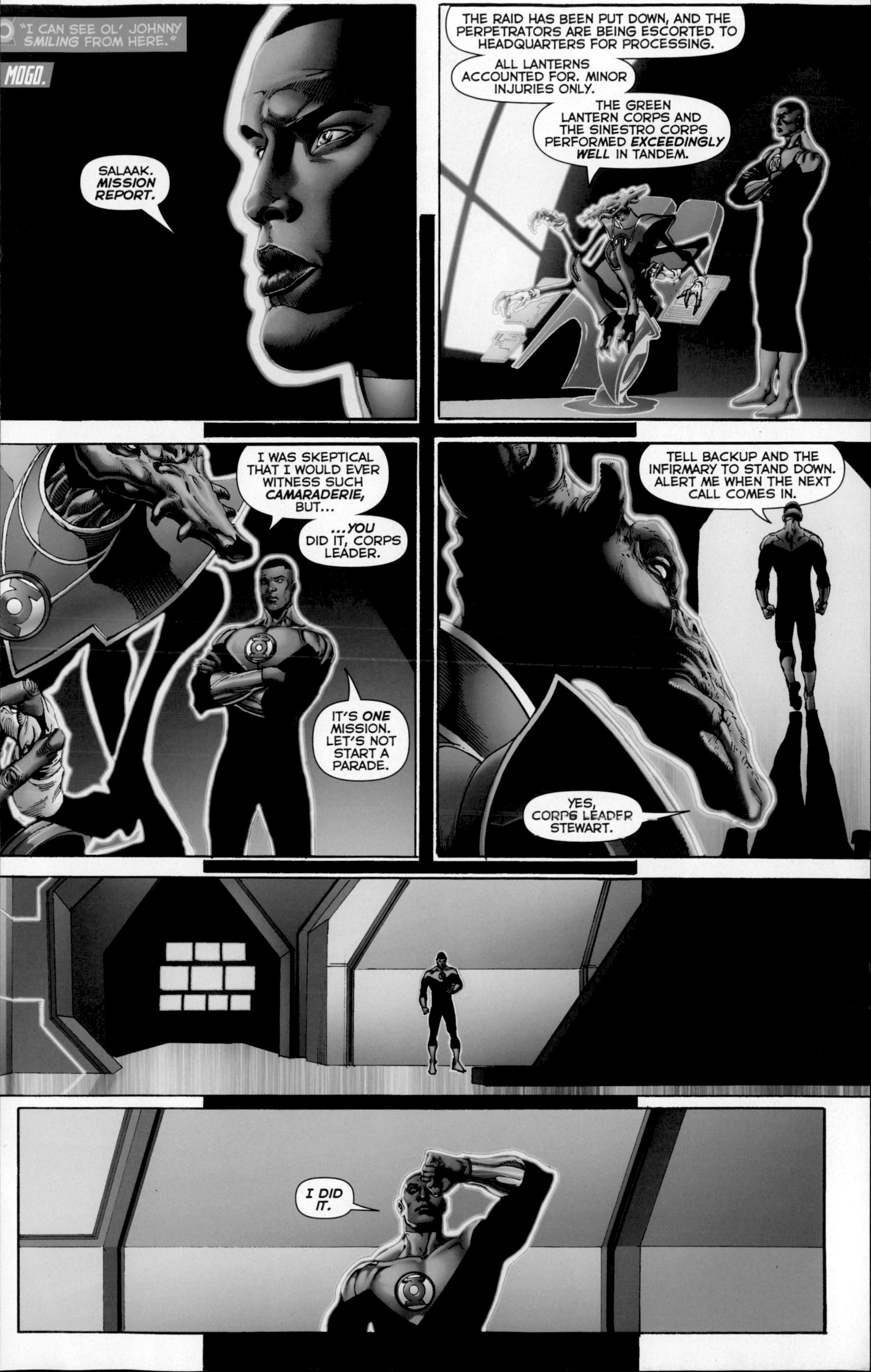
"I CAN SEE OL' JOHNNY SMILING FROM HERE."
MOGO.
SALAAK. MISSION REPORT.
THE RAID HAS BEEN PUT DOWN, AND THE PERPETRATORS ARE BEING ESCORTED TO HEADQUARTERS FOR PROCESSING.
ALL LANTERNS ACCOUNTED FOR. MINOR INJURIES ONLY.
THE GREEN LANTERN CORPS AND THE SINESTRO CORPS PERFORMED EXCEEDINGLY WELL IN TANDEM.
I WAS SKEPTICAL THAT I WOULD EVER WITNESS SUCH CAMARADERIE, BUT...
...YOU DID IT, CORPS LEADER.
IT'S ONE MISSION. LET'S NOT START A PARADE.
TELL BACKUP AND THE INFIRMARY TO STAND DOWN. ALERT ME WHEN THE NEXT CALL COMES IN.
YES, CORPS LEADER STEWART.
I DID IT.

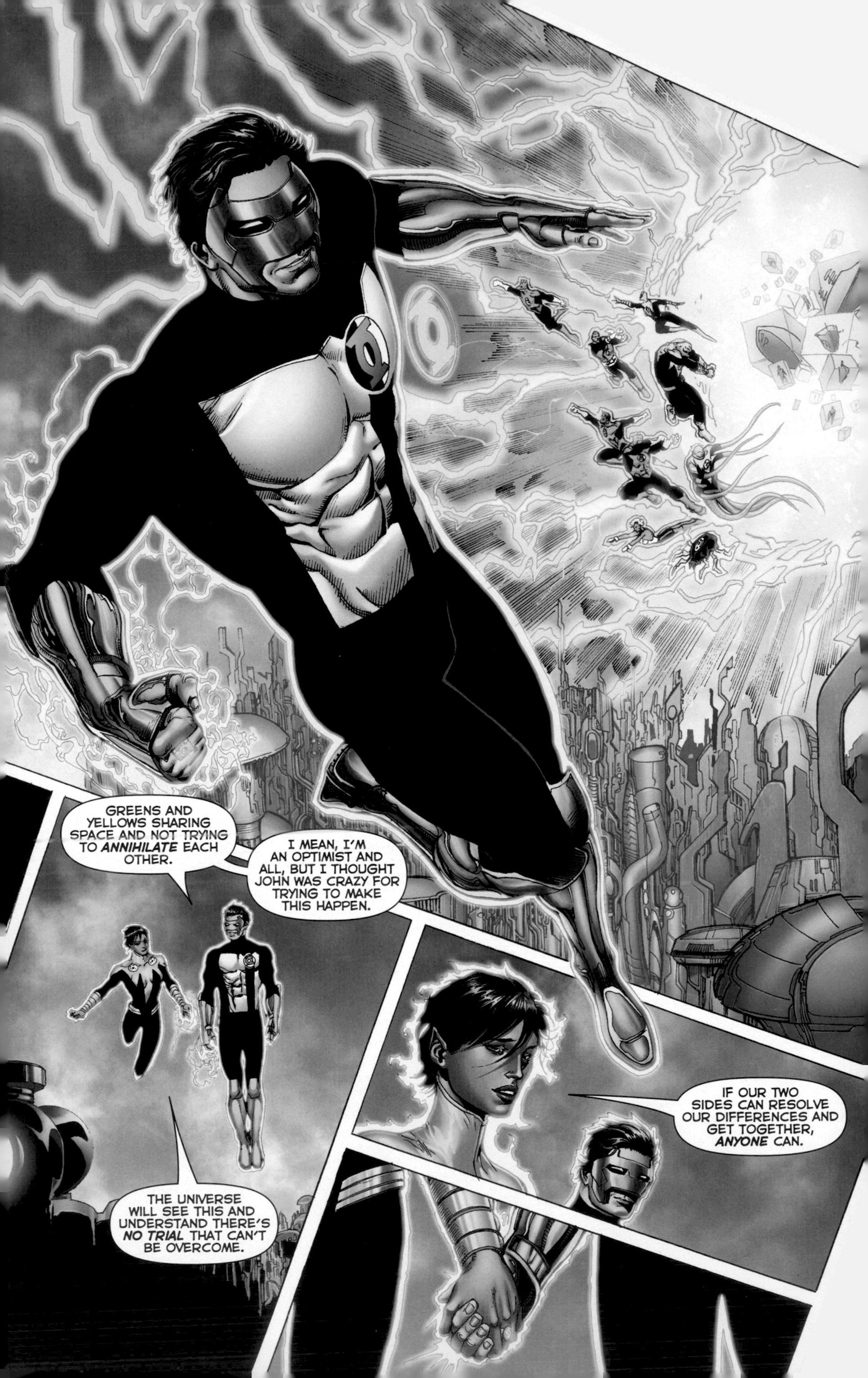
GREENS AND YELLOWS SHARING SPACE AND NOT TRYING TO *ANNIHILATE* EACH OTHER.
I MEAN, I'M AN OPTIMIST AND ALL, BUT I THOUGHT JOHN WAS CRAZY FOR TRYING TO MAKE THIS HAPPEN.
THE UNIVERSE WILL SEE THIS AND UNDERSTAND THERE'S *NO TRIAL* THAT CAN'T BE OVERCOME.
IF OUR TWO SIDES CAN RESOLVE OUR DIFFERENCES AND GET TOGETHER, *ANYONE* CAN.

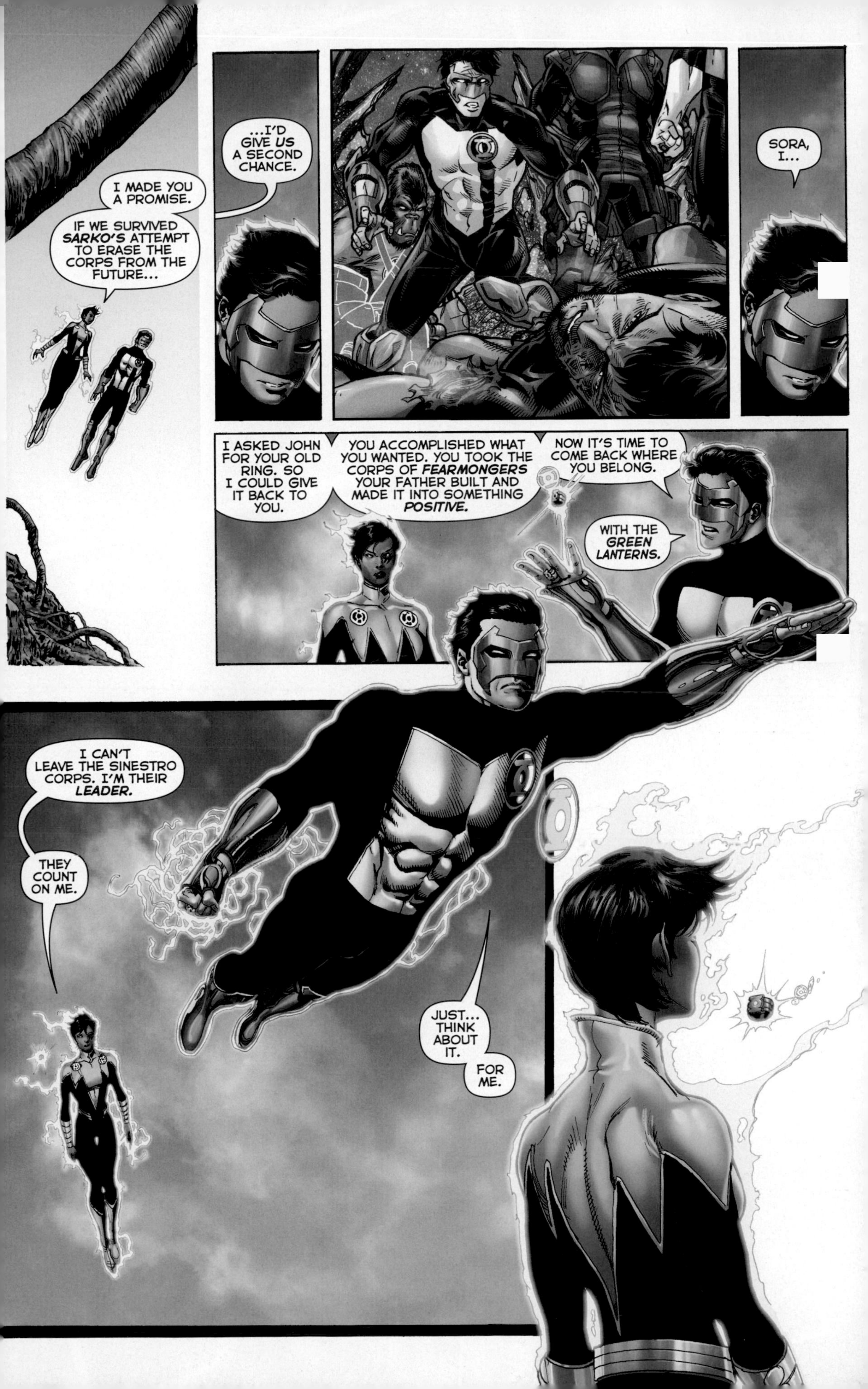
I MADE YOU A PROMISE.
IF WE SURVIVED SARKO'S ATTEMPT TO ERASE THE CORPS FROM THE FUTURE...
...I'D GIVE US A SECOND CHANCE.
SORA, I...
I ASKED JOHN FOR YOUR OLD RING. SO I COULD GIVE IT BACK TO YOU.
YOU ACCOMPLISHED WHAT YOU WANTED. YOU TOOK THE CORPS OF FEARMONGERS YOUR FATHER BUILT AND MADE IT INTO SOMETHING POSITIVE.
NOW IT'S TIME TO COME BACK WHERE YOU BELONG.
WITH THE GREEN LANTERNS.
I CAN'T LEAVE THE SINESTRO CORPS. I'M THEIR LEADER.
THEY COUNT ON ME.
JUST... THINK ABOUT IT.
FOR ME.

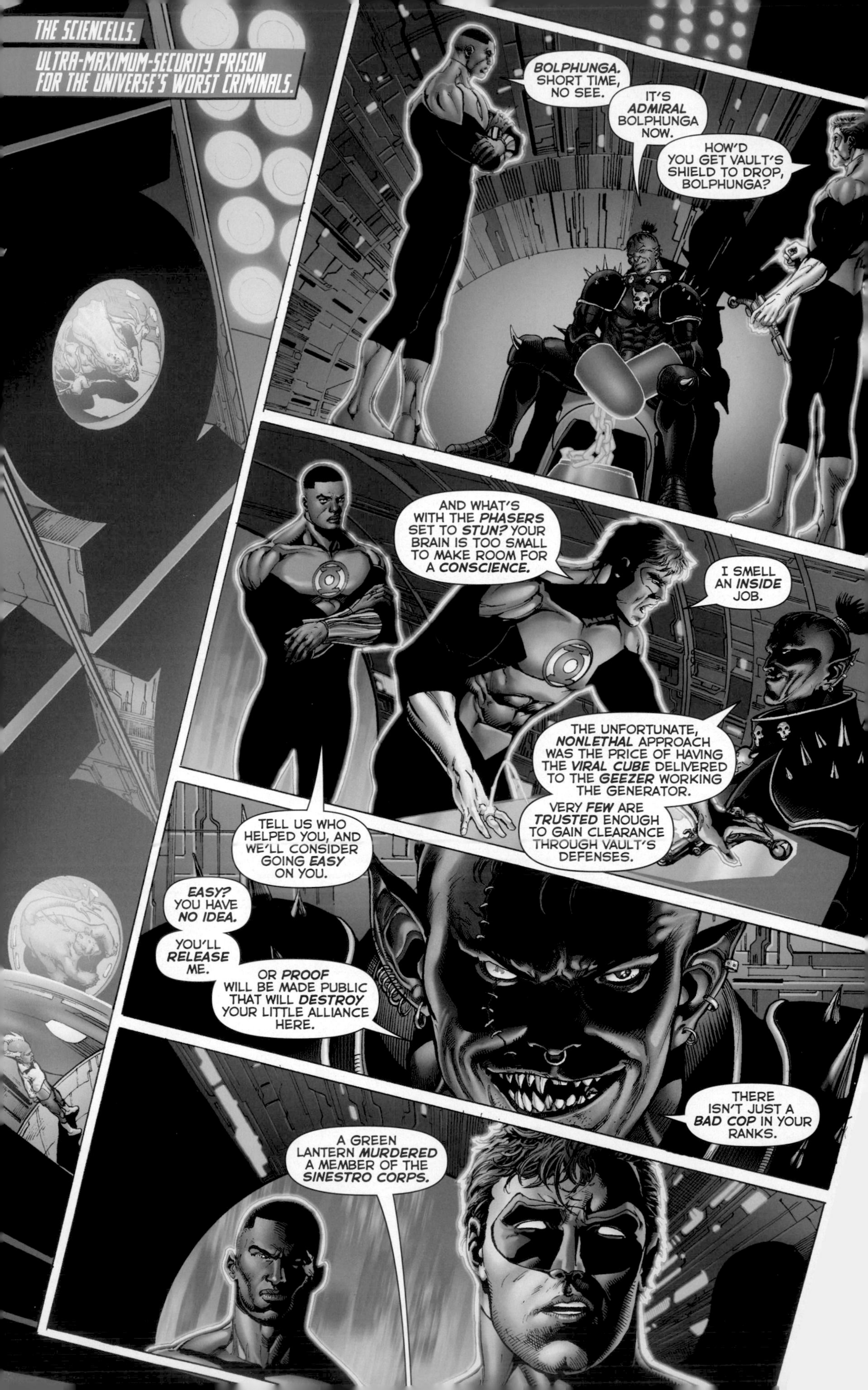
THE SCIENCELLS.
ULTRA-MAXIMUM-SECURITY PRISON FOR THE UNIVERSE'S WORST CRIMINALS.
BOLPHUNGA. SHORT TIME, NO SEE.
IT'S ADMIRAL BOLPHUNGA NOW.
HOW'D YOU GET VAULT'S SHIELD TO DROP, BOLPHUNGA?
AND WHAT'S WITH THE PHASERS SET TO STUN? YOUR BRAIN IS TOO SMALL TO MAKE ROOM FOR A CONSCIENCE.
I SMELL AN INSIDE JOB.
THE UNFORTUNATE, NONLETHAL APPROACH WAS THE PRICE OF HAVING THE VIRAL CUBE DELIVERED TO THE GEEZER WORKING THE GENERATOR.
VERY FEW ARE TRUSTED ENOUGH TO GAIN CLEARANCE THROUGH VAULT'S DEFENSES.
TELL US WHO HELPED YOU, AND WE'LL CONSIDER GOING EASY ON YOU.
EASY? YOU HAVE NO IDEA.
YOU'LL RELEASE ME.
OR PROOF WILL BE MADE PUBLIC THAT WILL DESTROY YOUR LITTLE ALLIANCE HERE.
THERE ISN'T JUST A BAD COP IN YOUR RANKS.
A GREEN LANTERN MURDERED A MEMBER OF THE SINESTRO CORPS.

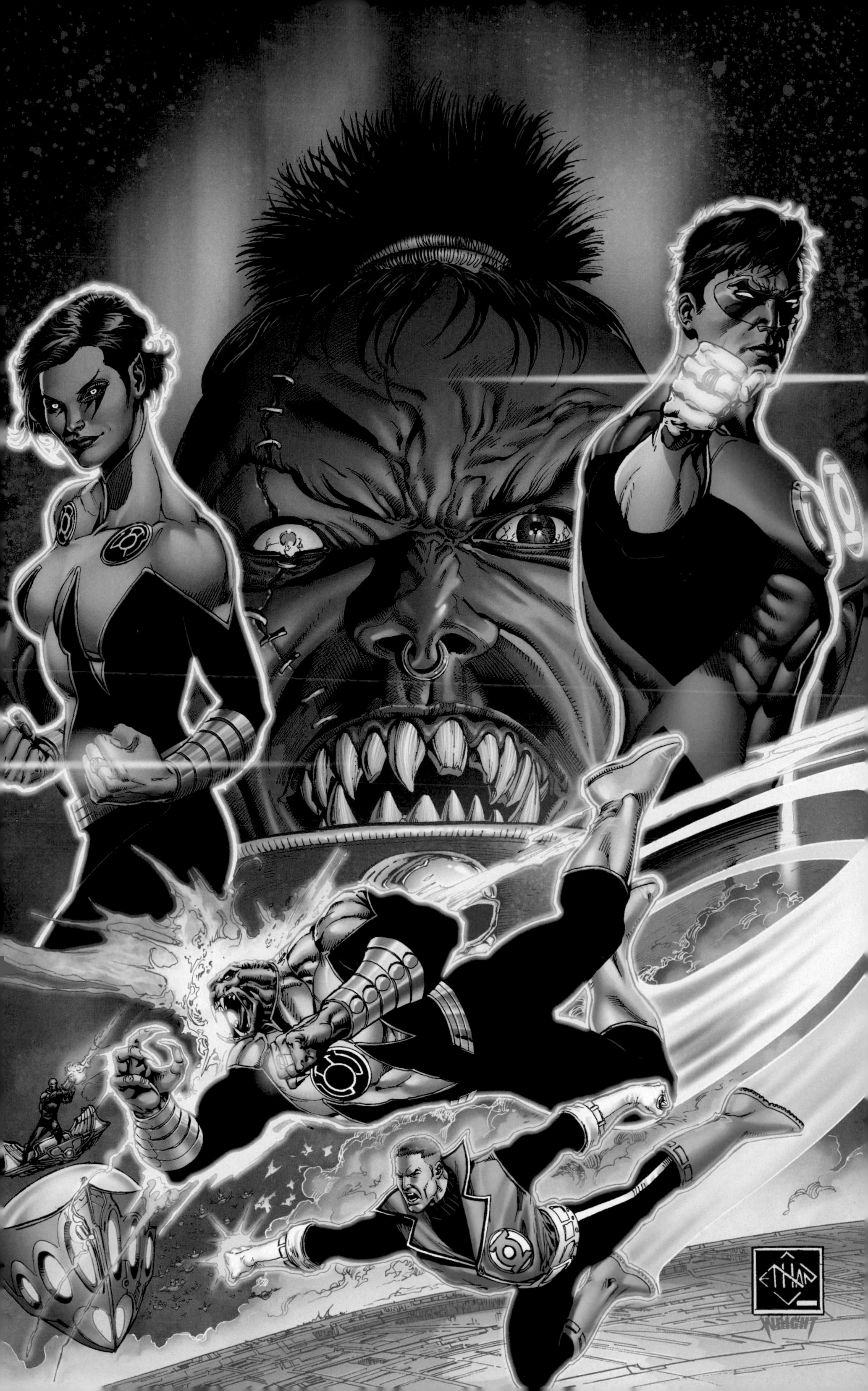

"FRACTURE PART 2: GUILTY BLOOD"

ETHAN VAN SCIVER artist * JASON WRIGHT colorist

cover art by ETHAN VAN SCIVER and JASON WRIGHT

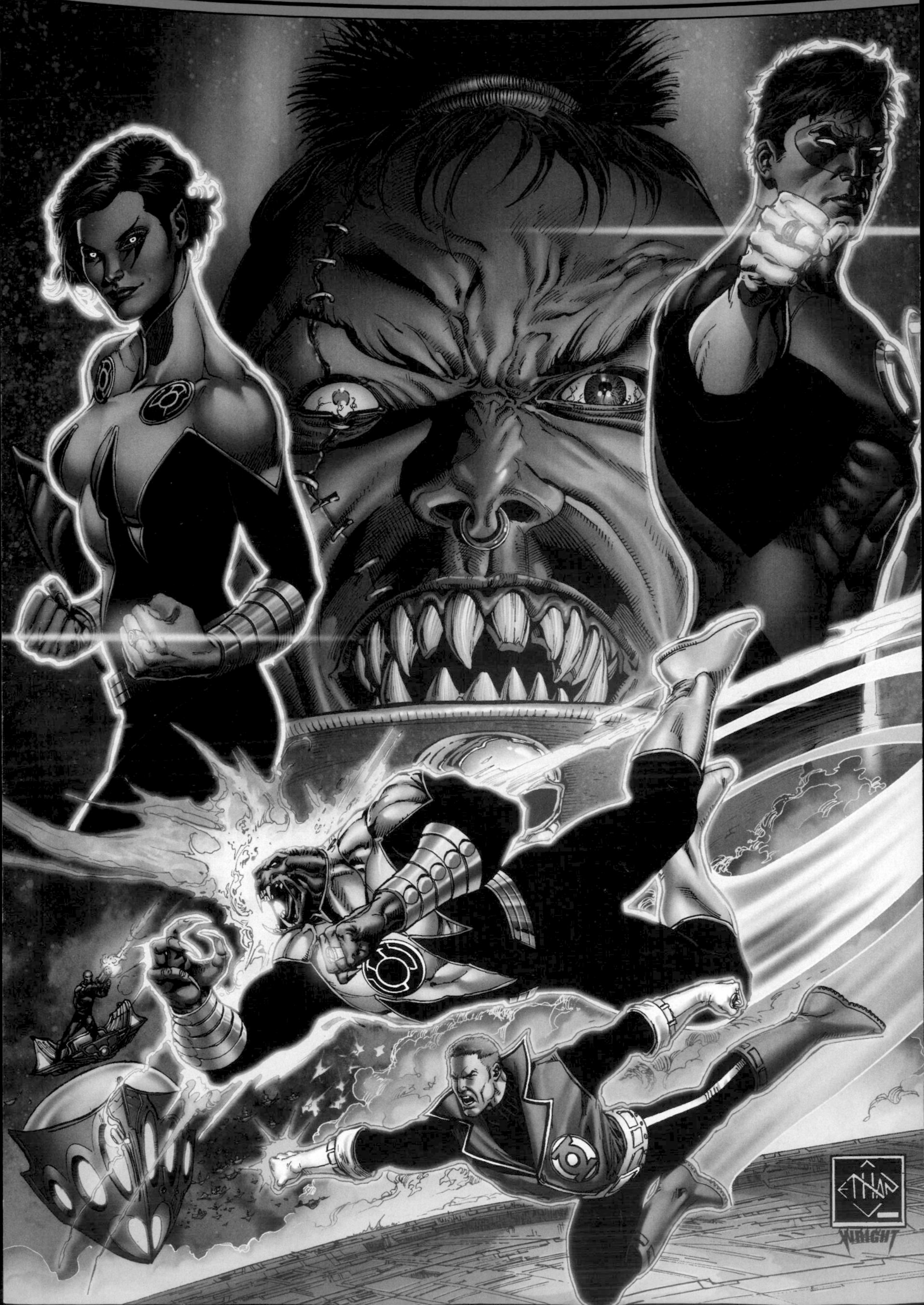

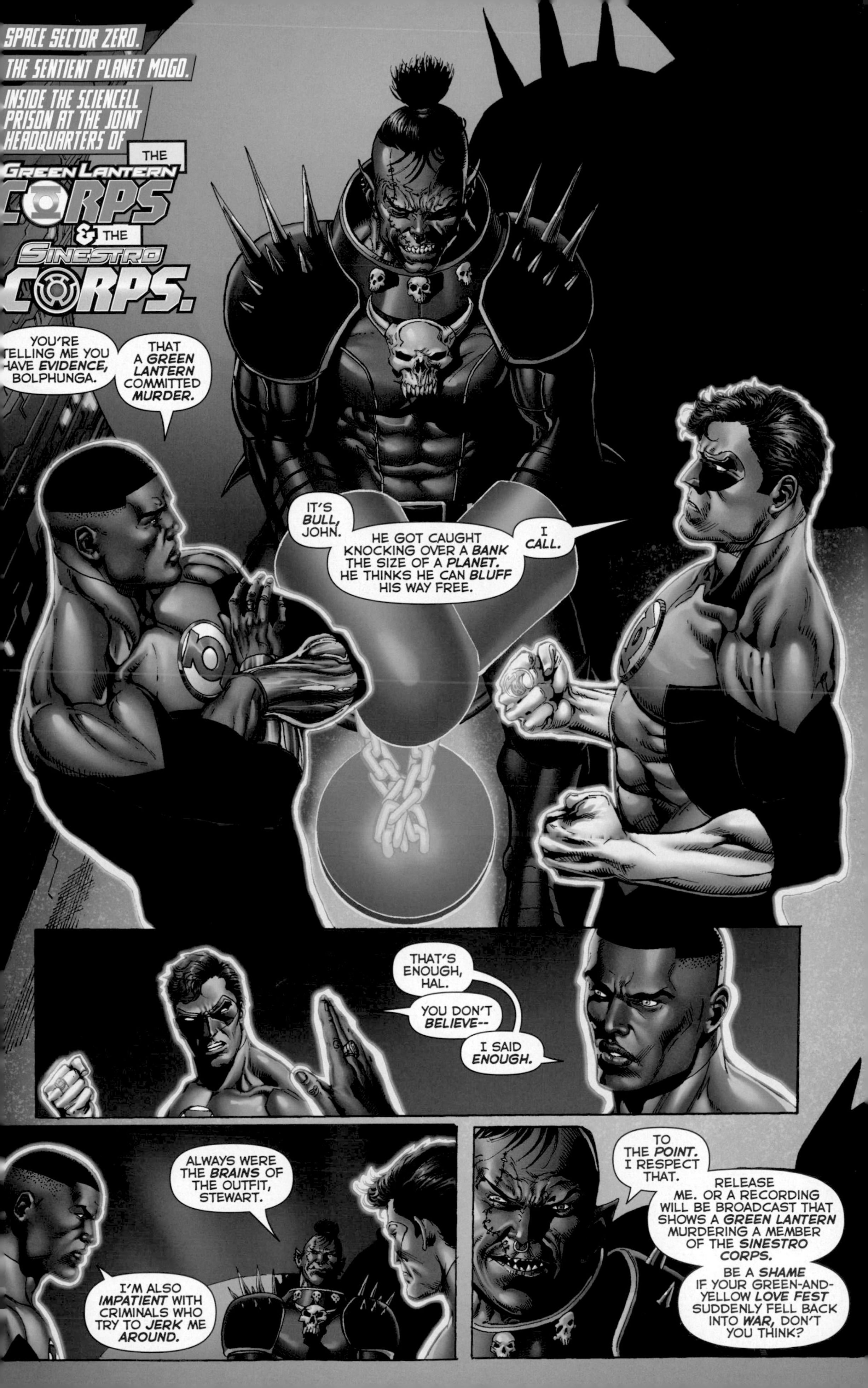
SPACE SECTOR ZERO.
THE SENTIENT PLANET MOGO.
INSIDE THE SCIENCELL PRISON AT THE JOINT HEADQUARTERS OF
THE GREEN LANTERN CORPS & THE SINESTRO CORPS.
YOU'RE TELLING ME YOU HAVE EVIDENCE, BOLPHUNGA.
THAT A GREEN LANTERN COMMITTED MURDER.
IT'S BULL, JOHN.
HE GOT CAUGHT KNOCKING OVER A BANK THE SIZE OF A PLANET. HE THINKS HE CAN BLUFF HIS WAY FREE.
I CALL.
THAT'S ENOUGH, HAL.
YOU DON'T BELIEVE--
I SAID ENOUGH.
ALWAYS WERE THE BRAINS OF THE OUTFIT, STEWART.
I'M ALSO IMPATIENT WITH CRIMINALS WHO TRY TO JERK ME AROUND.
TO THE POINT. I RESPECT THAT.
RELEASE ME. OR A RECORDING WILL BE BROADCAST THAT SHOWS A GREEN LANTERN MURDERING A MEMBER OF THE SINESTRO CORPS.
BE A SHAME IF YOUR GREEN-AND-YELLOW LOVE FEST SUDDENLY FELL BACK INTO WAR, DON'T YOU THINK?

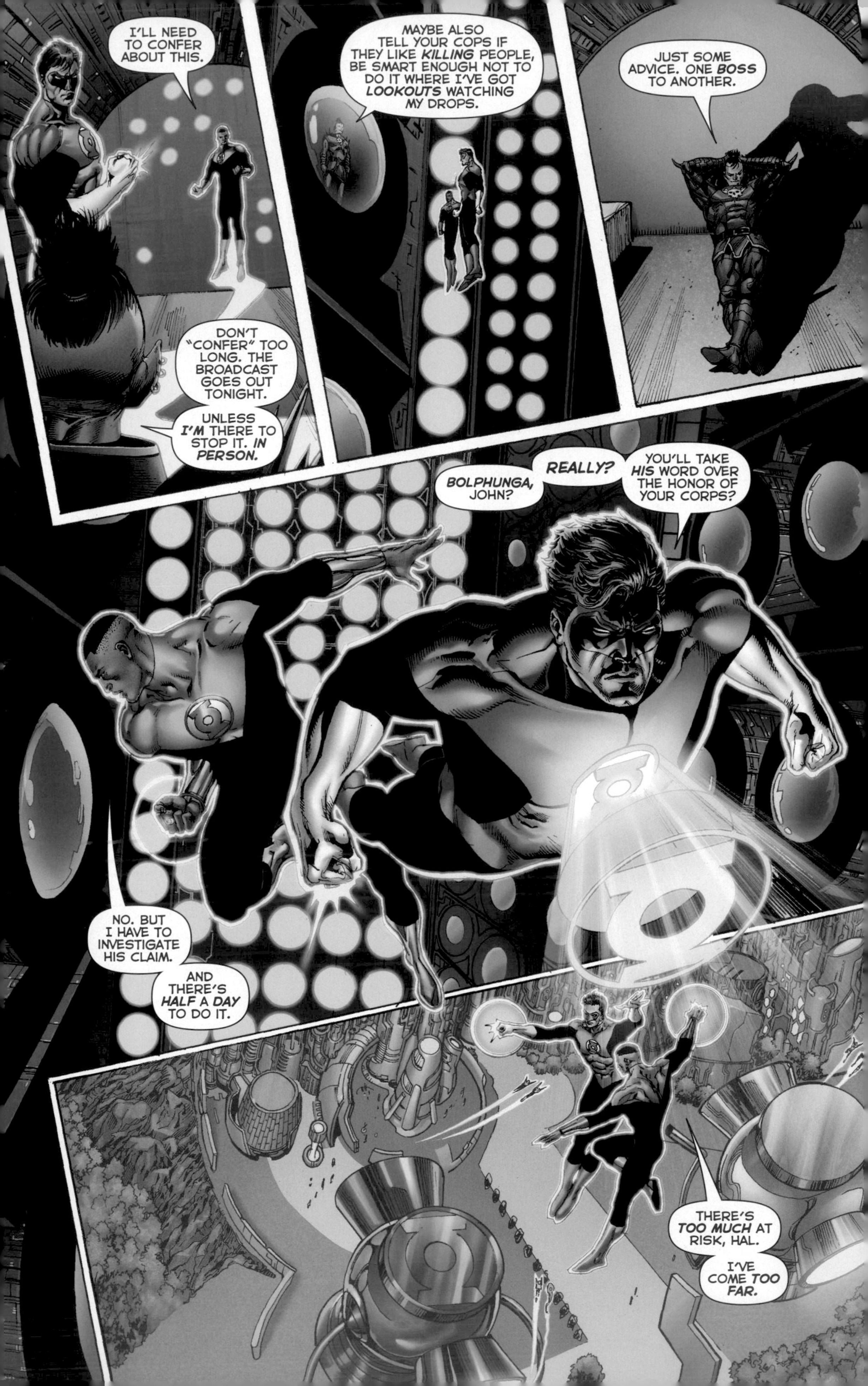

I'LL NEED TO CONFER ABOUT THIS.
DON'T "CONFER" TOO LONG. THE BROADCAST GOES OUT TONIGHT.
UNLESS I'M THERE TO STOP IT. IN PERSON.
MAYBE ALSO TELL YOUR COPS IF THEY LIKE KILLING PEOPLE, BE SMART ENOUGH NOT TO DO IT WHERE I'VE GOT LOOKOUTS WATCHING MY DROPS.
JUST SOME ADVICE. ONE BOSS TO ANOTHER.
BOLPHUNGA, JOHN?
REALLY?
YOU'LL TAKE HIS WORD OVER THE HONOR OF YOUR CORPS?
NO. BUT I HAVE TO INVESTIGATE HIS CLAIM.
AND THERE'S HALF A DAY TO DO IT.
THERE'S TOO MUCH AT RISK, HAL.
I'VE COME TOO FAR.

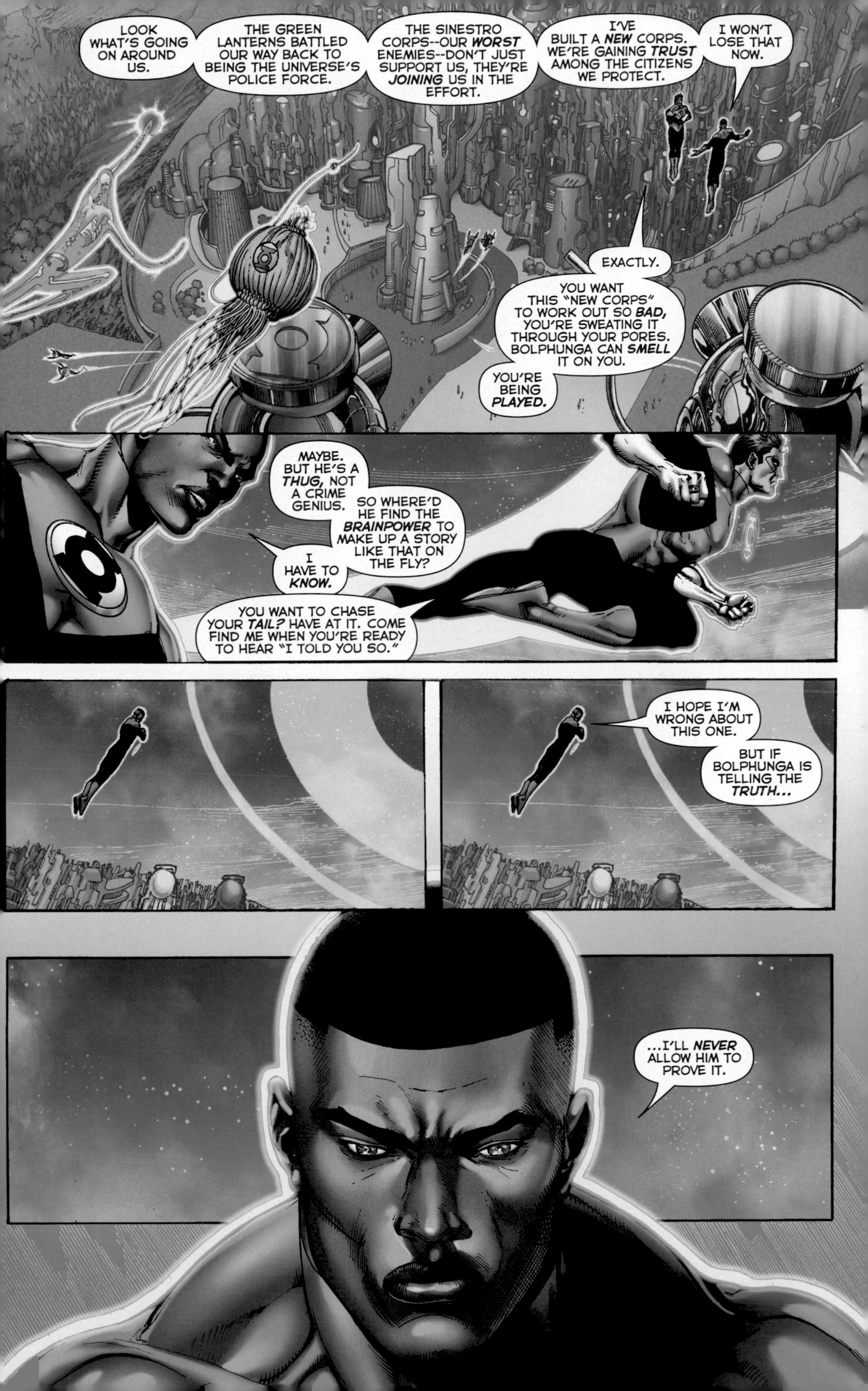

LOOK WHAT'S GOING ON AROUND US.
THE GREEN LANTERNS BATTLED OUR WAY BACK TO BEING THE UNIVERSE'S POLICE FORCE.
THE SINESTRO CORPS--OUR *WORST* ENEMIES--DON'T JUST SUPPORT US, THEY'RE *JOINING* US IN THE EFFORT.
I'VE BUILT A *NEW* CORPS. WE'RE GAINING *TRUST* AMONG THE CITIZENS WE PROTECT.
I WON'T LOSE THAT NOW.
EXACTLY.
YOU WANT THIS "NEW CORPS" TO WORK OUT SO *BAD,* YOU'RE SWEATING IT THROUGH YOUR PORES. BOLPHUNGA CAN *SMELL* IT ON YOU.
YOU'RE BEING *PLAYED.*
MAYBE. BUT HE'S A *THUG,* NOT A CRIME GENIUS.
SO WHERE'D HE FIND THE *BRAINPOWER* TO MAKE UP A STORY LIKE THAT ON THE FLY?
I HAVE TO *KNOW.*
YOU WANT TO CHASE YOUR *TAIL?* HAVE AT IT. COME FIND ME WHEN YOU'RE READY TO HEAR "I TOLD YOU SO."
I HOPE I'M WRONG ABOUT THIS ONE.
BUT IF BOLPHUNGA IS TELLING THE *TRUTH...*
...I'LL *NEVER* ALLOW HIM TO PROVE IT.

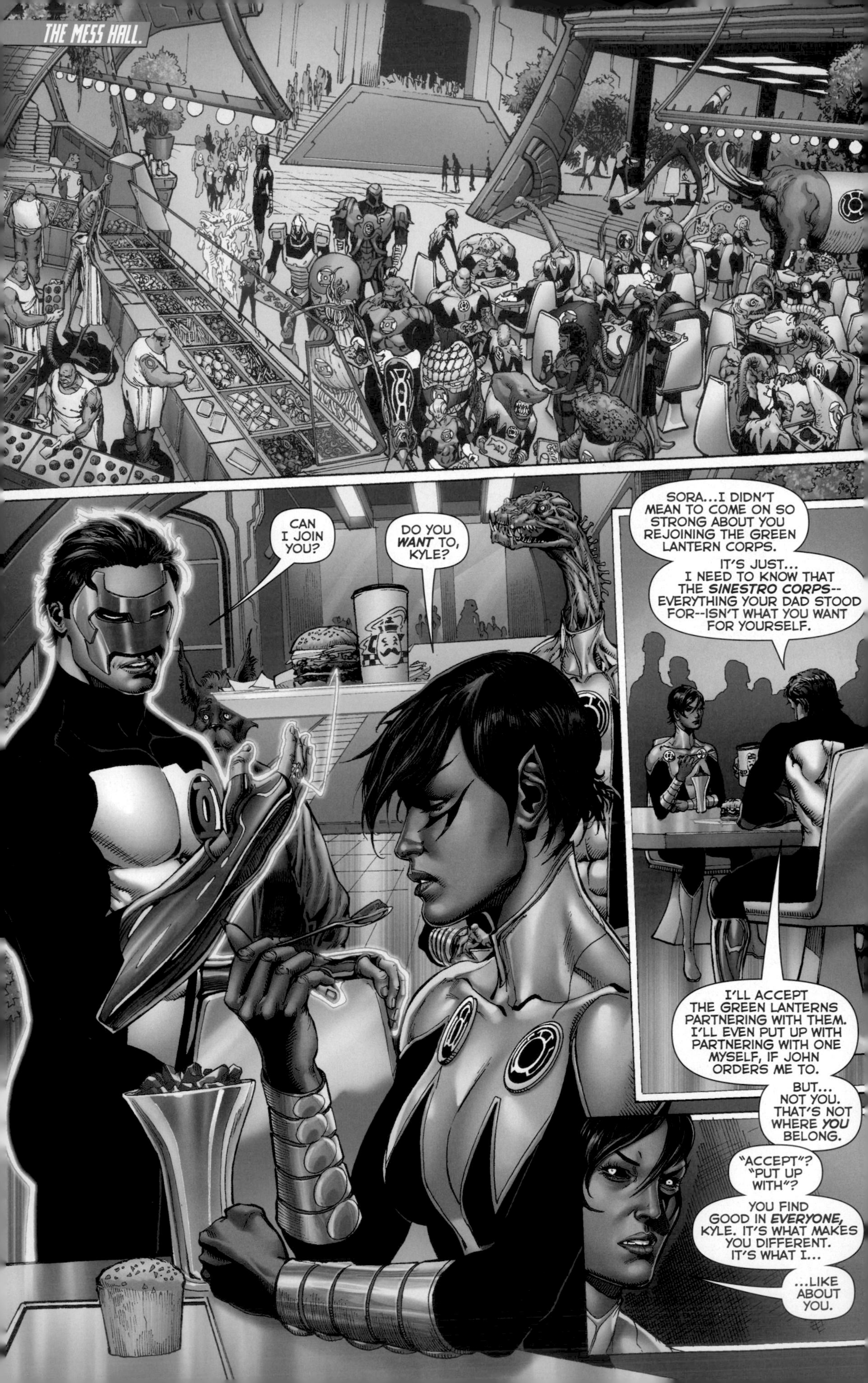
THE MESS HALL.
CAN I JOIN YOU?
DO YOU WANT TO, KYLE?
SORA...I DIDN'T MEAN TO COME ON SO STRONG ABOUT YOU REJOINING THE GREEN LANTERN CORPS.
IT'S JUST... I NEED TO KNOW THAT THE SINESTRO CORPS-- EVERYTHING YOUR DAD STOOD FOR--ISN'T WHAT YOU WANT FOR YOURSELF.
I'LL ACCEPT THE GREEN LANTERNS PARTNERING WITH THEM. I'LL EVEN PUT UP WITH PARTNERING WITH ONE MYSELF, IF JOHN ORDERS ME TO.
BUT... NOT YOU. THAT'S NOT WHERE YOU BELONG.
"ACCEPT"? "PUT UP WITH"?
YOU FIND GOOD IN EVERYONE, KYLE. IT'S WHAT MAKES YOU DIFFERENT. IT'S WHAT I...
...LIKE ABOUT YOU.

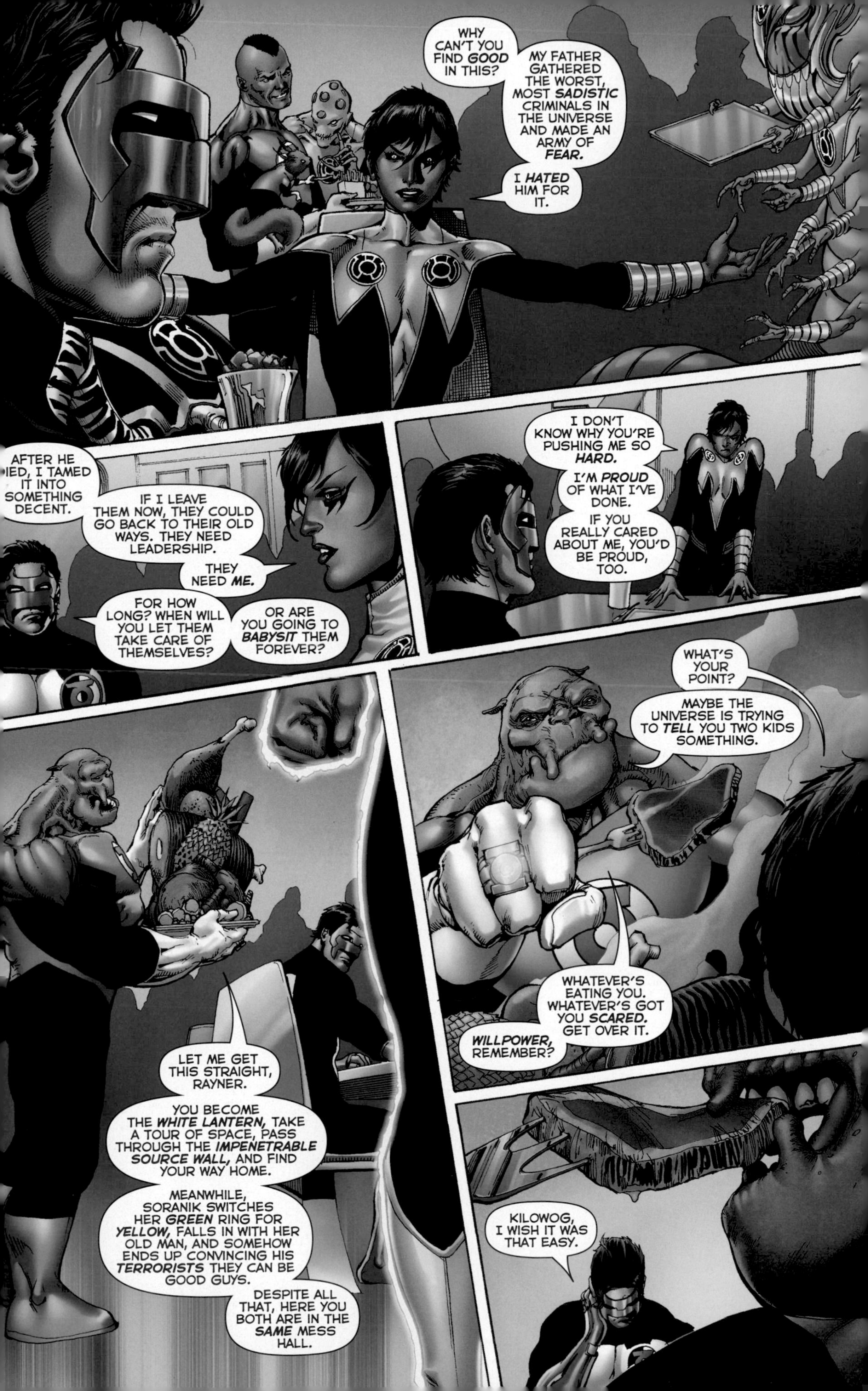
WHY CAN'T YOU FIND GOOD IN THIS?
MY FATHER GATHERED THE WORST, MOST SADISTIC CRIMINALS IN THE UNIVERSE AND MADE AN ARMY OF FEAR.
I HATED HIM FOR IT.
AFTER HE IED, I TAMED IT INTO SOMETHING DECENT.
IF I LEAVE THEM NOW, THEY COULD GO BACK TO THEIR OLD WAYS. THEY NEED LEADERSHIP.
THEY NEED ME.
FOR HOW LONG? WHEN WILL YOU LET THEM TAKE CARE OF THEMSELVES?
OR ARE YOU GOING TO BABYSIT THEM FOREVER?
I DON'T KNOW WHY YOU'RE PUSHING ME SO HARD.
I'M PROUD OF WHAT I'VE DONE.
IF YOU REALLY CARED ABOUT ME, YOU'D BE PROUD, TOO.
LET ME GET THIS STRAIGHT, RAYNER.
YOU BECOME THE WHITE LANTERN, TAKE A TOUR OF SPACE, PASS THROUGH THE IMPENETRABLE SOURCE WALL, AND FIND YOUR WAY HOME.
MEANWHILE, SORANIK SWITCHES HER GREEN RING FOR YELLOW, FALLS IN WITH HER OLD MAN, AND SOMEHOW ENDS UP CONVINCING HIS TERRORISTS THEY CAN BE GOOD GUYS.
DESPITE ALL THAT, HERE YOU BOTH ARE IN THE SAME MESS HALL.
WHAT'S YOUR POINT?
MAYBE THE UNIVERSE IS TRYING TO TELL YOU TWO KIDS SOMETHING.
WHATEVER'S EATING YOU. WHATEVER'S GOT YOU SCARED. GET OVER IT.
WILLPOWER, REMEMBER?
KILOWOG, I WISH IT WAS THAT EASY.

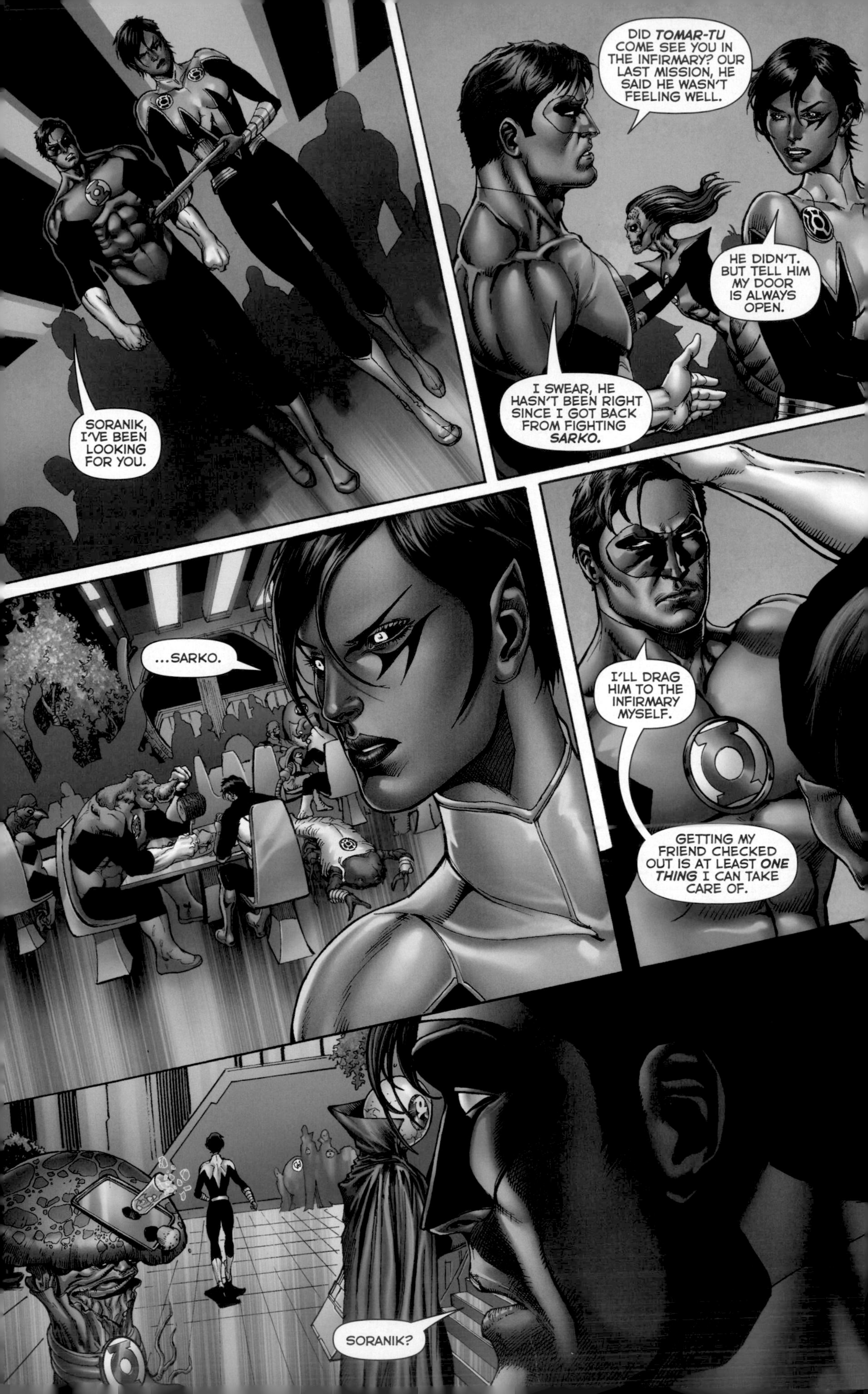
SORANIK, I'VE BEEN LOOKING FOR YOU.
DID TOMAR-TU COME SEE YOU IN THE INFIRMARY? OUR LAST MISSION, HE SAID HE WASN'T FEELING WELL.
HE DIDN'T. BUT TELL HIM MY DOOR IS ALWAYS OPEN.
I SWEAR, HE HASN'T BEEN RIGHT SINCE I GOT BACK FROM FIGHTING SARKO.
...SARKO.
I'LL DRAG HIM TO THE INFIRMARY MYSELF.
GETTING MY FRIEND CHECKED OUT IS AT LEAST ONE THING I CAN TAKE CARE OF.
SORANIK?

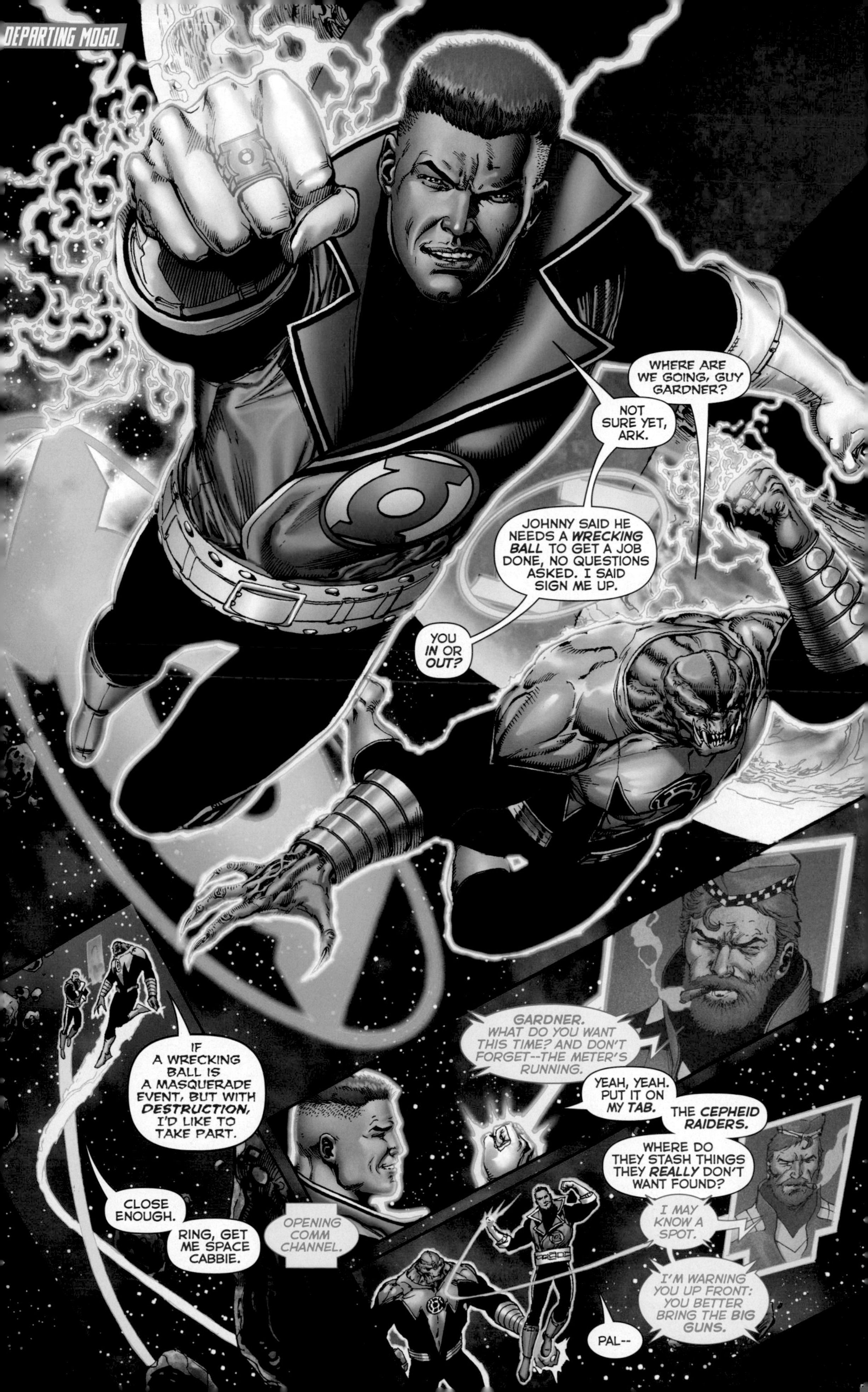
DEPARTING MOGO.
WHERE ARE WE GOING, GUY GARDNER?
NOT SURE YET, ARK.
JOHNNY SAID HE NEEDS A WRECKING BALL TO GET A JOB DONE, NO QUESTIONS ASKED. I SAID SIGN ME UP.
YOU IN OR OUT?
IF A WRECKING BALL IS A MASQUERADE EVENT, BUT WITH DESTRUCTION, I'D LIKE TO TAKE PART.
CLOSE ENOUGH.
RING, GET ME SPACE CABBIE.
OPENING COMM CHANNEL.
GARDNER. WHAT DO YOU WANT THIS TIME? AND DON'T FORGET--THE METER'S RUNNING.
YEAH, YEAH. PUT IT ON MY TAB.
THE CEPHEID RAIDERS.
WHERE DO THEY STASH THINGS THEY REALLY DON'T WANT FOUND?
I MAY KNOW A SPOT.
I'M WARNING YOU UP FRONT: YOU BETTER BRING THE BIG GUNS.
PAL--

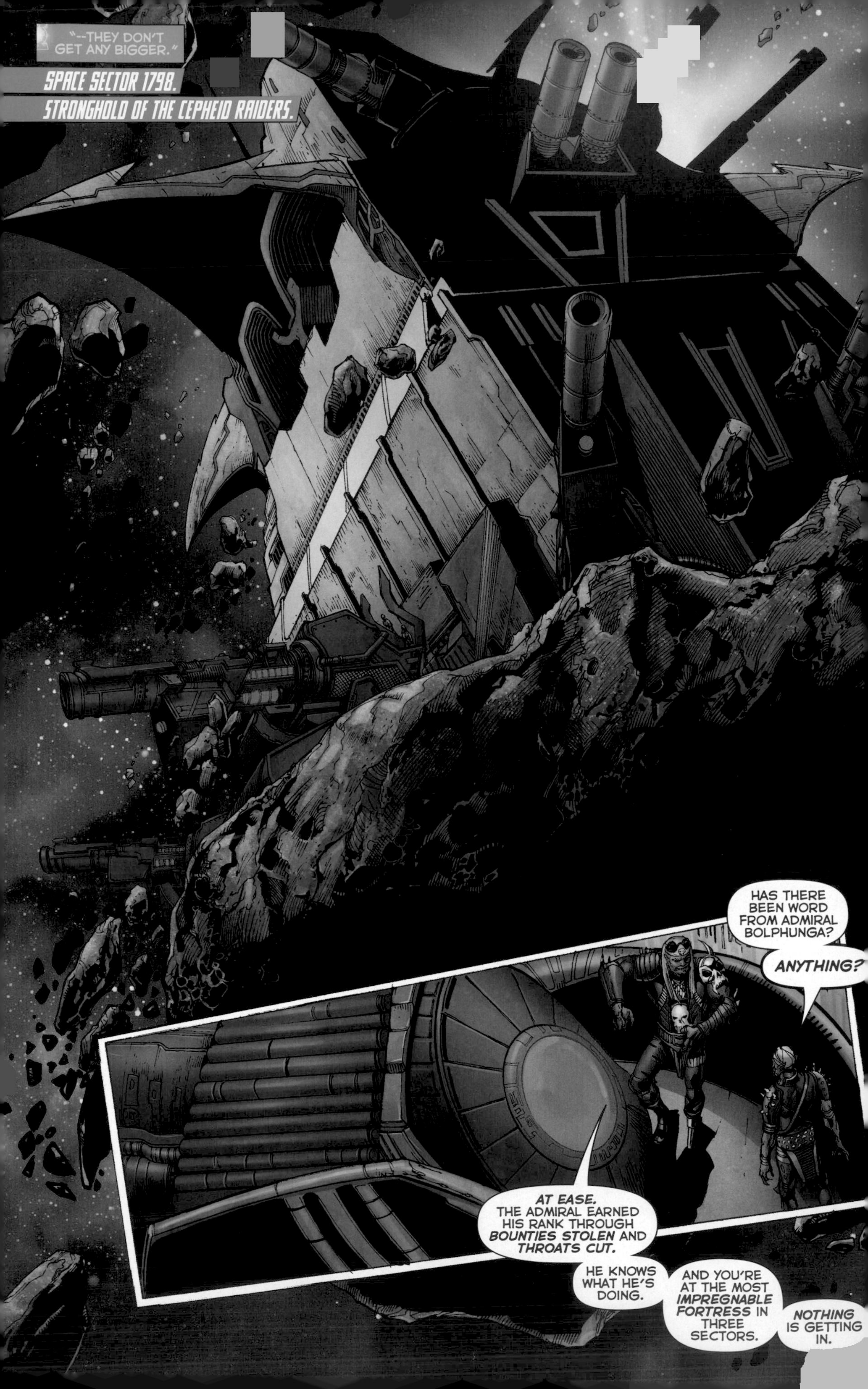
"--THEY DON'T GET ANY BIGGER."
SPACE SECTOR 1798.
STRONGHOLD OF THE CEPHEID RAIDERS.
HAS THERE BEEN WORD FROM ADMIRAL BOLPHUNGA?
ANYTHING?
AT EASE. THE ADMIRAL EARNED HIS RANK THROUGH BOUNTIES STOLEN AND THROATS CUT.
HE KNOWS WHAT HE'S DOING.
AND YOU'RE AT THE MOST IMPREGNABLE FORTRESS IN THREE SECTORS.
NOTHING IS GETTING IN.

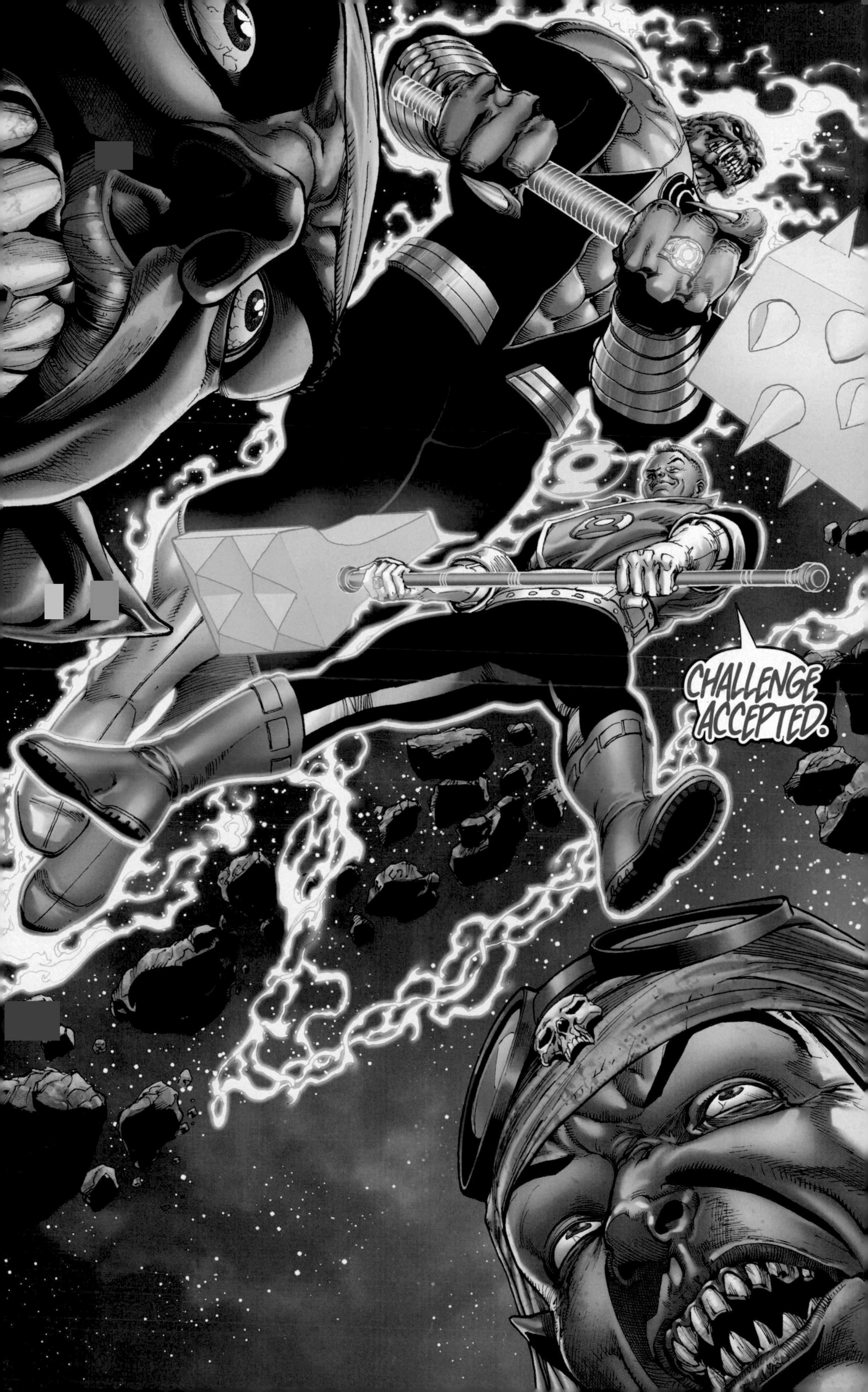
CHALLENGE ACCEPTED.

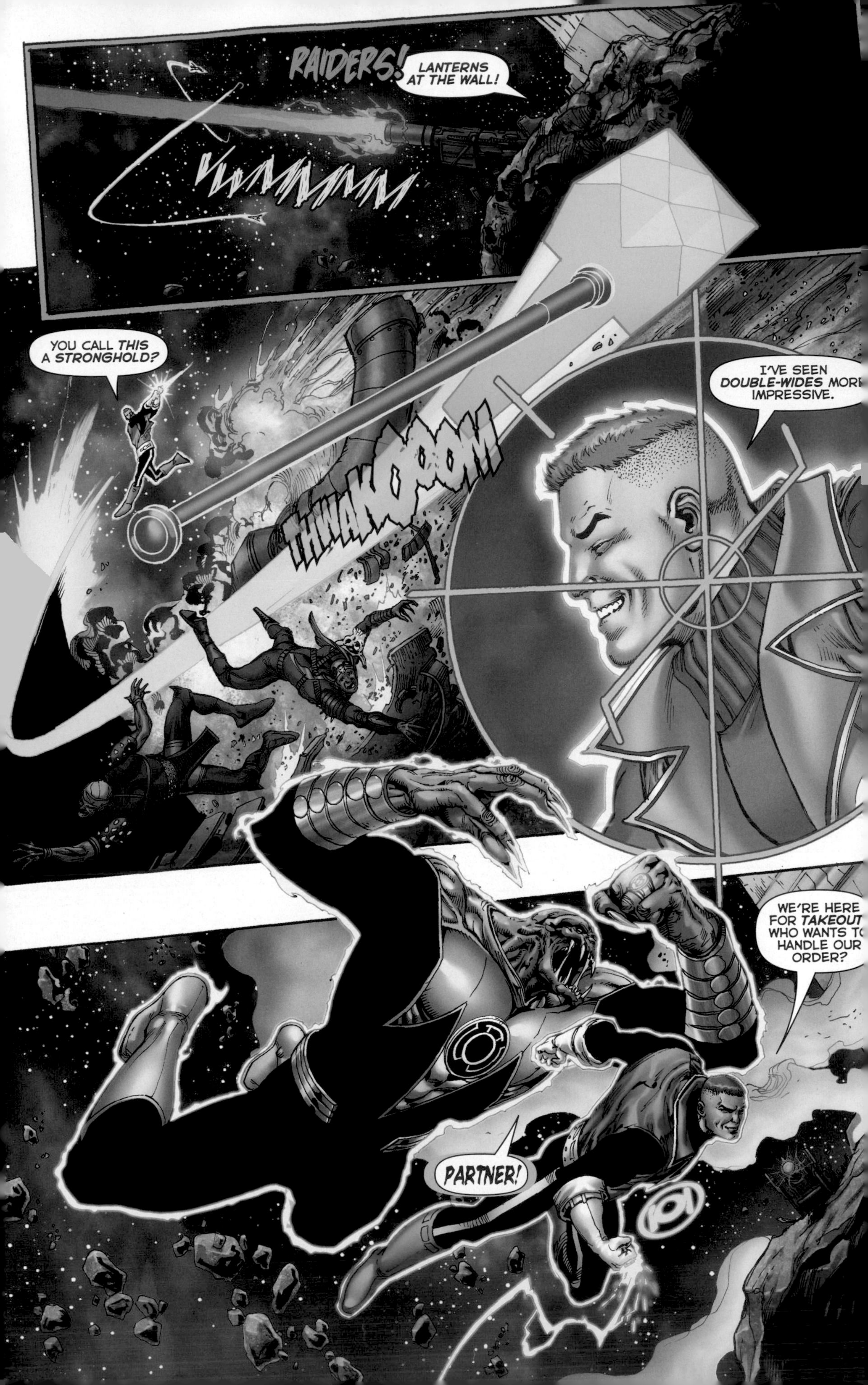
RAIDERS!
LANTERNS AT THE WALL!
VWAMMMM
YOU CALL THIS A STRONGHOLD?
I'VE SEEN DOUBLE-WIDES MORE IMPRESSIVE.
THWAKOOOM
WE'RE HERE FOR TAKEOUT. WHO WANTS TO HANDLE OUR ORDER?
PARTNER!

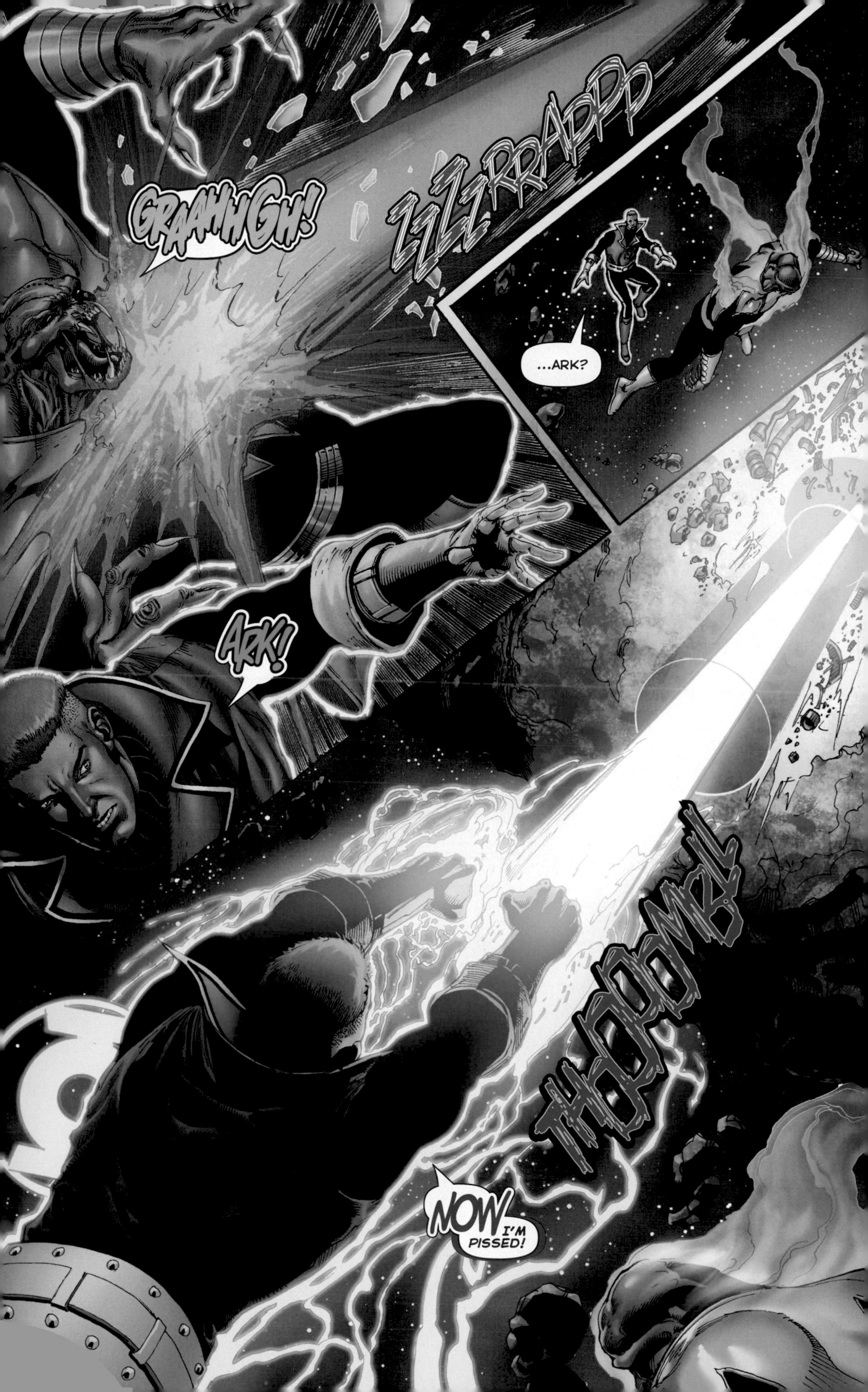
GRAAHHGH!
ZZZZRRAPPP
...ARK?
ARK!
THOOOMB!
NOW I'M PISSED!

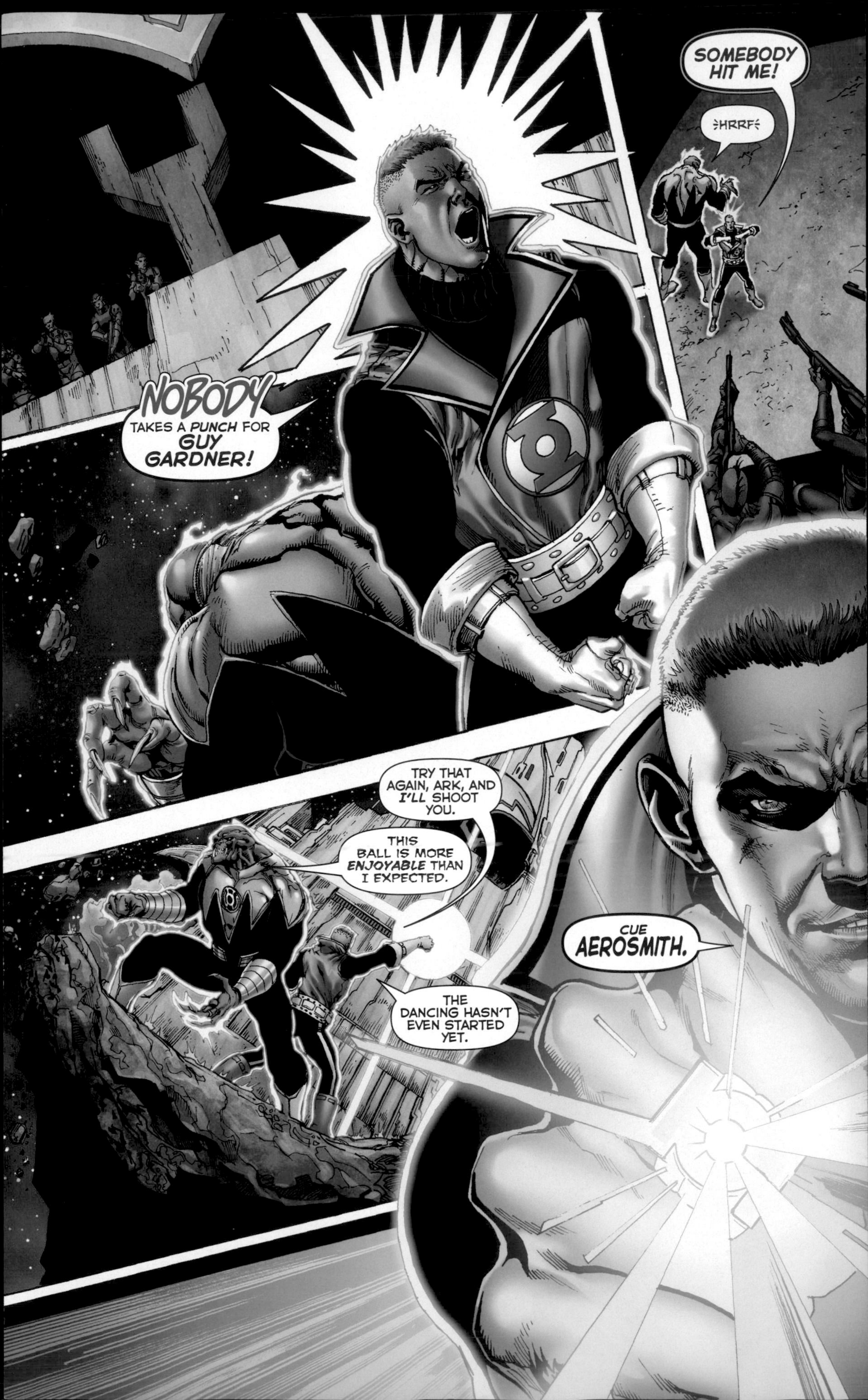
NOBODY TAKES A PUNCH FOR GUY GARDNER!
SOMEBODY HIT ME!
HRRF
TRY THAT AGAIN, ARK, AND I'LL SHOOT YOU.
THIS BALL IS MORE ENJOYABLE THAN I EXPECTED.
THE DANCING HASN'T EVEN STARTED YET.
CUE AEROSMITH.

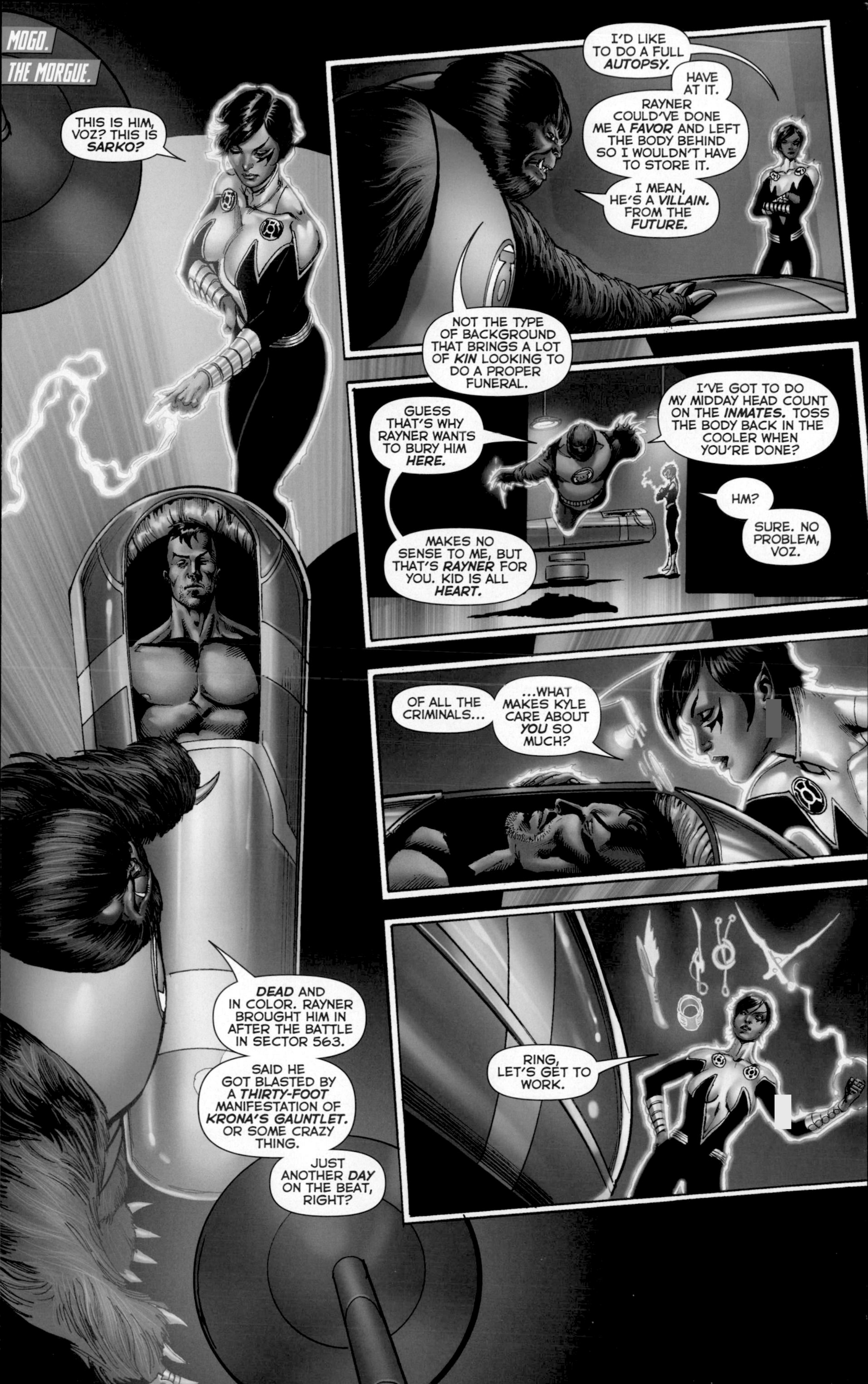

MOGO.
THE MORGUE.
THIS IS HIM, VOZ? THIS IS SARKO?
DEAD AND IN COLOR. RAYNER BROUGHT HIM IN AFTER THE BATTLE IN SECTOR 563.
SAID HE GOT BLASTED BY A THIRTY-FOOT MANIFESTATION OF KRONA'S GAUNTLET. OR SOME CRAZY THING.
JUST ANOTHER DAY ON THE BEAT, RIGHT?
I'D LIKE TO DO A FULL AUTOPSY.
HAVE AT IT.
RAYNER COULD'VE DONE ME A FAVOR AND LEFT THE BODY BEHIND SO I WOULDN'T HAVE TO STORE IT.
I MEAN, HE'S A VILLAIN. FROM THE FUTURE.
NOT THE TYPE OF BACKGROUND THAT BRINGS A LOT OF KIN LOOKING TO DO A PROPER FUNERAL.
GUESS THAT'S WHY RAYNER WANTS TO BURY HIM HERE.
MAKES NO SENSE TO ME, BUT THAT'S RAYNER FOR YOU. KID IS ALL HEART.
I'VE GOT TO DO MY MIDDAY HEAD COUNT ON THE INMATES. TOSS THE BODY BACK IN THE COOLER WHEN YOU'RE DONE?
HM?
SURE. NO PROBLEM, VOZ.
OF ALL THE CRIMINALS...
...WHAT MAKES KYLE CARE ABOUT YOU SO MUCH?
RING, LET'S GET TO WORK.

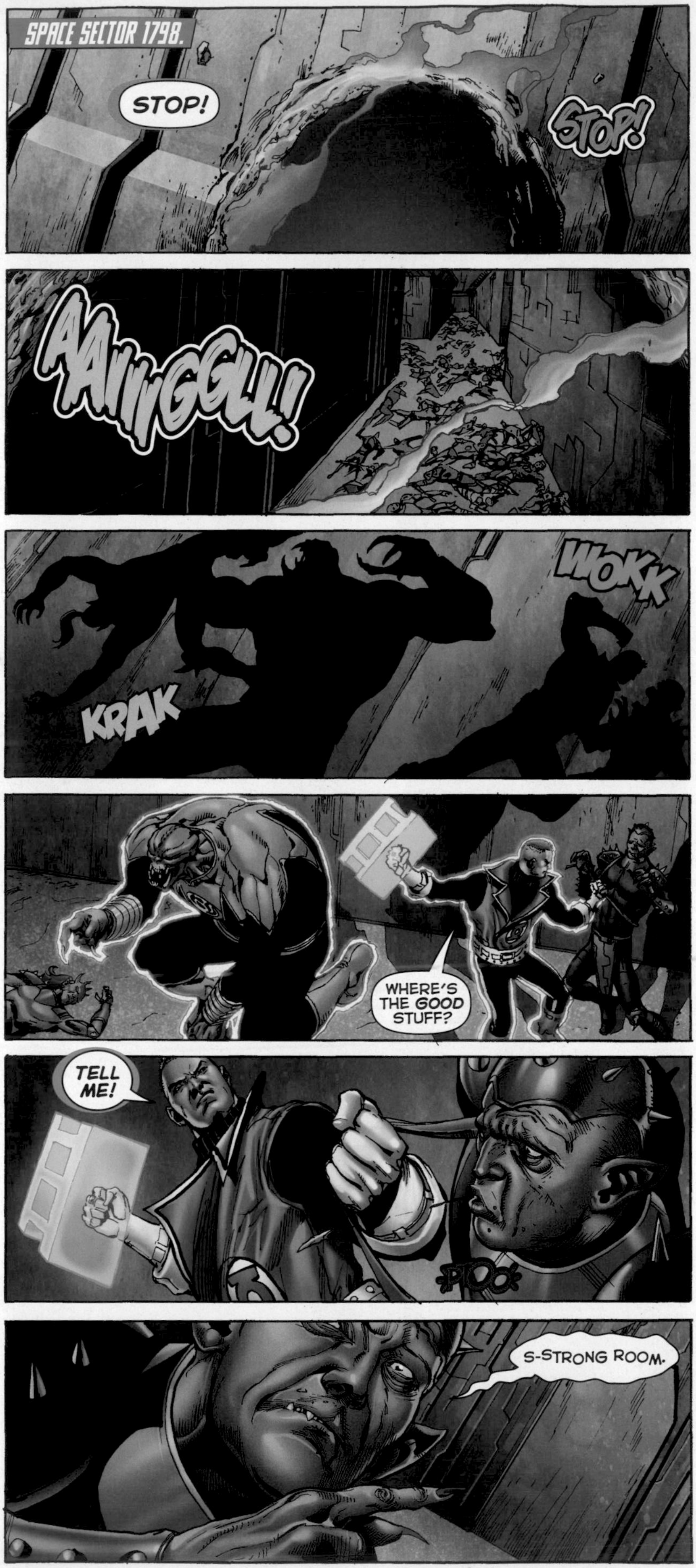
SPACE SECTOR 1798.
STOP!
STOP!
AAIIIGGLL!
WOKK
KRAK
WHERE'S THE GOOD STUFF?
TELL ME!
PTOO
S-STRONG ROOM.

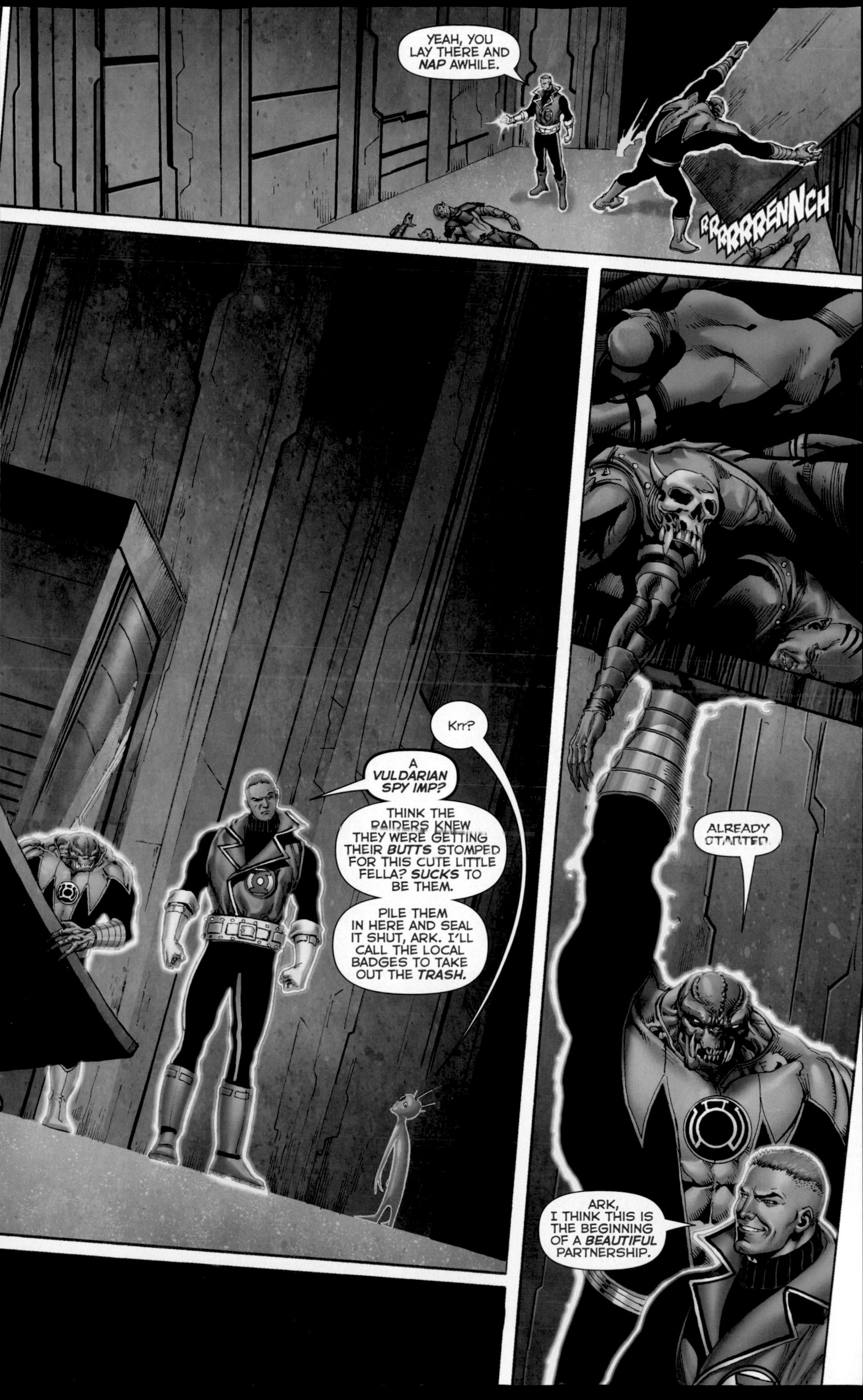
YEAH, YOU LAY THERE AND *NAP* AWHILE.
RRRRRRENNCH
Krr?
A *VULDARIAN SPY IMP?*
THINK THE RAIDERS KNEW THEY WERE GETTING THEIR *BUTTS* STOMPED FOR THIS CUTE LITTLE FELLA? *SUCKS* TO BE THEM.
PILE THEM IN HERE AND SEAL IT SHUT, ARK. I'LL CALL THE LOCAL BADGES TO TAKE OUT THE *TRASH.*
ALREADY STARTED.
ARK, I THINK THIS IS THE BEGINNING OF A *BEAUTIFUL* PARTNERSHIP.

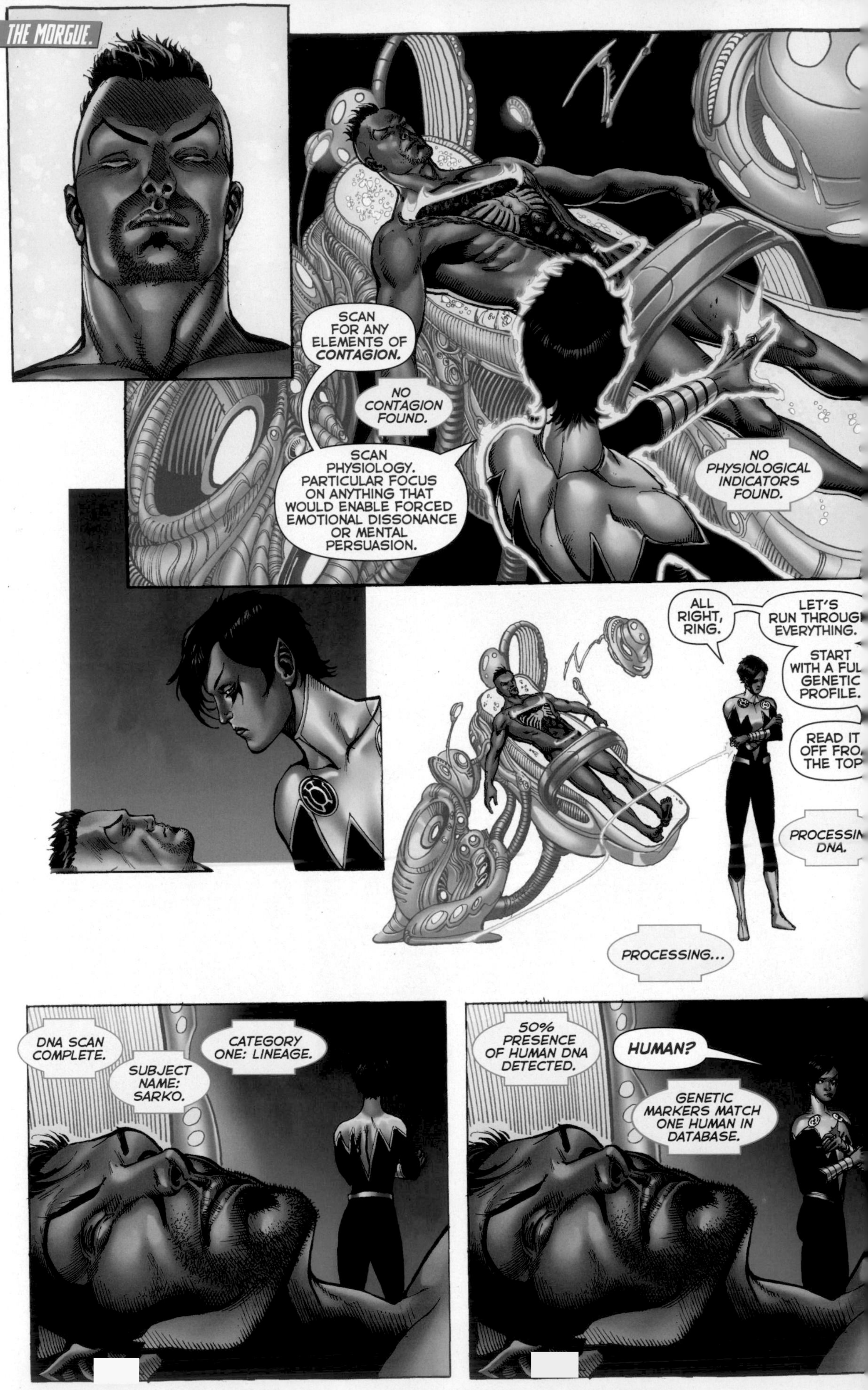
THE MORGUE.
SCAN FOR ANY ELEMENTS OF CONTAGION.
NO CONTAGION FOUND.
SCAN PHYSIOLOGY. PARTICULAR FOCUS ON ANYTHING THAT WOULD ENABLE FORCED EMOTIONAL DISSONANCE OR MENTAL PERSUASION.
NO PHYSIOLOGICAL INDICATORS FOUND.
ALL RIGHT, RING.
LET'S RUN THROUG EVERYTHING.
START WITH A FUL GENETIC PROFILE.
READ IT OFF FRO THE TOP
PROCESSIN DNA.
PROCESSING...
DNA SCAN COMPLETE.
SUBJECT NAME: SARKO.
CATEGORY ONE: LINEAGE.
50% PRESENCE OF HUMAN DNA DETECTED.
HUMAN?
GENETIC MARKERS MATCH ONE HUMAN IN DATABASE.

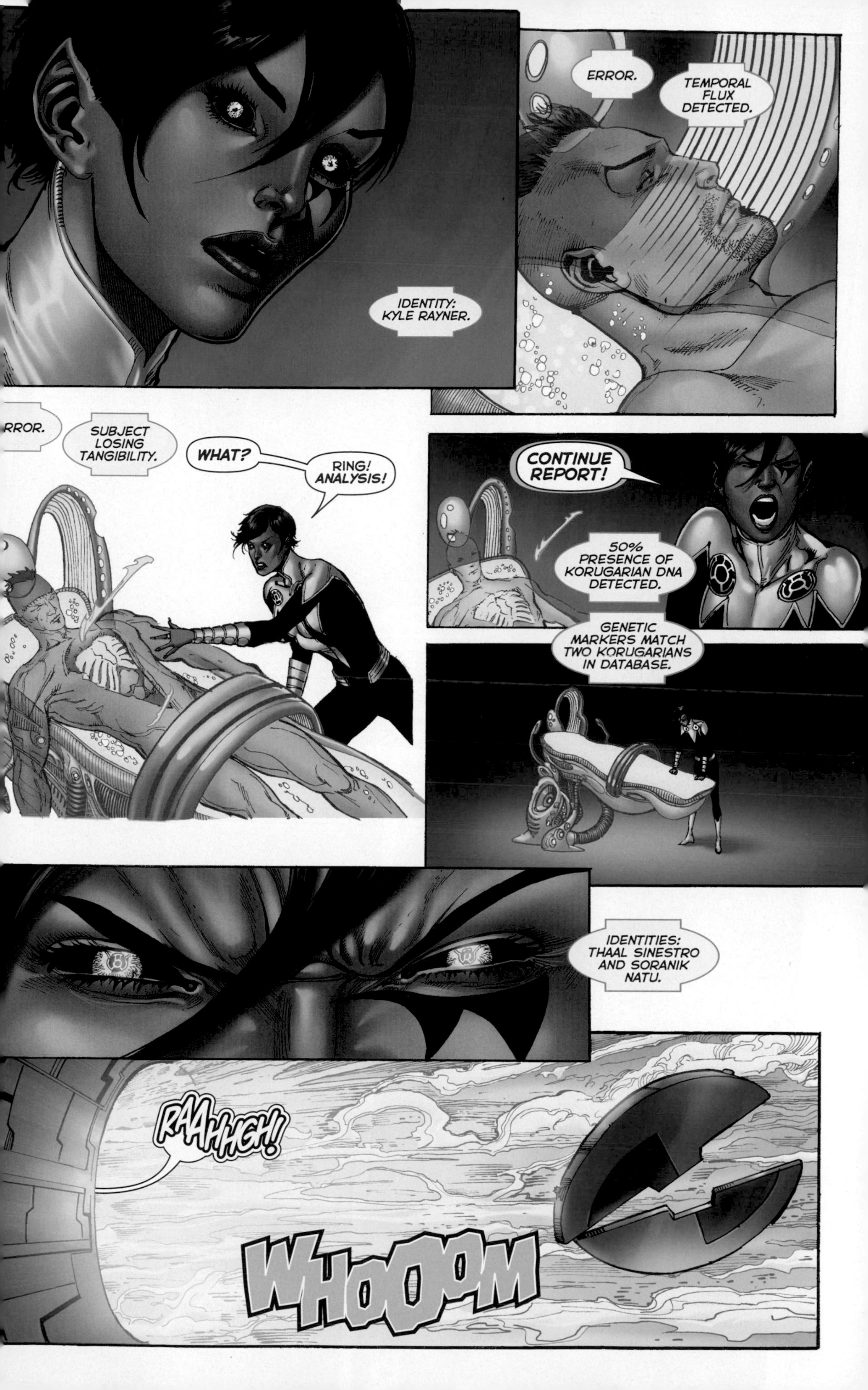

IDENTITY: KYLE RAYNER.
ERROR.
TEMPORAL FLUX DETECTED.
RROR.
SUBJECT LOSING TANGIBILITY.
WHAT?
RING! ANALYSIS!
CONTINUE REPORT!
50% PRESENCE OF KORUGARIAN DNA DETECTED.
GENETIC MARKERS MATCH TWO KORUGARIANS IN DATABASE.
IDENTITIES: THAAL SINESTRO AND SORANIK NATU.
RAAHHGH!
WHOOOM

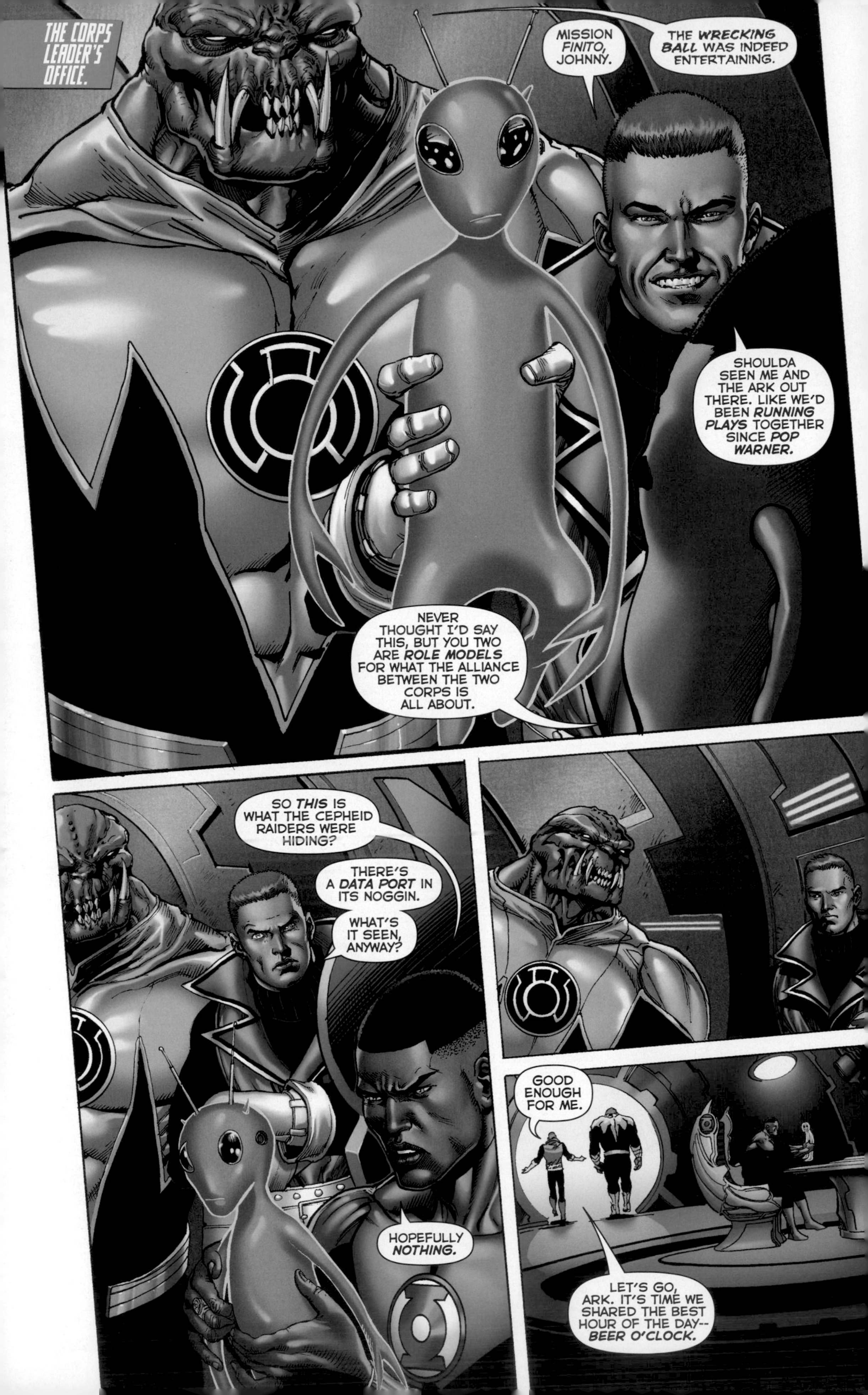
THE CORPS LEADER'S OFFICE.
MISSION FINITO, JOHNNY.
THE WRECKING BALL WAS INDEED ENTERTAINING.
SHOULDA SEEN ME AND THE ARK OUT THERE. LIKE WE'D BEEN RUNNING PLAYS TOGETHER SINCE POP WARNER.
NEVER THOUGHT I'D SAY THIS, BUT YOU TWO ARE ROLE MODELS FOR WHAT THE ALLIANCE BETWEEN THE TWO CORPS IS ALL ABOUT.
SO THIS IS WHAT THE CEPHEID RAIDERS WERE HIDING?
THERE'S A DATA PORT IN ITS NOGGIN.
WHAT'S IT SEEN, ANYWAY?
HOPEFULLY NOTHING.
GOOD ENOUGH FOR ME.
LET'S GO, ARK. IT'S TIME WE SHARED THE BEST HOUR OF THE DAY-- BEER O'CLOCK.

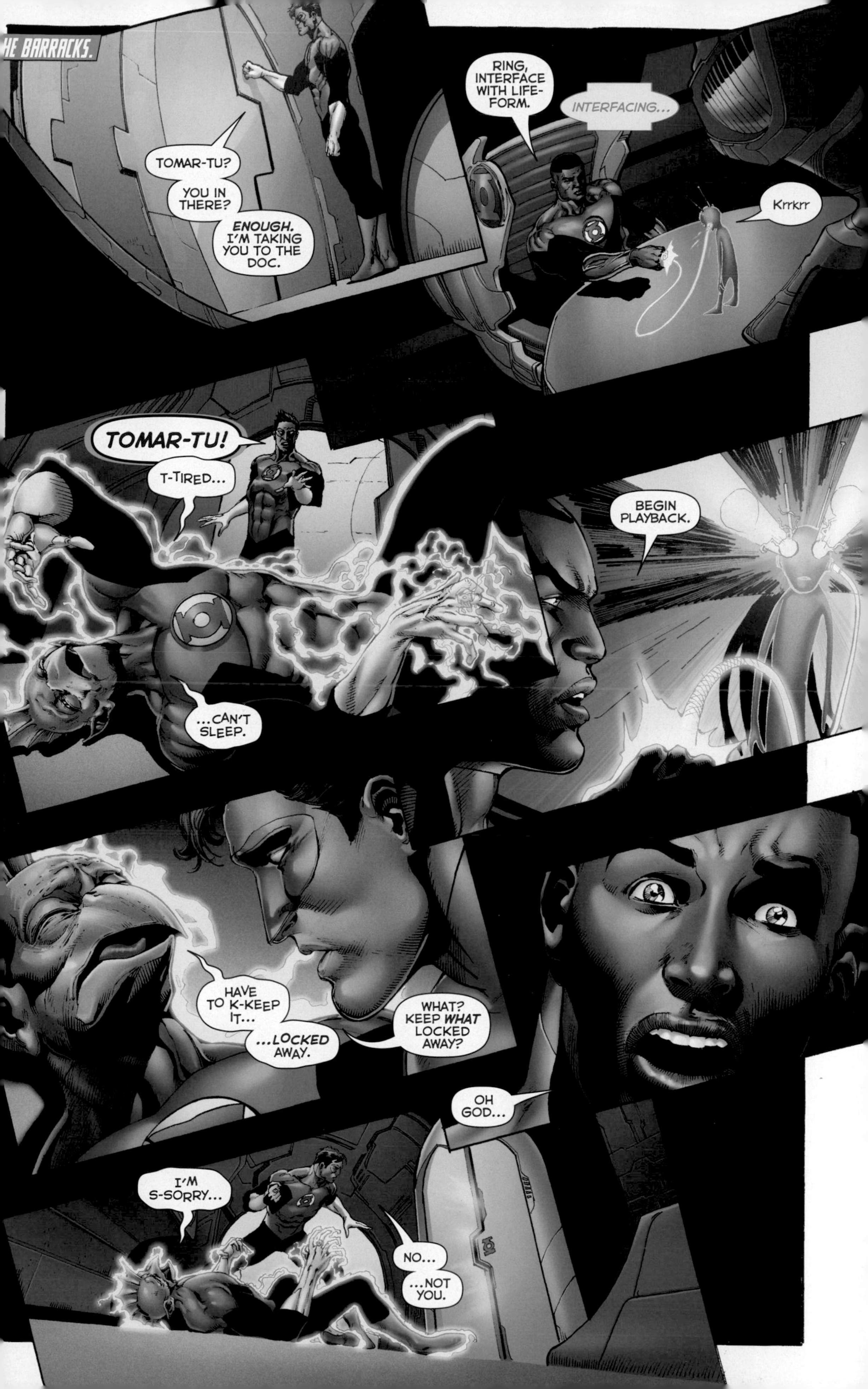
HE BARRACKS.
TOMAR-TU?
YOU IN THERE?
ENOUGH. I'M TAKING YOU TO THE DOC.
RING, INTERFACE WITH LIFE-FORM.
INTERFACING...
Krrkrr
TOMAR-TU!
T-TIRED...
...CAN'T SLEEP.
BEGIN PLAYBACK.
HAVE TO K-KEEP IT...
...LOCKED AWAY.
WHAT? KEEP WHAT LOCKED AWAY?
OH GOD...
I'M S-SORRY...
NO...
...NOT YOU.

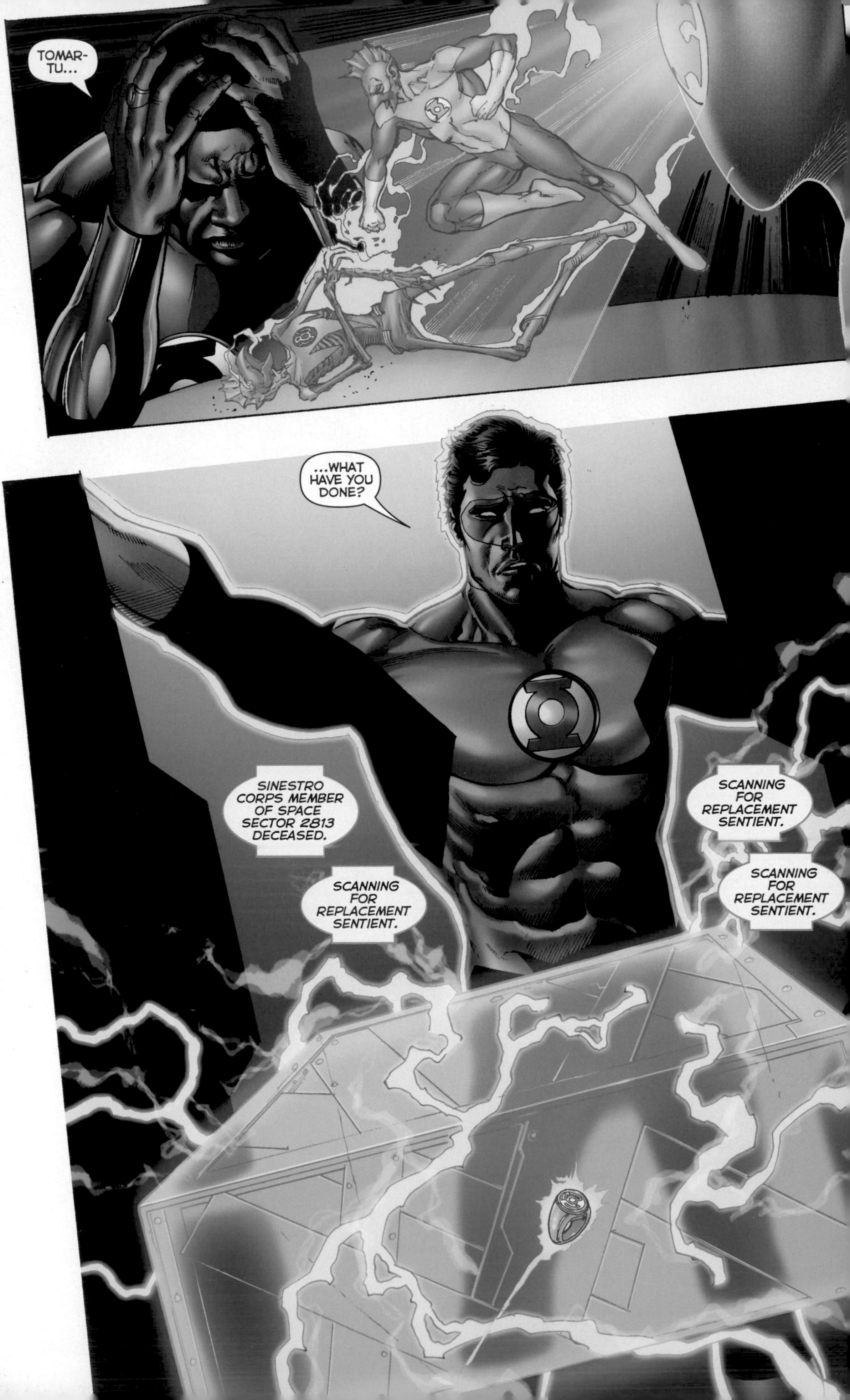
TOMAR-TU...
...WHAT HAVE YOU DONE?
SINESTRO CORPS MEMBER OF SPACE SECTOR 2813 DECEASED.
SCANNING FOR REPLACEMENT SENTIENT.
SCANNING FOR REPLACEMENT SENTIENT.
SCANNING FOR REPLACEMENT SENTIENT.

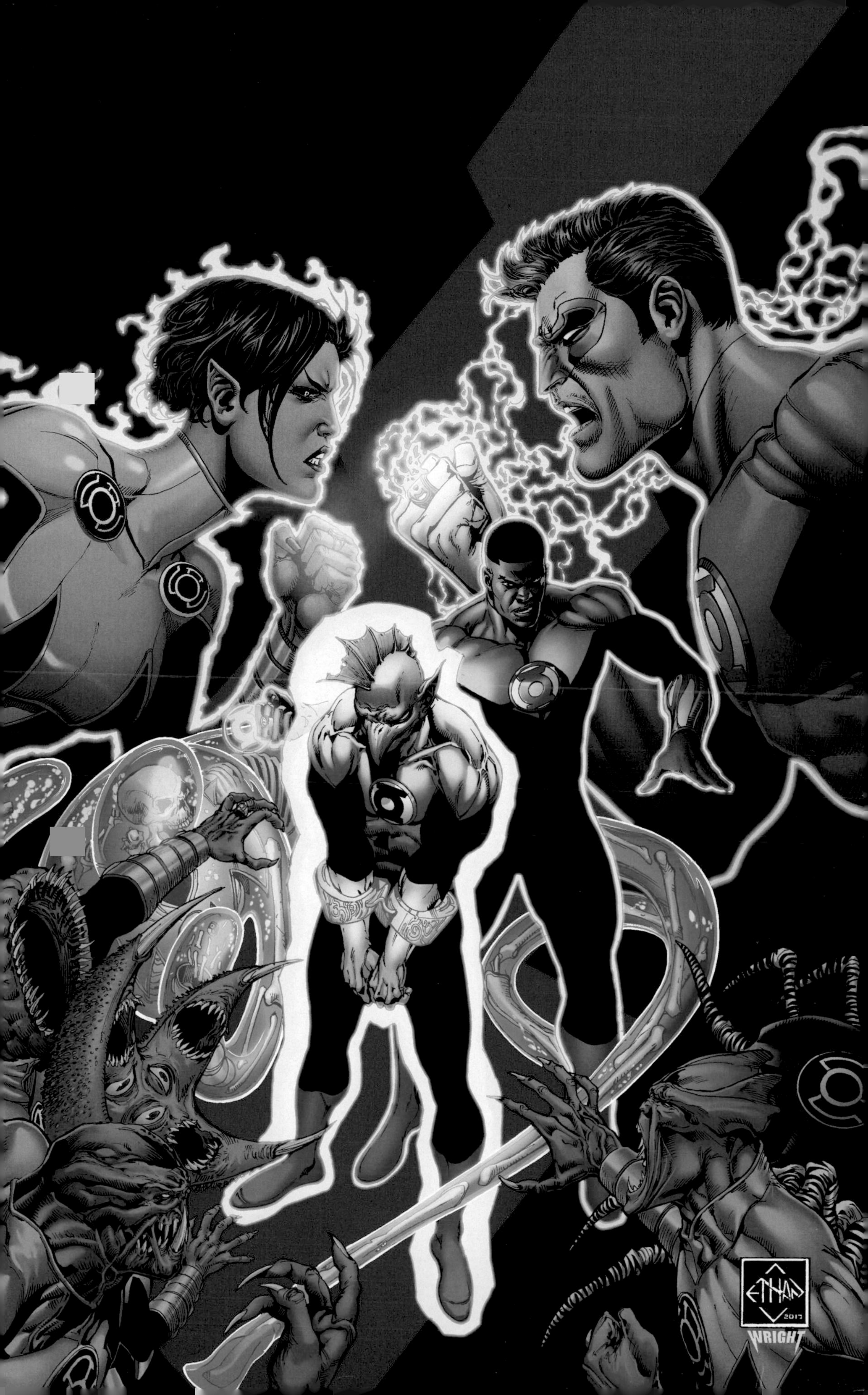
WRIGHT

"FRACTURE PART 3: DEAD LEGACY"

ETHAN VAN SCIVER artist * JASON WRIGHT colorist
cover art by ETHAN VAN SCIVER and JASON WRIGHT

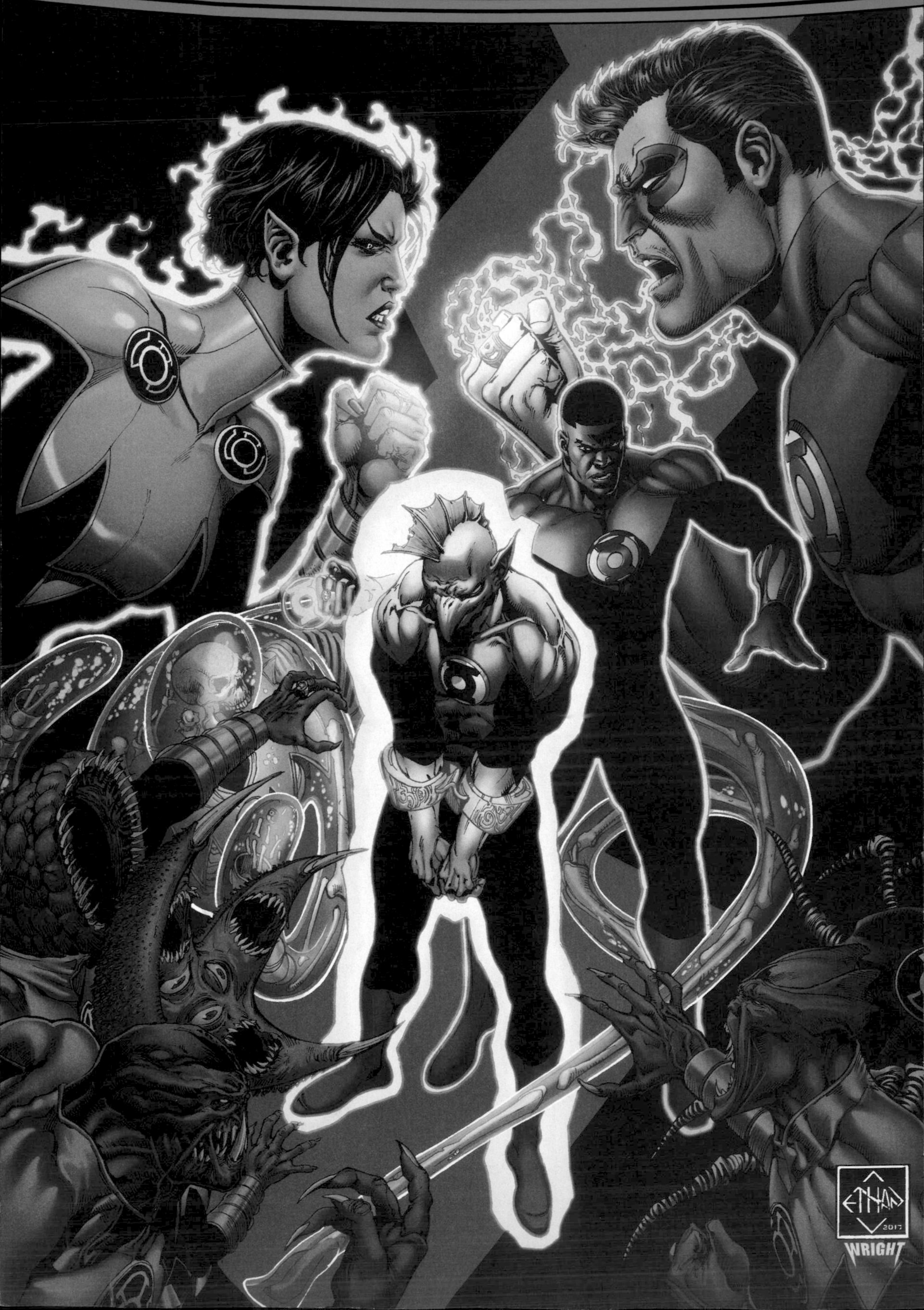
WRIGHT

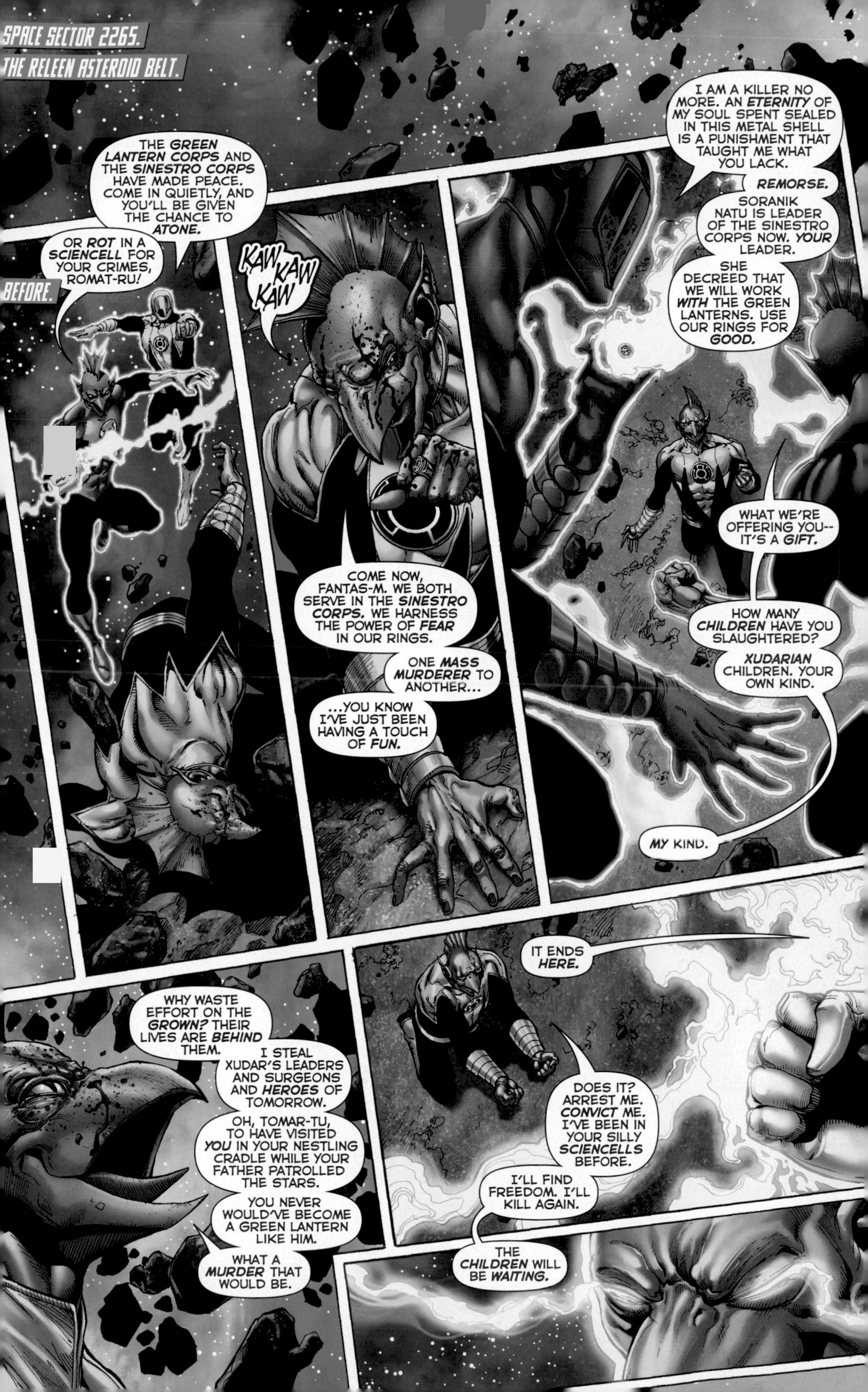
SPACE SECTOR 2265.
THE RELEEN ASTEROID BELT.
THE GREEN LANTERN CORPS AND THE SINESTRO CORPS HAVE MADE PEACE. COME IN QUIETLY, AND YOU'LL BE GIVEN THE CHANCE TO ATONE.
OR ROT IN A SCIENCELL FOR YOUR CRIMES, ROMAT-RU!
BEFORE.
KAW KAW KAW
COME NOW, FANTAS-M. WE BOTH SERVE IN THE SINESTRO CORPS. WE HARNESS THE POWER OF FEAR IN OUR RINGS.
ONE MASS MURDERER TO ANOTHER...
...YOU KNOW I'VE JUST BEEN HAVING A TOUCH OF FUN.
I AM A KILLER NO MORE. AN ETERNITY OF MY SOUL SPENT SEALED IN THIS METAL SHELL IS A PUNISHMENT THAT TAUGHT ME WHAT YOU LACK.
REMORSE.
SORANIK NATU IS LEADER OF THE SINESTRO CORPS NOW. YOUR LEADER.
SHE DECREED THAT WE WILL WORK WITH THE GREEN LANTERNS. USE OUR RINGS FOR GOOD.
WHAT WE'RE OFFERING YOU-- IT'S A GIFT.
HOW MANY CHILDREN HAVE YOU SLAUGHTERED?
XUDARIAN CHILDREN. YOUR OWN KIND.
MY KIND.
WHY WASTE EFFORT ON THE GROWN? THEIR LIVES ARE BEHIND THEM.
I STEAL XUDAR'S LEADERS AND SURGEONS AND HEROES OF TOMORROW.
OH, TOMAR-TU, TO HAVE VISITED YOU IN YOUR NESTLING CRADLE WHILE YOUR FATHER PATROLLED THE STARS.
YOU NEVER WOULD'VE BECOME A GREEN LANTERN LIKE HIM.
WHAT A MURDER THAT WOULD BE.
IT ENDS HERE.
DOES IT? ARREST ME. CONVICT ME. I'VE BEEN IN YOUR SILLY SCIENCELLS BEFORE.
I'LL FIND FREEDOM. I'LL KILL AGAIN.
THE CHILDREN WILL BE WAITING.

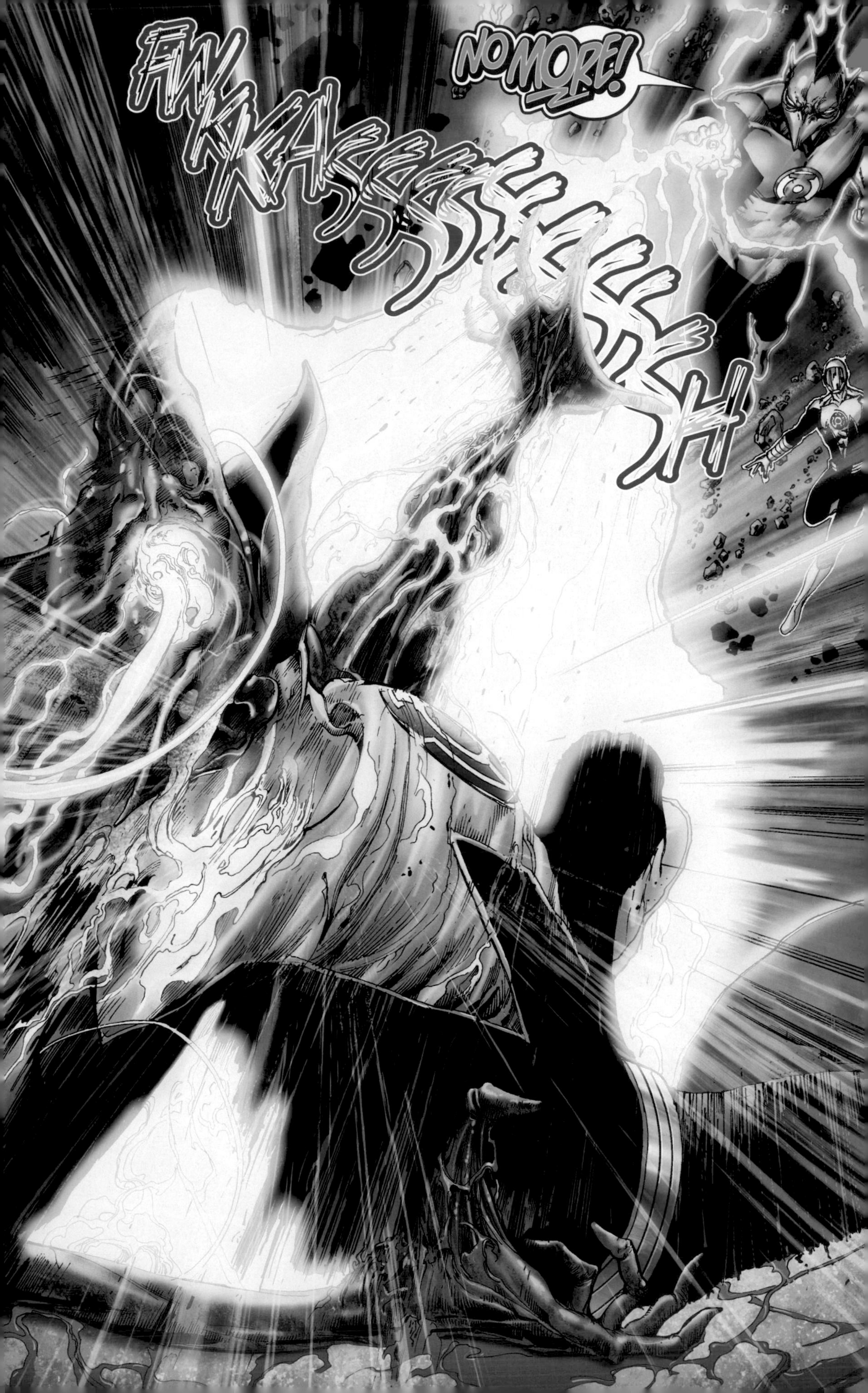

NO MORE!

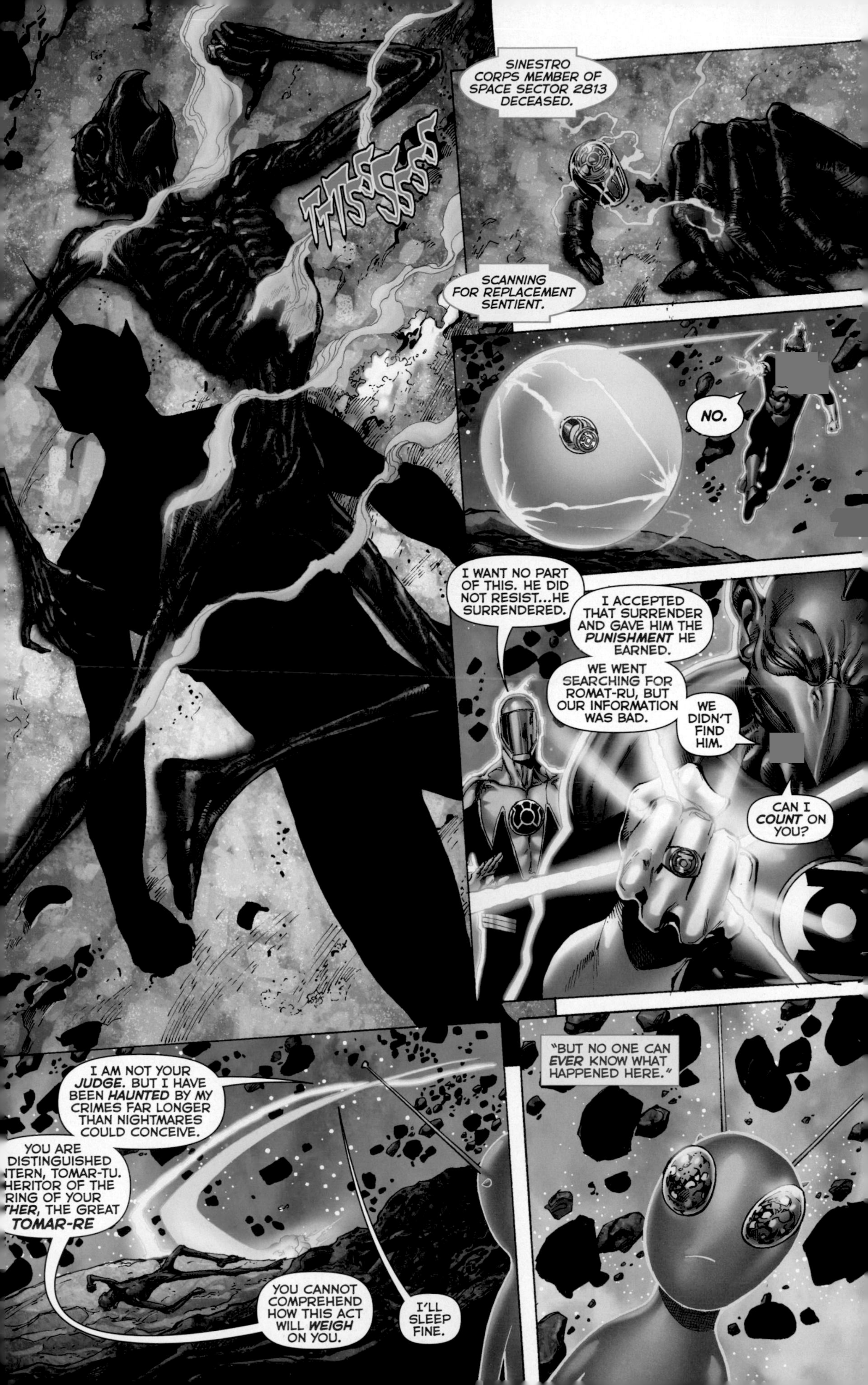

TTSSSSS
SINESTRO CORPS MEMBER OF SPACE SECTOR 2813 DECEASED.
SCANNING FOR REPLACEMENT SENTIENT.
NO.
I WANT NO PART OF THIS. HE DID NOT RESIST...HE SURRENDERED.
I ACCEPTED THAT SURRENDER AND GAVE HIM THE *PUNISHMENT* HE EARNED.
WE WENT SEARCHING FOR ROMAT-RU, BUT OUR INFORMATION WAS BAD.
WE DIDN'T FIND HIM.
CAN I *COUNT* ON YOU?
I AM NOT YOUR *JUDGE*. BUT I HAVE BEEN *HAUNTED* BY MY CRIMES FAR LONGER THAN NIGHTMARES COULD CONCEIVE.
YOU ARE DISTINGUISHED TERN, TOMAR-TU. HERITOR OF THE RING OF YOUR THER, THE GREAT TOMAR-RE
YOU CANNOT COMPREHEND HOW THIS ACT WILL *WEIGH* ON YOU.
I'LL SLEEP FINE.
"BUT NO ONE CAN *EVER* KNOW WHAT HAPPENED HERE."

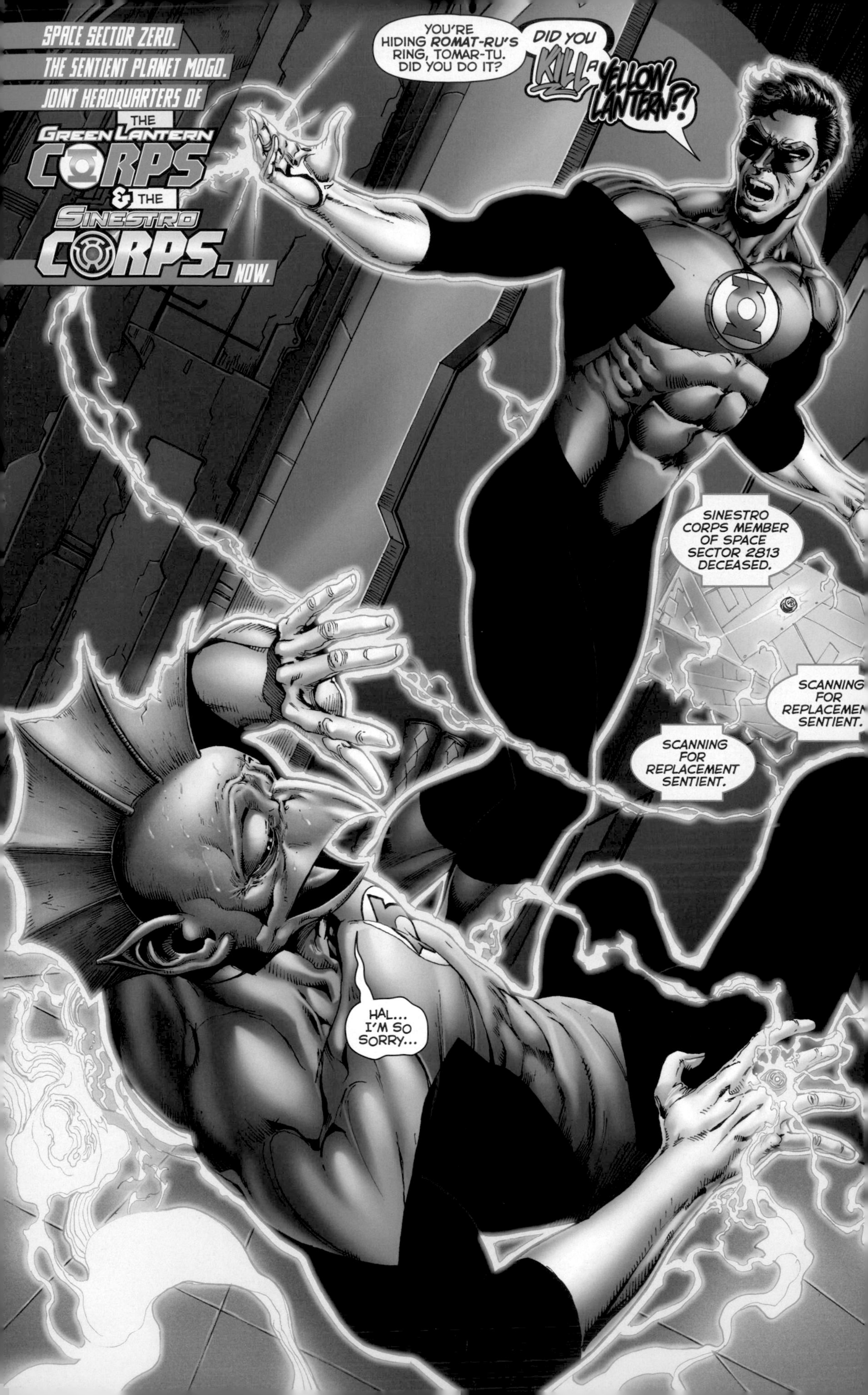

SPACE SECTOR ZERO.
THE SENTIENT PLANET MOGO.
JOINT HEADQUARTERS OF
THE GREEN LANTERN CORPS & THE SINESTRO CORPS. NOW.
YOU'RE HIDING ROMAT-RU'S RING, TOMAR-TU. DID YOU DO IT?
DID YOU KILL A YELLOW LANTERN?!
SINESTRO CORPS MEMBER OF SPACE SECTOR 2813 DECEASED.
SCANNING FOR REPLACEMENT SENTIENT.
SCANNING FOR REPLACEMENT SENTIENT.
HAL... I'M SO SORRY...

THAT'S NOT GOOD ENOUGH.

TOMAR-TU, GREEN LANTERN OF SPACE SECTOR 2813.

HAND OVER YOUR RING.

JOHN, HOLD ON. WE'RE TALKING ABOUT ROMAT-RU.

A SERIAL KILLER. OF KIDS.

THERE HAS TO BE AN EXPLANATION.

A VULDARIAN SPY IMP WITNESSED THE WHOLE THING, HAL. IT SHOWED ME THE EVIDENCE.

ROMAT-RU CHOSE A SCIENCECELL.

AND TOMAR-TU LIT HIM UP.

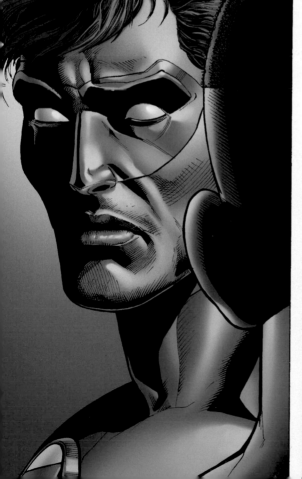

NO WAY.

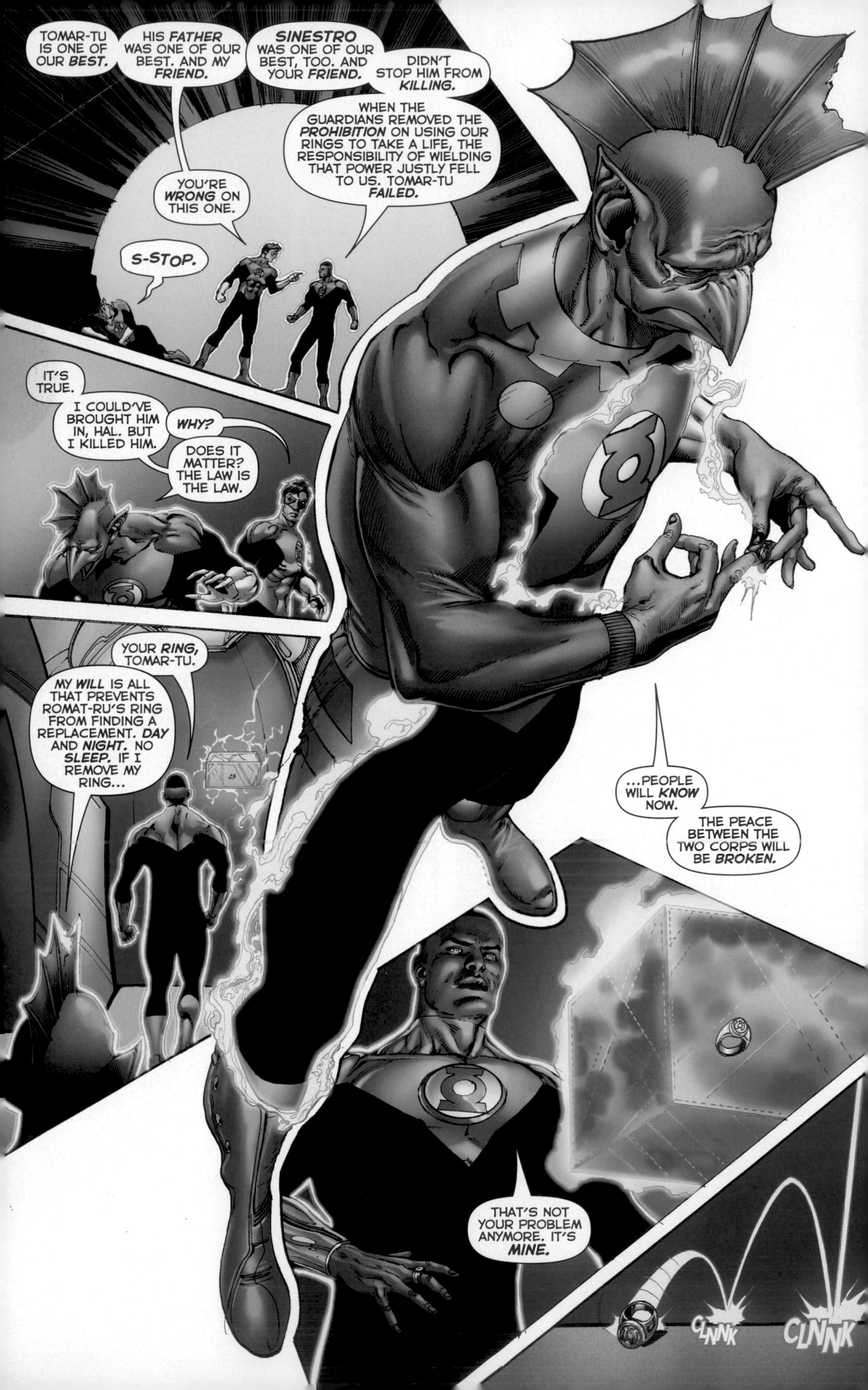
TOMAR-TU IS ONE OF OUR BEST.
HIS FATHER WAS ONE OF OUR BEST. AND MY FRIEND.
SINESTRO WAS ONE OF OUR BEST, TOO. AND YOUR FRIEND.
DIDN'T STOP HIM FROM KILLING.
WHEN THE GUARDIANS REMOVED THE PROHIBITION ON USING OUR RINGS TO TAKE A LIFE, THE RESPONSIBILITY OF WIELDING THAT POWER JUSTLY FELL TO US. TOMAR-TU FAILED.
YOU'RE WRONG ON THIS ONE.
S-STOP.
IT'S TRUE.
I COULD'VE BROUGHT HIM IN, HAL. BUT I KILLED HIM.
WHY?
DOES IT MATTER? THE LAW IS THE LAW.
YOUR RING, TOMAR-TU.
MY WILL IS ALL THAT PREVENTS ROMAT-RU'S RING FROM FINDING A REPLACEMENT. DAY AND NIGHT. NO SLEEP. IF I REMOVE MY RING...
...PEOPLE WILL KNOW NOW.
THE PEACE BETWEEN THE TWO CORPS WILL BE BROKEN.
THAT'S NOT YOUR PROBLEM ANYMORE. IT'S MINE.
CLNNK
CLNNK

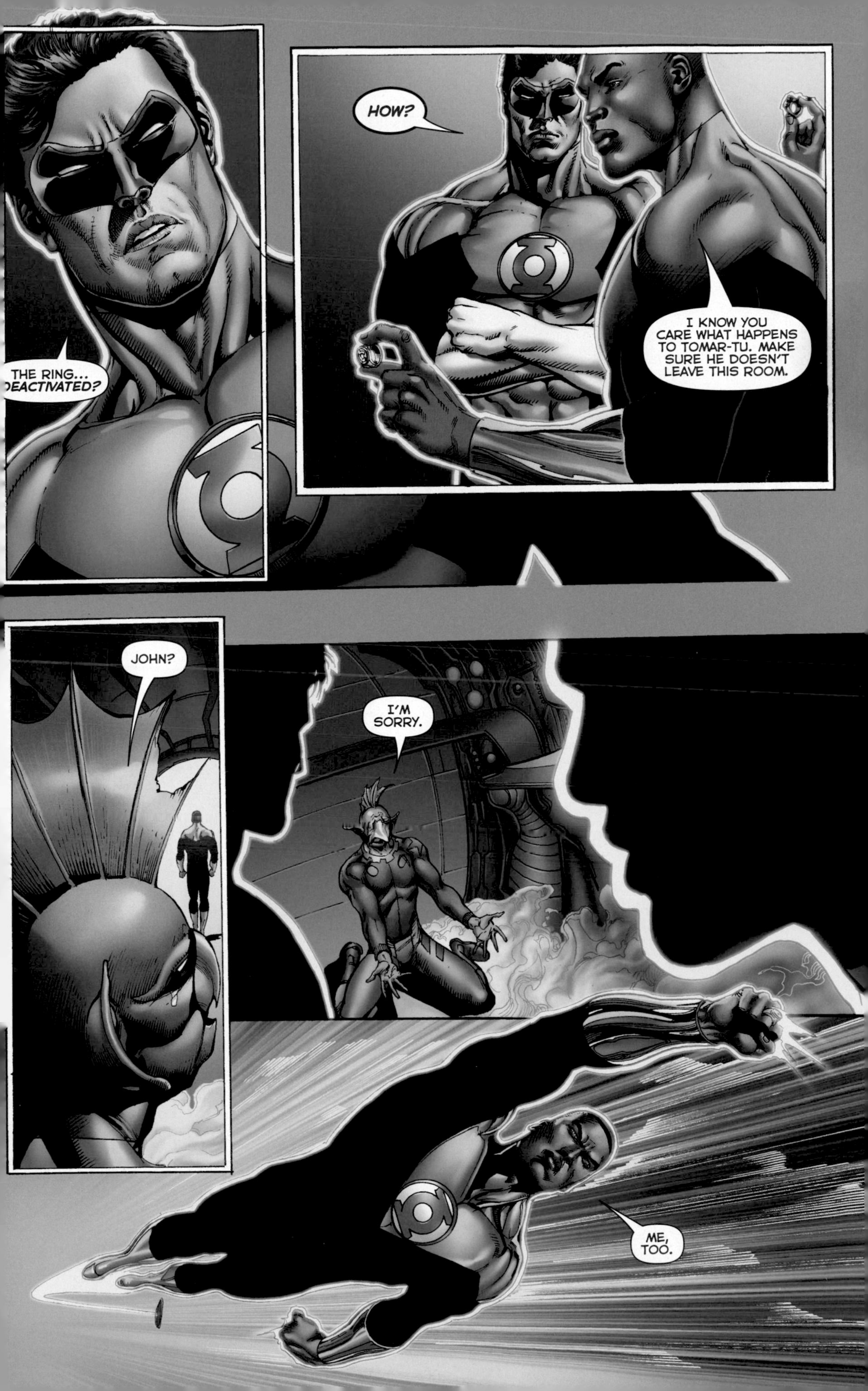
THE RING...
DEACTIVATED?
HOW?
I KNOW YOU CARE WHAT HAPPENS TO TOMAR-TU. MAKE SURE HE DOESN'T LEAVE THIS ROOM.
JOHN?
I'M SORRY.
ME, TOO.

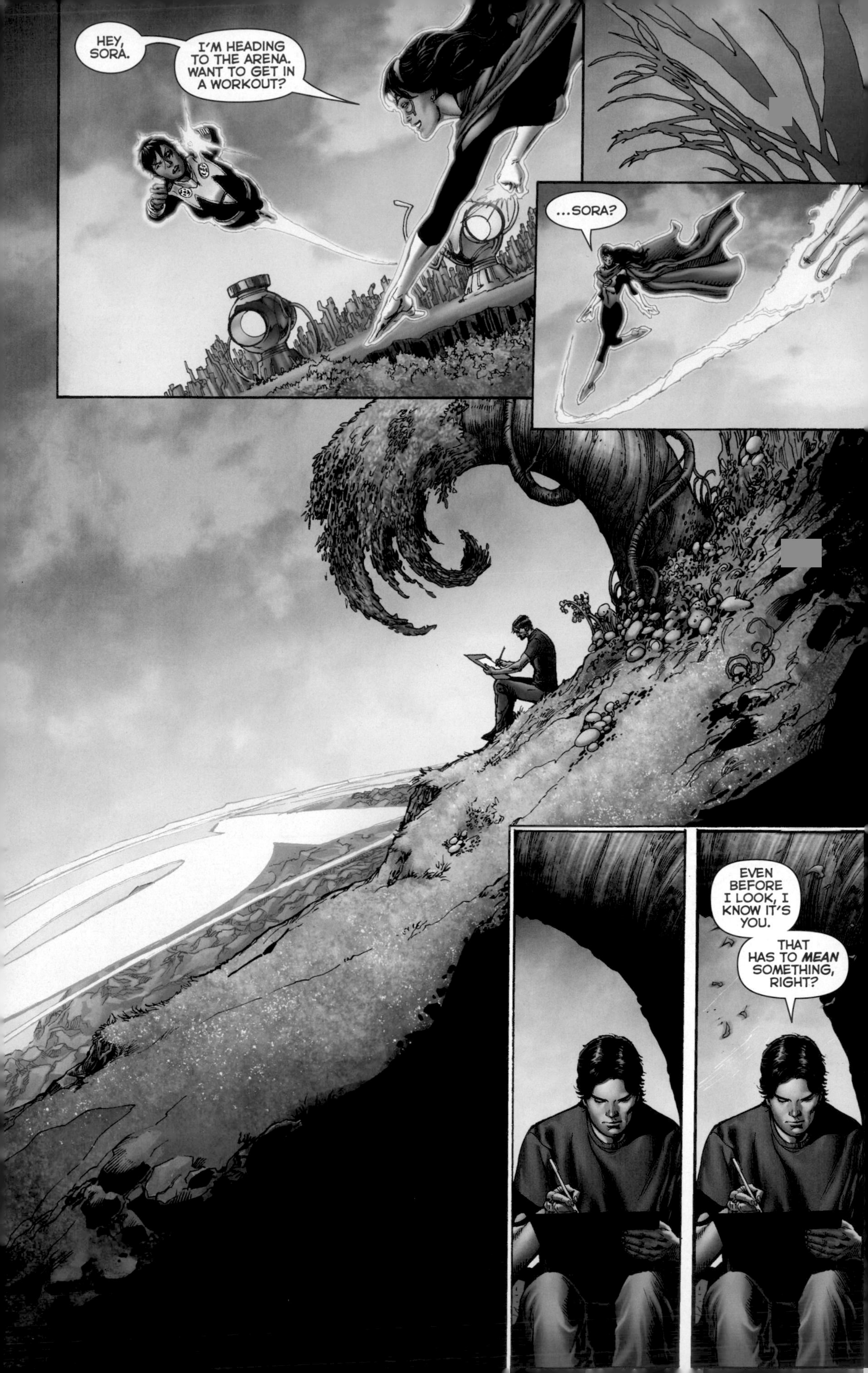
HEY, SORA.
I'M HEADING TO THE ARENA. WANT TO GET IN A WORKOUT?
...SORA?
EVEN BEFORE I LOOK, I KNOW IT'S YOU.
THAT HAS TO *MEAN* SOMETHING, RIGHT?

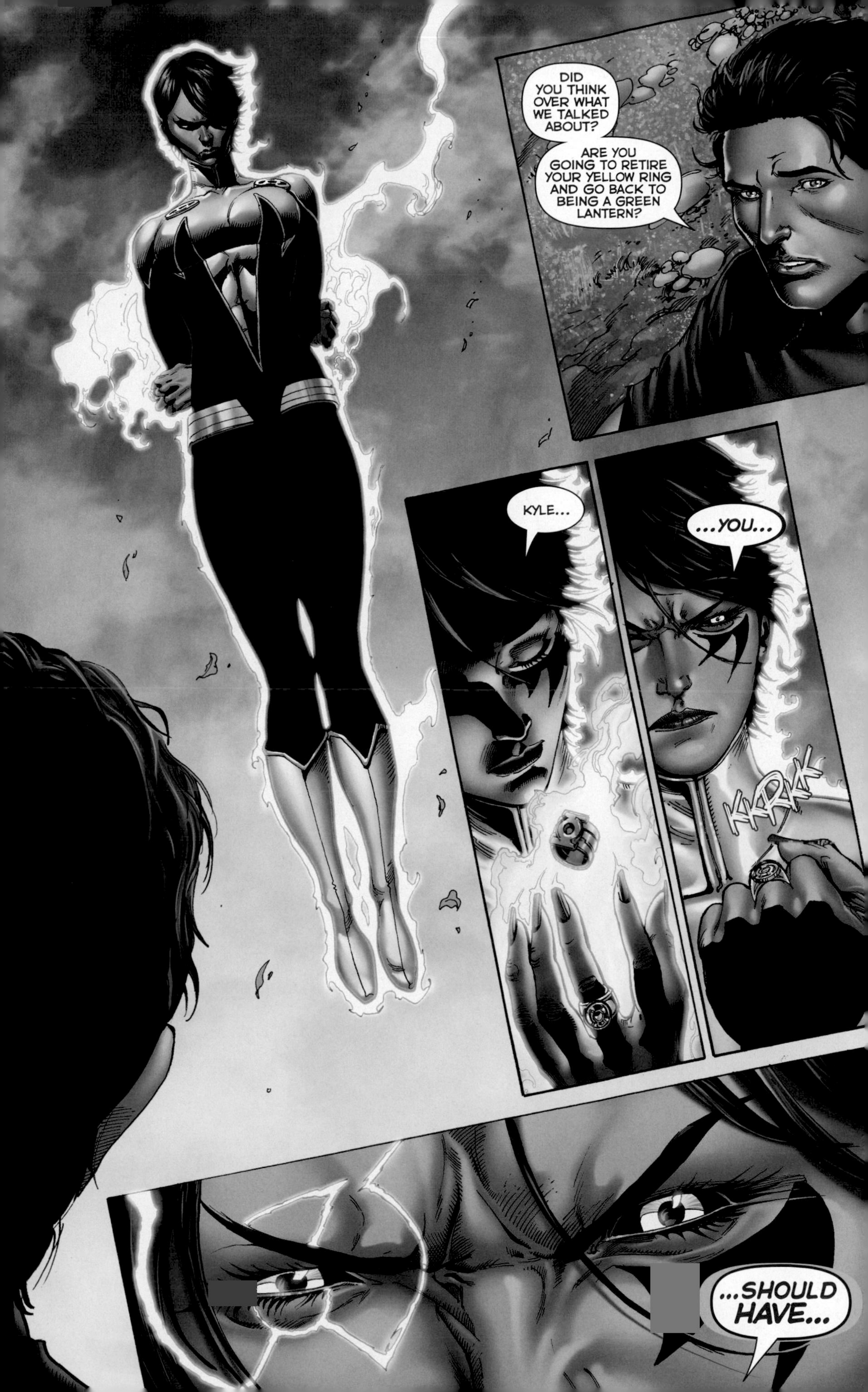
DID YOU THINK OVER WHAT WE TALKED ABOUT?
ARE YOU GOING TO RETIRE YOUR YELLOW RING AND GO BACK TO BEING A GREEN LANTERN?
KYLE...
...YOU...
KKRAK
...SHOULD HAVE...

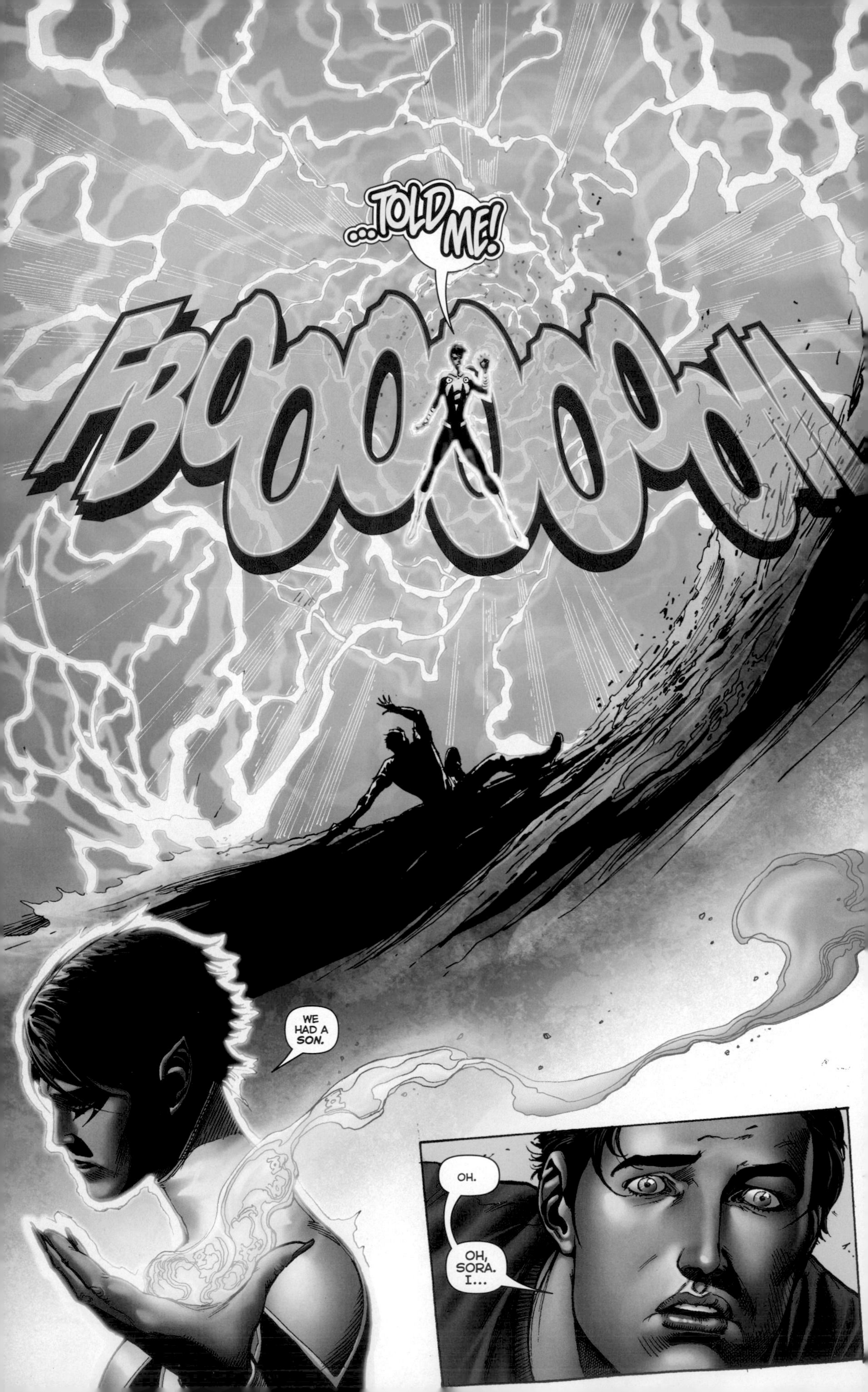
...TOLD ME!
FBOOOOOOM
WE HAD A SON.
OH.
OH, SORA. I...

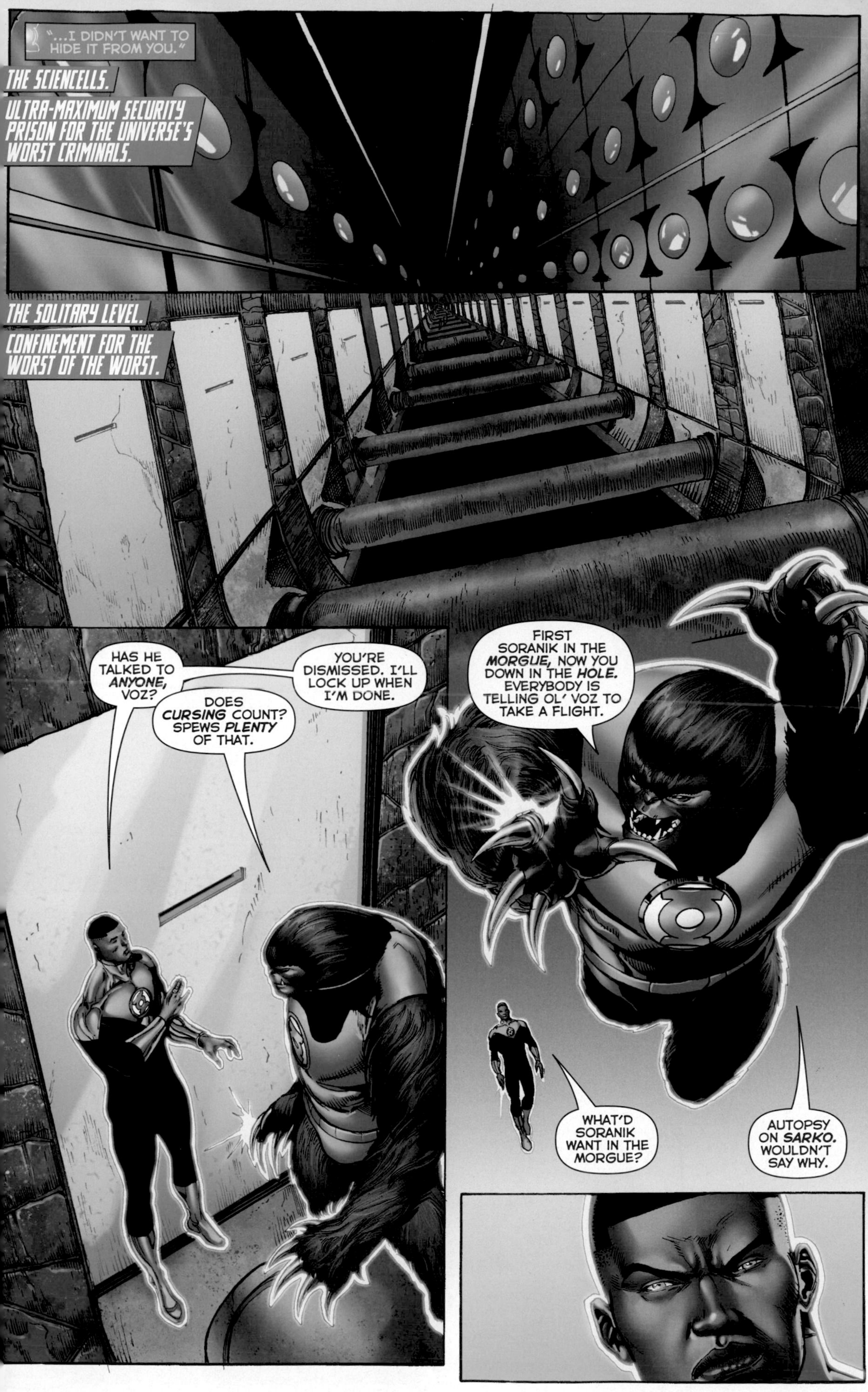
"...I DIDN'T WANT TO HIDE IT FROM YOU."
THE SCIENCELLS.
ULTRA-MAXIMUM SECURITY PRISON FOR THE UNIVERSE'S WORST CRIMINALS.
THE SOLITARY LEVEL.
CONFINEMENT FOR THE WORST OF THE WORST.
HAS HE TALKED TO ANYONE, VOZ?
DOES CURSING COUNT? SPEWS PLENTY OF THAT.
YOU'RE DISMISSED. I'LL LOCK UP WHEN I'M DONE.
FIRST SORANIK IN THE MORGUE, NOW YOU DOWN IN THE HOLE. EVERYBODY IS TELLING OL' VOZ TO TAKE A FLIGHT.
WHAT'D SORANIK WANT IN THE MORGUE?
AUTOPSY ON SARKO. WOULDN'T SAY WHY.

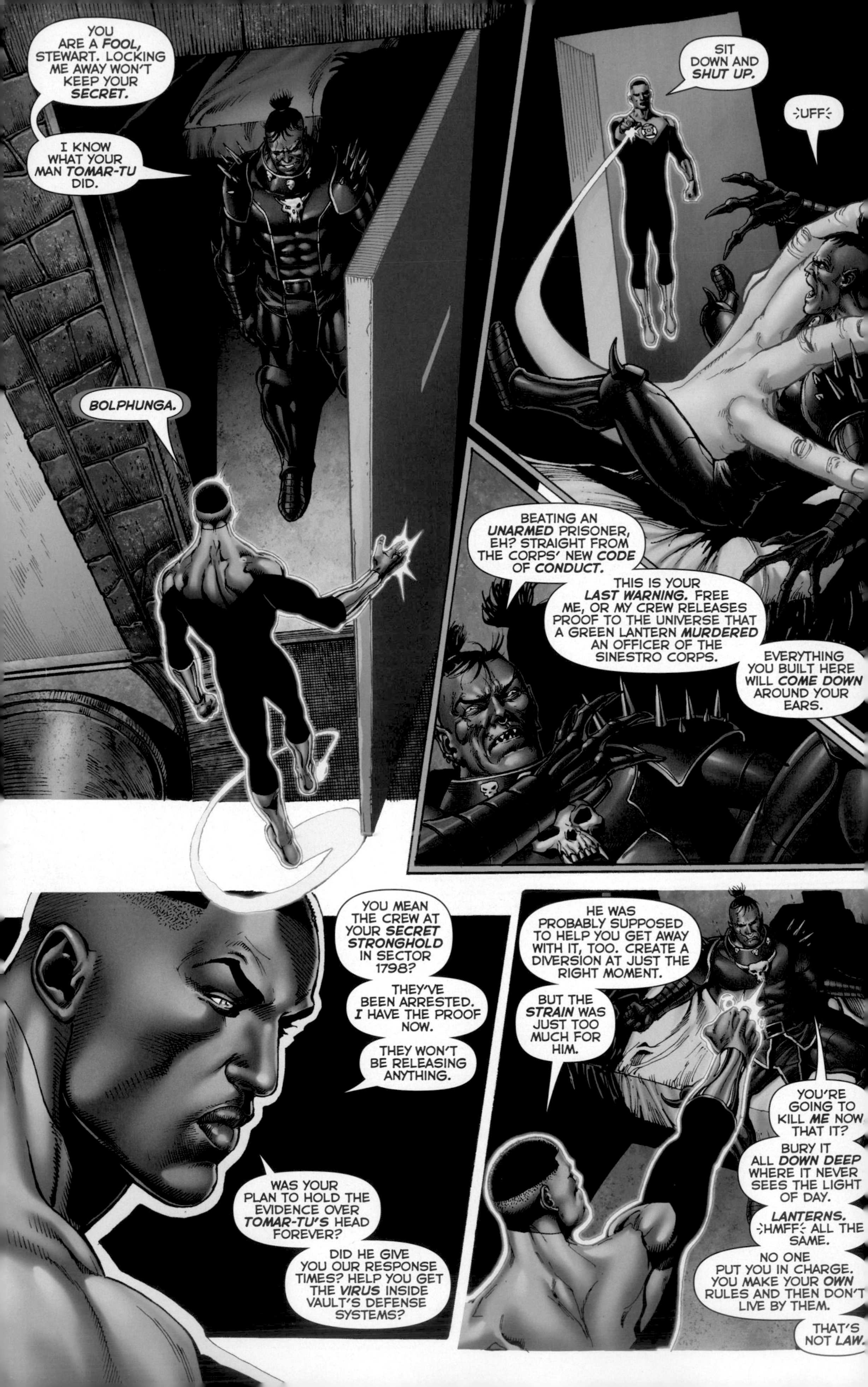
YOU ARE A FOOL, STEWART. LOCKING ME AWAY WON'T KEEP YOUR SECRET.
I KNOW WHAT YOUR MAN TOMAR-TU DID.
BOLPHUNGA.
SIT DOWN AND SHUT UP.
UFF
BEATING AN UNARMED PRISONER, EH? STRAIGHT FROM THE CORPS' NEW CODE OF CONDUCT.
THIS IS YOUR LAST WARNING. FREE ME, OR MY CREW RELEASES PROOF TO THE UNIVERSE THAT A GREEN LANTERN MURDERED AN OFFICER OF THE SINESTRO CORPS.
EVERYTHING YOU BUILT HERE WILL COME DOWN AROUND YOUR EARS.
YOU MEAN THE CREW AT YOUR SECRET STRONGHOLD IN SECTOR 1798?
THEY'VE BEEN ARRESTED. I HAVE THE PROOF NOW.
THEY WON'T BE RELEASING ANYTHING.
WAS YOUR PLAN TO HOLD THE EVIDENCE OVER TOMAR-TU'S HEAD FOREVER?
DID HE GIVE YOU OUR RESPONSE TIMES? HELP YOU GET THE VIRUS INSIDE VAULT'S DEFENSE SYSTEMS?
HE WAS PROBABLY SUPPOSED TO HELP YOU GET AWAY WITH IT, TOO. CREATE A DIVERSION AT JUST THE RIGHT MOMENT.
BUT THE STRAIN WAS JUST TOO MUCH FOR HIM.
YOU'RE GOING TO KILL ME NOW. THAT IT?
BURY IT ALL DOWN DEEP WHERE IT NEVER SEES THE LIGHT OF DAY.
LANTERNS. HMFF ALL THE SAME.
NO ONE PUT YOU IN CHARGE. YOU MAKE YOUR OWN RULES AND THEN DON'T LIVE BY THEM.
THAT'S NOT LAW.

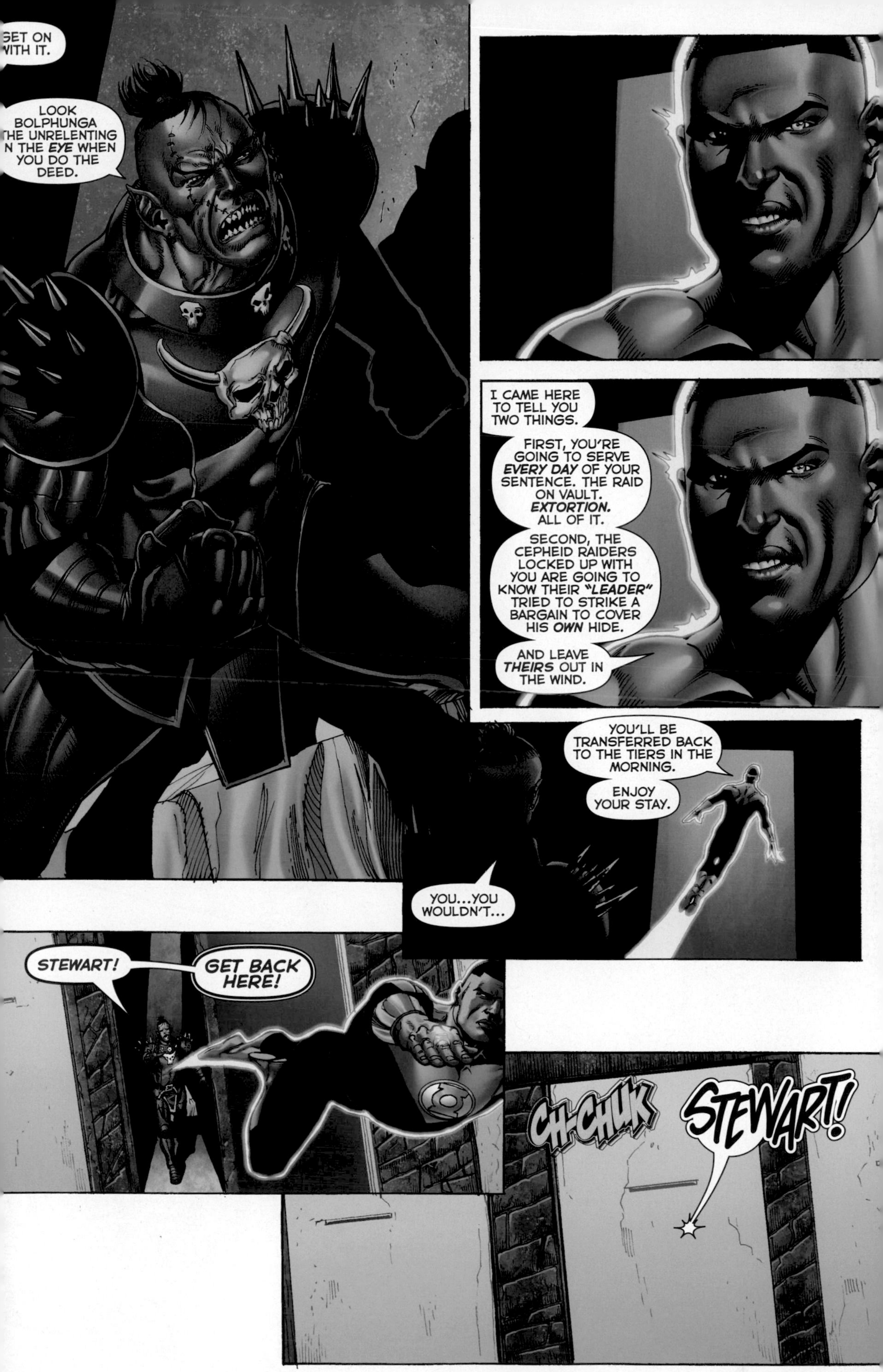

GET ON WITH IT.
LOOK BOLPHUNGA THE UNRELENTING IN THE EYE WHEN YOU DO THE DEED.
I CAME HERE TO TELL YOU TWO THINGS.
FIRST, YOU'RE GOING TO SERVE EVERY DAY OF YOUR SENTENCE. THE RAID ON VAULT. EXTORTION. ALL OF IT.
SECOND, THE CEPHEID RAIDERS LOCKED UP WITH YOU ARE GOING TO KNOW THEIR "LEADER" TRIED TO STRIKE A BARGAIN TO COVER HIS OWN HIDE.
AND LEAVE THEIRS OUT IN THE WIND.
YOU'LL BE TRANSFERRED BACK TO THE TIERS IN THE MORNING.
ENJOY YOUR STAY.
YOU...YOU WOULDN'T...
STEWART!
GET BACK HERE!
CH-CHUK
STEWART!

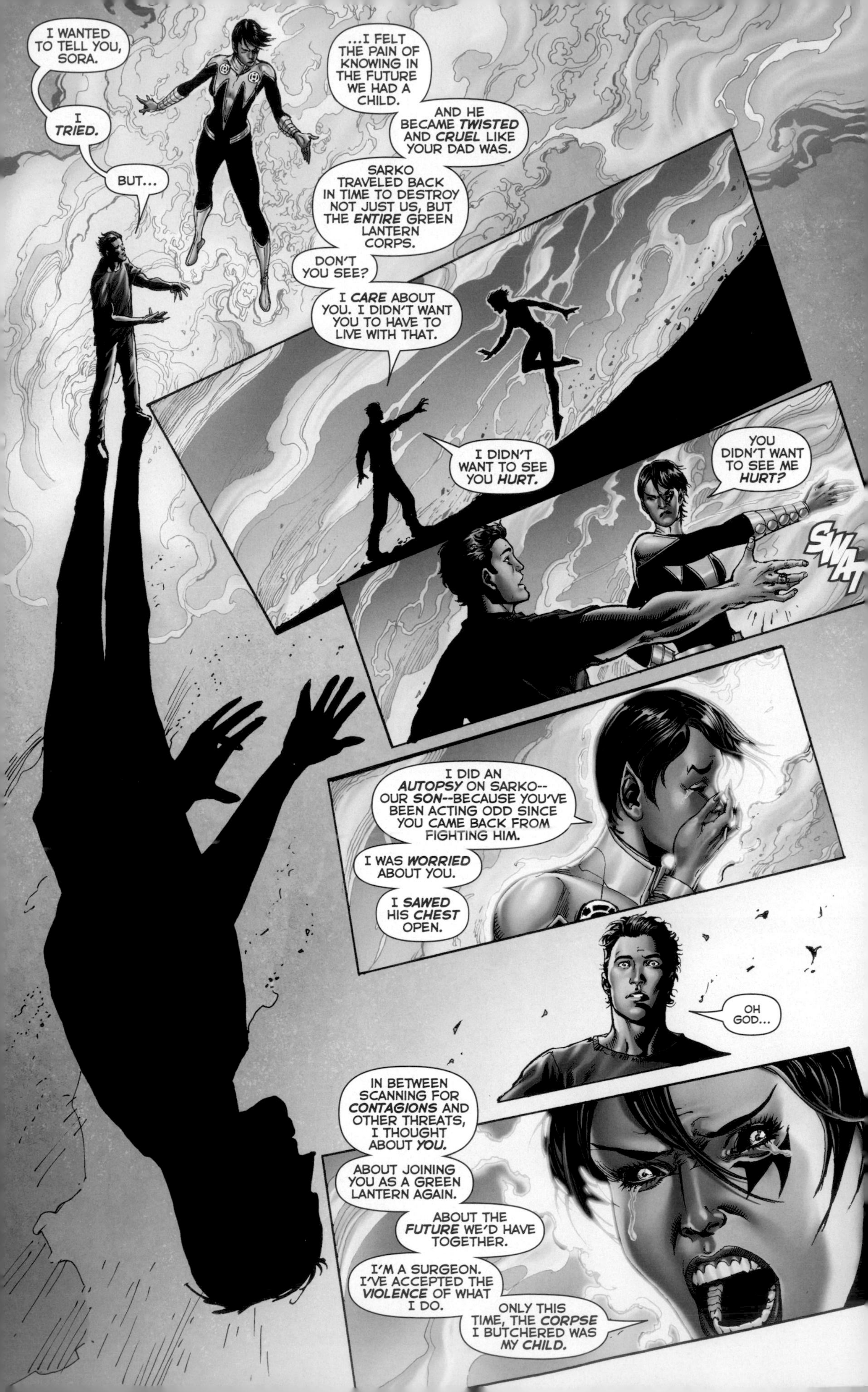
I WANTED TO TELL YOU, SORA.
I TRIED.
BUT...
...I FELT THE PAIN OF KNOWING IN THE FUTURE WE HAD A CHILD.
AND HE BECAME TWISTED AND CRUEL LIKE YOUR DAD WAS.
SARKO TRAVELED BACK IN TIME TO DESTROY NOT JUST US, BUT THE ENTIRE GREEN LANTERN CORPS.
DON'T YOU SEE?
I CARE ABOUT YOU. I DIDN'T WANT YOU TO HAVE TO LIVE WITH THAT.
I DIDN'T WANT TO SEE YOU HURT.
YOU DIDN'T WANT TO SEE ME HURT?
SWAT
I DID AN AUTOPSY ON SARKO-- OUR SON--BECAUSE YOU'VE BEEN ACTING ODD SINCE YOU CAME BACK FROM FIGHTING HIM.
I WAS WORRIED ABOUT YOU.
I SAWED HIS CHEST OPEN.
OH GOD...
IN BETWEEN SCANNING FOR CONTAGIONS AND OTHER THREATS, I THOUGHT ABOUT YOU.
ABOUT JOINING YOU AS A GREEN LANTERN AGAIN.
ABOUT THE FUTURE WE'D HAVE TOGETHER.
I'M A SURGEON. I'VE ACCEPTED THE VIOLENCE OF WHAT I DO.
ONLY THIS TIME, THE CORPSE I BUTCHERED WAS MY CHILD.

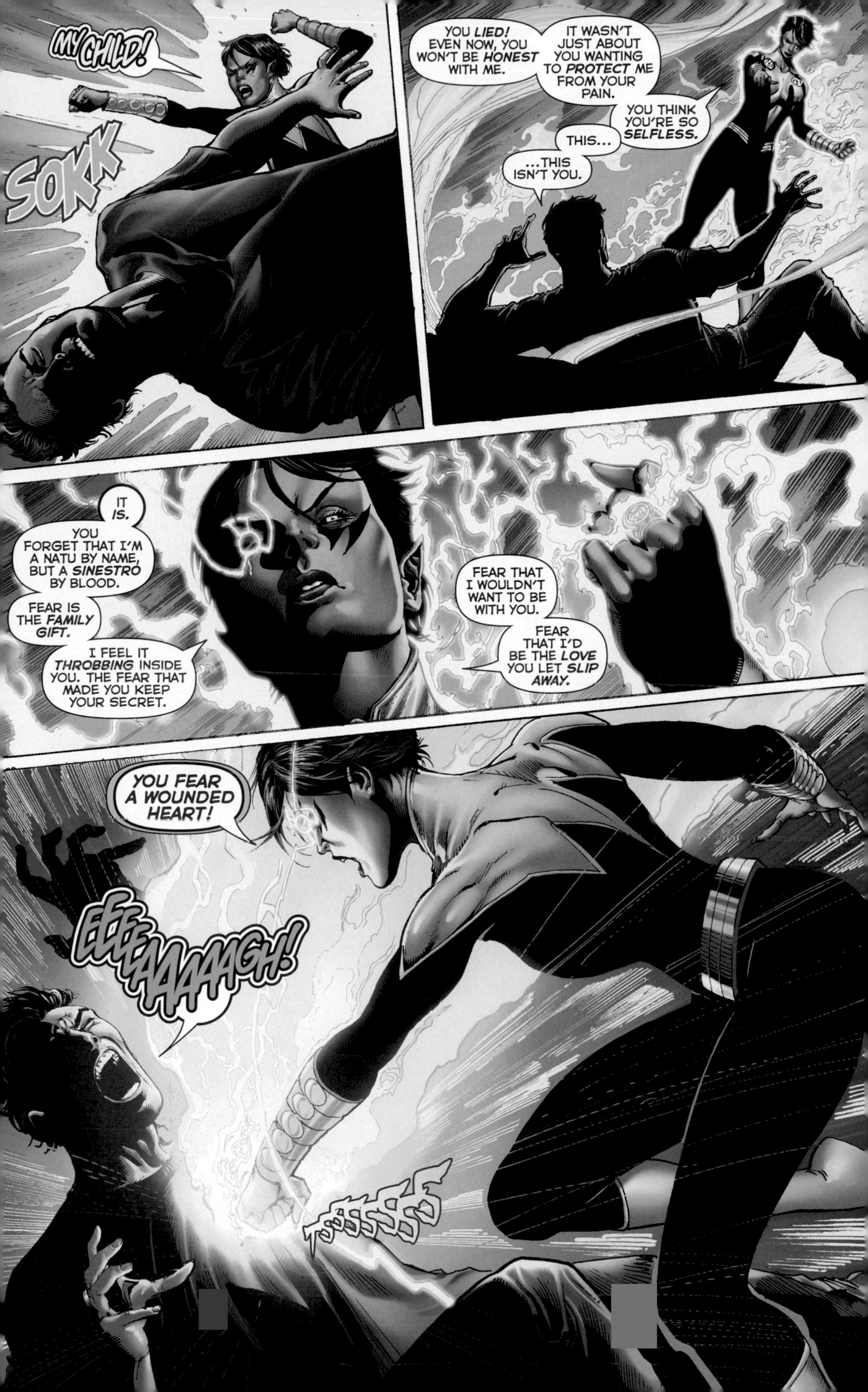
MY CHILD!
SOKK
YOU LIED! EVEN NOW, YOU WON'T BE HONEST WITH ME.
IT WASN'T JUST ABOUT YOU WANTING TO PROTECT ME FROM YOUR PAIN.
YOU THINK YOU'RE SO SELFLESS.
THIS...
...THIS ISN'T YOU.
IT IS.
YOU FORGET THAT I'M A NATU BY NAME, BUT A SINESTRO BY BLOOD.
FEAR IS THE FAMILY GIFT.
I FEEL IT THROBBING INSIDE YOU. THE FEAR THAT MADE YOU KEEP YOUR SECRET.
FEAR THAT I WOULDN'T WANT TO BE WITH YOU.
FEAR THAT I'D BE THE LOVE YOU LET SLIP AWAY.
YOU FEAR A WOUNDED HEART!
EEEEAAAAAAGH!
TSSSSSS

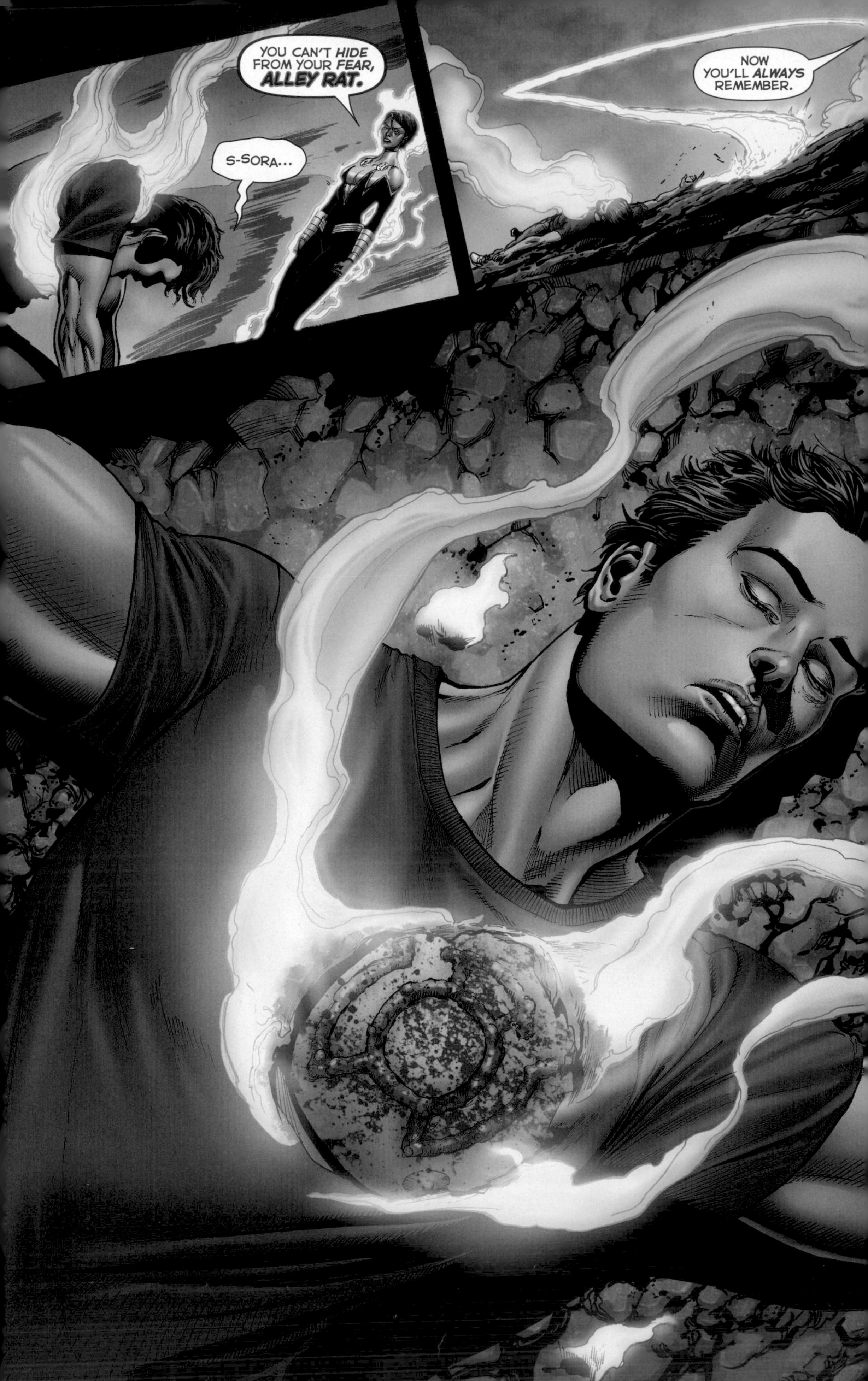
YOU CAN'T HIDE FROM YOUR FEAR, ALLEY RAT.
S-SORA...
NOW YOU'LL ALWAYS REMEMBER.

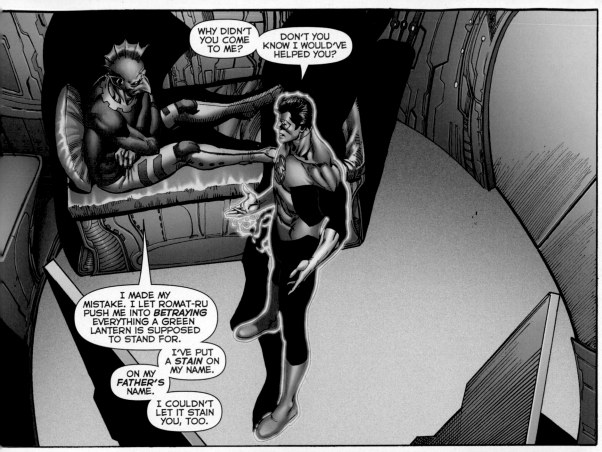

WHY DIDN'T YOU COME TO ME?

DON'T YOU KNOW I WOULD'VE HELPED YOU?

I MADE MY MISTAKE. I LET ROMAT-RU PUSH ME INTO *BETRAYING* EVERYTHING A GREEN LANTERN IS SUPPOSED TO STAND FOR.

I'VE PUT A *STAIN* ON MY NAME.

ON MY *FATHER'S* NAME.

I COULDN'T LET IT STAIN YOU, TOO.

BUT IF YOU'D JUST ADMITTED TO IT. IF YOU HADN'T GOTTEN MIXED UP WITH BOLPHUNGA.

IF I'D *KNOWN.*

IT ISN'T YOUR FAULT, HAL.

I DID THIS. I ACCEPT MY PUNISHMENT.

I'M GLAD IT'S OVER.

FANTAS-M WAS RIGHT. THE *WEIGHT* OF IT. OF KEEPING IT HIDDEN.

A GREEN LANTERN ISN'T MEANT TO LIVE IN THE DARK.

WE BELONG IN THE *LIGHT.*

THERE'S *ALWAYS* REDEMPTION, TOMAR-TU.

I'LL BE THERE WITH YOU.

IN BRIGHTEST DAY, IN BLACKEST NIGHT.

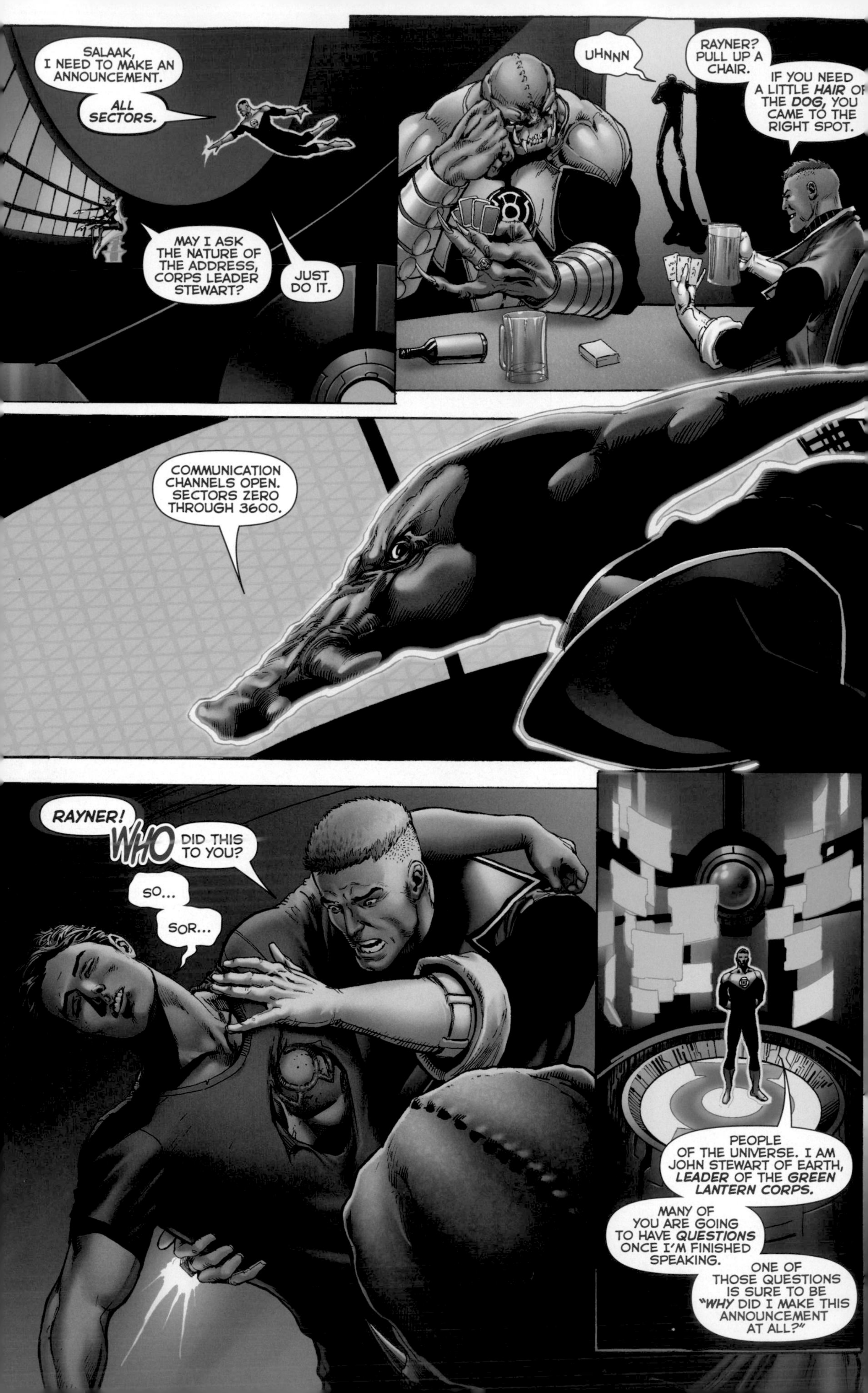
SALAAK, I NEED TO MAKE AN ANNOUNCEMENT.
ALL SECTORS.
MAY I ASK THE NATURE OF THE ADDRESS, CORPS LEADER STEWART?
JUST DO IT.
UHNNN
RAYNER? PULL UP A CHAIR.
IF YOU NEED A LITTLE HAIR OF THE DOG, YOU CAME TO THE RIGHT SPOT.
COMMUNICATION CHANNELS OPEN. SECTORS ZERO THROUGH 3600.
RAYNER!
WHO DID THIS TO YOU?
SO...
SOR...
PEOPLE OF THE UNIVERSE. I AM JOHN STEWART OF EARTH, LEADER OF THE GREEN LANTERN CORPS.
MANY OF YOU ARE GOING TO HAVE QUESTIONS ONCE I'M FINISHED SPEAKING.
ONE OF THOSE QUESTIONS IS SURE TO BE "WHY DID I MAKE THIS ANNOUNCEMENT AT ALL?"

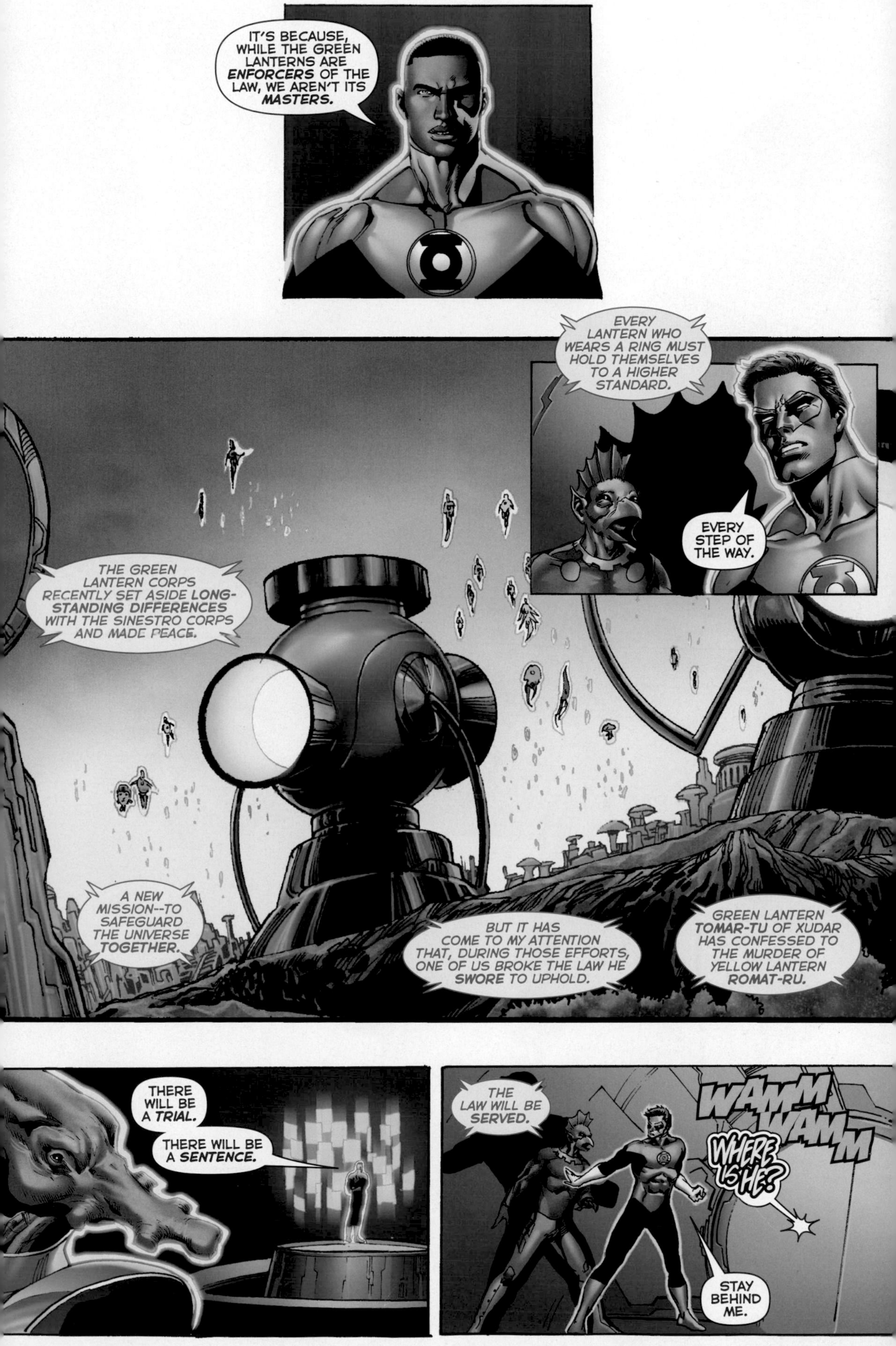
IT'S BECAUSE, WHILE THE GREEN LANTERNS ARE ENFORCERS OF THE LAW, WE AREN'T ITS MASTERS.
EVERY LANTERN WHO WEARS A RING MUST HOLD THEMSELVES TO A HIGHER STANDARD.
EVERY STEP OF THE WAY.
THE GREEN LANTERN CORPS RECENTLY SET ASIDE LONG-STANDING DIFFERENCES WITH THE SINESTRO CORPS AND MADE PEACE.
A NEW MISSION--TO SAFEGUARD THE UNIVERSE TOGETHER.
BUT IT HAS COME TO MY ATTENTION THAT, DURING THOSE EFFORTS, ONE OF US BROKE THE LAW HE SWORE TO UPHOLD.
GREEN LANTERN TOMAR-TU OF XUDAR HAS CONFESSED TO THE MURDER OF YELLOW LANTERN ROMAT-RU.
THERE WILL BE A TRIAL.
THERE WILL BE A SENTENCE.
THE LAW WILL BE SERVED.
WAMM WAMM
WHERE IS HE?
STAY BEHIND ME.

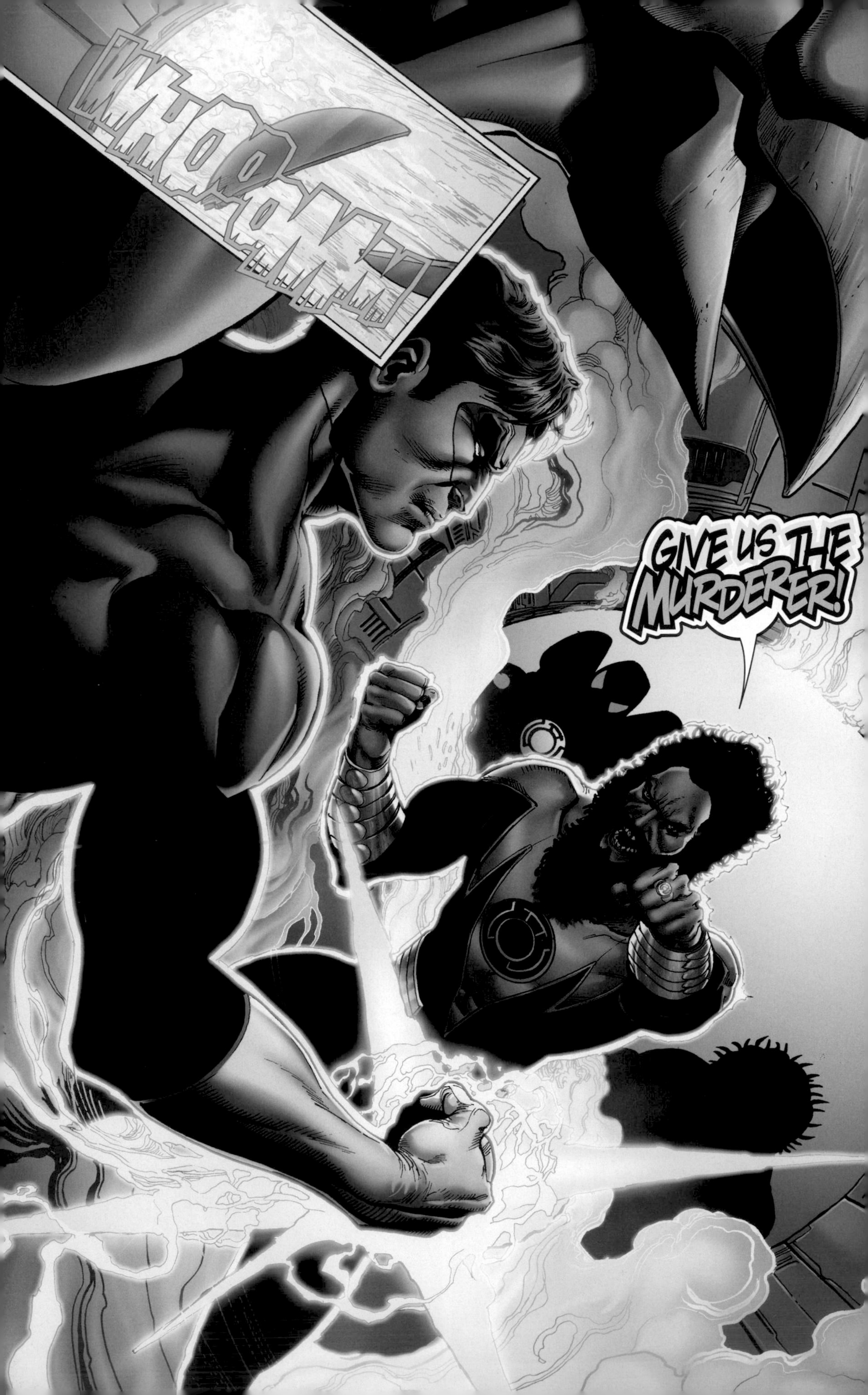
WHOOOM
GIVE US THE MURDERER!

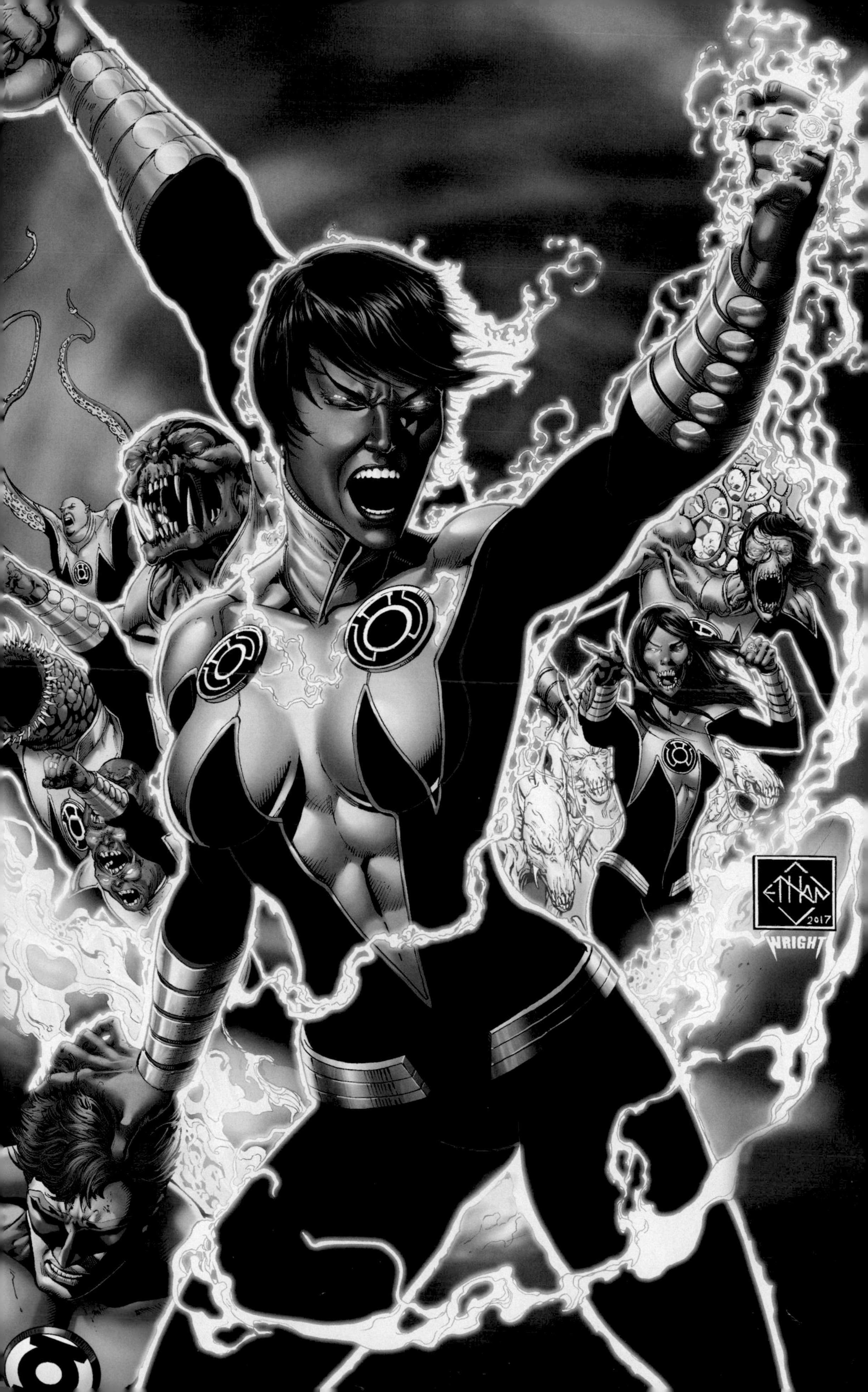
ETHAN
2017
WRIGHT

"FRACTURE PART 4: THE LONG WAR"
ETHAN VAN SCIVER artist * JASON WRIGHT colorist
cover art by ETHAN VAN SCIVER and JASON WRIGHT

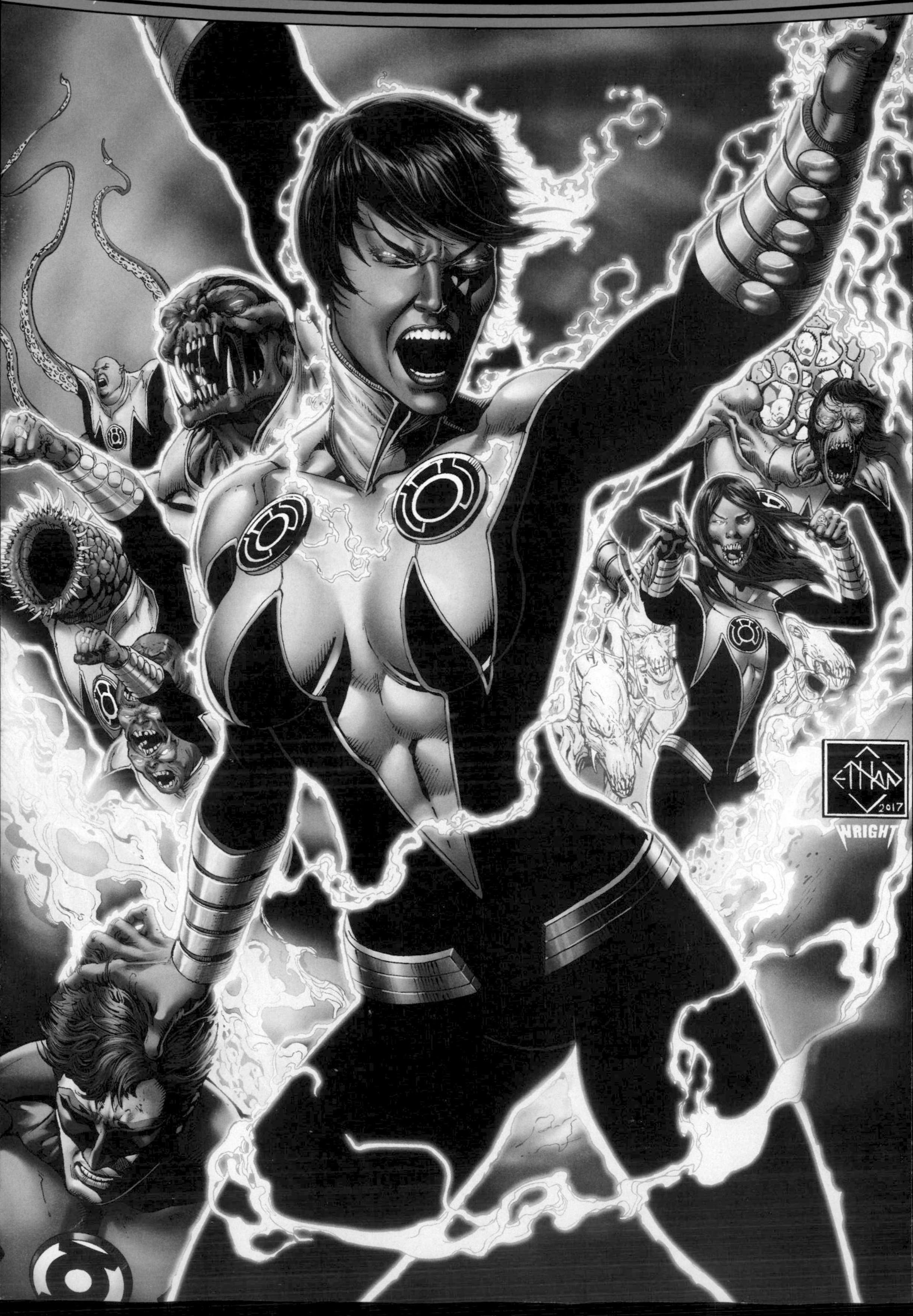
ETHAN
2017
WRIGHT

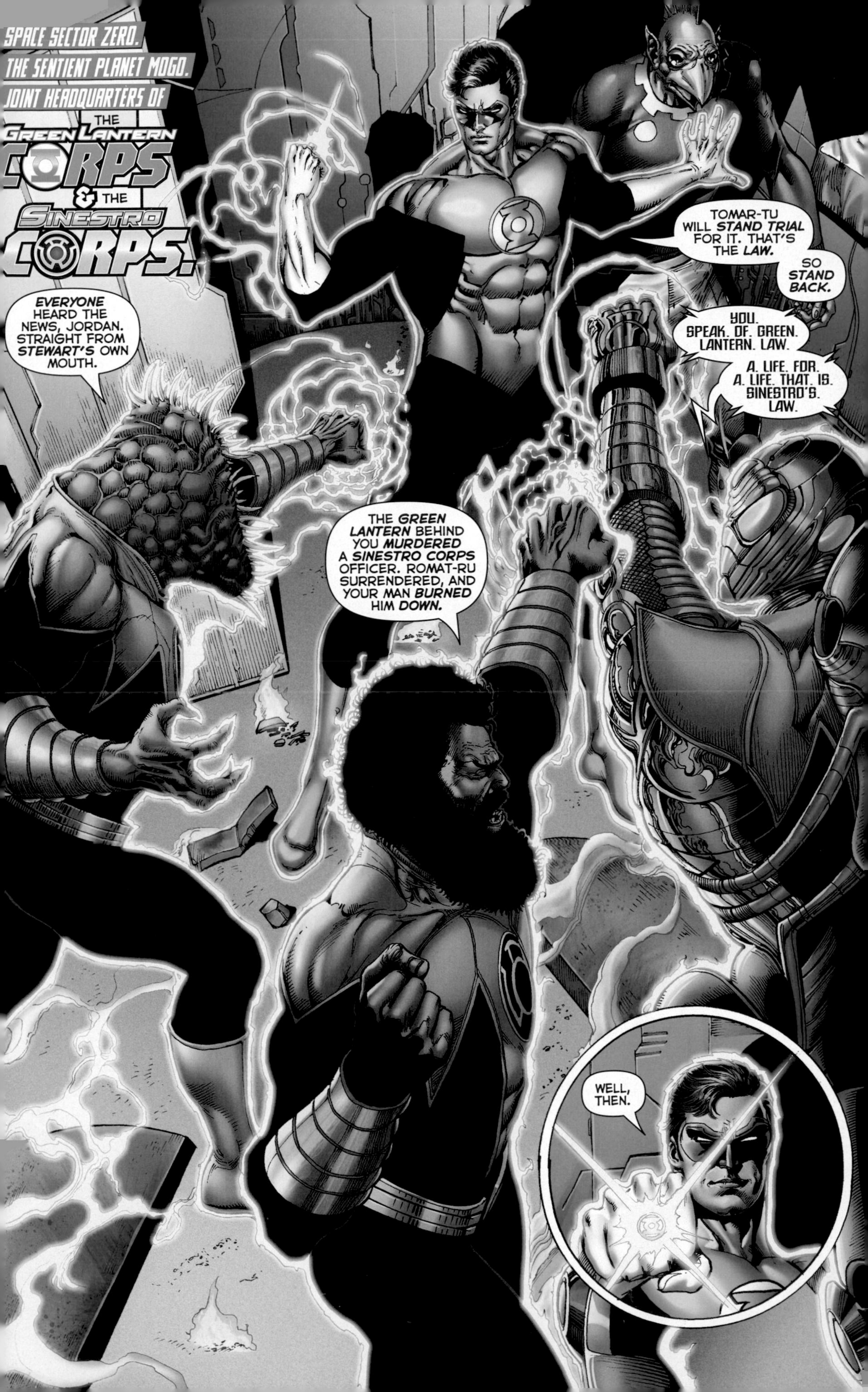
SPACE SECTOR ZERO.
THE SENTIENT PLANET MOGO.
JOINT HEADQUARTERS OF
THE GREEN LANTERN CORPS & THE SINESTRO CORPS.
EVERYONE HEARD THE NEWS, JORDAN. STRAIGHT FROM STEWART'S OWN MOUTH.
TOMAR-TU WILL STAND TRIAL FOR IT. THAT'S THE LAW.
SO STAND BACK.
YOU. SPEAK. OF. GREEN. LANTERN. LAW.
A. LIFE. FOR. A. LIFE. THAT. IS. SINESTRO'S. LAW.
THE GREEN LANTERN BEHIND YOU MURDERED A SINESTRO CORPS OFFICER. ROMAT-RU SURRENDERED, AND YOUR MAN BURNED HIM DOWN.
WELL, THEN.

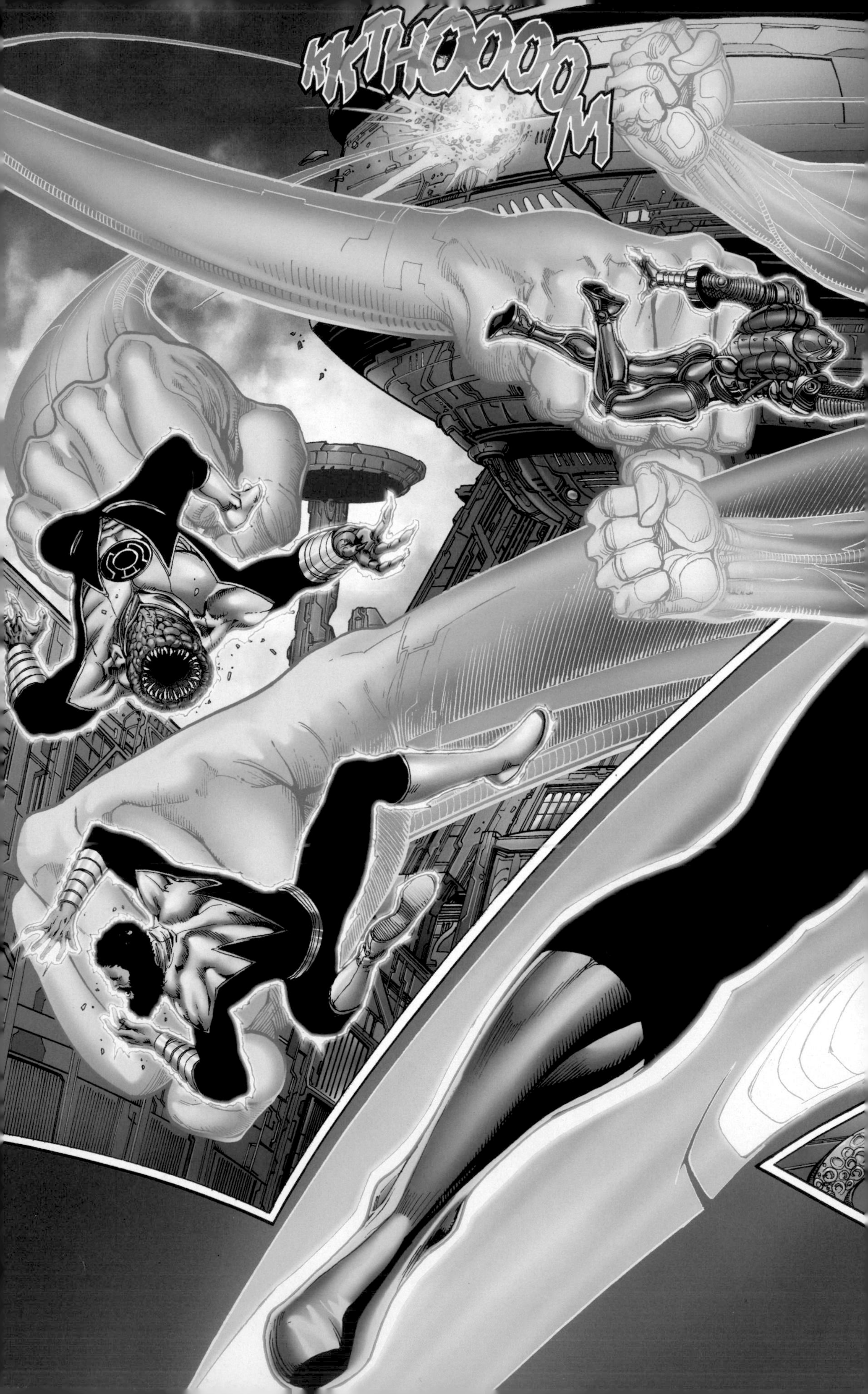
KKTHOOOOOM

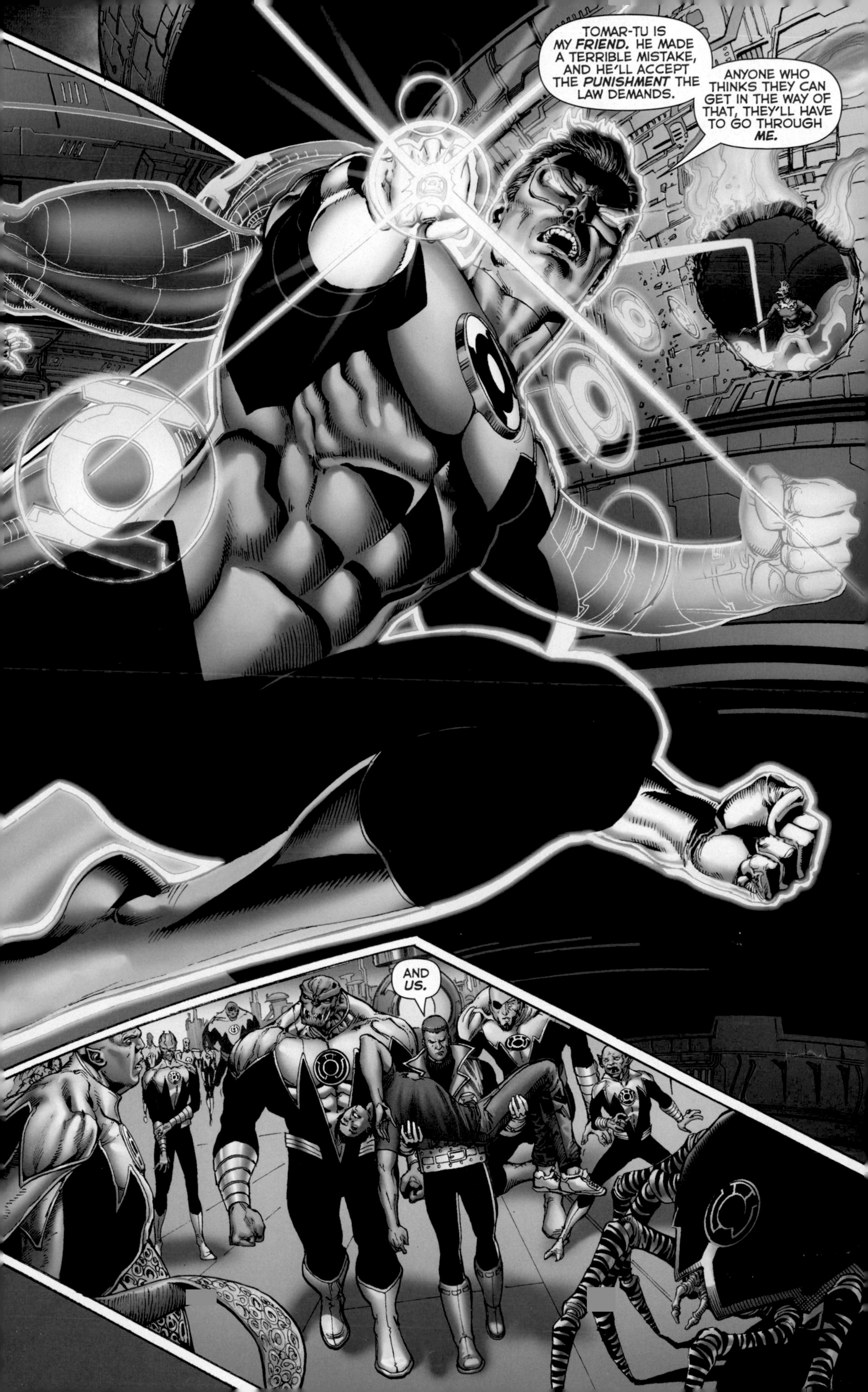
TOMAR-TU IS MY FRIEND. HE MADE A TERRIBLE MISTAKE, AND HE'LL ACCEPT THE PUNISHMENT THE LAW DEMANDS.
ANYONE WHO THINKS THEY CAN GET IN THE WAY OF THAT, THEY'LL HAVE TO GO THROUGH ME.
AND US.

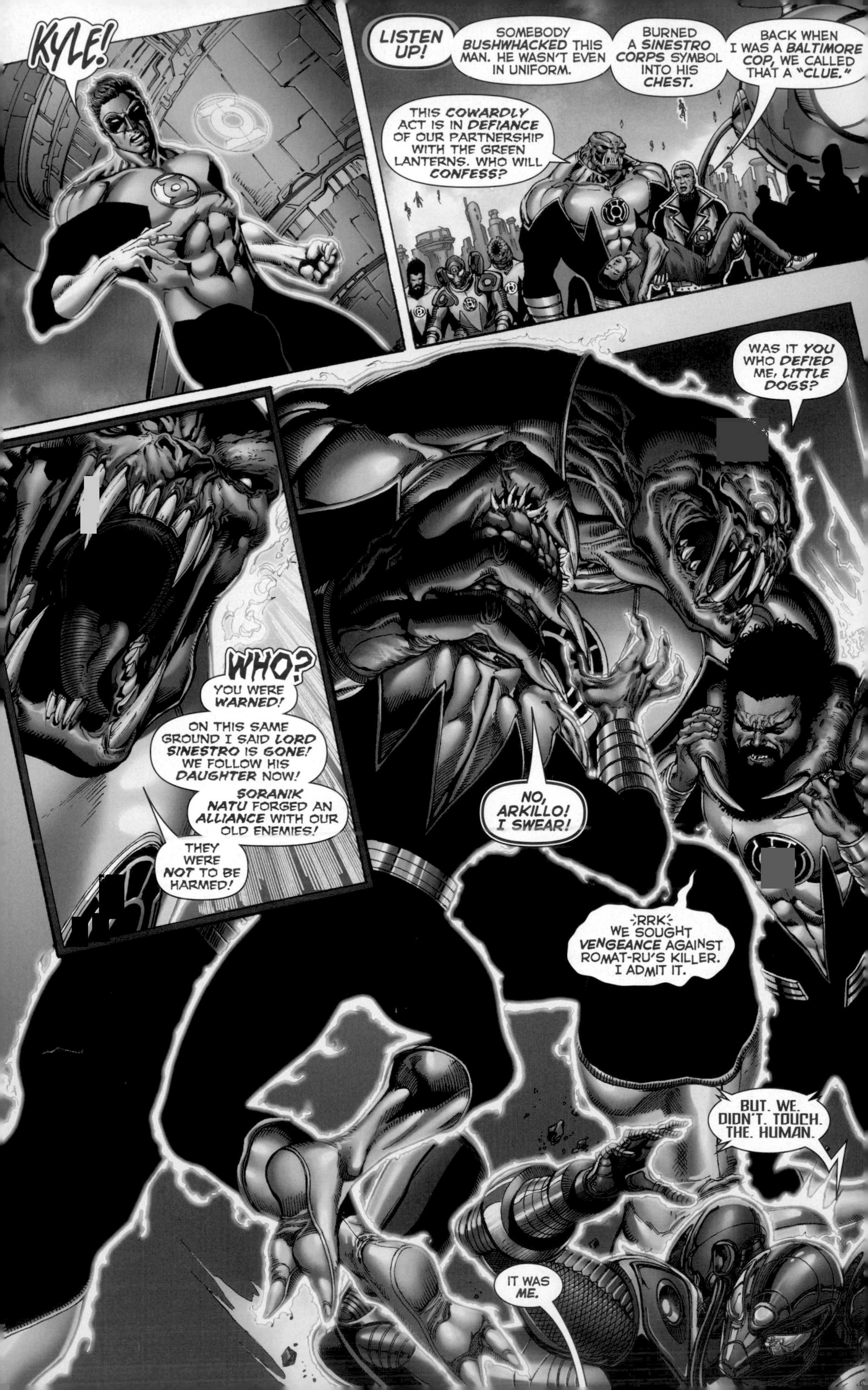
KYLE!
LISTEN UP!
SOMEBODY BUSHWHACKED THIS MAN. HE WASN'T EVEN IN UNIFORM.
BURNED A SINESTRO CORPS SYMBOL INTO HIS CHEST.
BACK WHEN I WAS A BALTIMORE COP, WE CALLED THAT A "CLUE."
THIS COWARDLY ACT IS IN DEFIANCE OF OUR PARTNERSHIP WITH THE GREEN LANTERNS. WHO WILL CONFESS?
WAS IT YOU WHO DEFIED ME, LITTLE DOGS?
WHO?
YOU WERE WARNED!
ON THIS SAME GROUND I SAID LORD SINESTRO IS GONE! WE FOLLOW HIS DAUGHTER NOW!
SORANIK NATU FORGED AN ALLIANCE WITH OUR OLD ENEMIES!
THEY WERE NOT TO BE HARMED!
NO, ARKILLO! I SWEAR!
-RRK- WE SOUGHT VENGEANCE AGAINST ROMAT-RU'S KILLER. I ADMIT IT.
BUT. WE. DIDN'T. TOUCH. THE. HUMAN.
IT WAS ME.

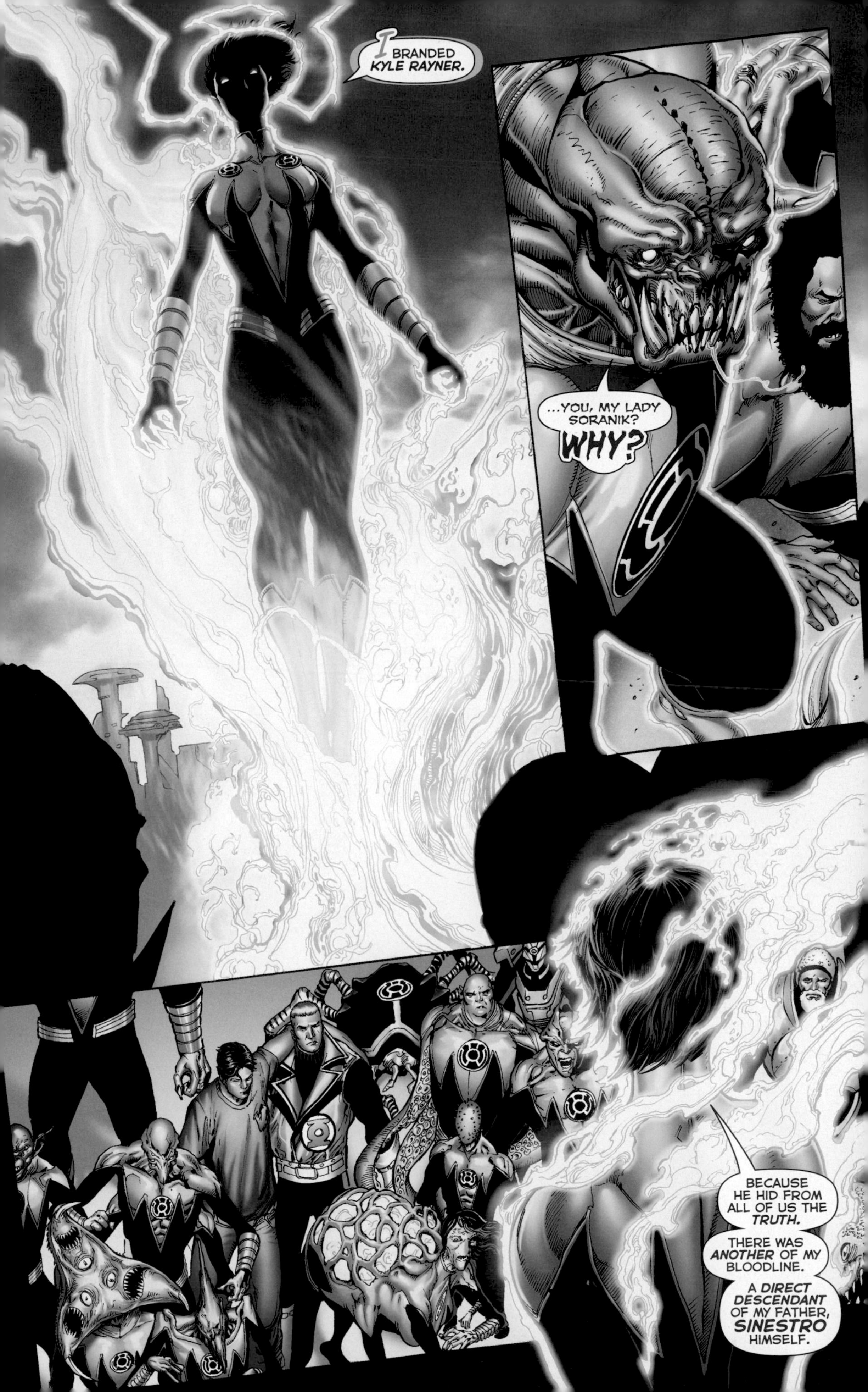
I BRANDED KYLE RAYNER.
...YOU, MY LADY SORANIK? WHY?
BECAUSE HE HID FROM ALL OF US THE TRUTH.
THERE WAS ANOTHER OF MY BLOODLINE.
A DIRECT DESCENDANT OF MY FATHER, SINESTRO HIMSELF.

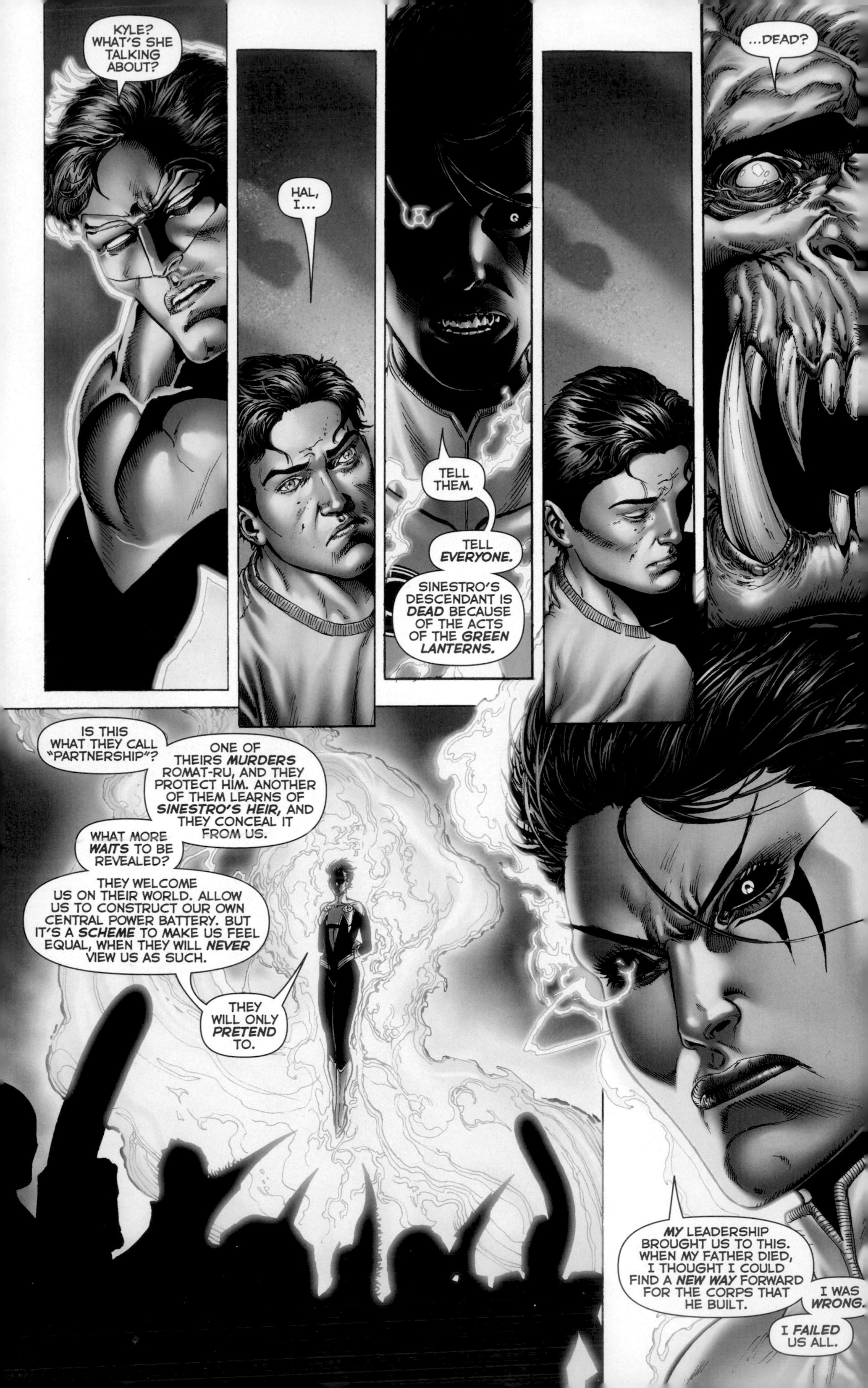
KYLE? WHAT'S SHE TALKING ABOUT?
HAL, I...
TELL THEM.
TELL EVERYONE.
SINESTRO'S DESCENDANT IS DEAD BECAUSE OF THE ACTS OF THE GREEN LANTERNS.
...DEAD?
IS THIS WHAT THEY CALL "PARTNERSHIP"?
ONE OF THEIRS MURDERS ROMAT-RU, AND THEY PROTECT HIM. ANOTHER OF THEM LEARNS OF SINESTRO'S HEIR, AND THEY CONCEAL IT FROM US.
WHAT MORE WAITS TO BE REVEALED?
THEY WELCOME US ON THEIR WORLD. ALLOW US TO CONSTRUCT OUR OWN CENTRAL POWER BATTERY. BUT IT'S A SCHEME TO MAKE US FEEL EQUAL, WHEN THEY WILL NEVER VIEW US AS SUCH.
THEY WILL ONLY PRETEND TO.
MY LEADERSHIP BROUGHT US TO THIS. WHEN MY FATHER DIED, I THOUGHT I COULD FIND A NEW WAY FORWARD FOR THE CORPS THAT HE BUILT.
I WAS WRONG.
I FAILED US ALL.

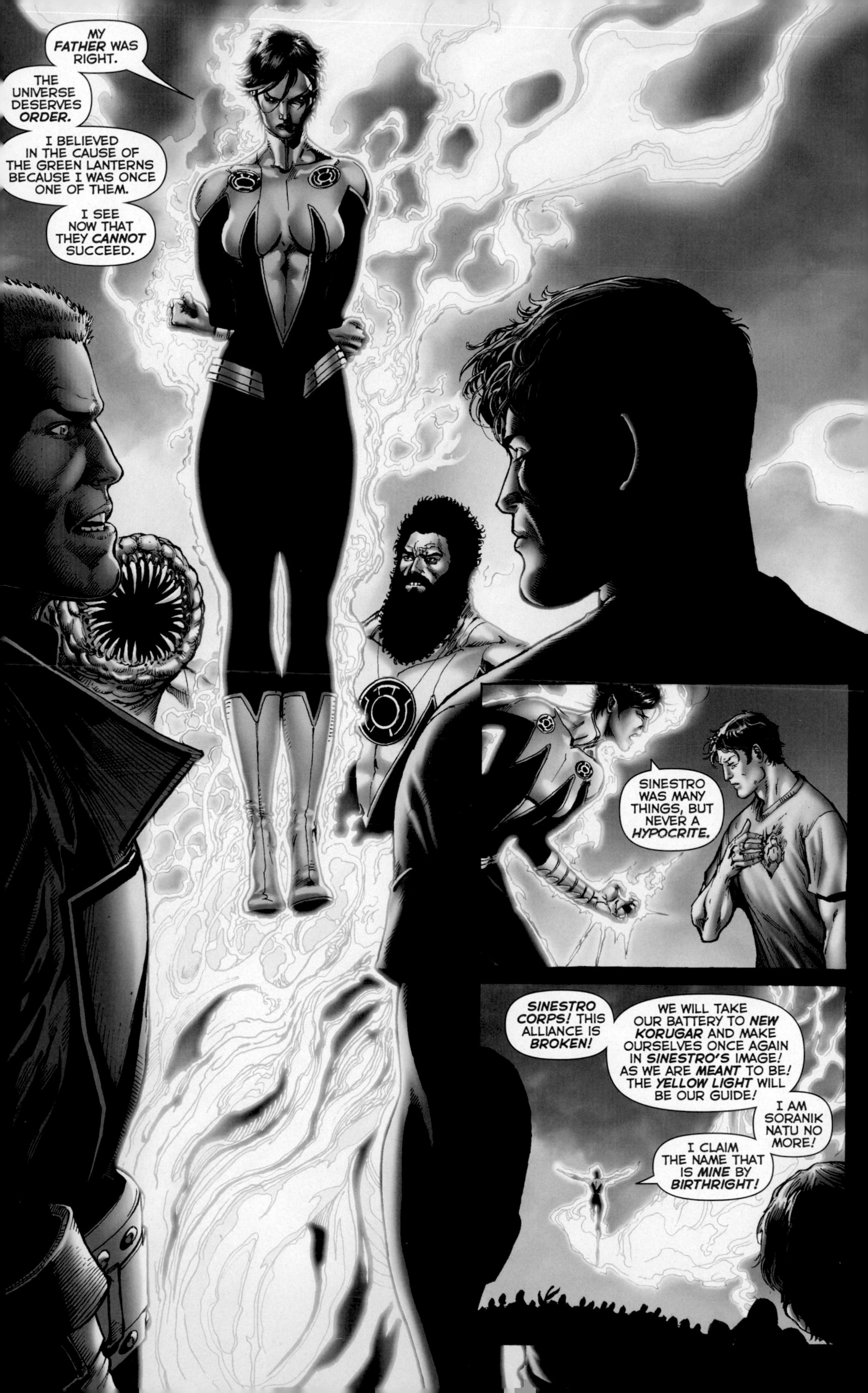
MY FATHER WAS RIGHT.
THE UNIVERSE DESERVES ORDER.
I BELIEVED IN THE CAUSE OF THE GREEN LANTERNS BECAUSE I WAS ONCE ONE OF THEM.
I SEE NOW THAT THEY CANNOT SUCCEED.
SINESTRO WAS MANY THINGS, BUT NEVER A HYPOCRITE.
SINESTRO CORPS! THIS ALLIANCE IS BROKEN!
WE WILL TAKE OUR BATTERY TO NEW KORUGAR AND MAKE OURSELVES ONCE AGAIN IN SINESTRO'S IMAGE! AS WE ARE MEANT TO BE! THE YELLOW LIGHT WILL BE OUR GUIDE!
I AM SORANIK NATU NO MORE!
I CLAIM THE NAME THAT IS MINE BY BIRTHRIGHT!

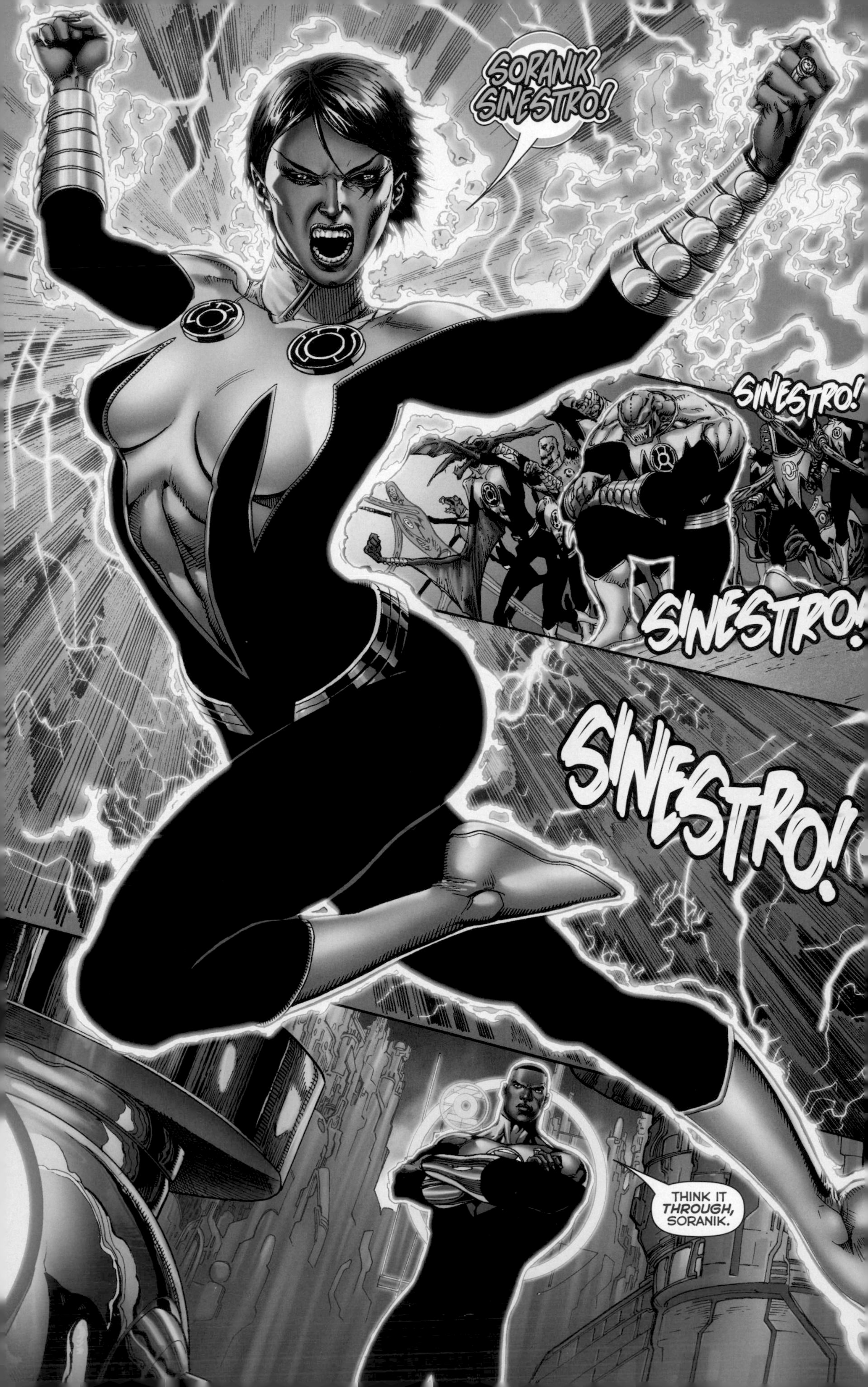
SORANIK SINESTRO!
SINESTRO!
SINESTRO!
SINESTRO!
THINK IT THROUGH, SORANIK.

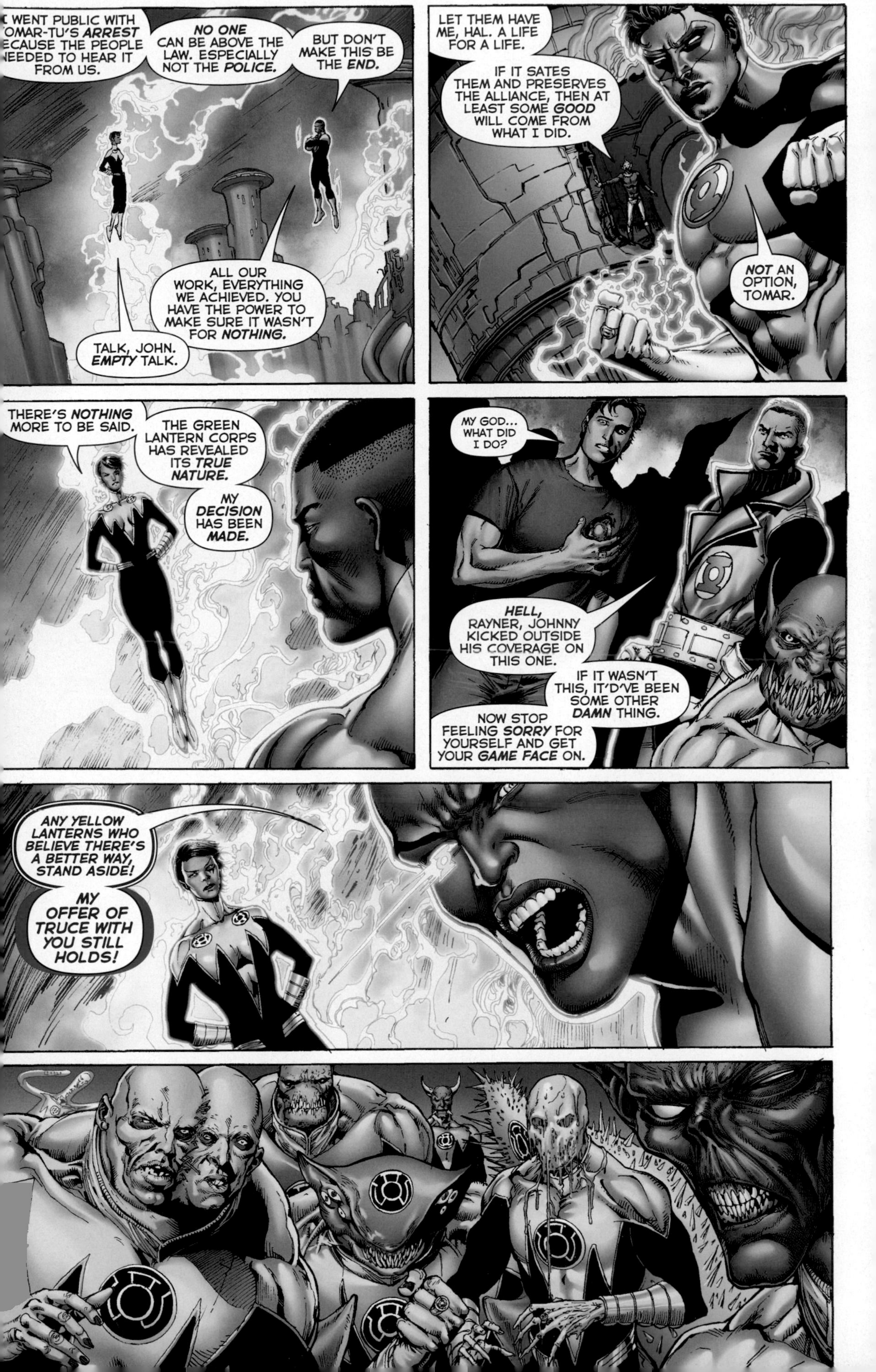

I WENT PUBLIC WITH OMAR-TU'S ARREST ECAUSE THE PEOPLE EEDED TO HEAR IT FROM US.
NO ONE CAN BE ABOVE THE LAW. ESPECIALLY NOT THE POLICE.
BUT DON'T MAKE THIS BE THE END.
ALL OUR WORK, EVERYTHING WE ACHIEVED. YOU HAVE THE POWER TO MAKE SURE IT WASN'T FOR NOTHING.
TALK, JOHN. EMPTY TALK.
LET THEM HAVE ME, HAL. A LIFE FOR A LIFE.
IF IT SATES THEM AND PRESERVES THE ALLIANCE, THEN AT LEAST SOME GOOD WILL COME FROM WHAT I DID.
NOT AN OPTION, TOMAR.
THERE'S NOTHING MORE TO BE SAID.
THE GREEN LANTERN CORPS HAS REVEALED ITS TRUE NATURE.
MY DECISION HAS BEEN MADE.
MY GOD... WHAT DID I DO?
HELL, RAYNER, JOHNNY KICKED OUTSIDE HIS COVERAGE ON THIS ONE.
IF IT WASN'T THIS, IT'D'VE BEEN SOME OTHER DAMN THING.
NOW STOP FEELING SORRY FOR YOURSELF AND GET YOUR GAME FACE ON.
ANY YELLOW LANTERNS WHO BELIEVE THERE'S A BETTER WAY, STAND ASIDE!
MY OFFER OF TRUCE WITH YOU STILL HOLDS!

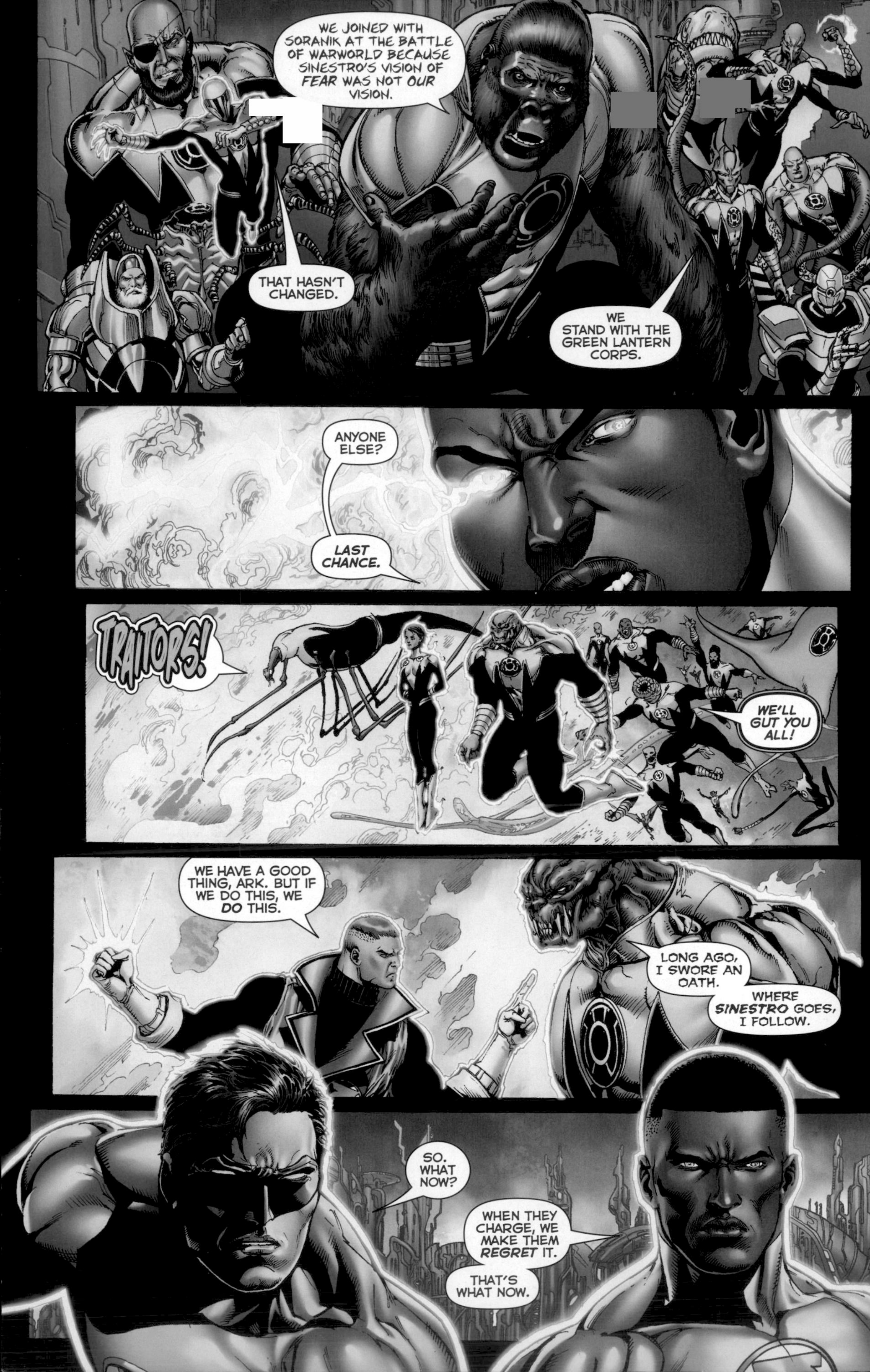
WE JOINED WITH SORANIK AT THE BATTLE OF WARWORLD BECAUSE SINESTRO'S VISION OF FEAR WAS NOT OUR VISION.
THAT HASN'T CHANGED.
WE STAND WITH THE GREEN LANTERN CORPS.
ANYONE ELSE?
LAST CHANCE.
TRAITORS!
WE'LL GUT YOU ALL!
WE HAVE A GOOD THING, ARK. BUT IF WE DO THIS, WE DO THIS.
LONG AGO, I SWORE AN OATH.
WHERE SINESTRO GOES, I FOLLOW.
SO. WHAT NOW?
WHEN THEY CHARGE, WE MAKE THEM REGRET IT.
THAT'S WHAT NOW.

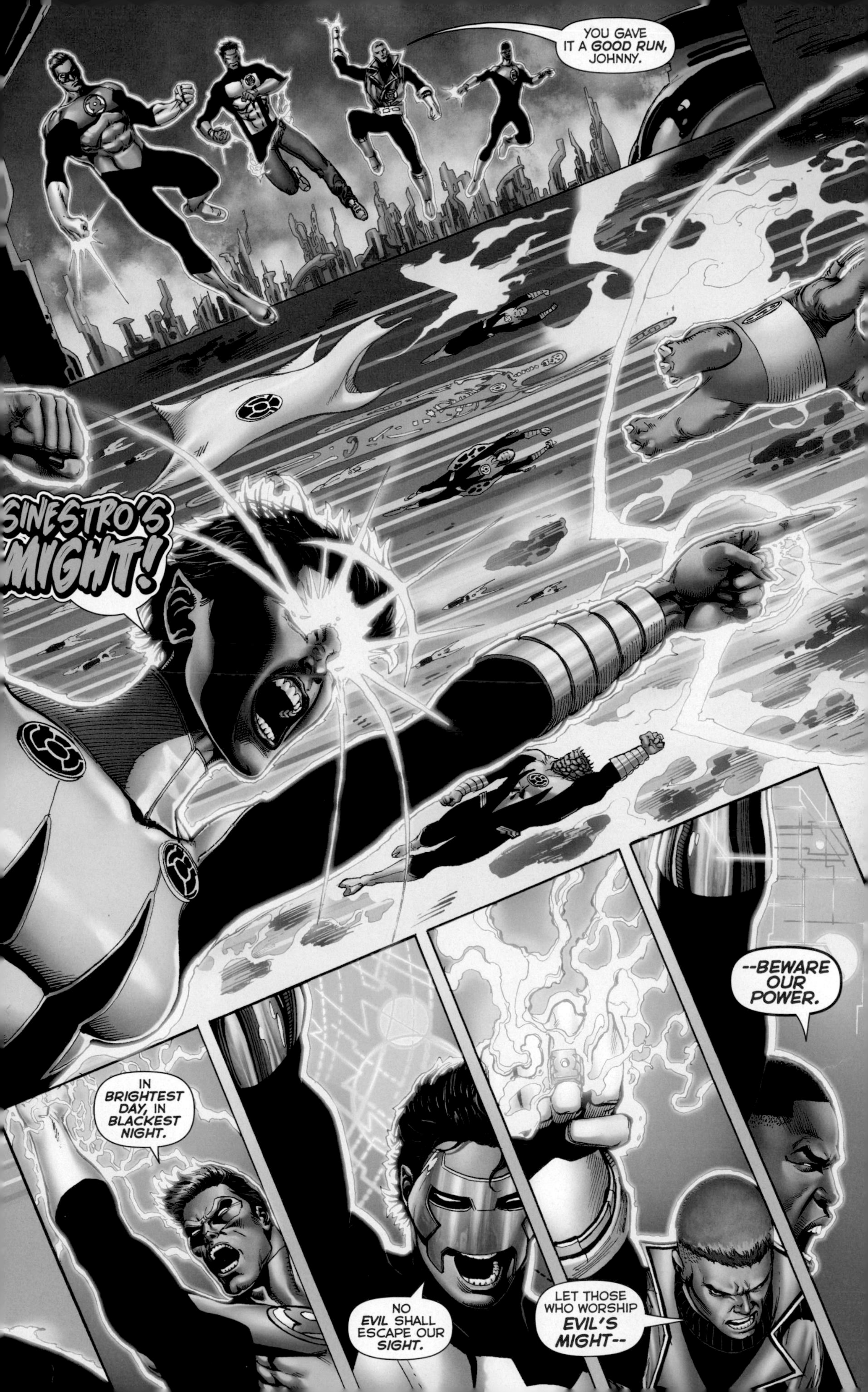
YOU GAVE IT A GOOD RUN, JOHNNY.
SINESTRO'S MIGHT!
IN BRIGHTEST DAY, IN BLACKEST NIGHT.
NO EVIL SHALL ESCAPE OUR SIGHT.
LET THOSE WHO WORSHIP EVIL'S MIGHT--
--BEWARE OUR POWER.

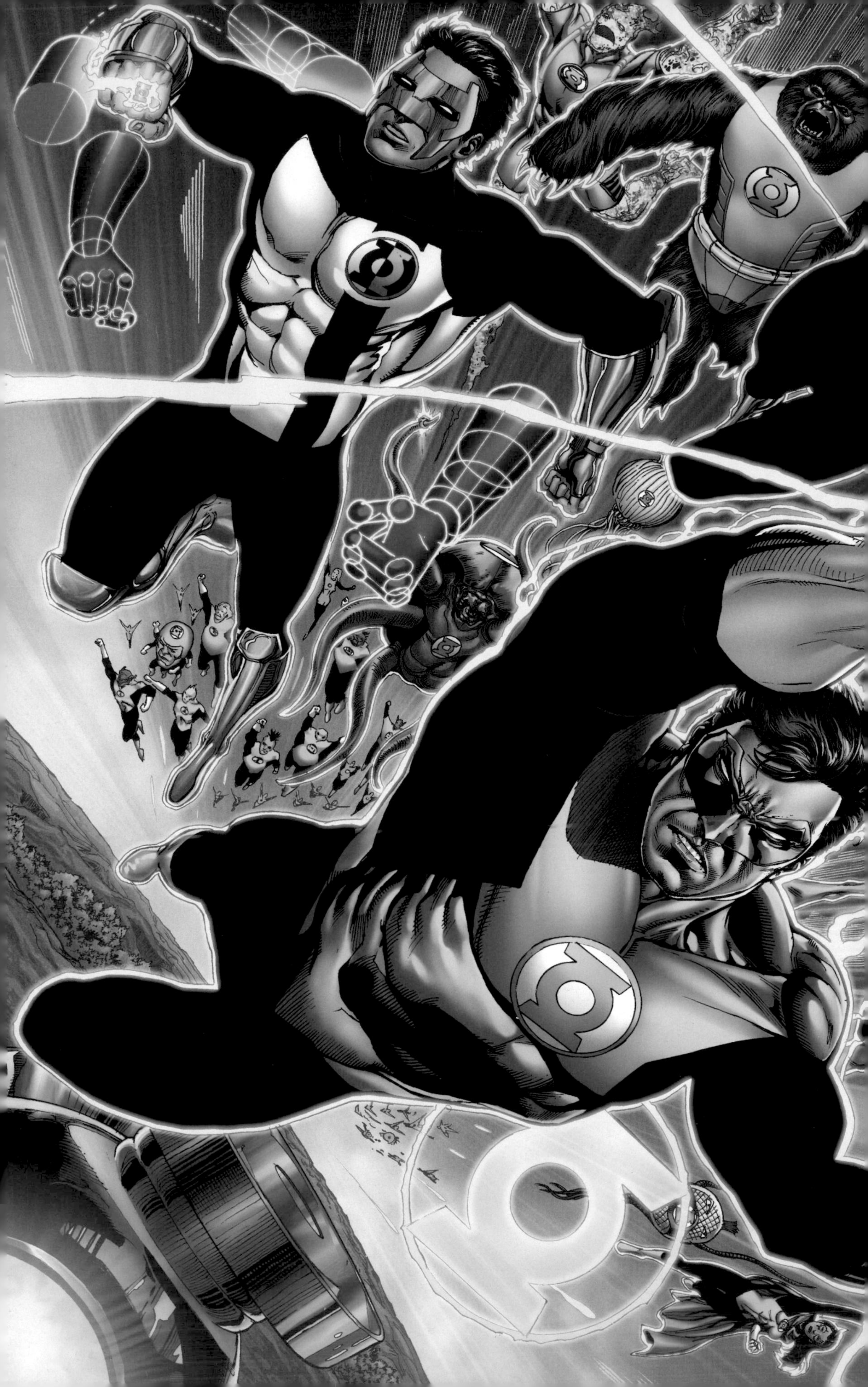

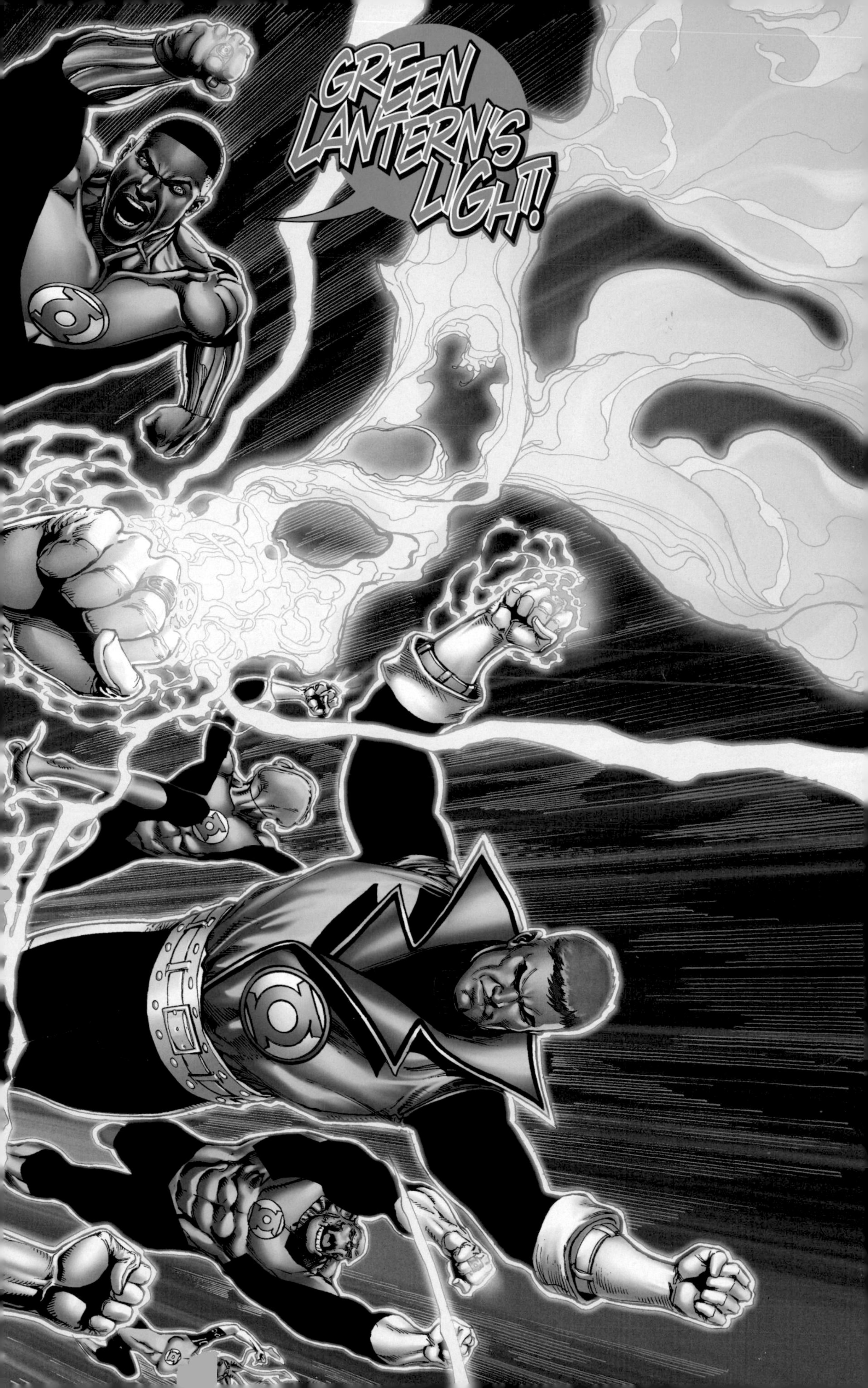
GREEN LANTERN'S LIGHT!

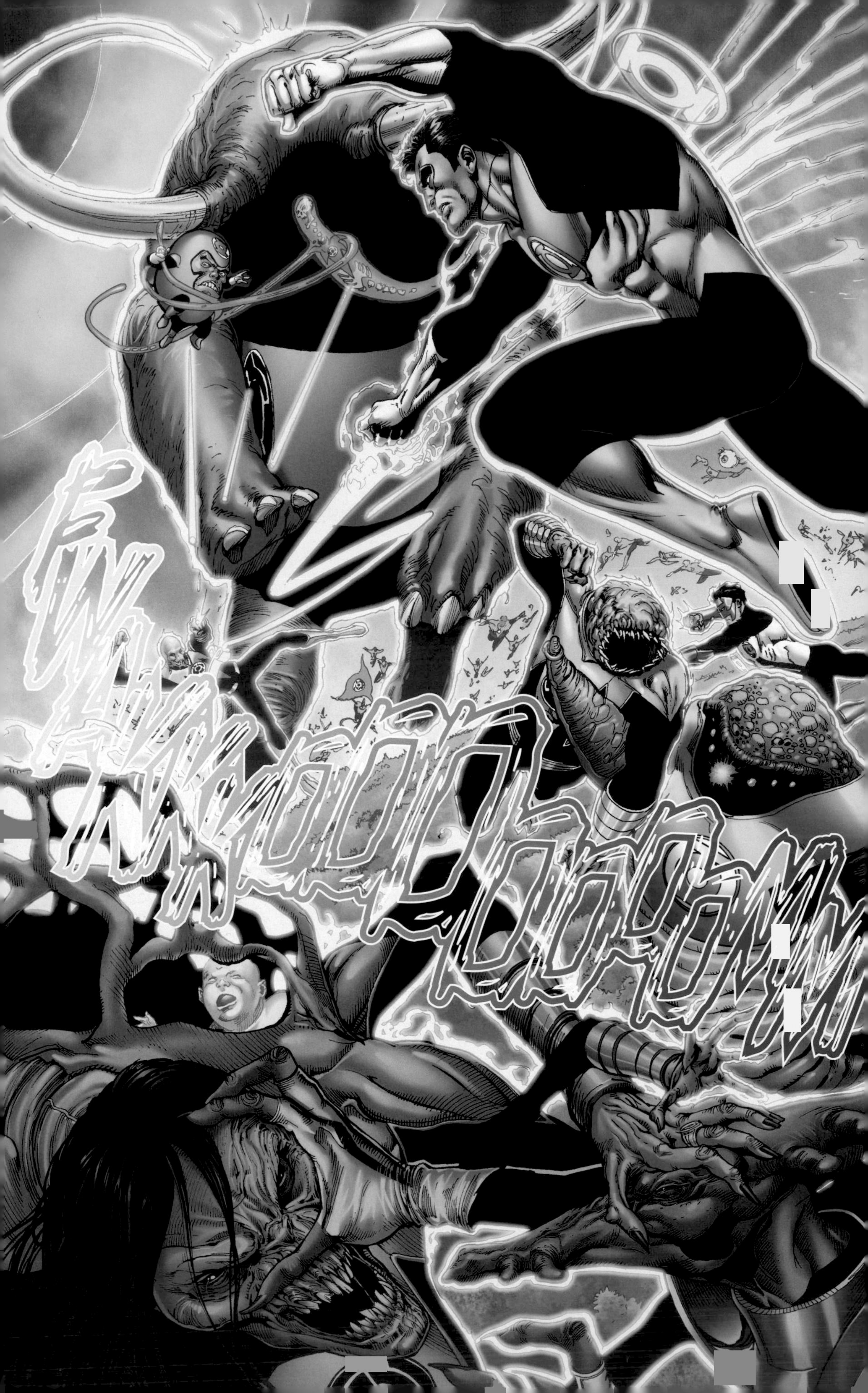

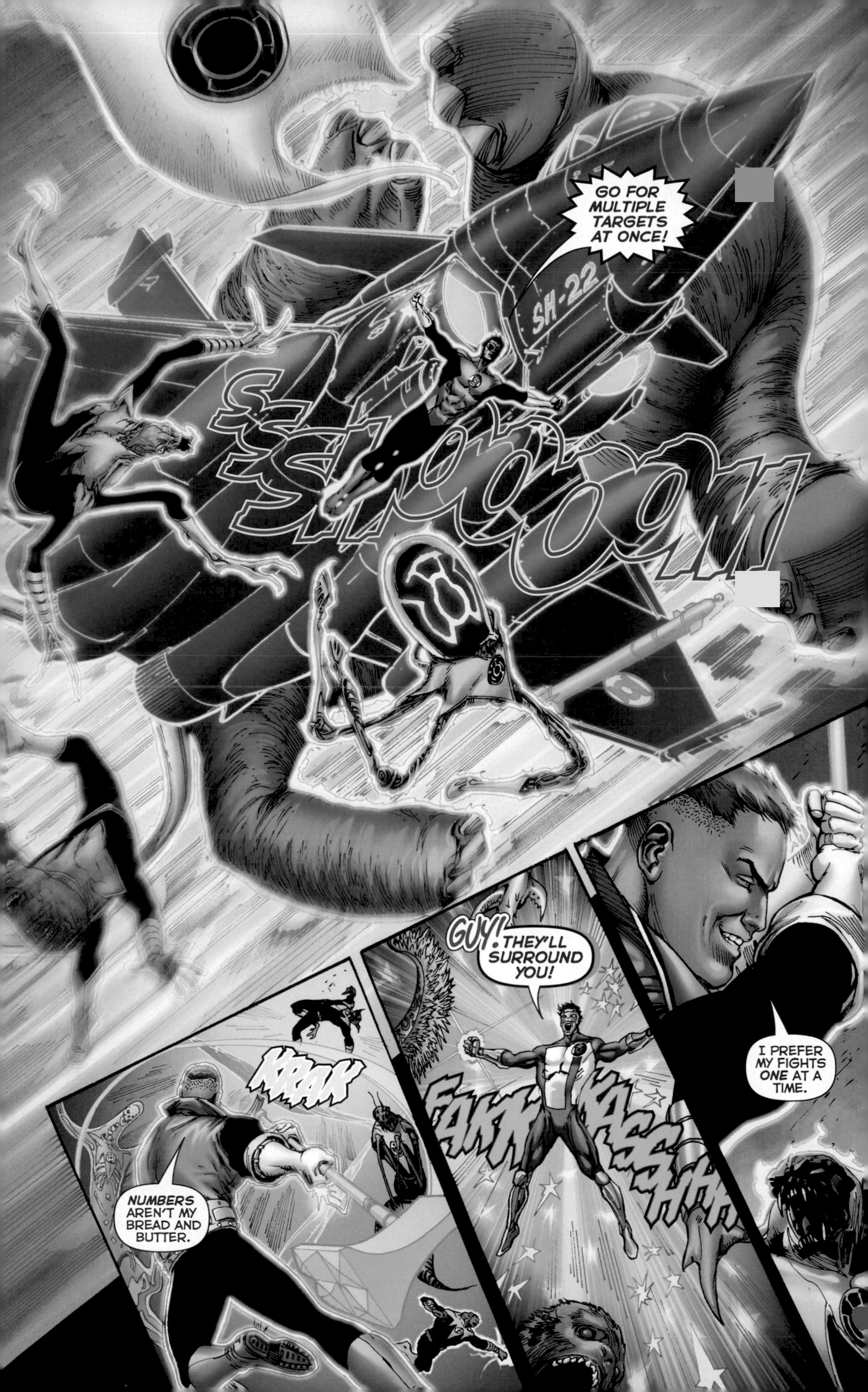
GO FOR MULTIPLE TARGETS AT ONCE!
SH-22
NUMBERS AREN'T MY BREAD AND BUTTER.
KRAK
GUY! THEY'LL SURROUND YOU!
I PREFER MY FIGHTS ONE AT A TIME.

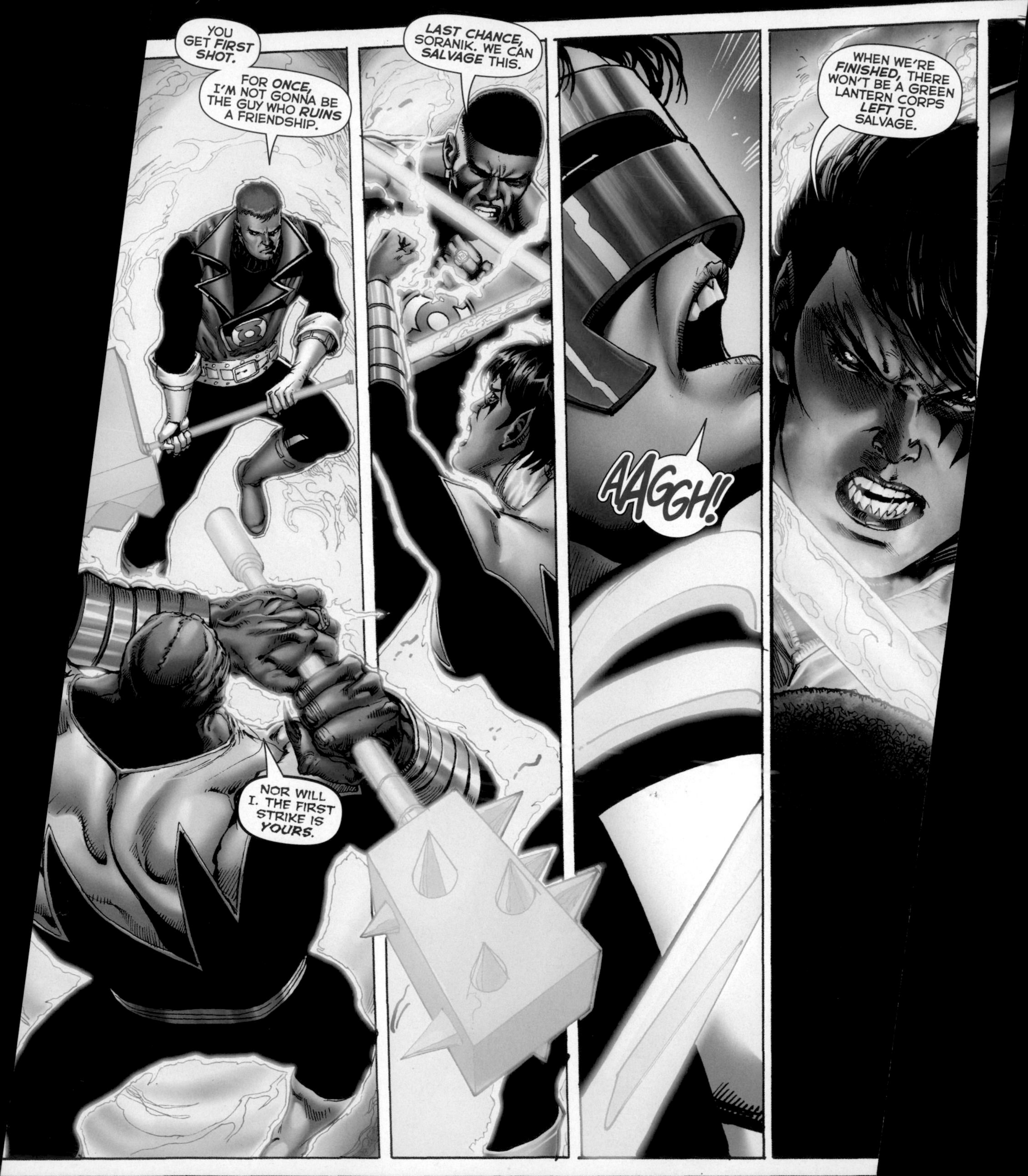
YOU GET FIRST SHOT.
FOR ONCE, I'M NOT GONNA BE THE GUY WHO RUINS A FRIENDSHIP.
NOR WILL I. THE FIRST STRIKE IS YOURS.
LAST CHANCE, SORANIK. WE CAN SALVAGE THIS.
AAGGH!
WHEN WE'RE FINISHED, THERE WON'T BE A GREEN LANTERN CORPS LEFT TO SALVAGE.

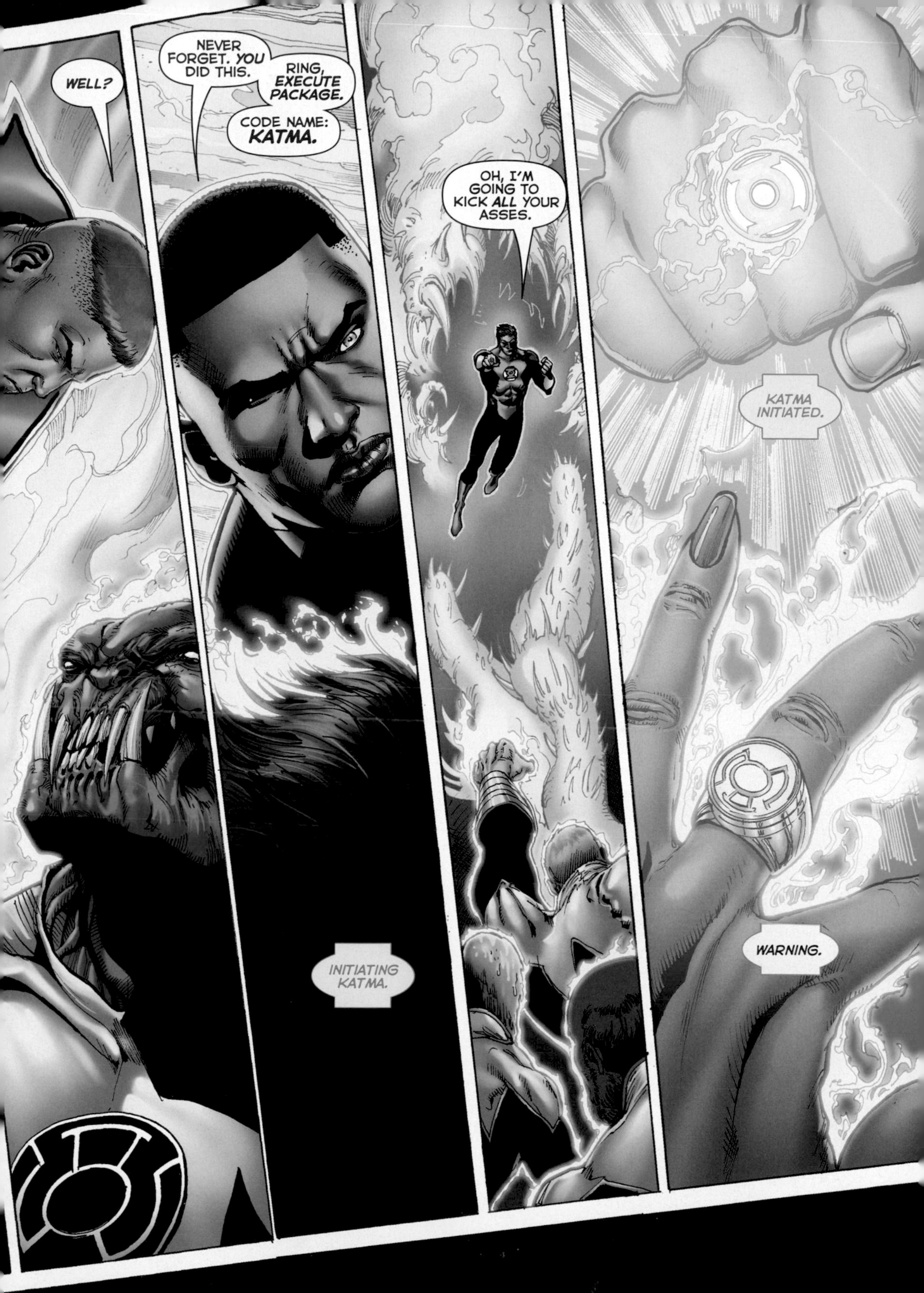
WELL?
NEVER FORGET. YOU DID THIS.
RING, EXECUTE PACKAGE.
CODE NAME: KATMA.
INITIATING KATMA.
OH, I'M GOING TO KICK ALL YOUR ASSES.
KATMA INITIATED.
WARNING.

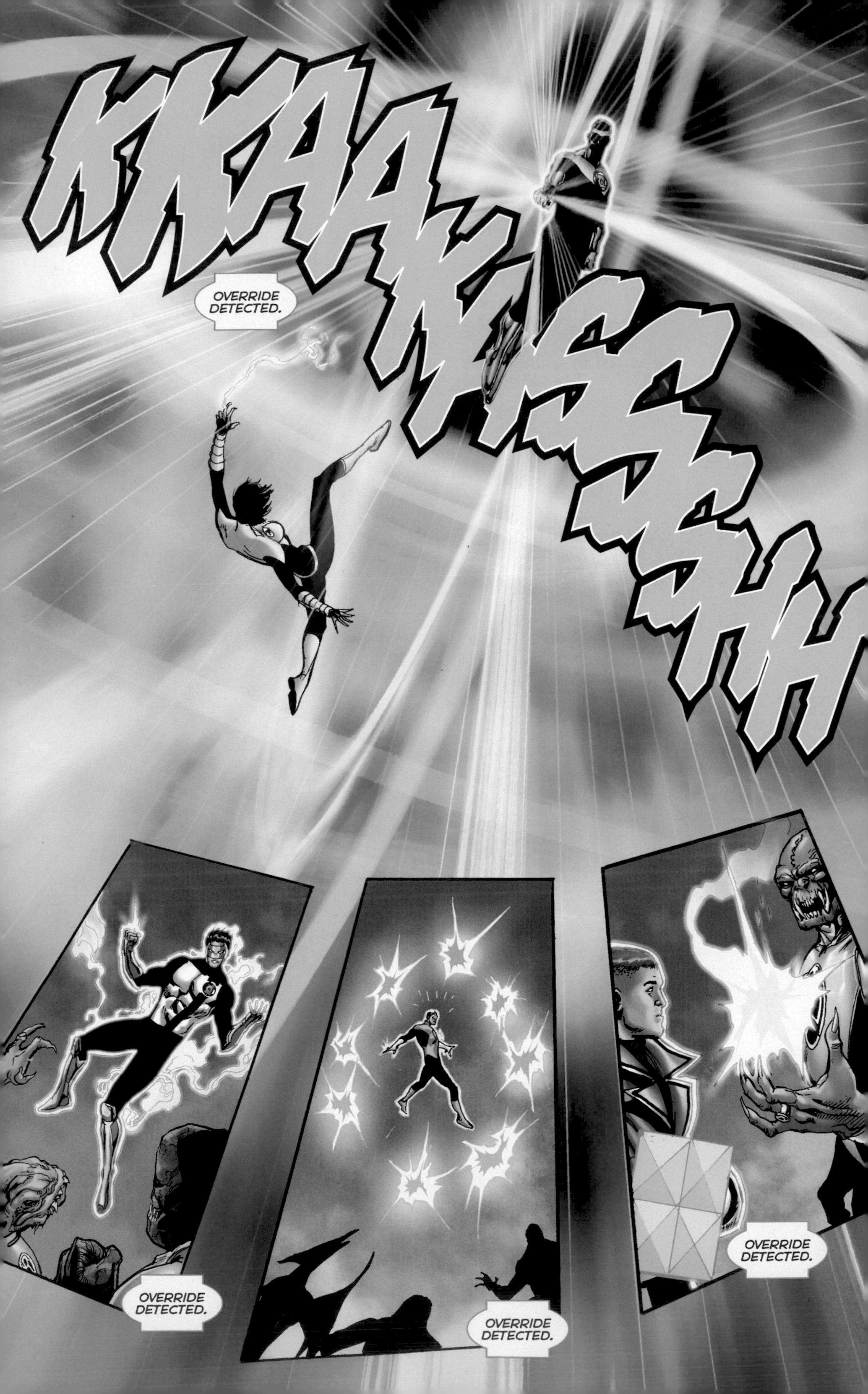
KKAAKKSSSHH
OVERRIDE DETECTED.
OVERRIDE DETECTED.
OVERRIDE DETECTED.
OVERRIDE DETECTED.

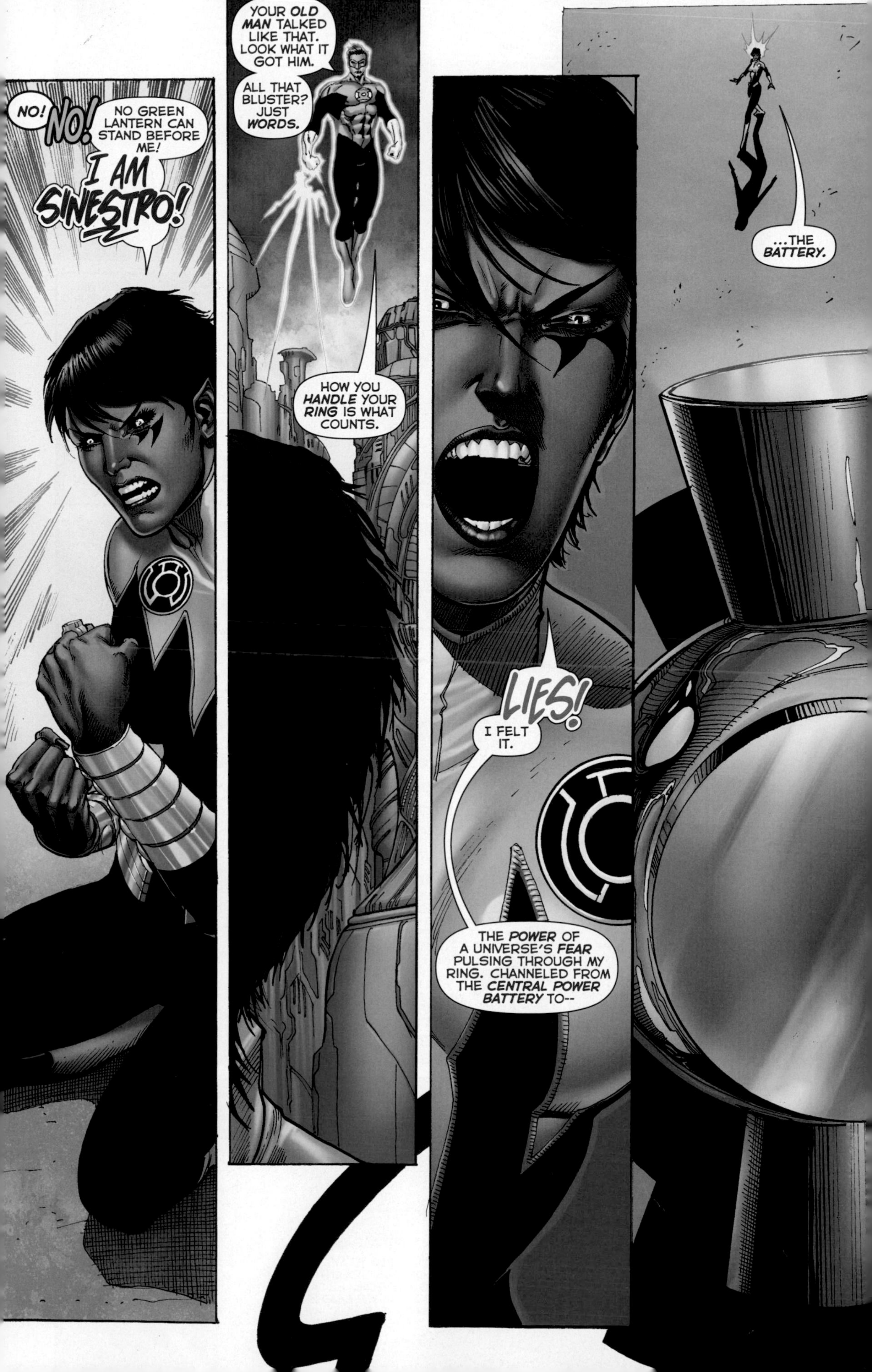
NO! NO!
NO GREEN LANTERN CAN STAND BEFORE ME!
I AM SINESTRO!
YOUR OLD MAN TALKED LIKE THAT. LOOK WHAT IT GOT HIM.
ALL THAT BLUSTER? JUST WORDS.
HOW YOU HANDLE YOUR RING IS WHAT COUNTS.
LIES!
I FELT IT.
THE POWER OF A UNIVERSE'S FEAR PULSING THROUGH MY RING. CHANNELED FROM THE CENTRAL POWER BATTERY TO--
...THE BATTERY.

YOU DID THIS!

STEWART?

YOUR OFFER OF PEACE WAS A FARCE FROM THE START.

WHEN WE HELPED BUILD YOUR NEW BATTERY, I INSTALLED A SAFETY MEASURE.

IT TRANSFERRED FROM THE BATTERY TO EVERY YELLOW RING, MAKING THEM INEFFECTIVE AGAINST WILL.

THINK OF IT AS A GREEN IMPURITY.

JOHNNY, I JUST FELL IN LOVE WITH YOU.

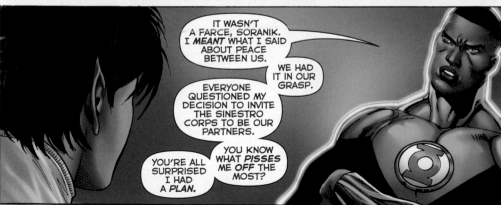

IT WASN'T A FARCE, SORANIK. I MEANT WHAT I SAID ABOUT PEACE BETWEEN US.

WE HAD IT IN OUR GRASP.

EVERYONE QUESTIONED MY DECISION TO INVITE THE SINESTRO CORPS TO BE OUR PARTNERS.

YOU'RE ALL SURPRISED I HAD A PLAN.

YOU KNOW WHAT PISSES ME OFF THE MOST?

THIS ISN'T THE END.

YOU WANT TO GO? GO.

BUT STAY ON THE STRAIGHT AND NARROW. BECAUSE THE GREEN LANTERN CORPS CAN--AND WILL-- TAKE YOU DOWN.

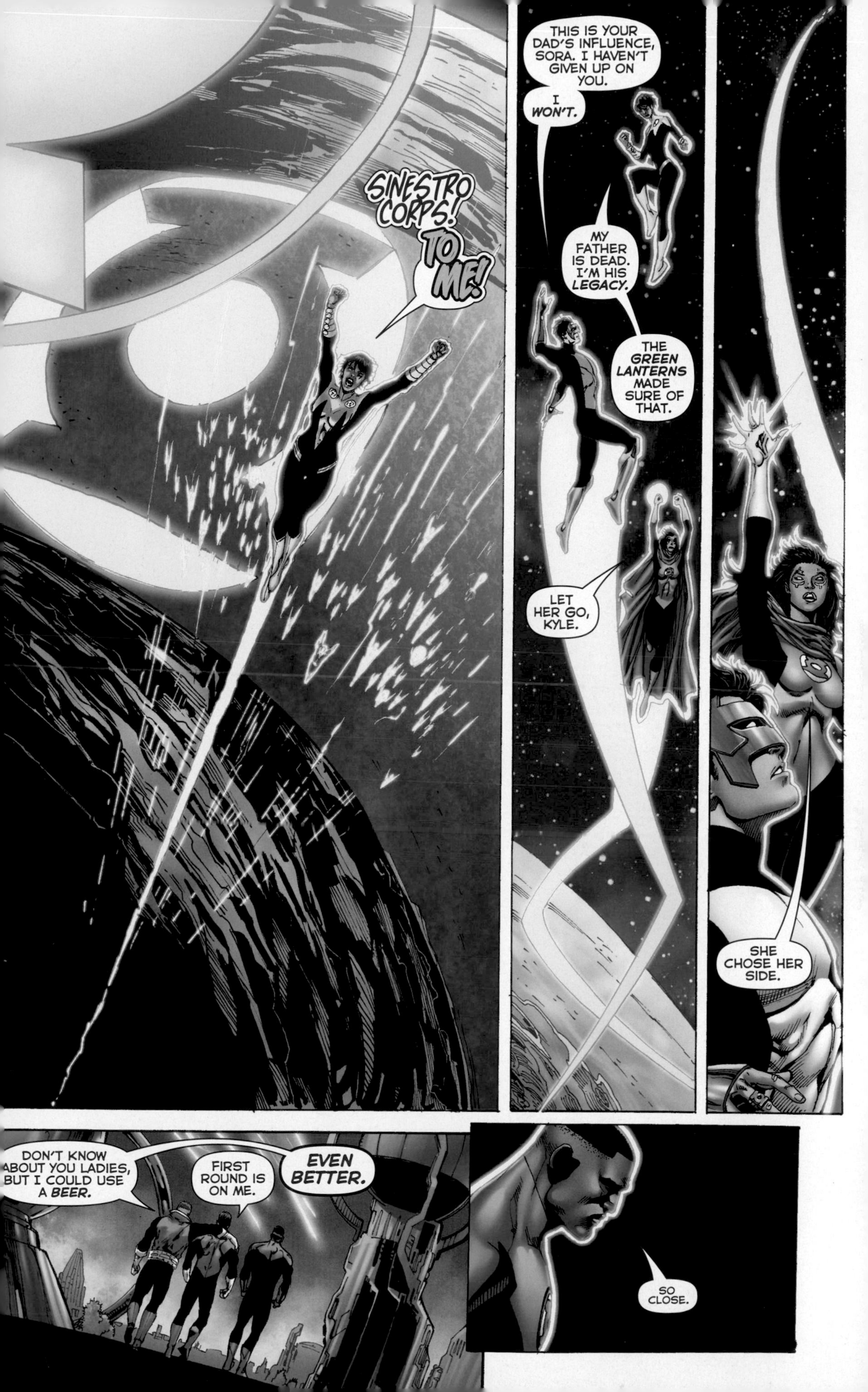
SINESTRO CORPS! TO ME!
THIS IS YOUR DAD'S INFLUENCE, SORA. I HAVEN'T GIVEN UP ON YOU.
I WON'T.
MY FATHER IS DEAD. I'M HIS LEGACY.
THE GREEN LANTERNS MADE SURE OF THAT.
LET HER GO, KYLE.
SHE CHOSE HER SIDE.
DON'T KNOW ABOUT YOU LADIES, BUT I COULD USE A BEER.
FIRST ROUND IS ON ME.
EVEN BETTER.
SO CLOSE.

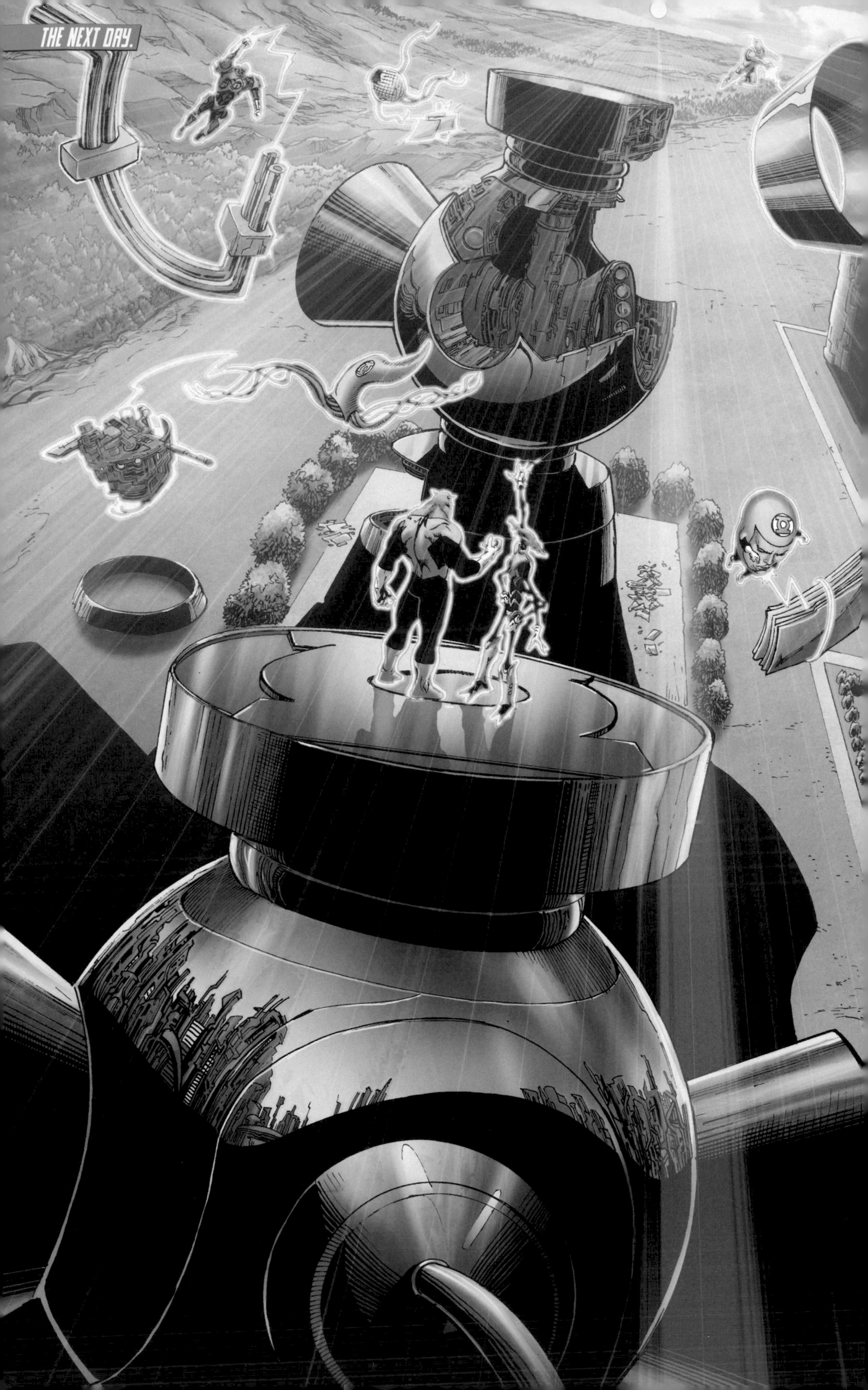
THE NEXT DAY.

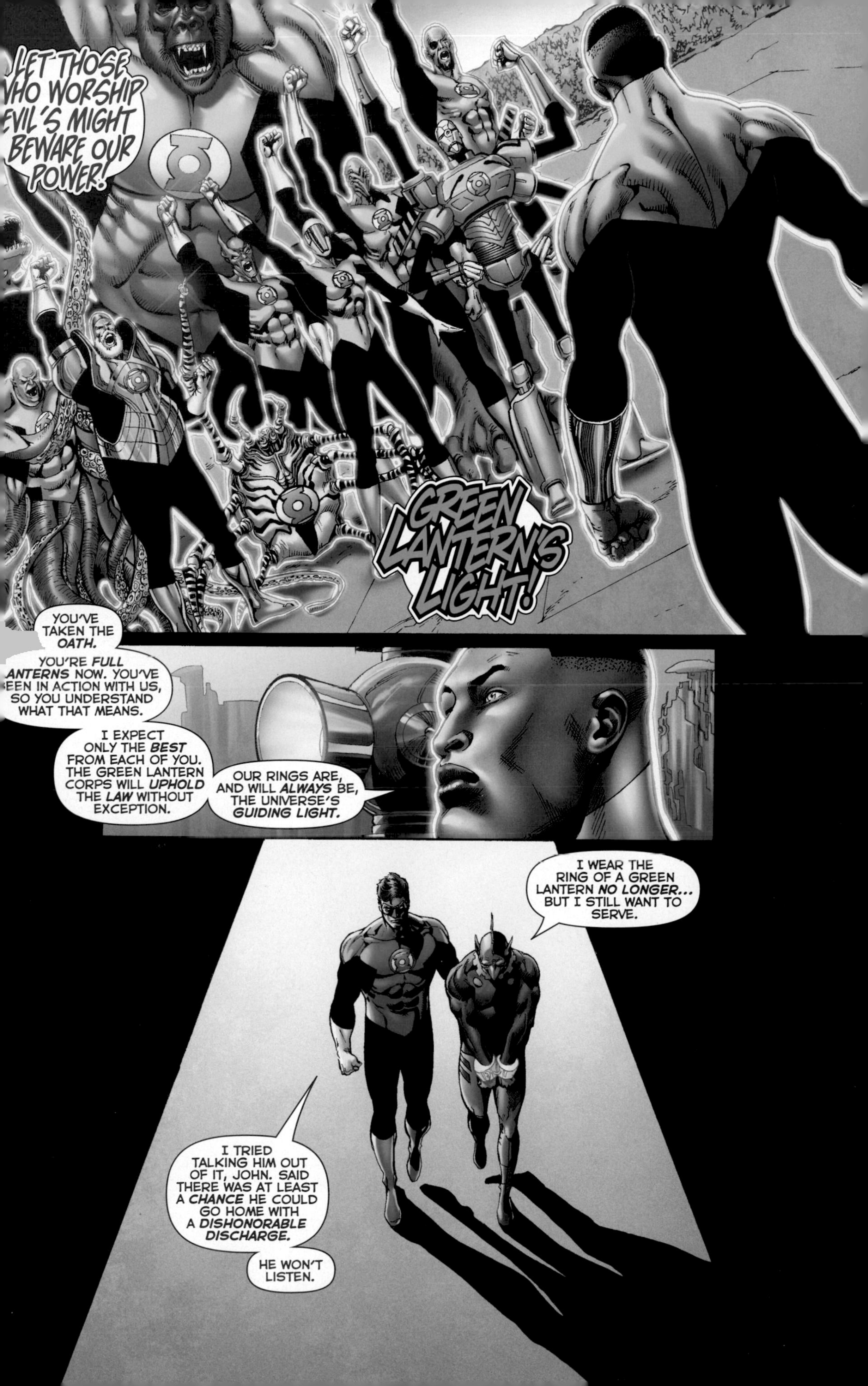
LET THOSE WHO WORSHIP EVIL'S MIGHT BEWARE OUR POWER!
GREEN LANTERN'S LIGHT!
YOU'VE TAKEN THE OATH.
YOU'RE FULL LANTERNS NOW. YOU'VE BEEN IN ACTION WITH US, SO YOU UNDERSTAND WHAT THAT MEANS.
I EXPECT ONLY THE BEST FROM EACH OF YOU. THE GREEN LANTERN CORPS WILL UPHOLD THE LAW WITHOUT EXCEPTION.
OUR RINGS ARE, AND WILL ALWAYS BE, THE UNIVERSE'S GUIDING LIGHT.
I WEAR THE RING OF A GREEN LANTERN NO LONGER... BUT I STILL WANT TO SERVE.
I TRIED TALKING HIM OUT OF IT, JOHN. SAID THERE WAS AT LEAST A CHANCE HE COULD GO HOME WITH A DISHONORABLE DISCHARGE.
HE WON'T LISTEN.

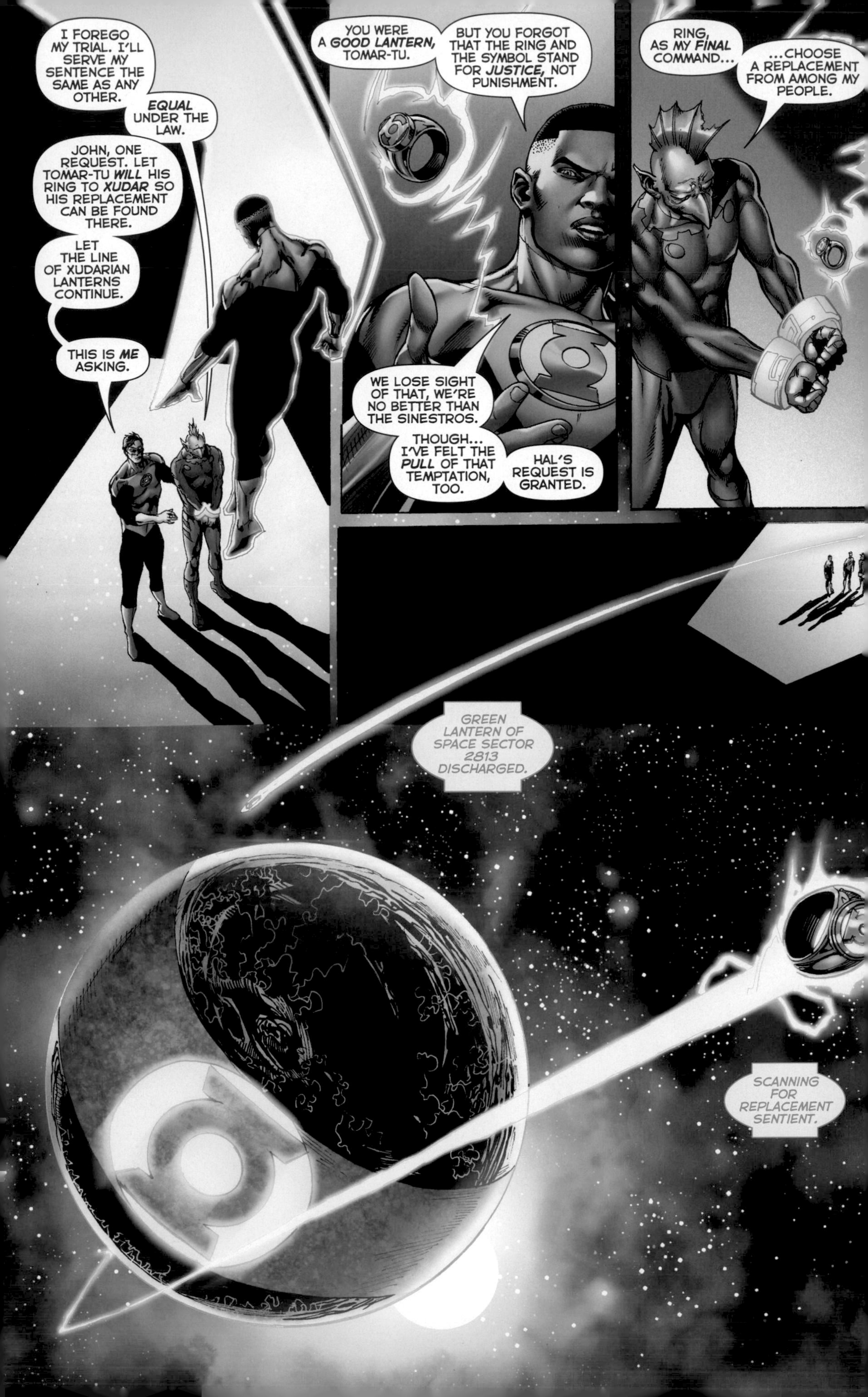
I FOREGO MY TRIAL. I'LL SERVE MY SENTENCE THE SAME AS ANY OTHER.
EQUAL UNDER THE LAW.
JOHN, ONE REQUEST. LET TOMAR-TU WILL HIS RING TO XUDAR SO HIS REPLACEMENT CAN BE FOUND THERE.
LET THE LINE OF XUDARIAN LANTERNS CONTINUE.
THIS IS ME ASKING.
YOU WERE A GOOD LANTERN, TOMAR-TU.
BUT YOU FORGOT THAT THE RING AND THE SYMBOL STAND FOR JUSTICE, NOT PUNISHMENT.
WE LOSE SIGHT OF THAT, WE'RE NO BETTER THAN THE SINESTROS.
THOUGH... I'VE FELT THE PULL OF THAT TEMPTATION, TOO.
HAL'S REQUEST IS GRANTED.
RING, AS MY FINAL COMMAND...
...CHOOSE A REPLACEMENT FROM AMONG MY PEOPLE.
GREEN LANTERN OF SPACE SECTOR 2813 DISCHARGED.
SCANNING FOR REPLACEMENT SENTIENT.

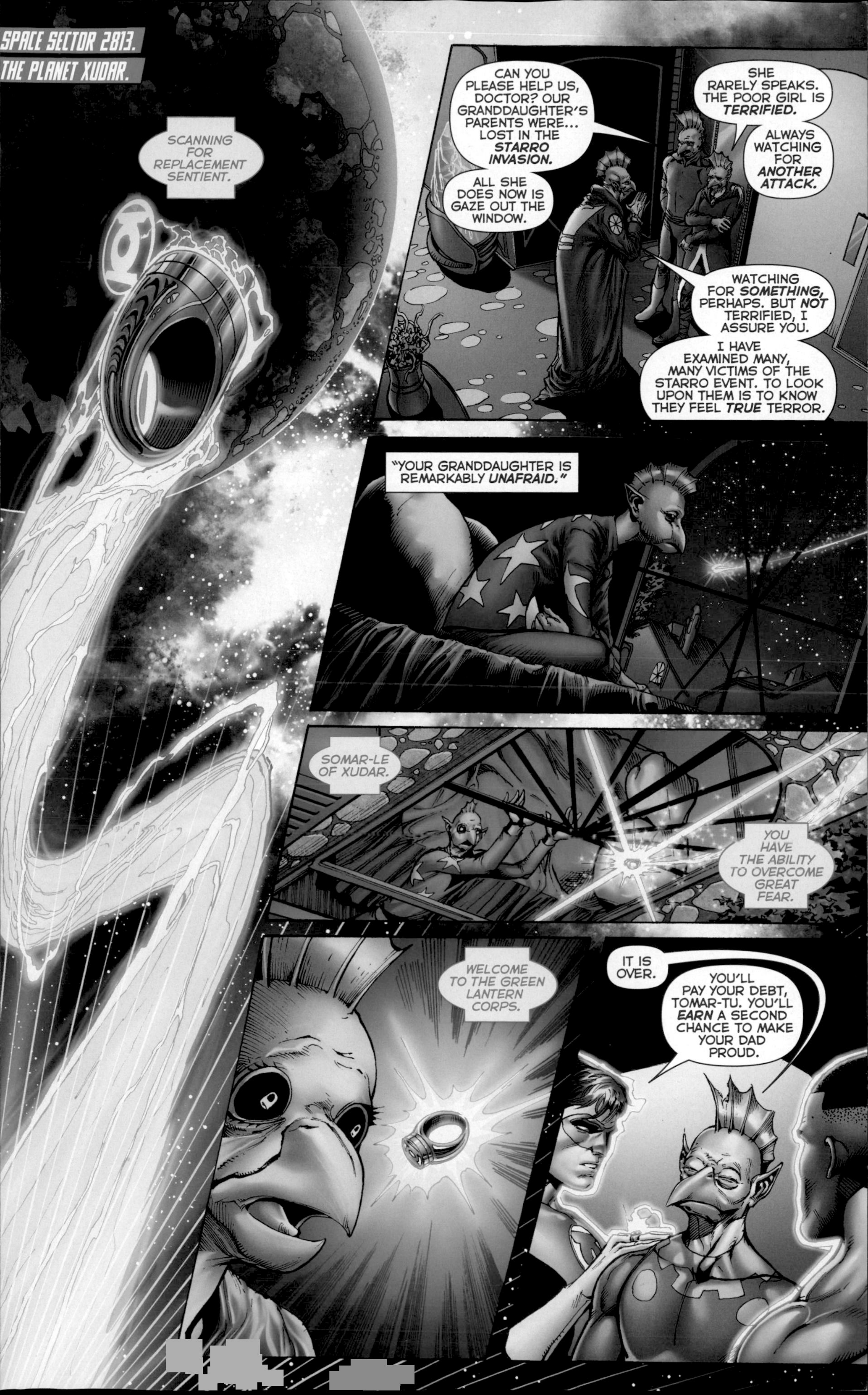
SPACE SECTOR 2813.
THE PLANET XUDAR.
SCANNING FOR REPLACEMENT SENTIENT.
CAN YOU PLEASE HELP US, DOCTOR? OUR GRANDDAUGHTER'S PARENTS WERE... LOST IN THE STARRO INVASION.
ALL SHE DOES NOW IS GAZE OUT THE WINDOW.
SHE RARELY SPEAKS. THE POOR GIRL IS TERRIFIED.
ALWAYS WATCHING FOR ANOTHER ATTACK.
WATCHING FOR SOMETHING, PERHAPS. BUT NOT TERRIFIED, I ASSURE YOU.
I HAVE EXAMINED MANY, MANY VICTIMS OF THE STARRO EVENT. TO LOOK UPON THEM IS TO KNOW THEY FEEL TRUE TERROR.
"YOUR GRANDDAUGHTER IS REMARKABLY UNAFRAID."
SOMAR-LE OF XUDAR.
YOU HAVE THE ABILITY TO OVERCOME GREAT FEAR.
WELCOME TO THE GREEN LANTERN CORPS.
IT IS OVER.
YOU'LL PAY YOUR DEBT, TOMAR-TU. YOU'LL EARN A SECOND CHANCE TO MAKE YOUR DAD PROUD.

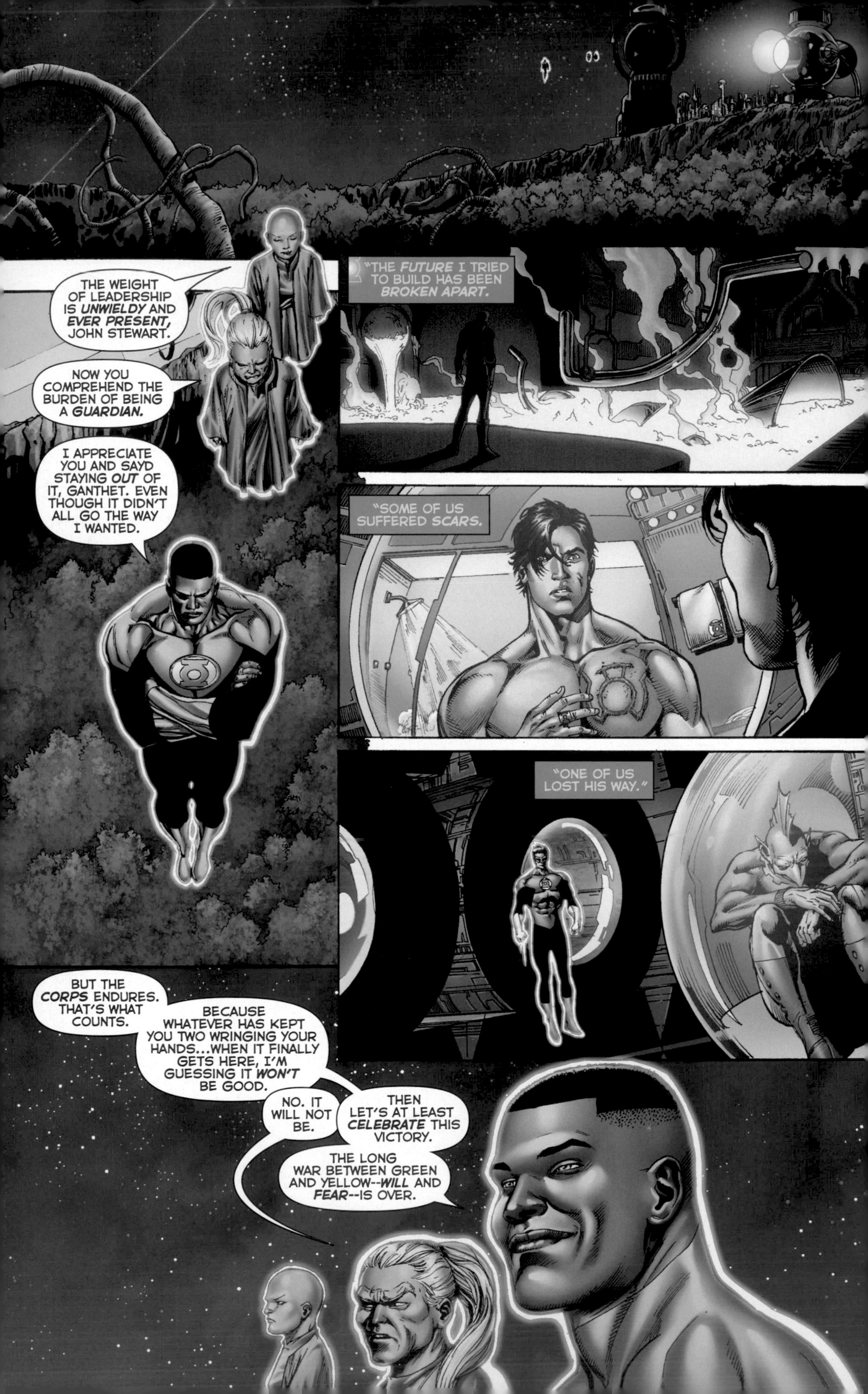
THE WEIGHT OF LEADERSHIP IS UNWIELDY AND EVER PRESENT, JOHN STEWART.
NOW YOU COMPREHEND THE BURDEN OF BEING A GUARDIAN.
I APPRECIATE YOU AND SAYD STAYING OUT OF IT, GANTHET. EVEN THOUGH IT DIDN'T ALL GO THE WAY I WANTED.
"THE FUTURE I TRIED TO BUILD HAS BEEN BROKEN APART.
"SOME OF US SUFFERED SCARS.
"ONE OF US LOST HIS WAY."
BUT THE CORPS ENDURES. THAT'S WHAT COUNTS.
BECAUSE WHATEVER HAS KEPT YOU TWO WRINGING YOUR HANDS...WHEN IT FINALLY GETS HERE, I'M GUESSING IT WON'T BE GOOD.
NO. IT WILL NOT BE.
THEN LET'S AT LEAST CELEBRATE THIS VICTORY.
THE LONG WAR BETWEEN GREEN AND YELLOW--WILL AND FEAR--IS OVER.

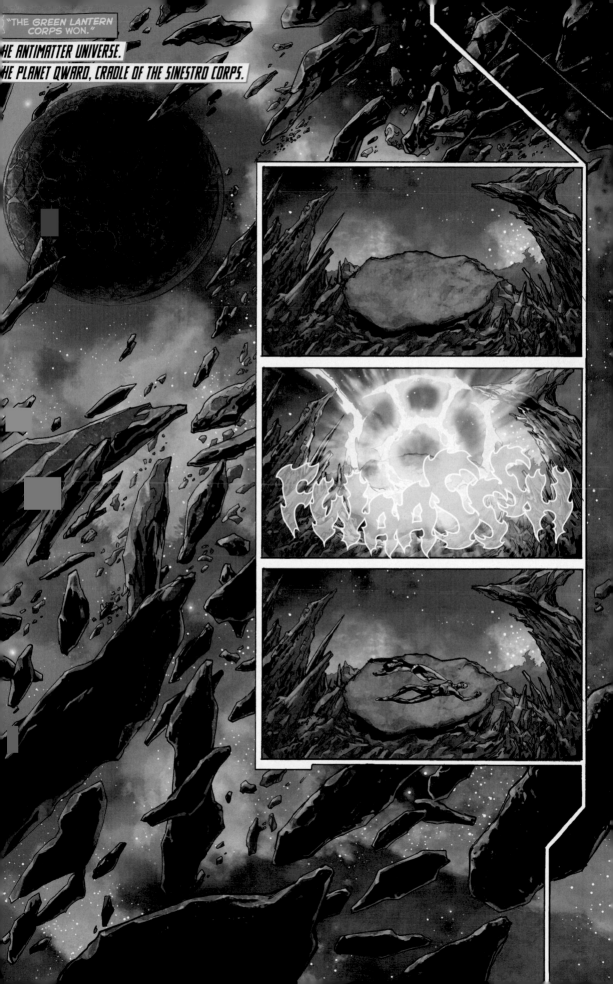

"THE *GREEN LANTERN CORPS* WON."

THE ANTIMATTER UNIVERSE.
THE PLANET QWARD, CRADLE OF THE SINESTRO CORPS.

FWAAASSH

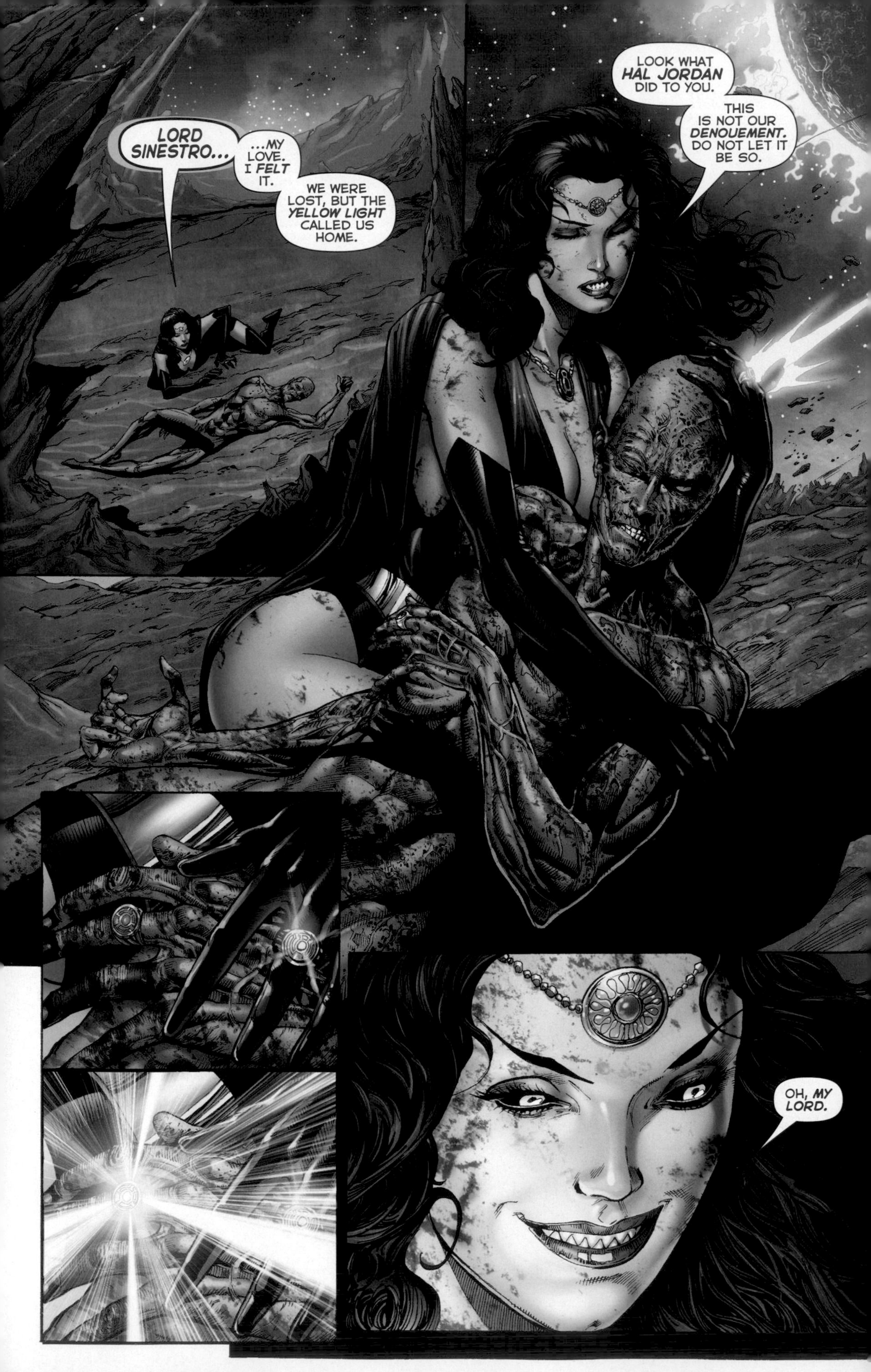
LORD SINESTRO...
...MY LOVE. I FELT IT.
WE WERE LOST, BUT THE YELLOW LIGHT CALLED US HOME.
LOOK WHAT HAL JORDAN DID TO YOU.
THIS IS NOT OUR DENOUEMENT. DO NOT LET IT BE SO.
OH, MY LORD.

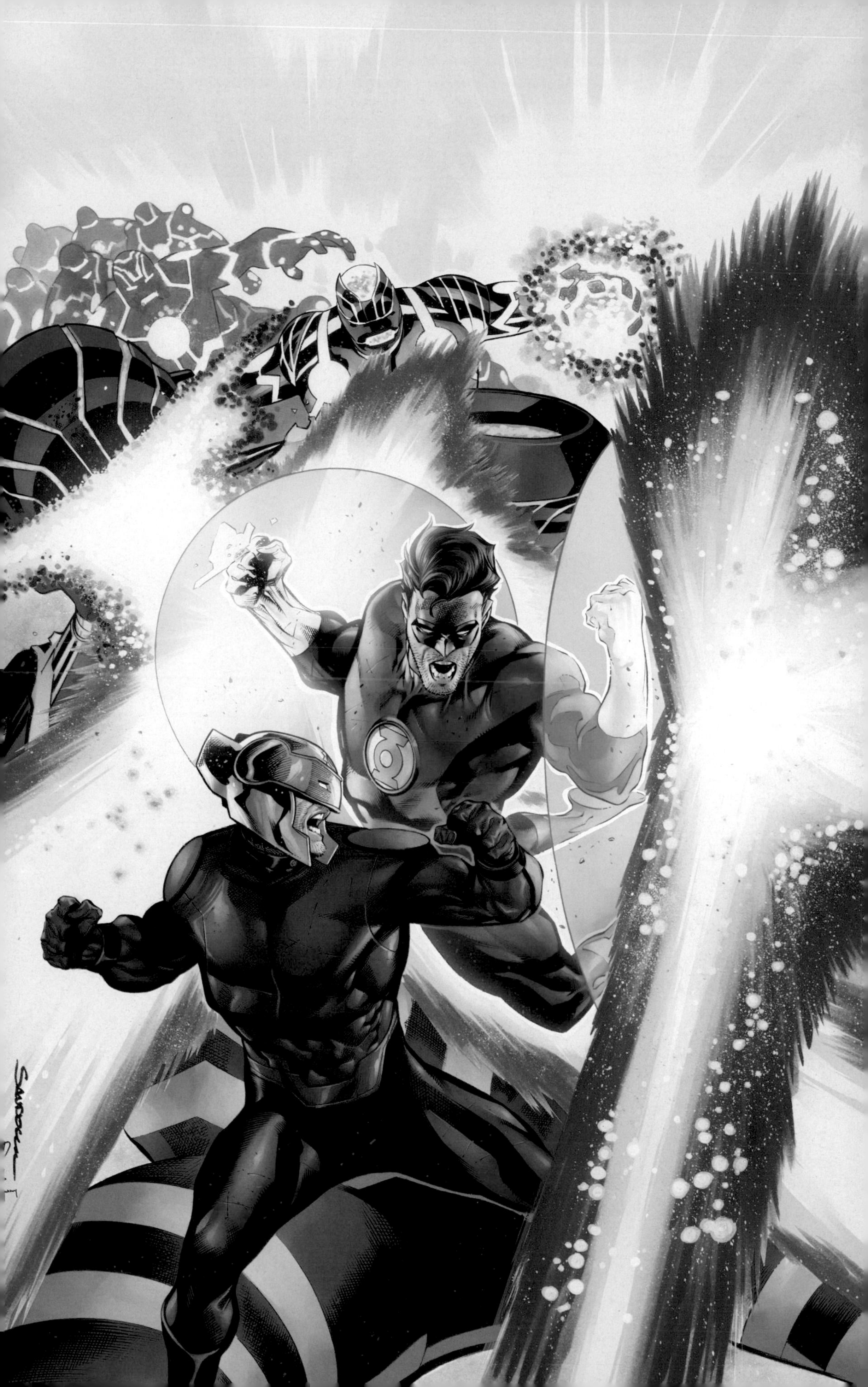

"FALL OF THE GODS PART ONE: A SHOT FROM THE DARK"

RAFA SANDOVAL penciller * JORDI TARRAGONA inker * TOMEU MOREY colorist
cover art by RAFA SANDOVAL, JORDI TARRAGONA, and TOMEU MOREY

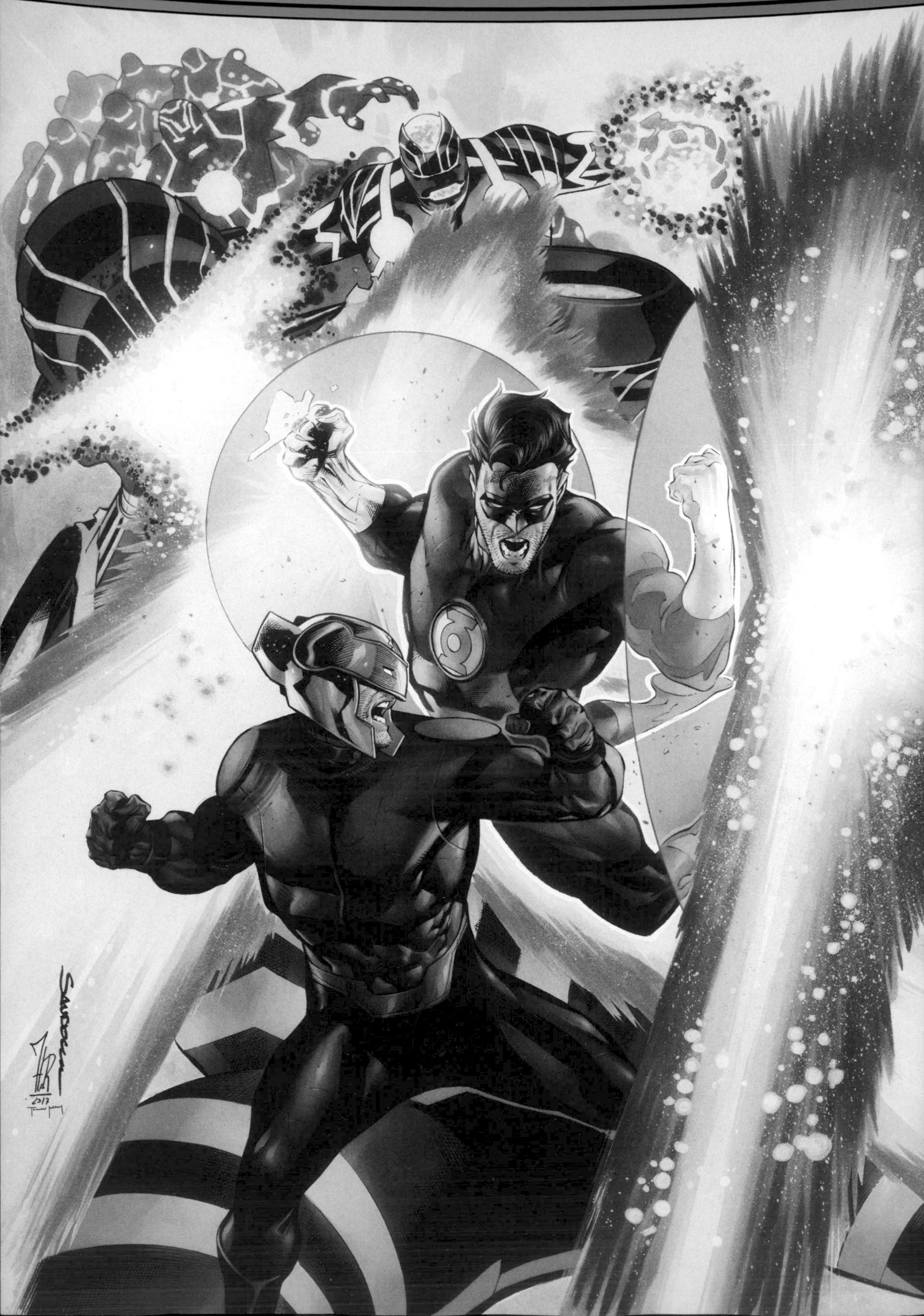

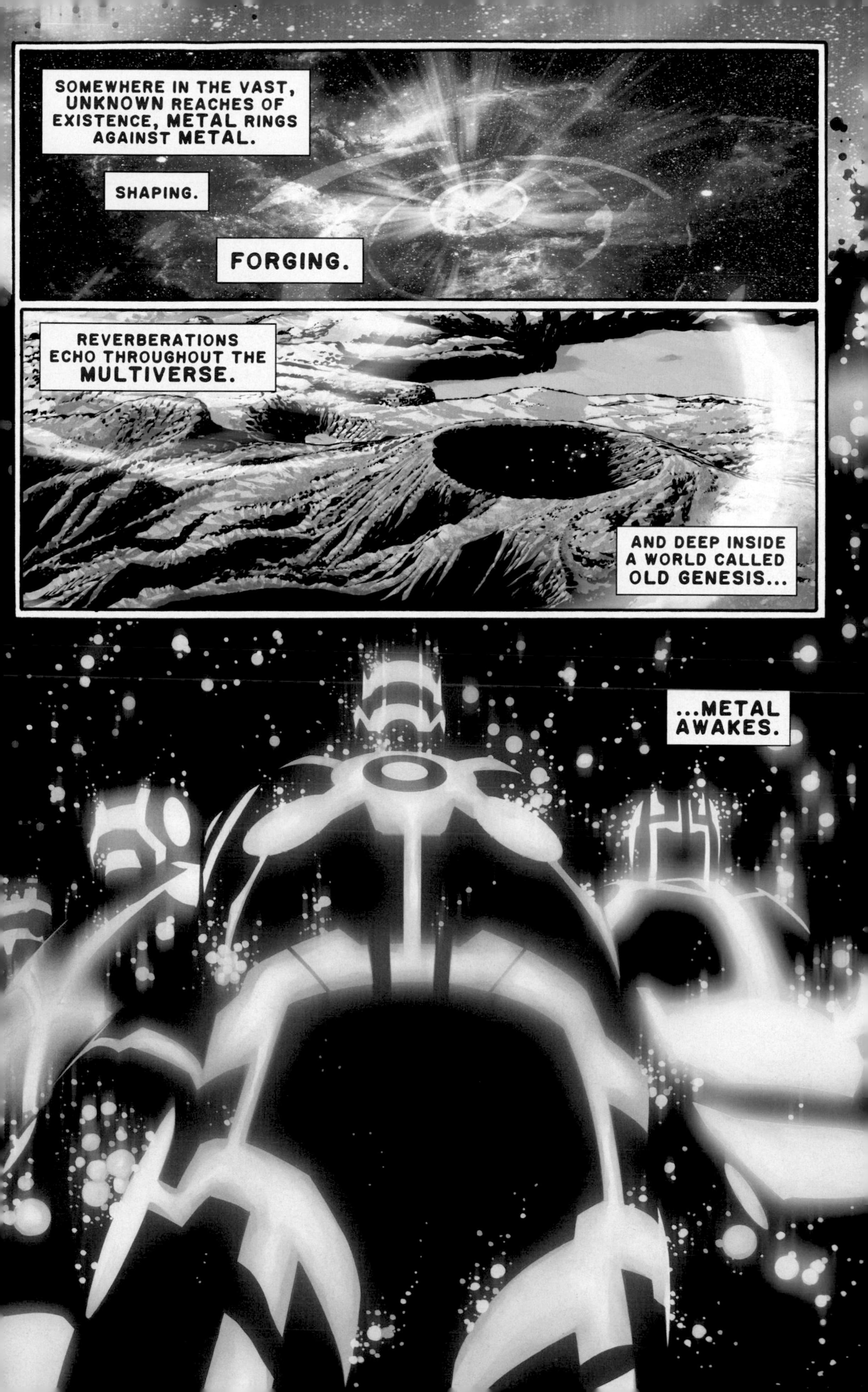
SOMEWHERE IN THE VAST, UNKNOWN REACHES OF EXISTENCE, METAL RINGS AGAINST METAL.
SHAPING.
FORGING.
REVERBERATIONS ECHO THROUGHOUT THE MULTIVERSE.
AND DEEP INSIDE A WORLD CALLED OLD GENESIS...
...METAL AWAKES.

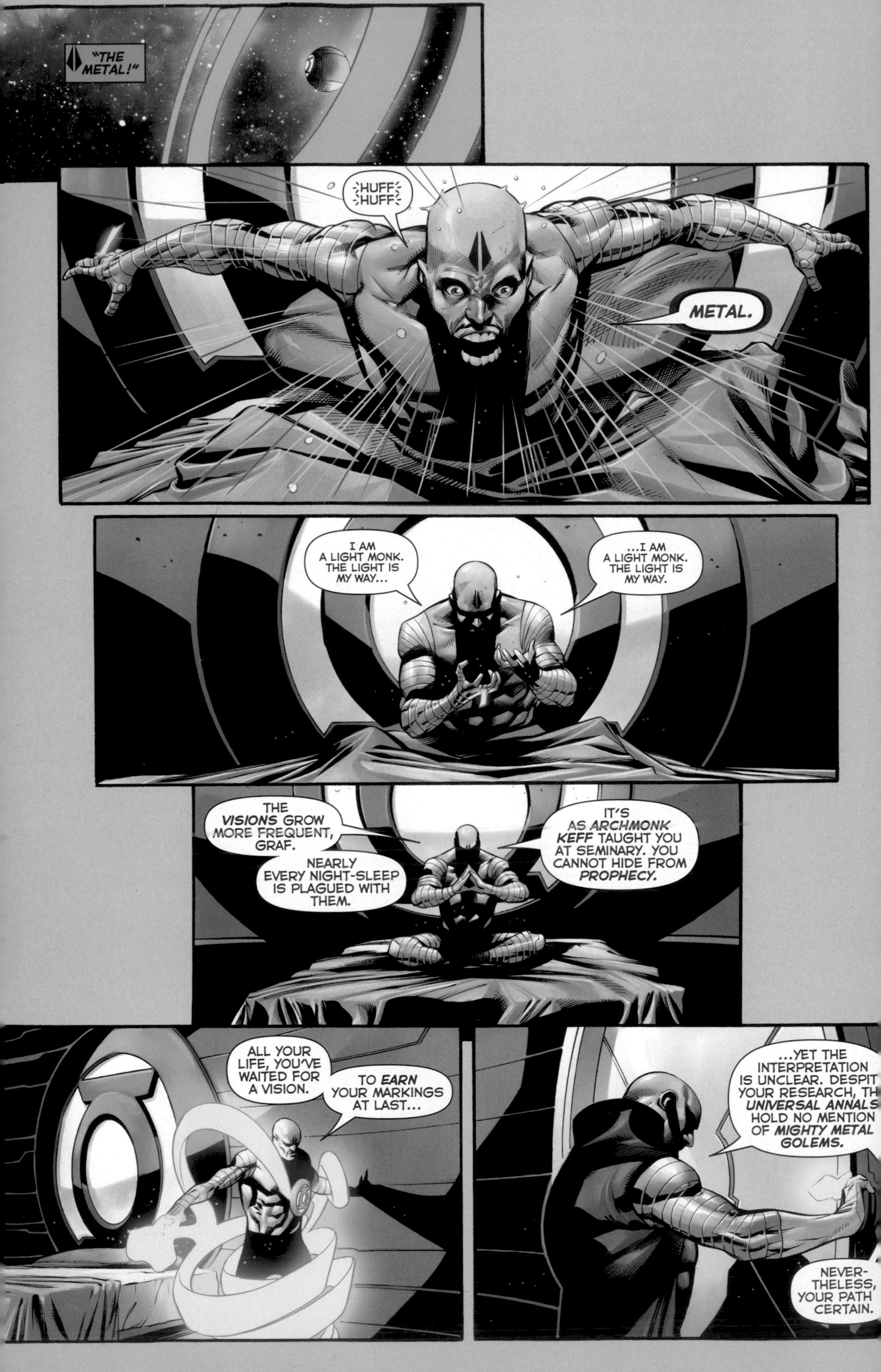
"THE METAL!"
HUFF HUFF
METAL.
I AM A LIGHT MONK. THE LIGHT IS MY WAY...
...I AM A LIGHT MONK. THE LIGHT IS MY WAY.
THE VISIONS GROW MORE FREQUENT, GRAF.
NEARLY EVERY NIGHT-SLEEP IS PLAGUED WITH THEM.
IT'S AS ARCHMONK KEFF TAUGHT YOU AT SEMINARY. YOU CANNOT HIDE FROM PROPHECY.
ALL YOUR LIFE, YOU'VE WAITED FOR A VISION.
TO EARN YOUR MARKINGS AT LAST...
...YET THE INTERPRETATION IS UNCLEAR. DESPIT YOUR RESEARCH, TH UNIVERSAL ANNALS HOLD NO MENTION OF MIGHTY METAL GOLEMS.
NEVER-THELESS, YOUR PATH CERTAIN.

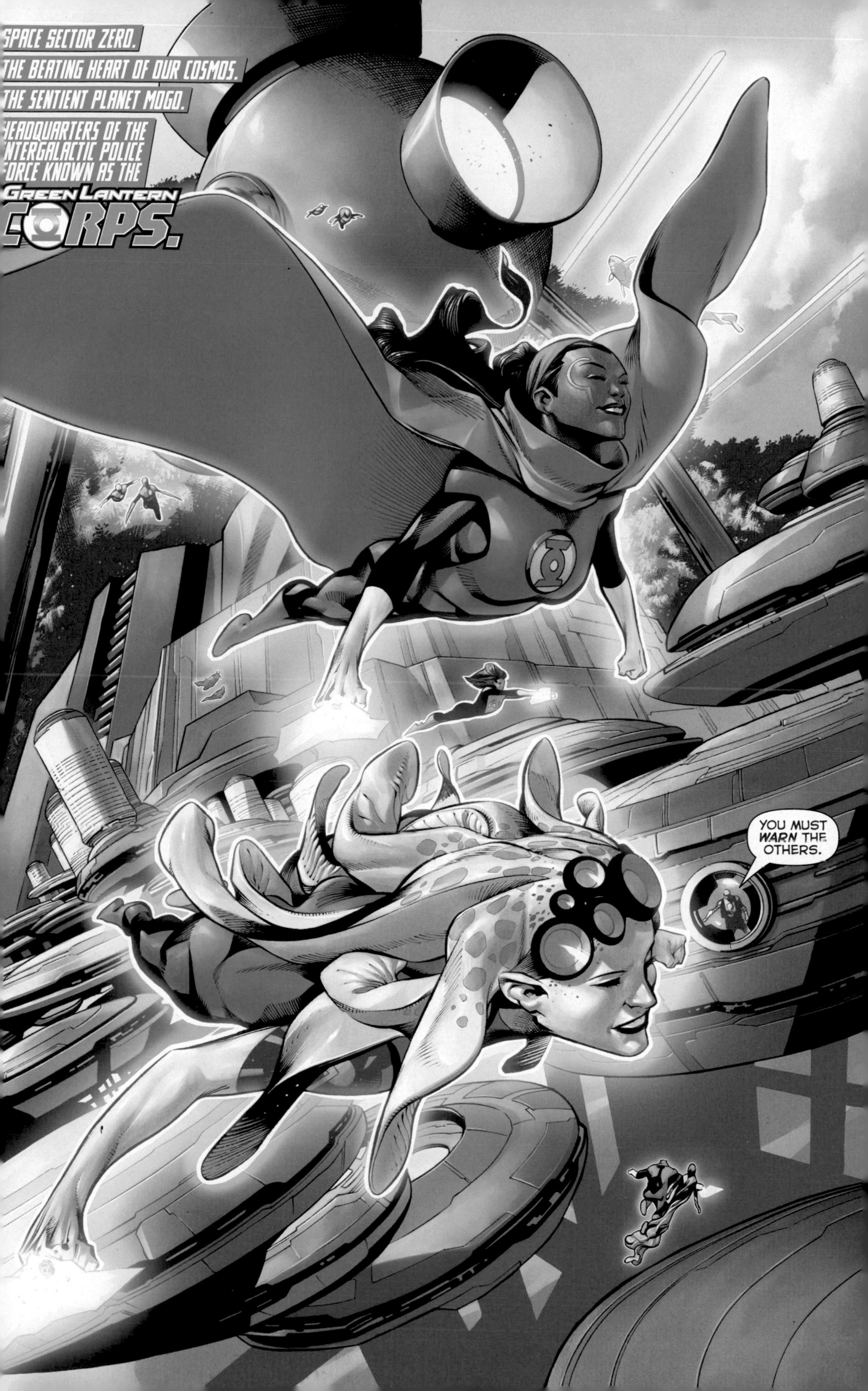
SPACE SECTOR ZERO.
THE BEATING HEART OF OUR COSMOS.
THE SENTIENT PLANET MOGO.
HEADQUARTERS OF THE INTERGALACTIC POLICE FORCE KNOWN AS THE
GREEN LANTERN CORPS.
YOU MUST WARN THE OTHERS.

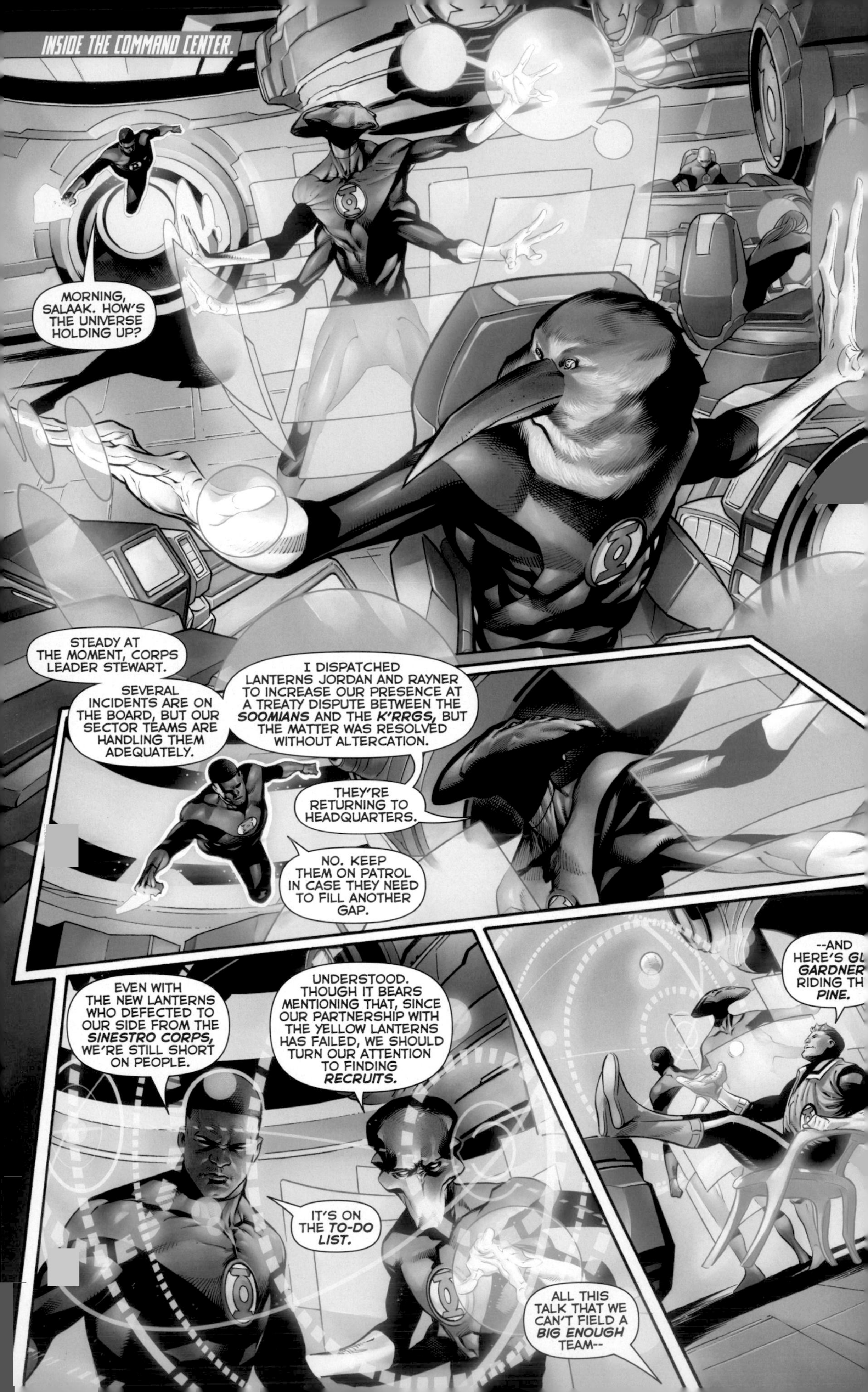
INSIDE THE COMMAND CENTER.
MORNING, SALAAK. HOW'S THE UNIVERSE HOLDING UP?
STEADY AT THE MOMENT, CORPS LEADER STEWART.
SEVERAL INCIDENTS ARE ON THE BOARD, BUT OUR SECTOR TEAMS ARE HANDLING THEM ADEQUATELY.
I DISPATCHED LANTERNS JORDAN AND RAYNER TO INCREASE OUR PRESENCE AT A TREATY DISPUTE BETWEEN THE SOOMIANS AND THE K'RRGS, BUT THE MATTER WAS RESOLVED WITHOUT ALTERCATION.
THEY'RE RETURNING TO HEADQUARTERS.
NO. KEEP THEM ON PATROL IN CASE THEY NEED TO FILL ANOTHER GAP.
EVEN WITH THE NEW LANTERNS WHO DEFECTED TO OUR SIDE FROM THE SINESTRO CORPS, WE'RE STILL SHORT ON PEOPLE.
UNDERSTOOD. THOUGH IT BEARS MENTIONING THAT, SINCE OUR PARTNERSHIP WITH THE YELLOW LANTERNS HAS FAILED, WE SHOULD TURN OUR ATTENTION TO FINDING RECRUITS.
IT'S ON THE TO-DO LIST.
ALL THIS TALK THAT WE CAN'T FIELD A BIG ENOUGH TEAM--
--AND HERE'S GU GARDNER RIDING TH PINE.

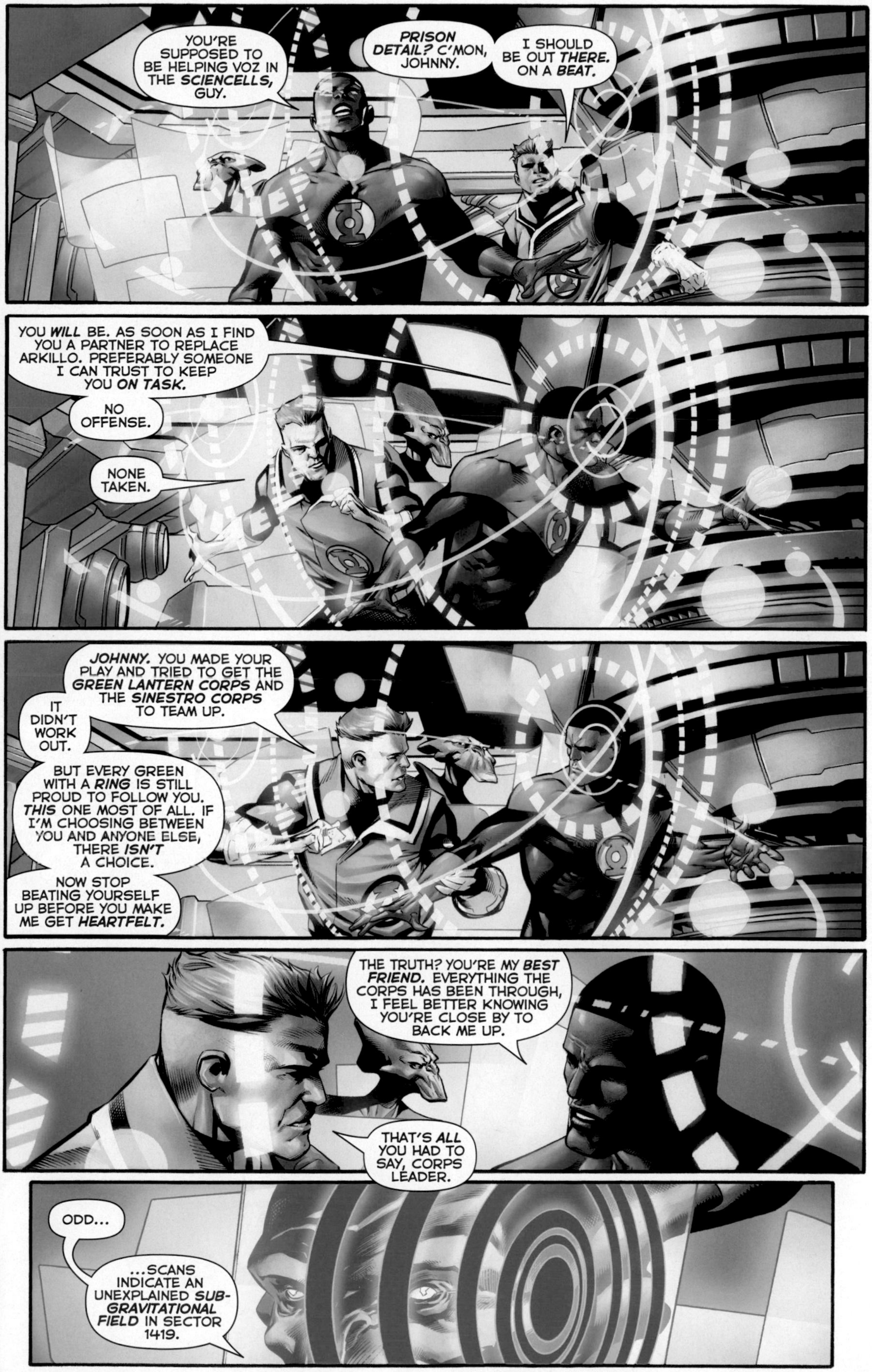
YOU'RE SUPPOSED TO BE HELPING VOZ IN THE SCIENCELLS, GUY.
PRISON DETAIL? C'MON, JOHNNY.
I SHOULD BE OUT THERE. ON A BEAT.
YOU WILL BE. AS SOON AS I FIND YOU A PARTNER TO REPLACE ARKILLO. PREFERABLY SOMEONE I CAN TRUST TO KEEP YOU ON TASK.
NO OFFENSE.
NONE TAKEN.
JOHNNY. YOU MADE YOUR PLAY AND TRIED TO GET THE GREEN LANTERN CORPS AND THE SINESTRO CORPS TO TEAM UP.
IT DIDN'T WORK OUT.
BUT EVERY GREEN WITH A RING IS STILL PROUD TO FOLLOW YOU. THIS ONE MOST OF ALL. IF I'M CHOOSING BETWEEN YOU AND ANYONE ELSE, THERE ISN'T A CHOICE.
NOW STOP BEATING YOURSELF UP BEFORE YOU MAKE ME GET HEARTFELT.
THE TRUTH? YOU'RE MY BEST FRIEND. EVERYTHING THE CORPS HAS BEEN THROUGH, I FEEL BETTER KNOWING YOU'RE CLOSE BY TO BACK ME UP.
THAT'S ALL YOU HAD TO SAY, CORPS LEADER.
ODD...
...SCANS INDICATE AN UNEXPLAINED SUB-GRAVITATIONAL FIELD IN SECTOR 1419.

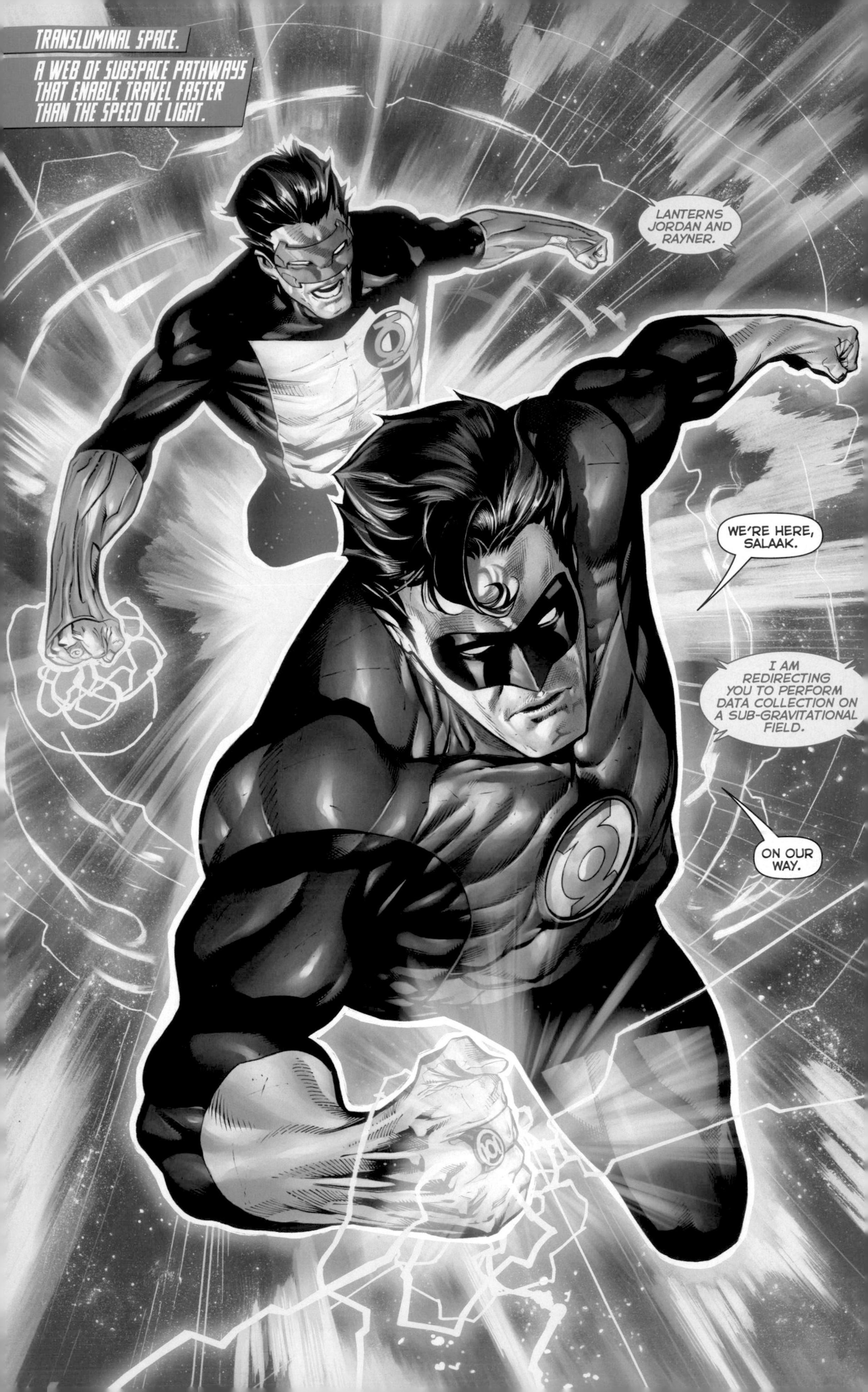
TRANSLUMINAL SPACE.
A WEB OF SUBSPACE PATHWAYS THAT ENABLE TRAVEL FASTER THAN THE SPEED OF LIGHT.
LANTERNS JORDAN AND RAYNER.
WE'RE HERE, SALAAK.
I AM REDIRECTING YOU TO PERFORM DATA COLLECTION ON A SUB-GRAVITATIONAL FIELD.
ON OUR WAY.

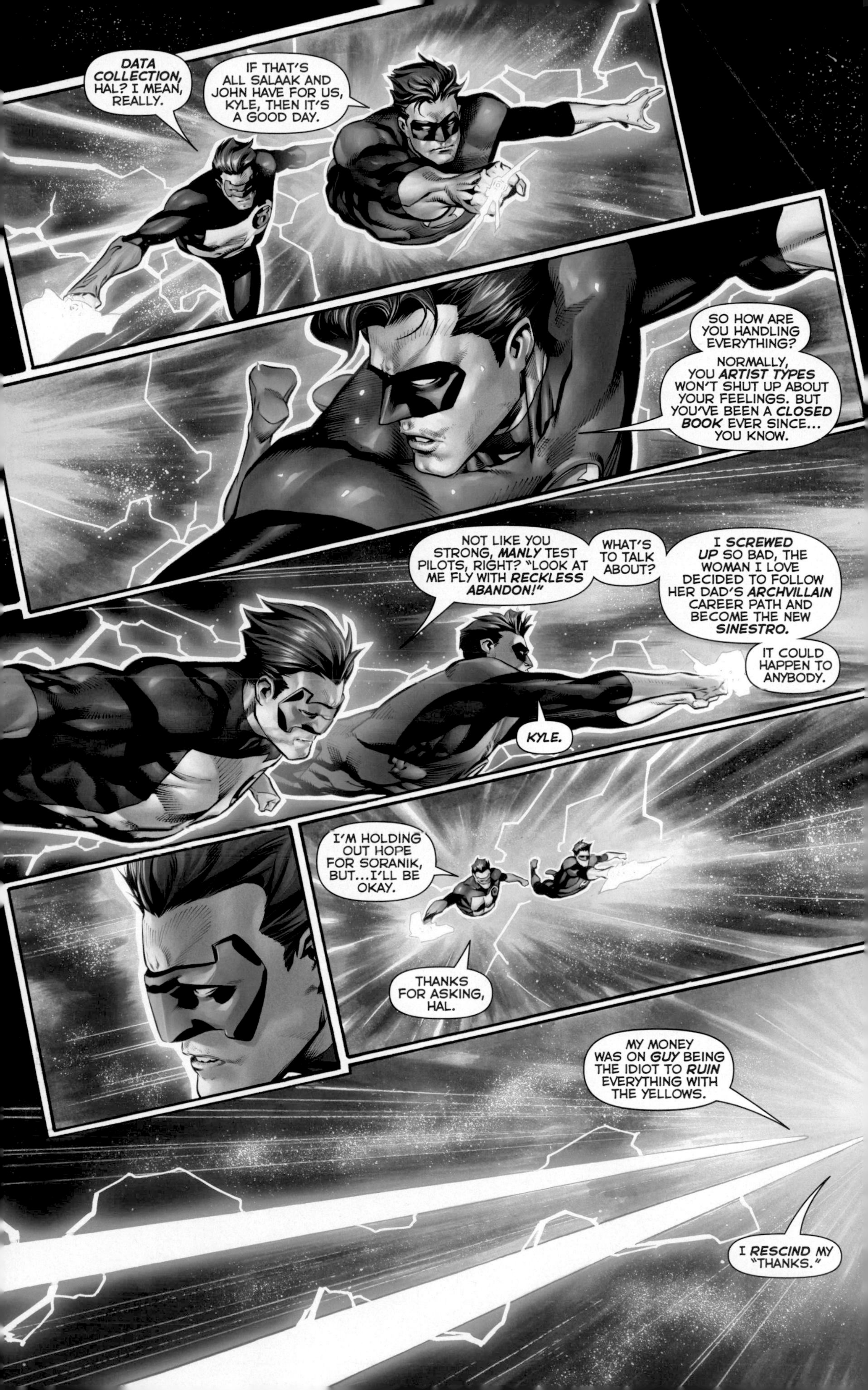
DATA COLLECTION, HAL? I MEAN, REALLY.
IF THAT'S ALL SALAAK AND JOHN HAVE FOR US, KYLE, THEN IT'S A GOOD DAY.
SO HOW ARE YOU HANDLING EVERYTHING?
NORMALLY, YOU ARTIST TYPES WON'T SHUT UP ABOUT YOUR FEELINGS. BUT YOU'VE BEEN A CLOSED BOOK EVER SINCE... YOU KNOW.
NOT LIKE YOU STRONG, MANLY TEST PILOTS, RIGHT? "LOOK AT ME FLY WITH RECKLESS ABANDON!"
WHAT'S TO TALK ABOUT?
I SCREWED UP SO BAD, THE WOMAN I LOVE DECIDED TO FOLLOW HER DAD'S ARCHVILLAIN CAREER PATH AND BECOME THE NEW SINESTRO.
IT COULD HAPPEN TO ANYBODY.
KYLE.
I'M HOLDING OUT HOPE FOR SORANIK, BUT...I'LL BE OKAY.
THANKS FOR ASKING, HAL.
MY MONEY WAS ON GUY BEING THE IDIOT TO RUIN EVERYTHING WITH THE YELLOWS.
I RESCIND MY "THANKS."

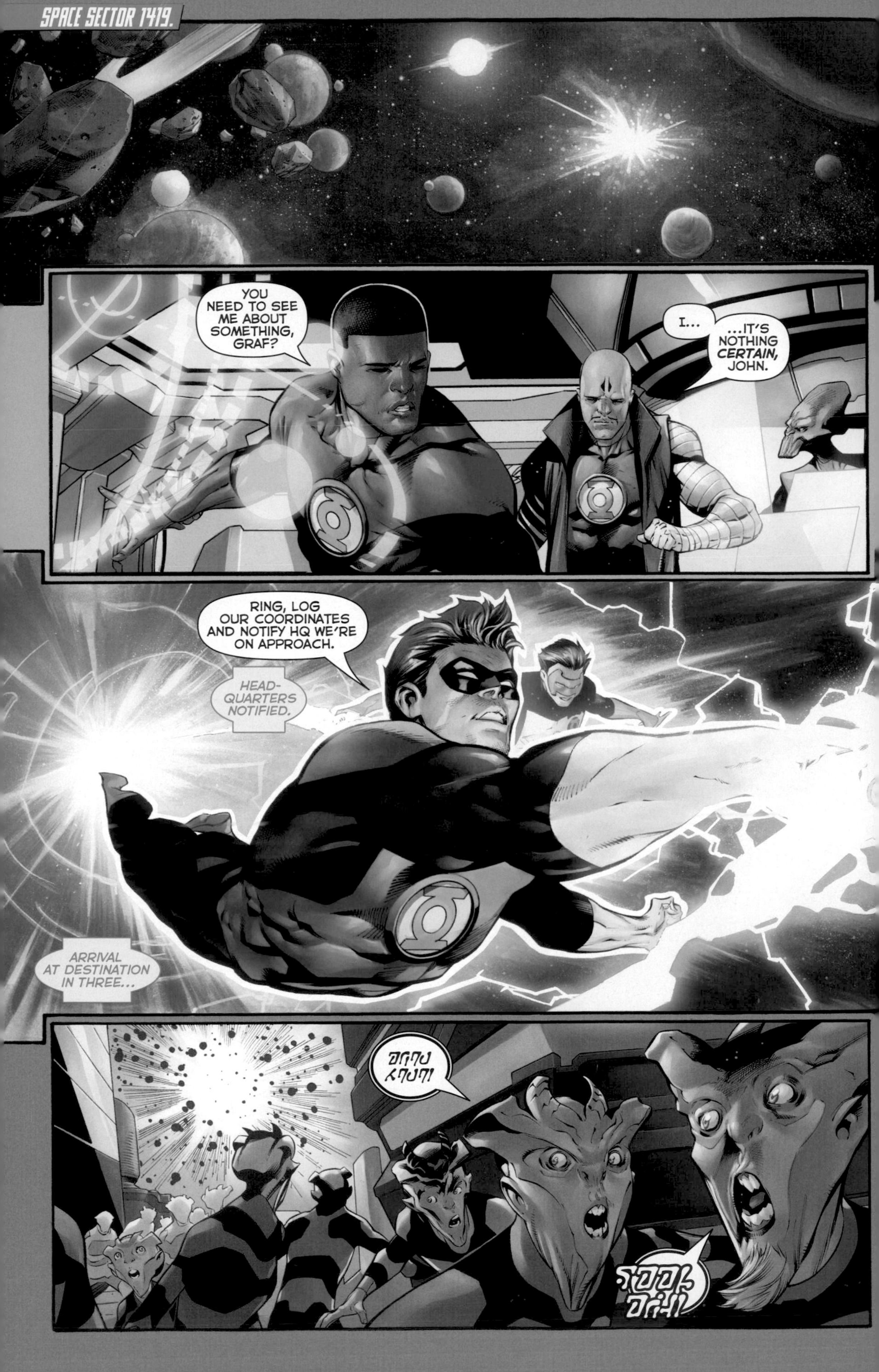
SPACE SECTOR 1419.
YOU NEED TO SEE ME ABOUT SOMETHING, GRAF?
I...
...IT'S NOTHING CERTAIN, JOHN.
RING, LOG OUR COORDINATES AND NOTIFY HQ WE'RE ON APPROACH.
HEAD-QUARTERS NOTIFIED.
ARRIVAL AT DESTINATION IN THREE...

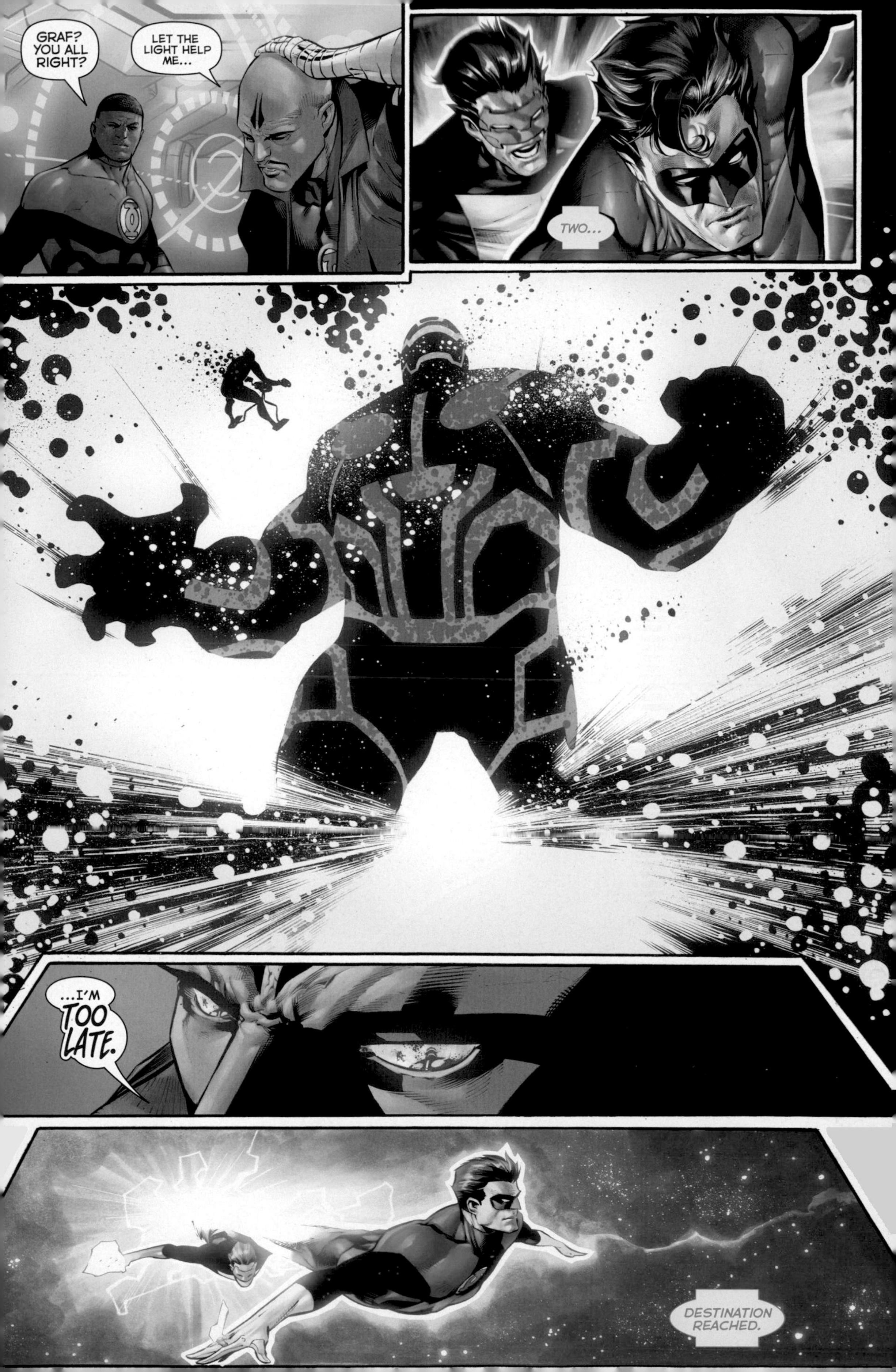
GRAF? YOU ALL RIGHT?
LET THE LIGHT HELP ME...
TWO...
...I'M TOO LATE.
DESTINATION REACHED.

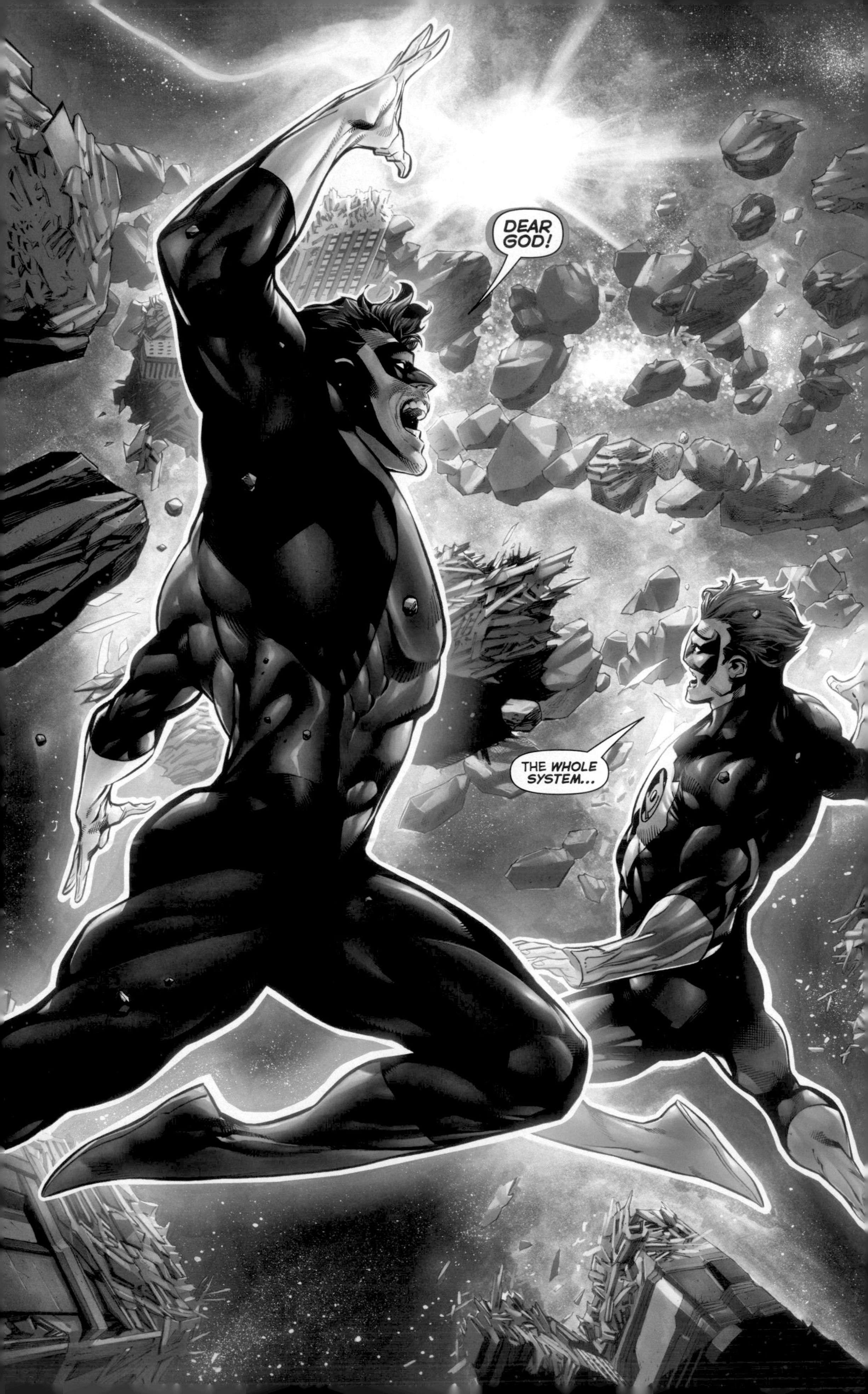
DEAR GOD!
THE WHOLE SYSTEM...

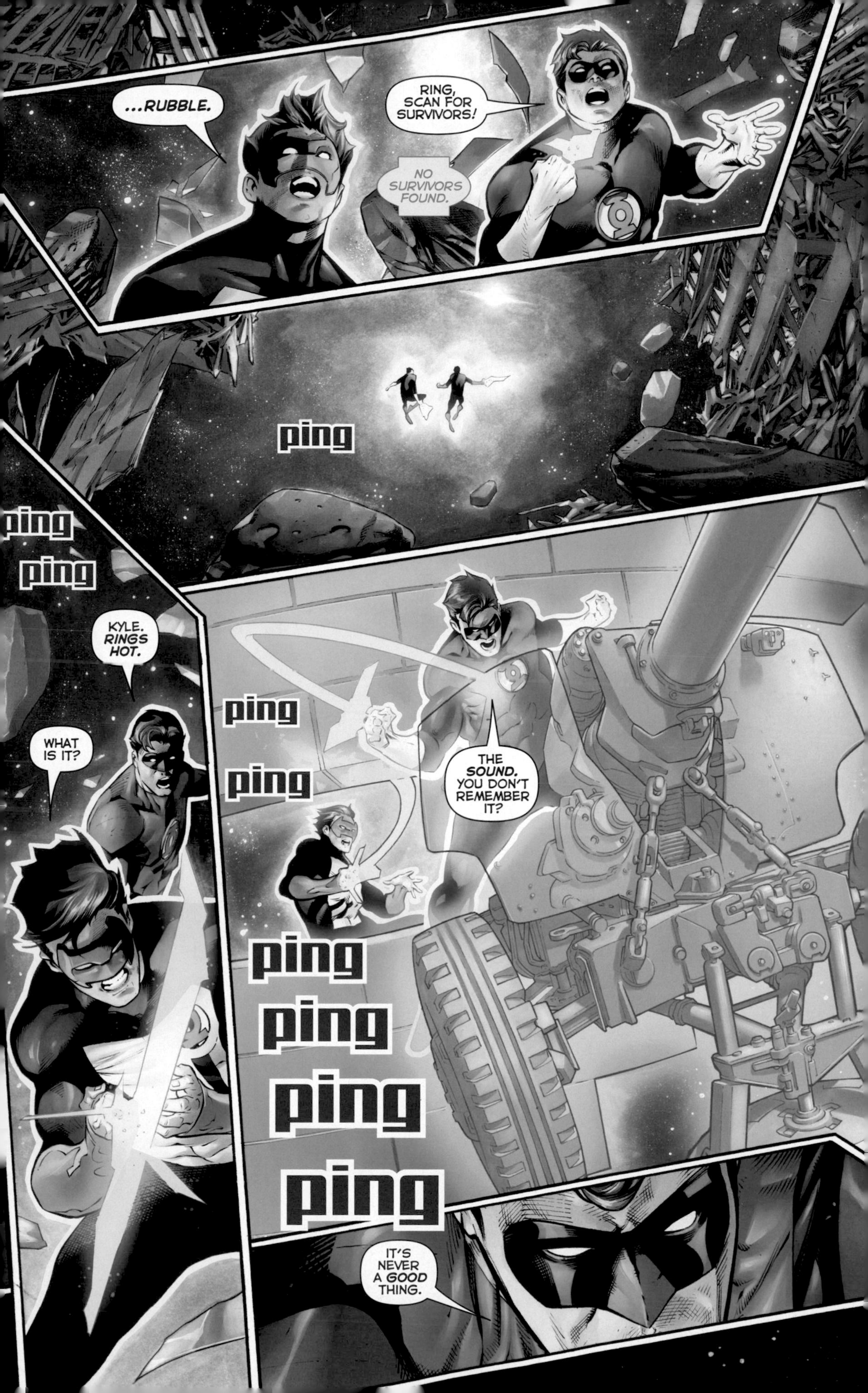
...RUBBLE.
RING, SCAN FOR SURVIVORS!
NO SURVIVORS FOUND.
ping
ping
ping
KYLE. RINGS HOT.
WHAT IS IT?
ping
ping
THE SOUND. YOU DON'T REMEMBER IT?
ping
ping
ping
ping
IT'S NEVER A GOOD THING.

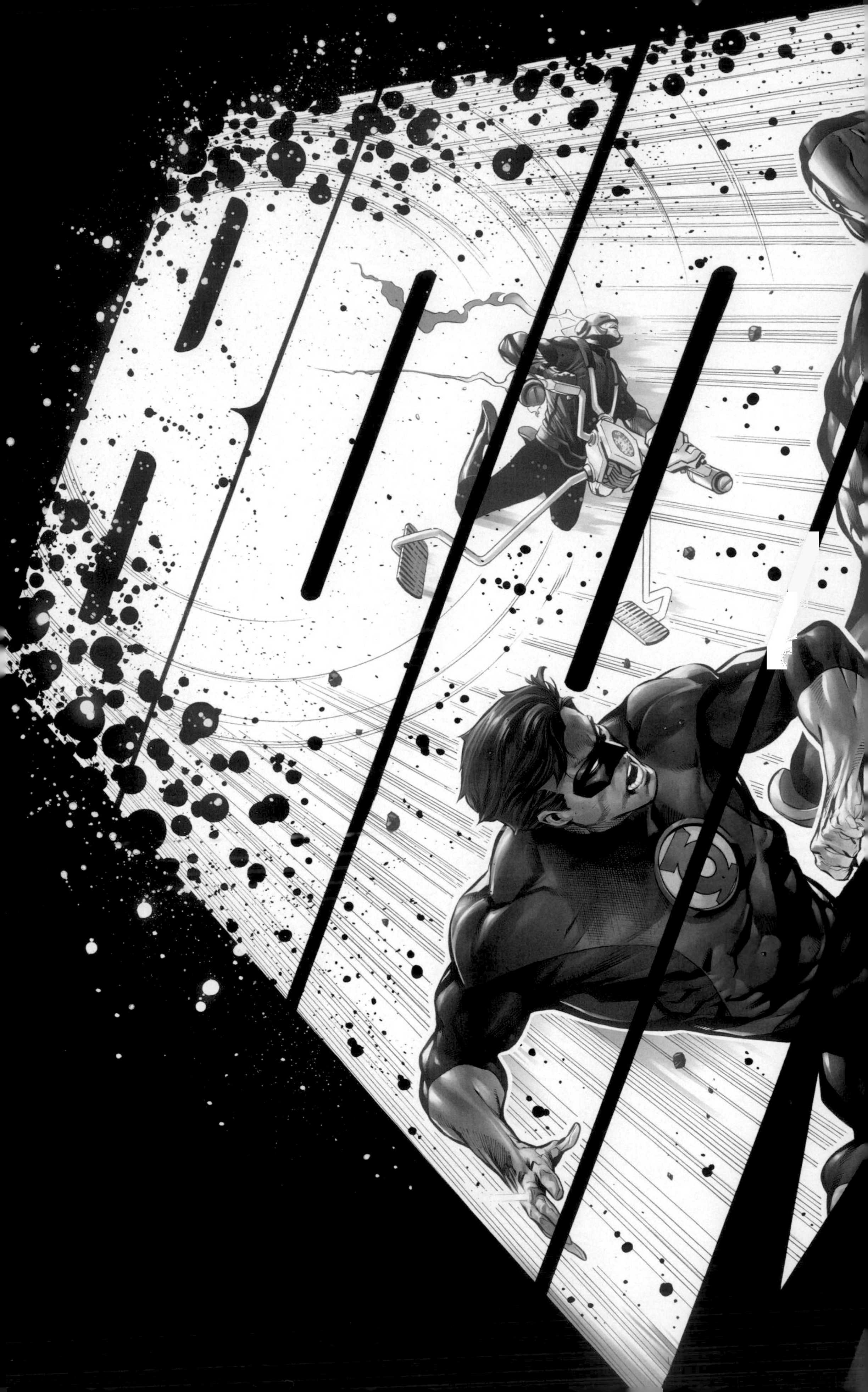

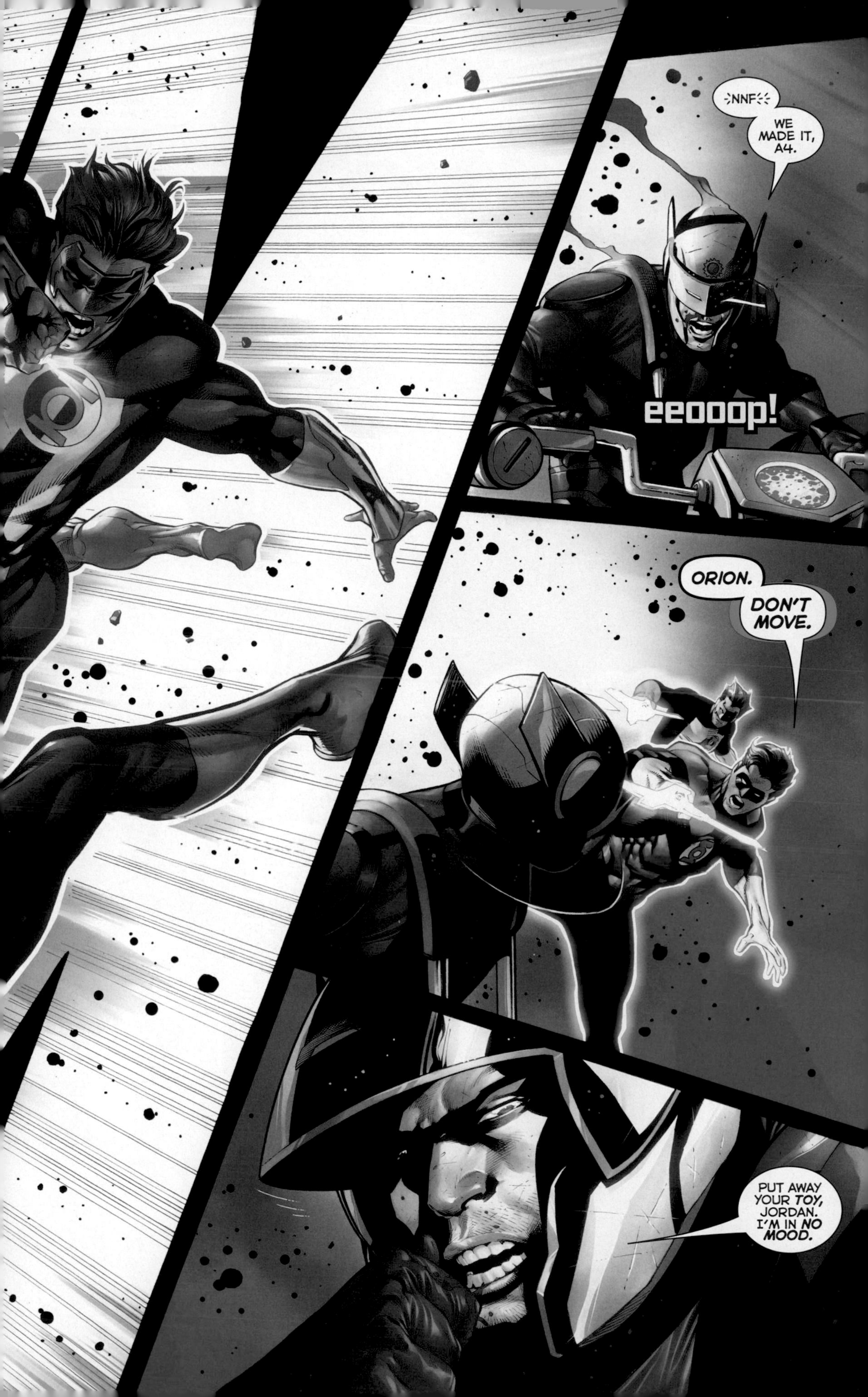
NNF
WE MADE IT, A4.
eeooop!
ORION.
DON'T MOVE.
PUT AWAY YOUR TOY, JORDAN. I'M IN NO MOOD.

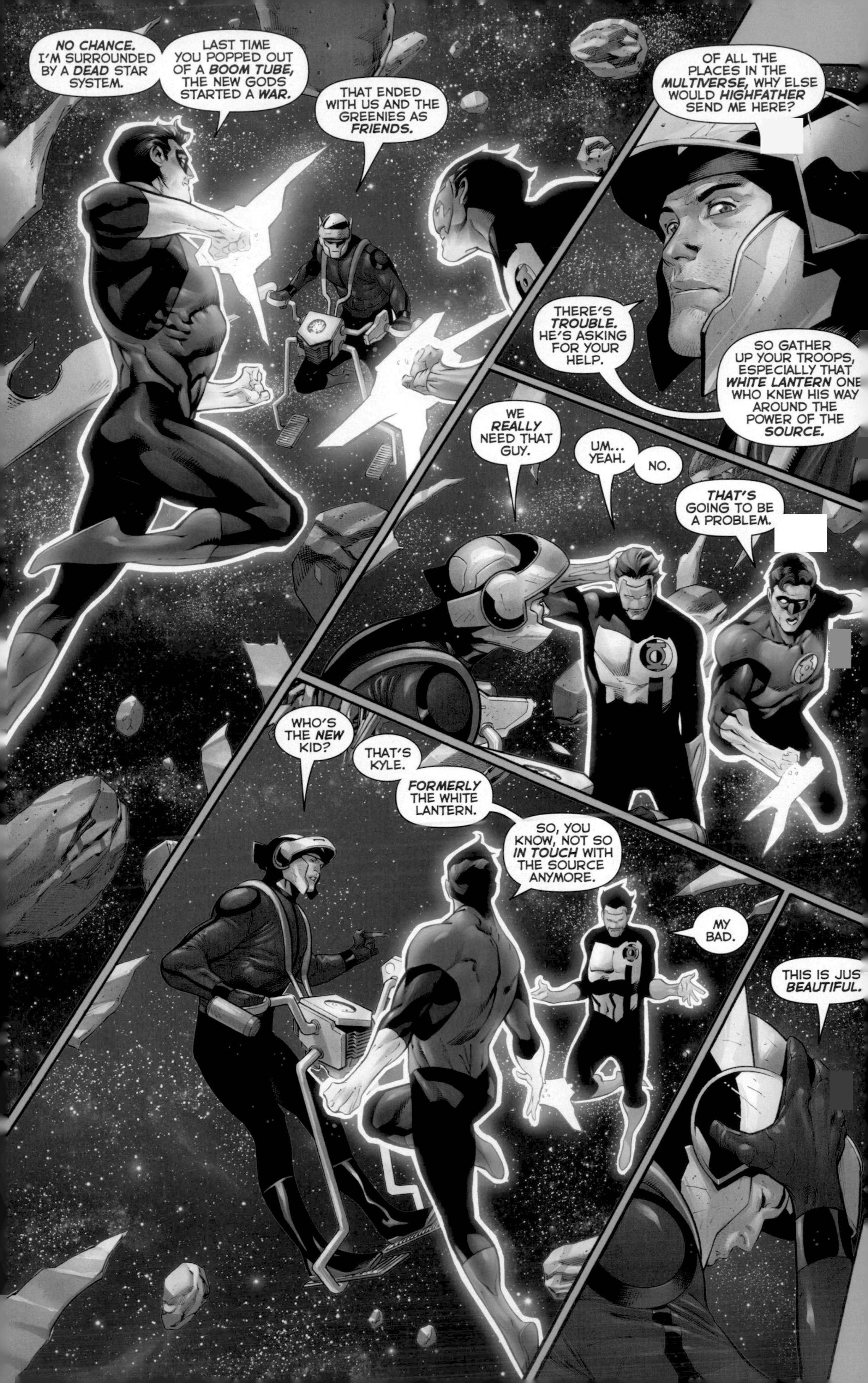
NO CHANCE. I'M SURROUNDED BY A DEAD STAR SYSTEM.
LAST TIME YOU POPPED OUT OF A BOOM TUBE, THE NEW GODS STARTED A WAR.
THAT ENDED WITH US AND THE GREENIES AS FRIENDS.
OF ALL THE PLACES IN THE MULTIVERSE, WHY ELSE WOULD HIGHFATHER SEND ME HERE?
THERE'S TROUBLE. HE'S ASKING FOR YOUR HELP.
SO GATHER UP YOUR TROOPS, ESPECIALLY THAT WHITE LANTERN ONE WHO KNEW HIS WAY AROUND THE POWER OF THE SOURCE.
WE REALLY NEED THAT GUY.
UM... YEAH.
NO.
THAT'S GOING TO BE A PROBLEM.
WHO'S THE NEW KID?
THAT'S KYLE.
FORMERLY THE WHITE LANTERN.
SO, YOU KNOW, NOT SO IN TOUCH WITH THE SOURCE ANYMORE.
MY BAD.
THIS IS JUS BEAUTIFUL.

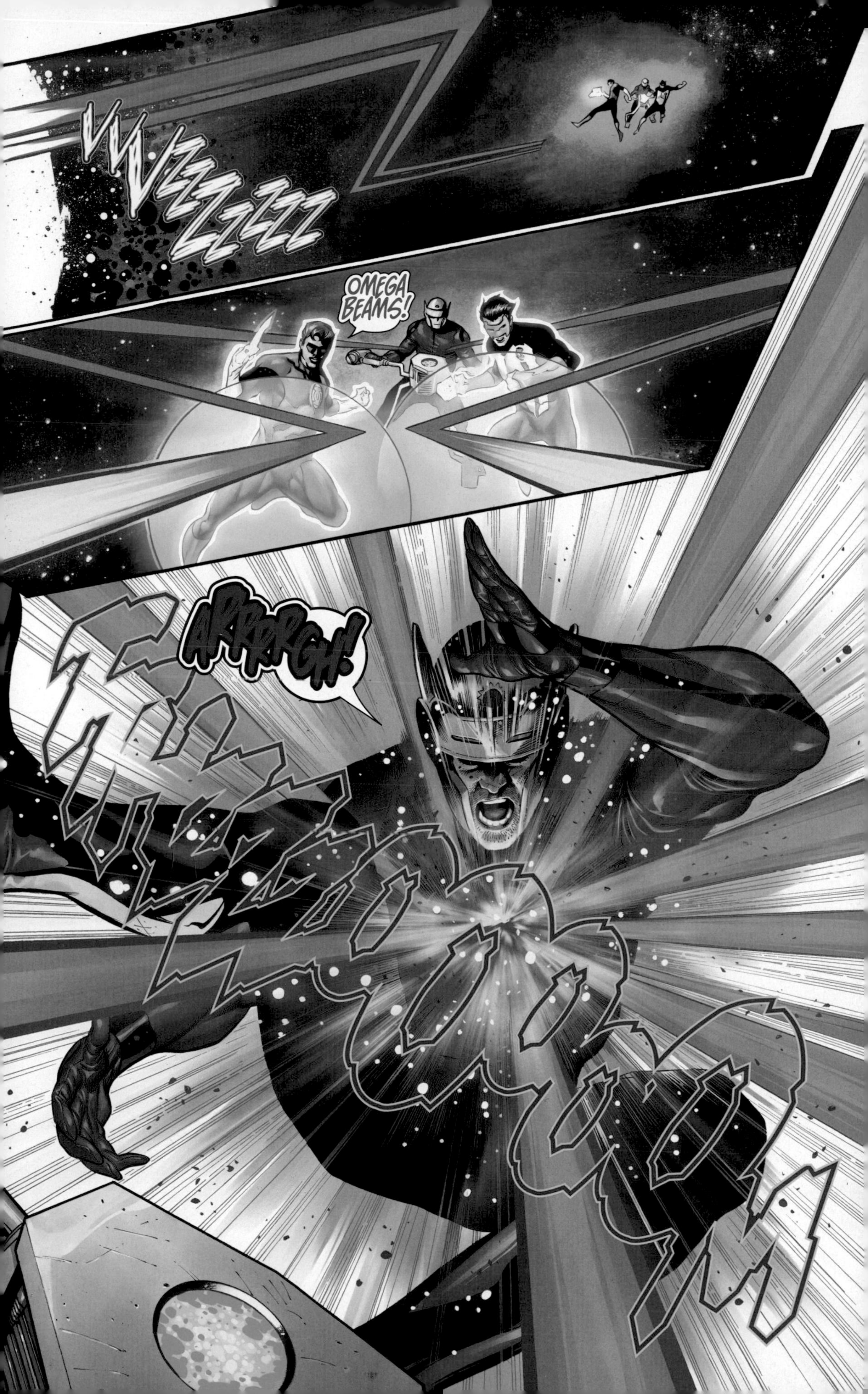
VVVZZZZZZZ
OMEGA BEAMS!
ARRRRGH!
ZZOOOOOOM

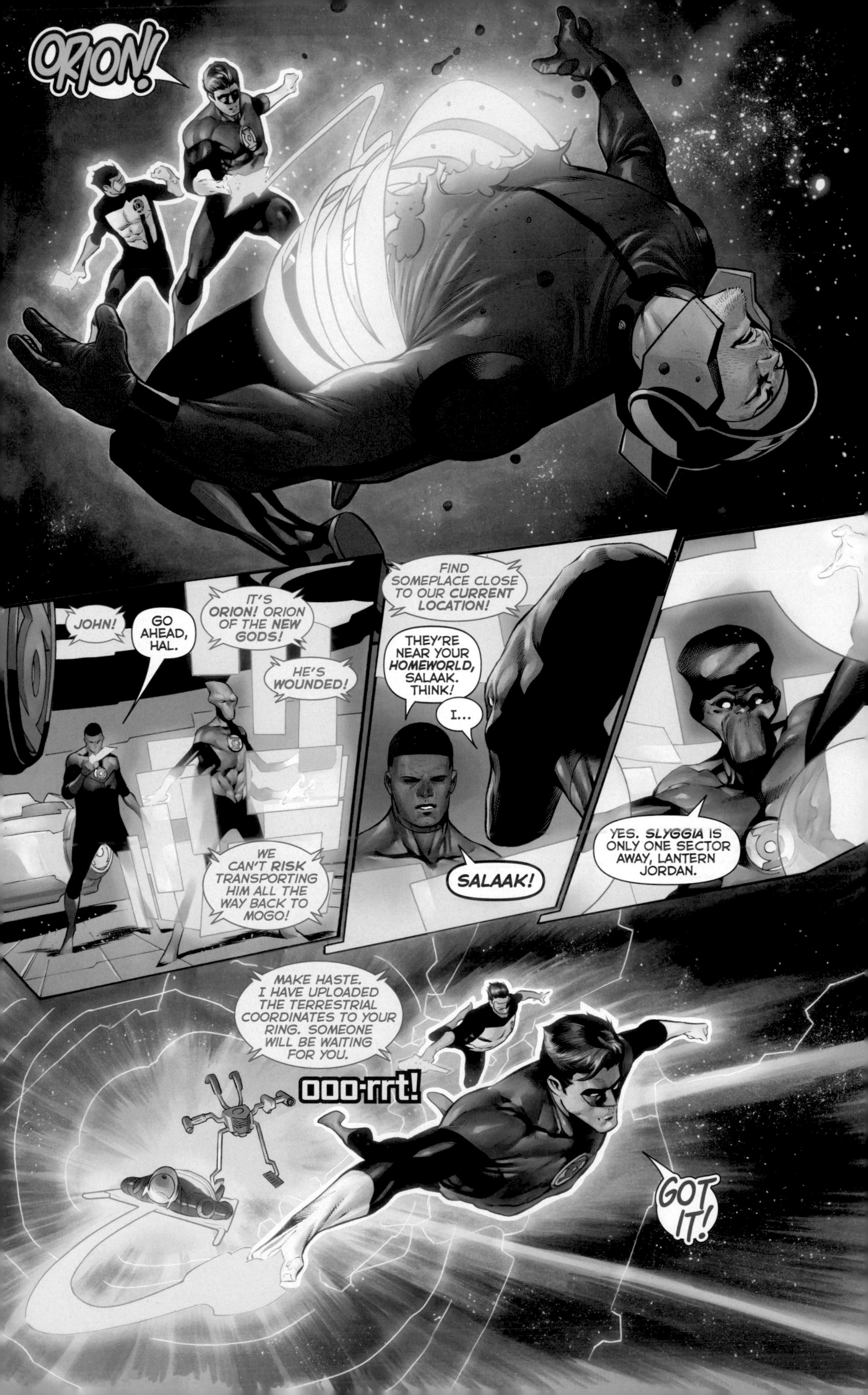
ORION!
JOHN!
GO AHEAD, HAL.
IT'S ORION! ORION OF THE NEW GODS!
HE'S WOUNDED!
WE CAN'T RISK TRANSPORTING HIM ALL THE WAY BACK TO MOGO!
FIND SOMEPLACE CLOSE TO OUR CURRENT LOCATION!
THEY'RE NEAR YOUR HOMEWORLD, SALAAK. THINK!
I...
SALAAK!
YES. SLYGGIA IS ONLY ONE SECTOR AWAY, LANTERN JORDAN.
MAKE HASTE. I HAVE UPLOADED THE TERRESTRIAL COORDINATES TO YOUR RING. SOMEONE WILL BE WAITING FOR YOU.
OOO-RRT!
GOT IT!

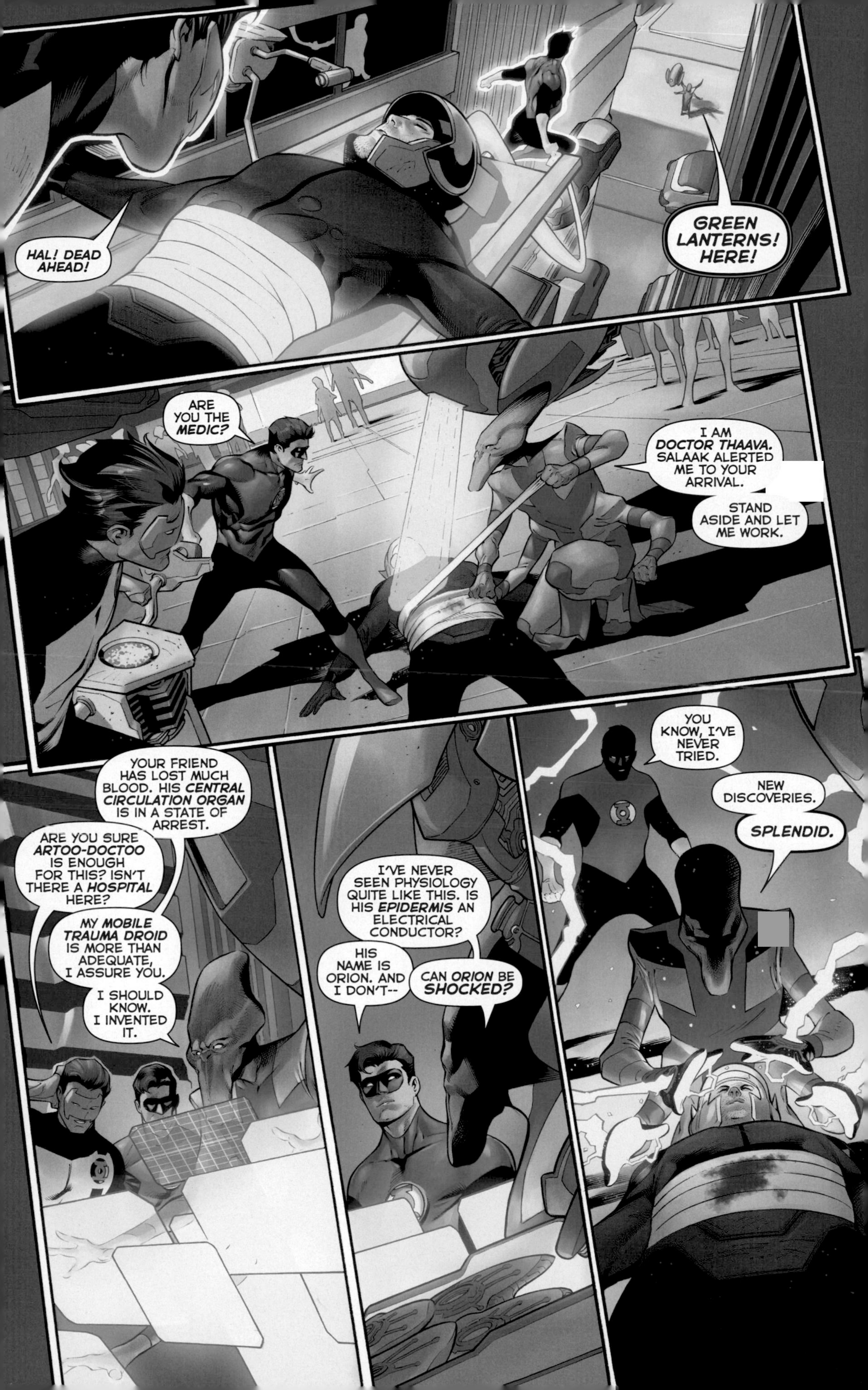
HAL! DEAD AHEAD!
GREEN LANTERNS! HERE!
ARE YOU THE MEDIC?
I AM DOCTOR THAAVA. SALAAK ALERTED ME TO YOUR ARRIVAL.
STAND ASIDE AND LET ME WORK.
YOUR FRIEND HAS LOST MUCH BLOOD. HIS CENTRAL CIRCULATION ORGAN IS IN A STATE OF ARREST.
ARE YOU SURE ARTOO-DOCTOO IS ENOUGH FOR THIS? ISN'T THERE A HOSPITAL HERE?
MY MOBILE TRAUMA DROID IS MORE THAN ADEQUATE, I ASSURE YOU.
I SHOULD KNOW. I INVENTED IT.
I'VE NEVER SEEN PHYSIOLOGY QUITE LIKE THIS. IS HIS EPIDERMIS AN ELECTRICAL CONDUCTOR?
HIS NAME IS ORION. AND I DON'T--
CAN ORION BE SHOCKED?
YOU KNOW, I'VE NEVER TRIED.
NEW DISCOVERIES.
SPLENDID.

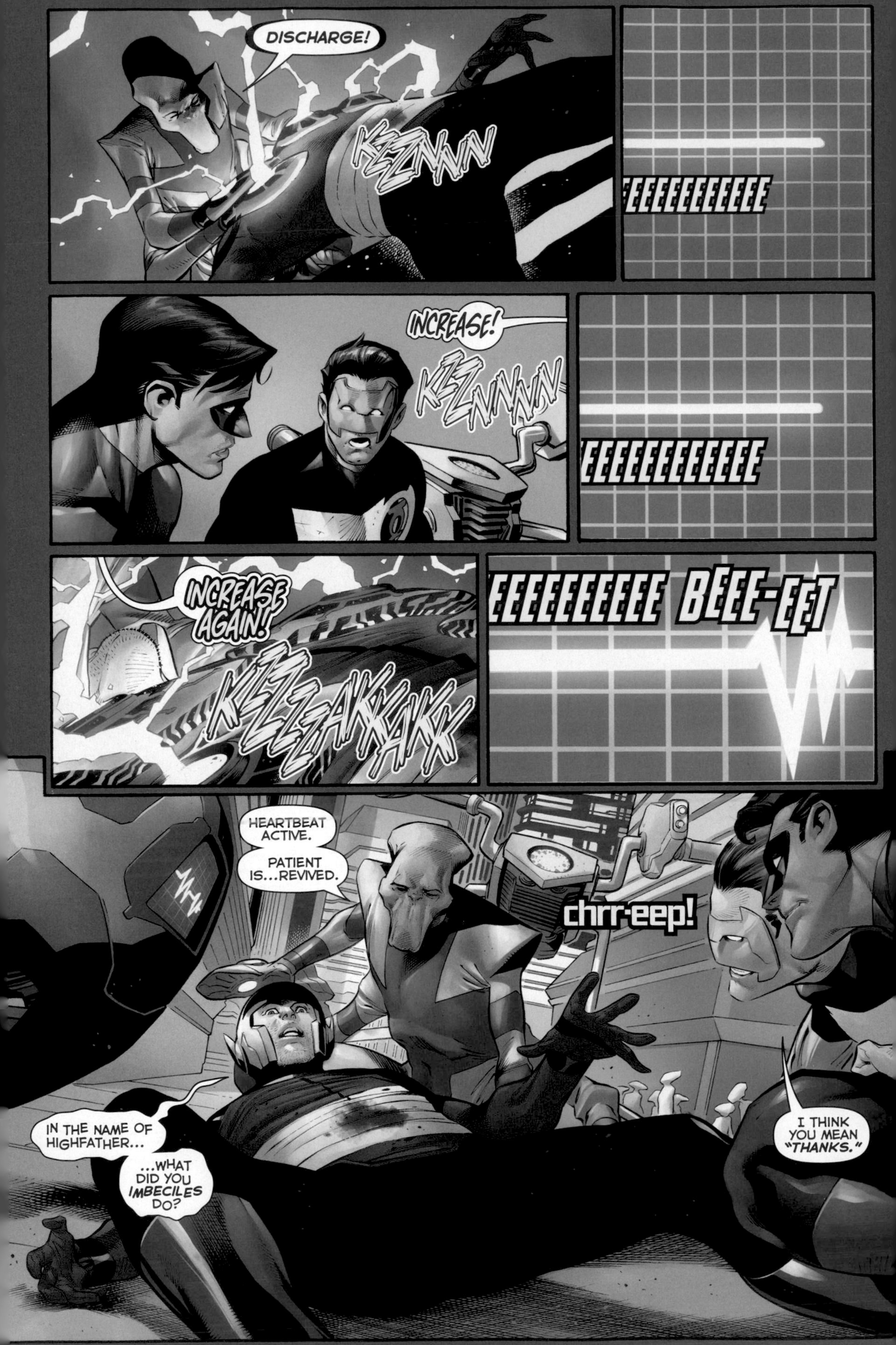
DISCHARGE!
KEZNNN
EEEEEEEEEEEE
INCREASE!
KEZNNNN
EEEEEEEEEEEE
INCREASE AGAIN!
KZZZAKKAKK
EEEEEEEEEE BEEE-EET
HEARTBEAT ACTIVE.
PATIENT IS...REVIVED.
chrr-eep!
IN THE NAME OF HIGHFATHER...
...WHAT DID YOU IMBECILES DO?
I THINK YOU MEAN "THANKS."

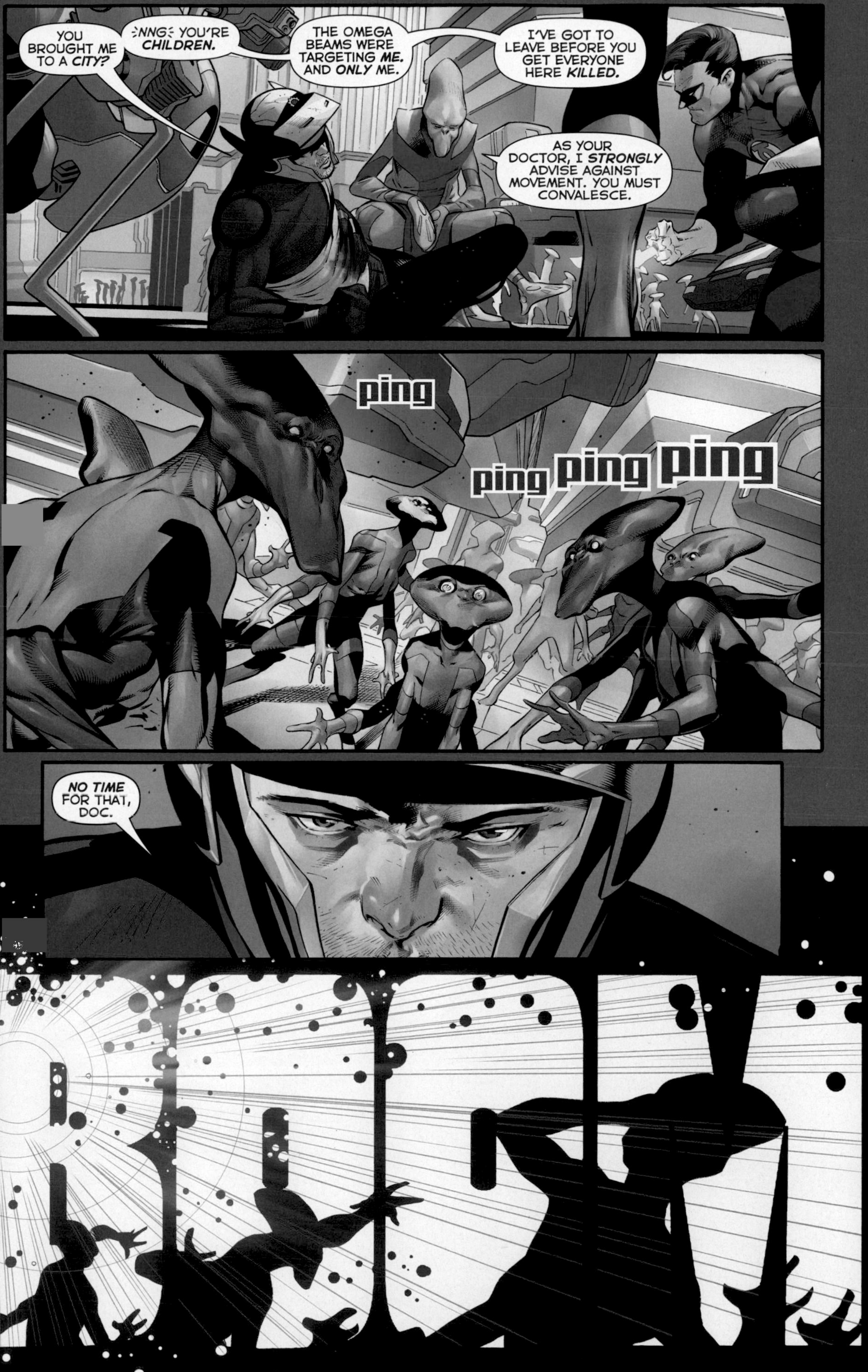
YOU BROUGHT ME TO A *CITY?*
NNG YOU'RE *CHILDREN.*
THE OMEGA BEAMS WERE TARGETING *ME.* AND *ONLY* ME.
I'VE GOT TO LEAVE BEFORE YOU GET EVERYONE HERE *KILLED.*
AS YOUR DOCTOR, I *STRONGLY* ADVISE AGAINST MOVEMENT. YOU MUST CONVALESCE.
ping
ping ping ping
NO TIME FOR THAT, DOC.

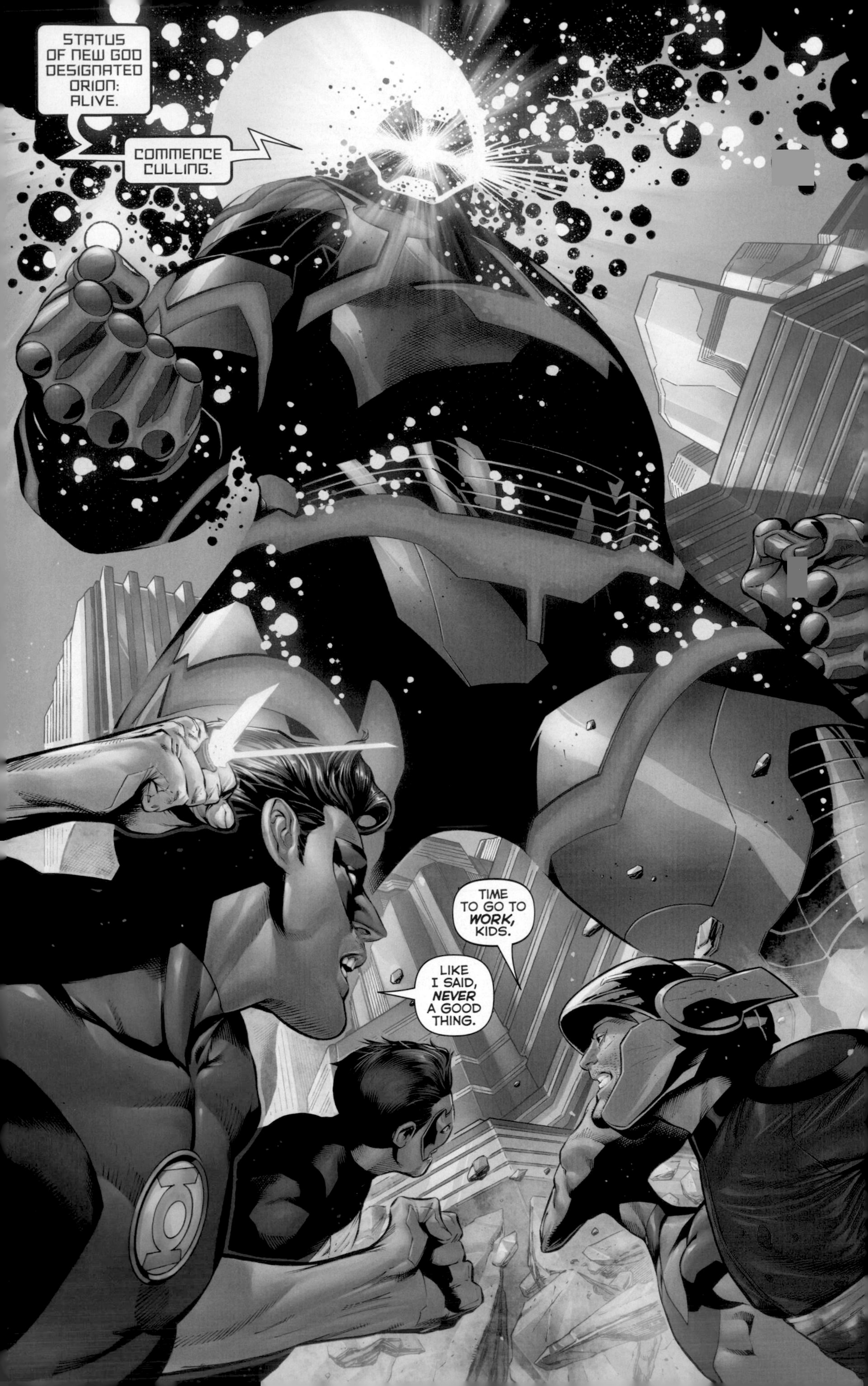
STATUS OF NEW GOD DESIGNATED ORION: ALIVE.
COMMENCE CULLING.
TIME TO GO TO WORK, KIDS.
LIKE I SAID, NEVER A GOOD THING.

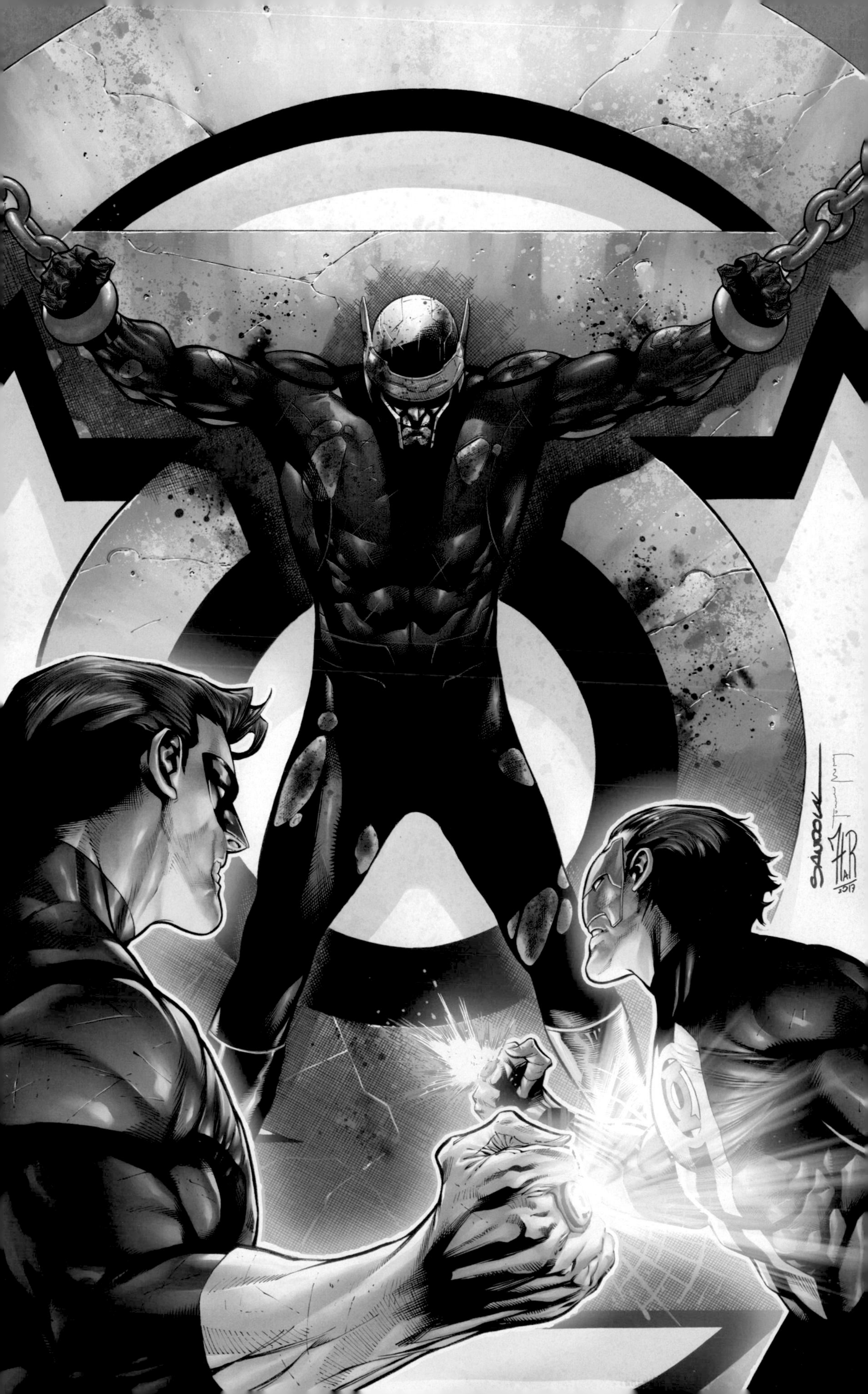

"FALL OF THE GODS PART TWO: ALL HEART"

RAFA SANDOVAL penciller * JORDI TARRAGONA inker * TOMEU MOREY colorist

cover art by RAFA SANDOVAL, JORDI TARRAGONA, and TOMEU MOREY

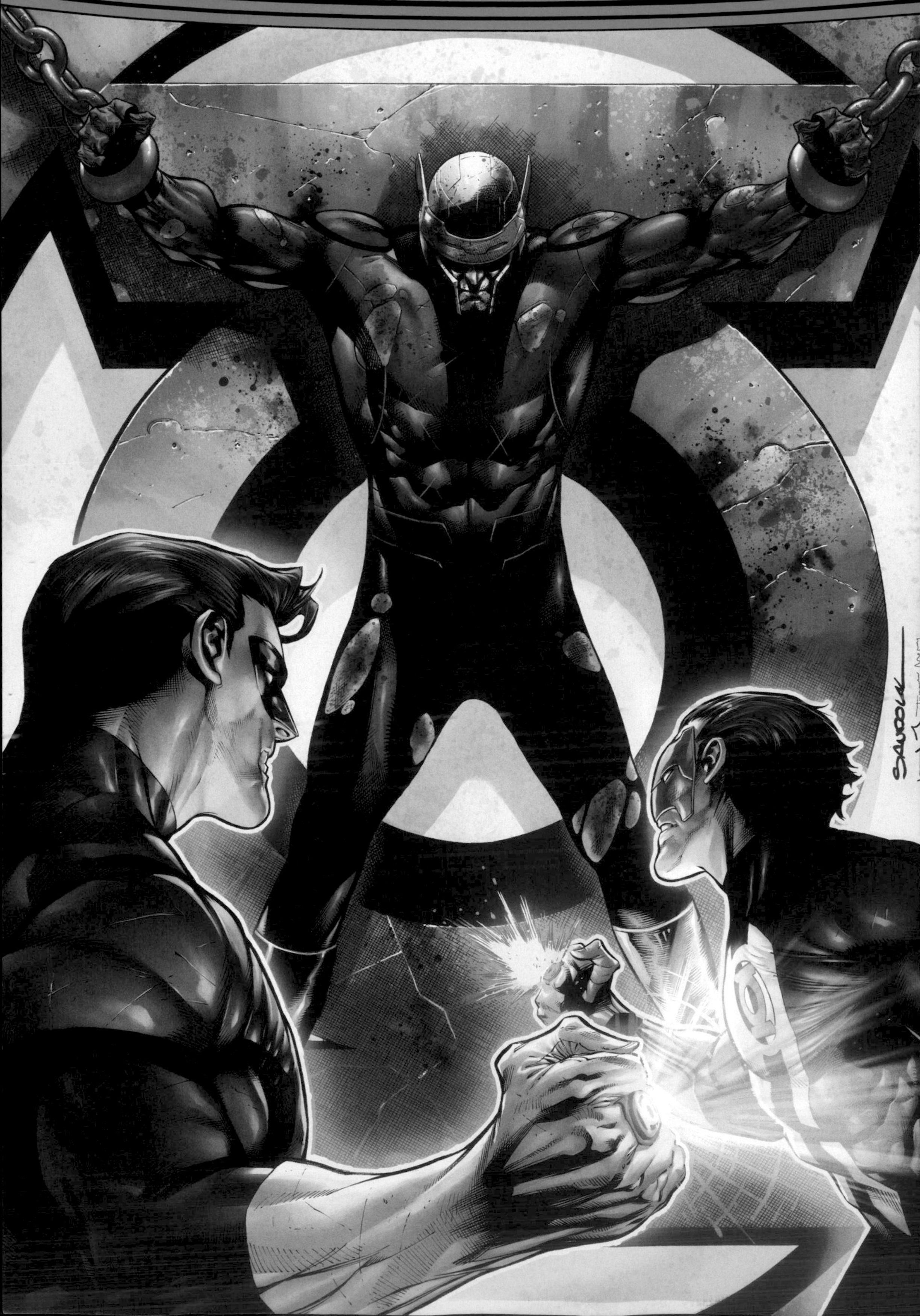

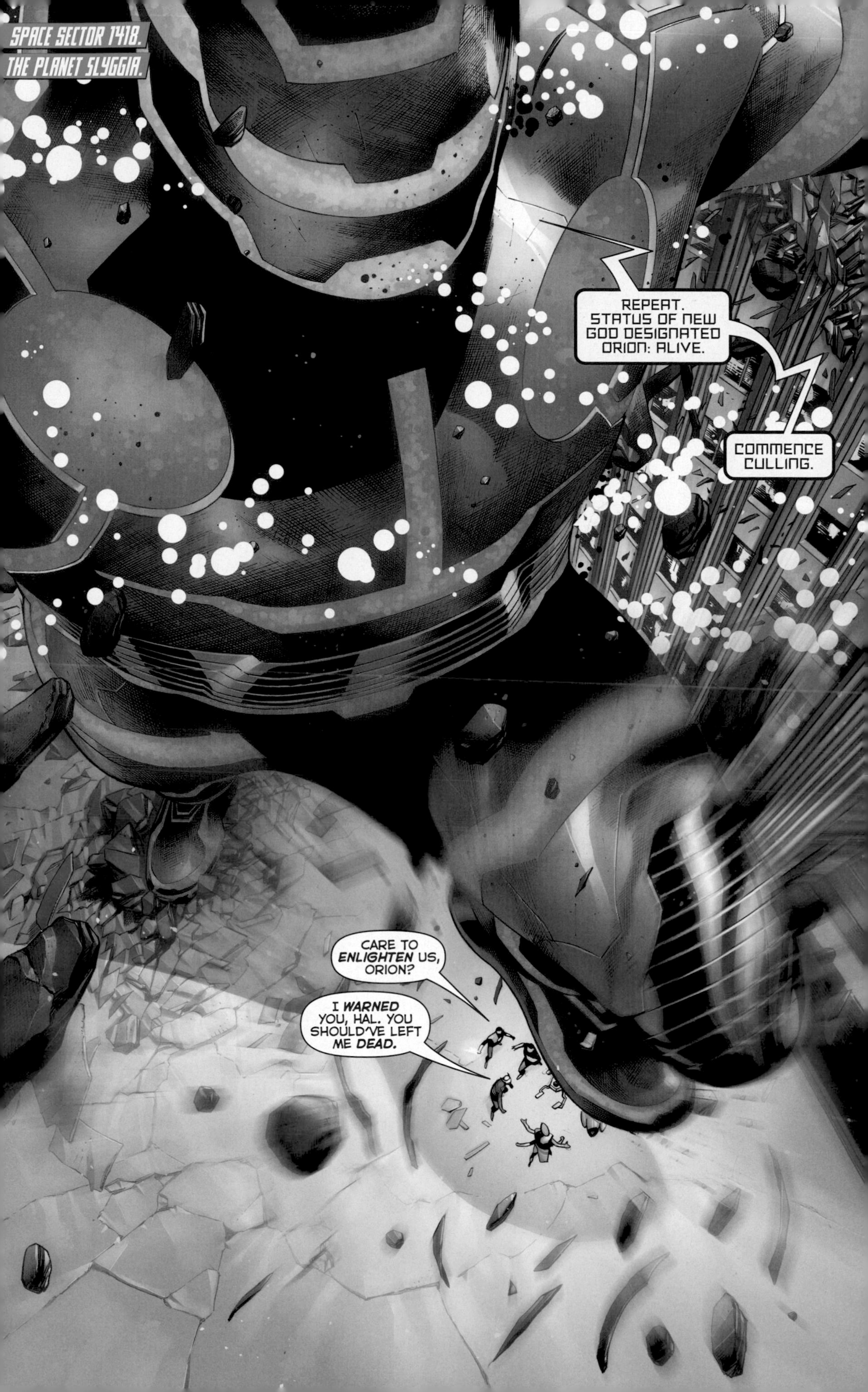

SPACE SECTOR 1418.
THE PLANET SLYGGIA.
REPEAT. STATUS OF NEW GOD DESIGNATED ORION: ALIVE.
COMMENCE CULLING.
CARE TO ENLIGHTEN US, ORION?
I WARNED YOU, HAL. YOU SHOULD'VE LEFT ME DEAD.

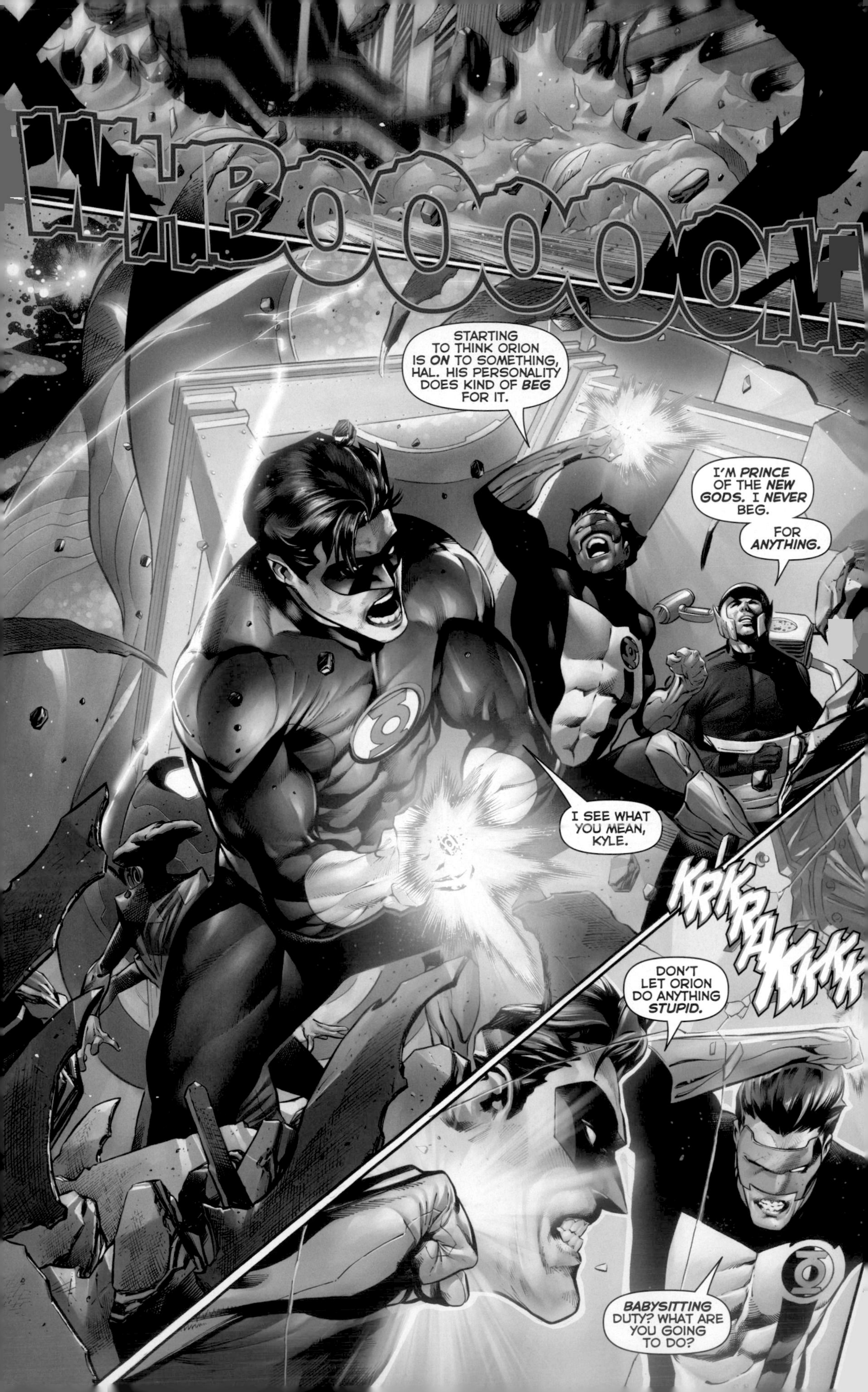
WHBOOOOOM
STARTING TO THINK ORION IS *ON* TO SOMETHING, HAL. HIS PERSONALITY DOES KIND OF *BEG* FOR IT.
I'M *PRINCE* OF THE *NEW GODS.* I NEVER BEG.
FOR *ANYTHING.*
I SEE WHAT YOU MEAN, KYLE.
DON'T LET ORION DO ANYTHING *STUPID.*
BABYSITTING DUTY? WHAT ARE YOU GOING TO DO?

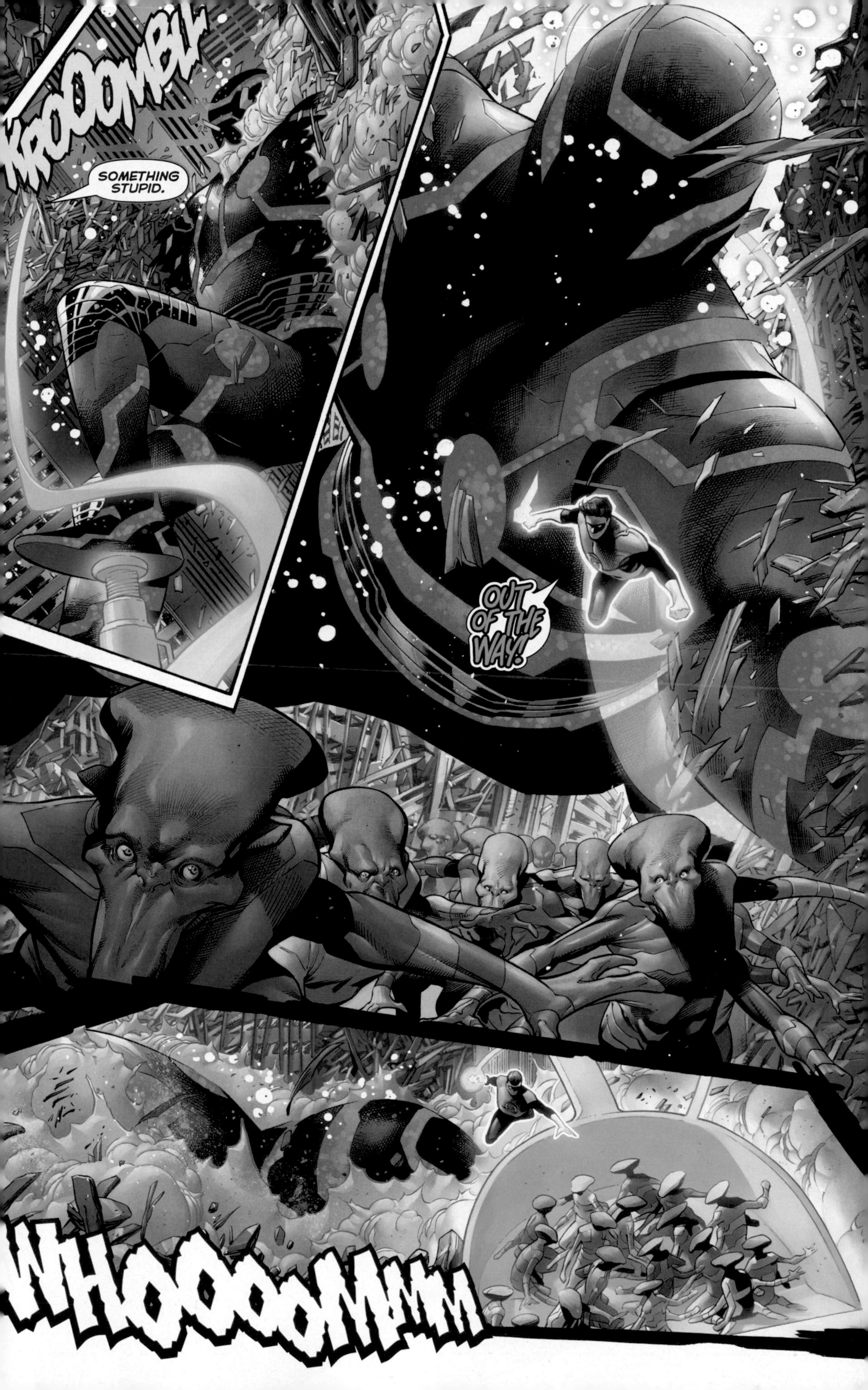
KROOOMBL
SOMETHING STUPID.
OUT OF THE WAY!
WHOOOOMMM

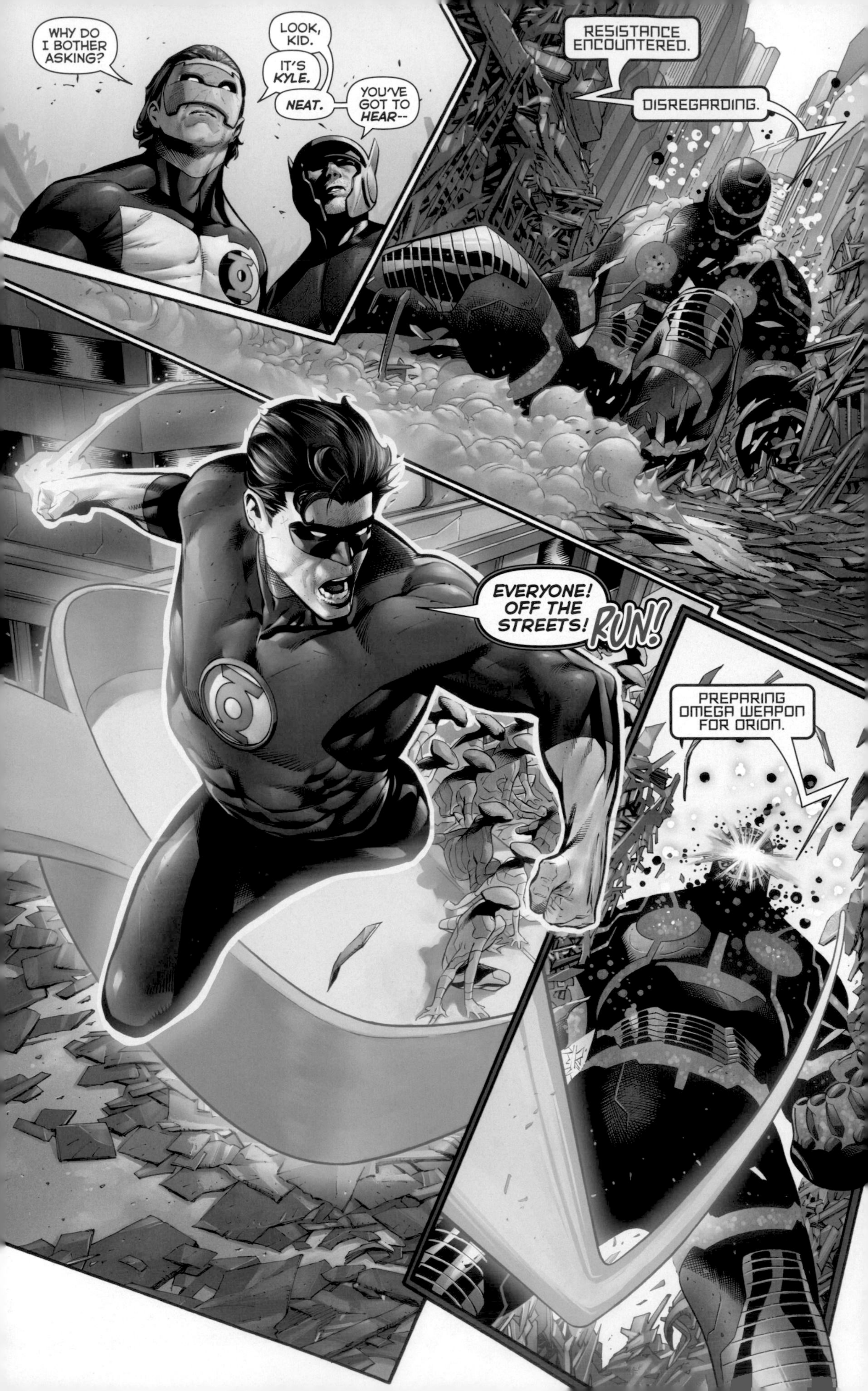
WHY DO I BOTHER ASKING?
LOOK, KID.
IT'S KYLE.
NEAT.
YOU'VE GOT TO HEAR--
RESISTANCE ENCOUNTERED.
DISREGARDING.
EVERYONE! OFF THE STREETS!
RUN!
PREPARING OMEGA WEAPON FOR ORION.

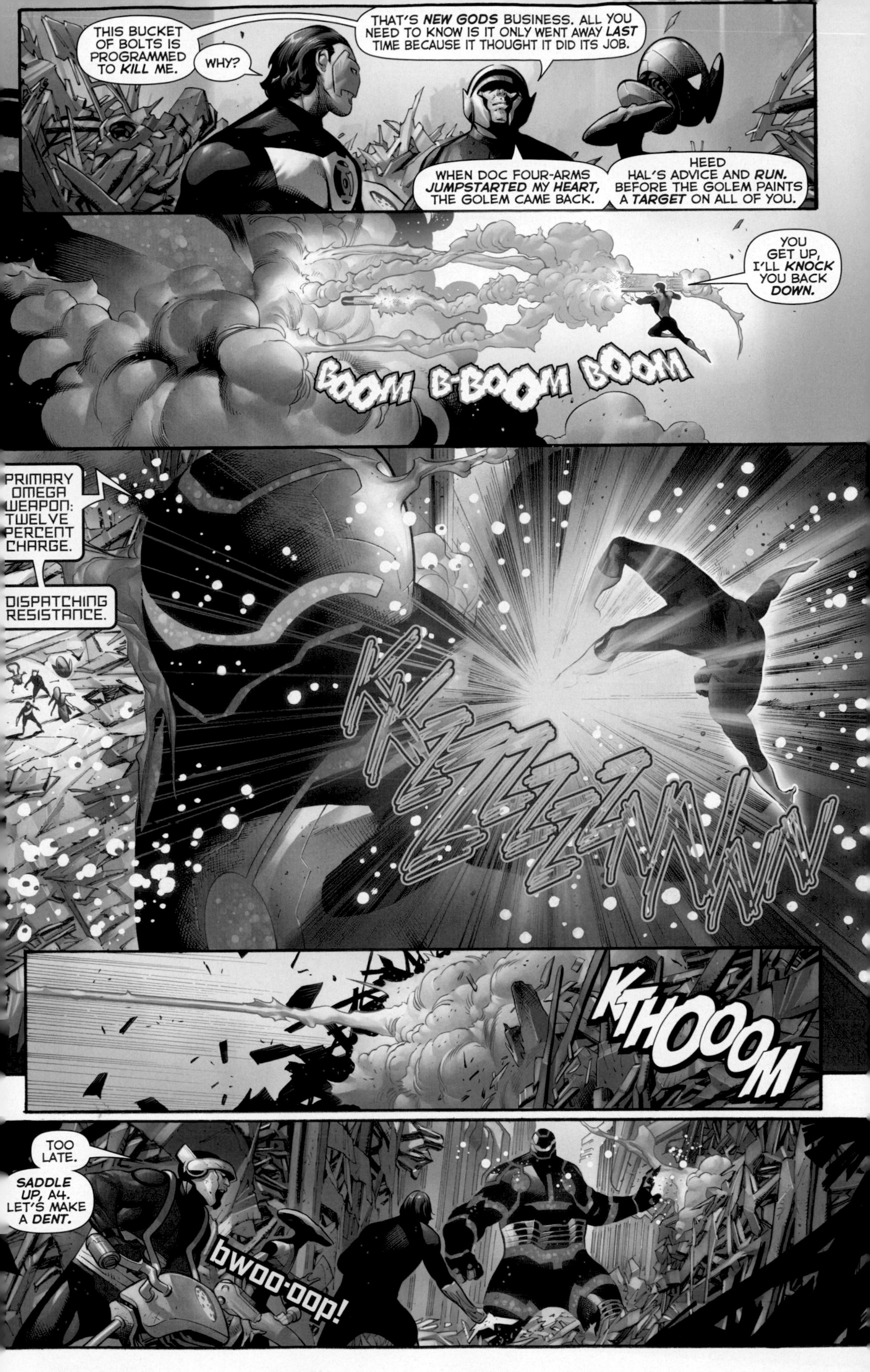
THIS BUCKET OF BOLTS IS PROGRAMMED TO KILL ME.
WHY?
THAT'S NEW GODS BUSINESS. ALL YOU NEED TO KNOW IS IT ONLY WENT AWAY LAST TIME BECAUSE IT THOUGHT IT DID ITS JOB.
WHEN DOC FOUR-ARMS JUMPSTARTED MY HEART, THE GOLEM CAME BACK.
HEED HAL'S ADVICE AND RUN. BEFORE THE GOLEM PAINTS A TARGET ON ALL OF YOU.
YOU GET UP, I'LL KNOCK YOU BACK DOWN.
BOOM B-BOOM BOOM
PRIMARY OMEGA WEAPON: TWELVE PERCENT CHARGE.
DISPATCHING RESISTANCE.
KTHOOOM
TOO LATE.
SADDLE UP, A4. LET'S MAKE A DENT.
bwoo-oop!

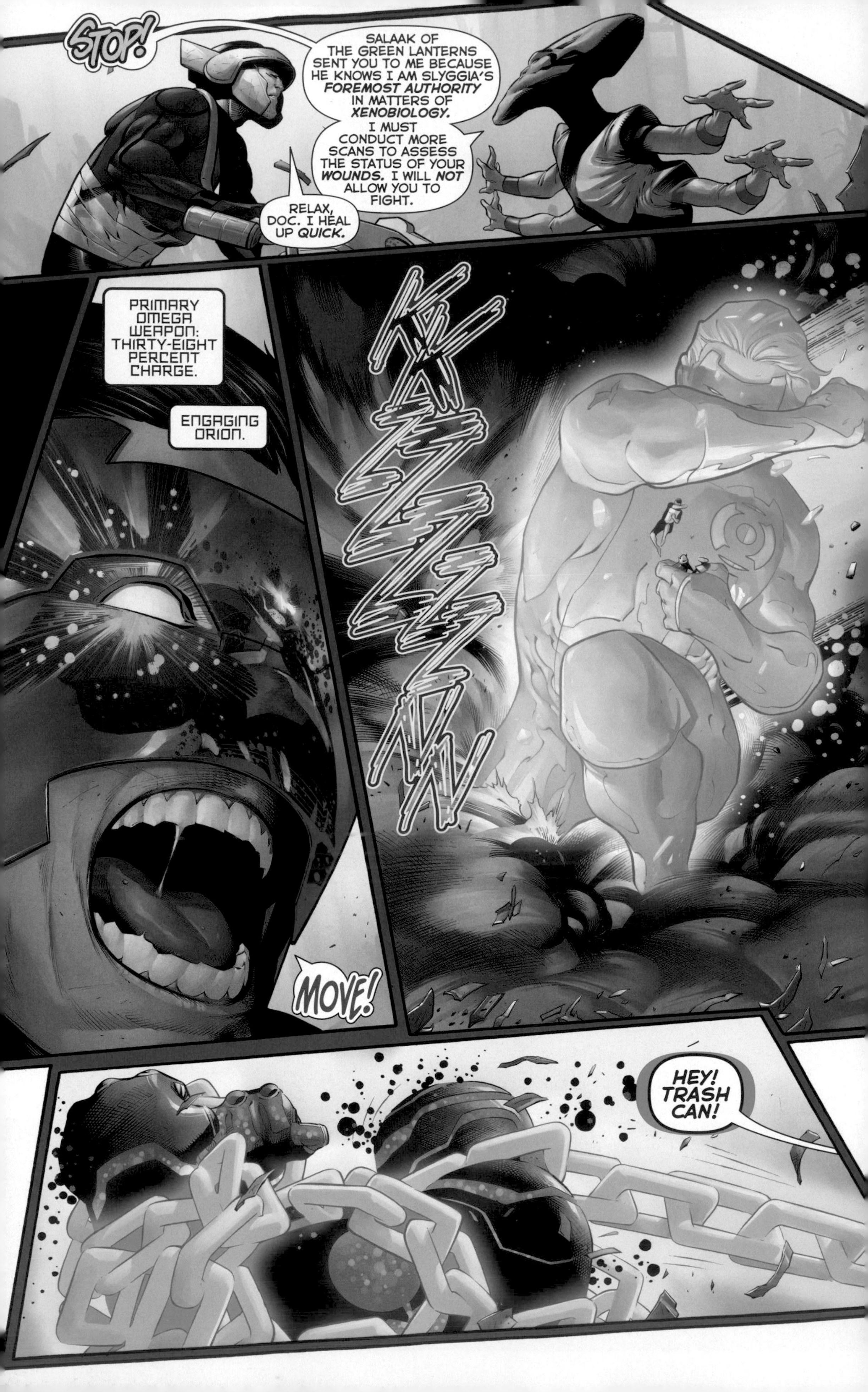
STOP!
SALAAK OF THE GREEN LANTERNS SENT YOU TO ME BECAUSE HE KNOWS I AM SLYGGIA'S FOREMOST AUTHORITY IN MATTERS OF XENOBIOLOGY.
I MUST CONDUCT MORE SCANS TO ASSESS THE STATUS OF YOUR WOUNDS. I WILL NOT ALLOW YOU TO FIGHT.
RELAX, DOC. I HEAL UP QUICK.
PRIMARY OMEGA WEAPON: THIRTY-EIGHT PERCENT CHARGE.
ENGAGING ORION.
MOVE!
HEY! TRASH CAN!

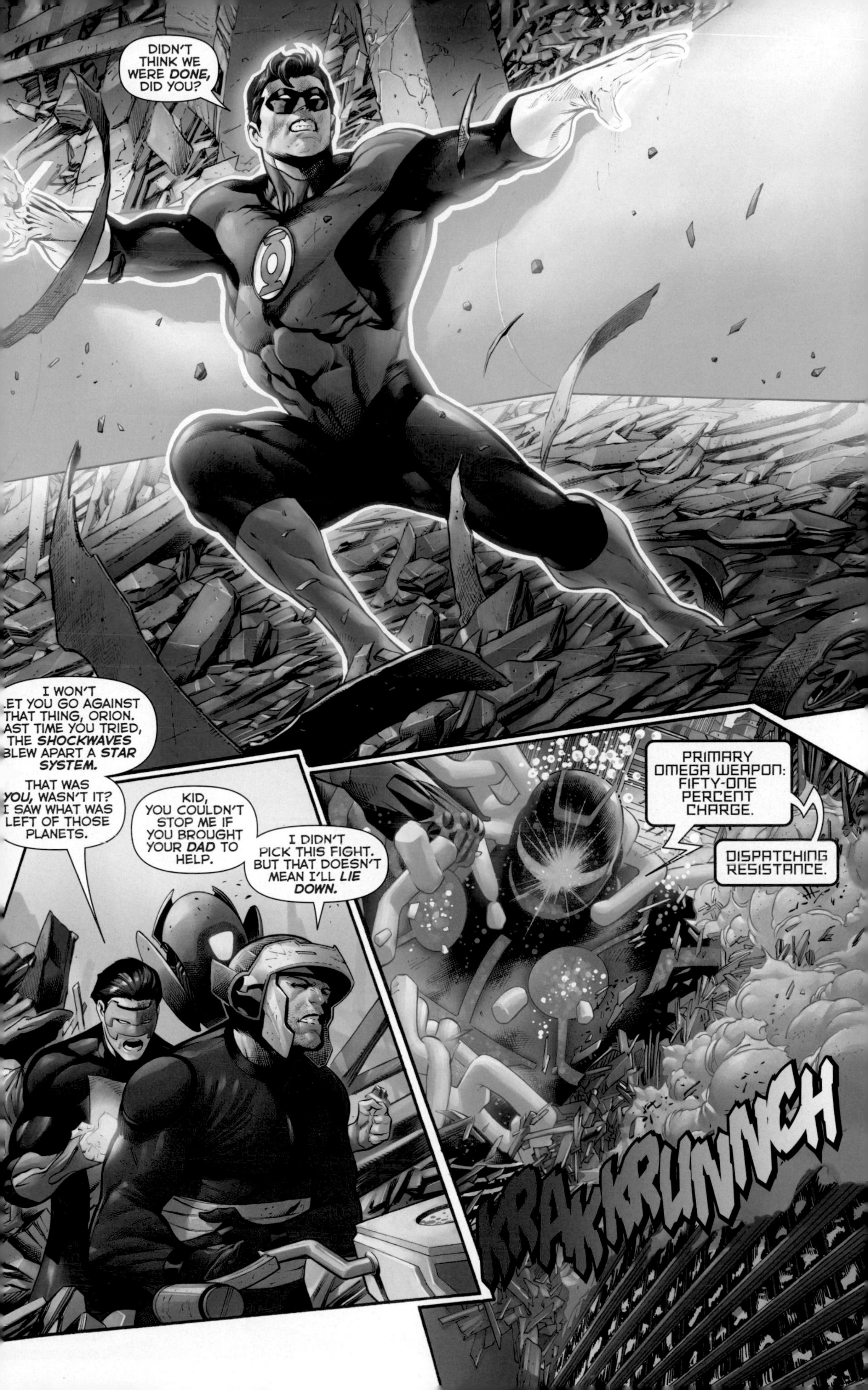
DIDN'T THINK WE WERE DONE, DID YOU?
I WON'T LET YOU GO AGAINST THAT THING, ORION. LAST TIME YOU TRIED, THE SHOCKWAVES BLEW APART A STAR SYSTEM.
THAT WAS YOU, WASN'T IT? I SAW WHAT WAS LEFT OF THOSE PLANETS.
KID, YOU COULDN'T STOP ME IF YOU BROUGHT YOUR DAD TO HELP.
I DIDN'T PICK THIS FIGHT. BUT THAT DOESN'T MEAN I'LL LIE DOWN.
PRIMARY OMEGA WEAPON: FIFTY-ONE PERCENT CHARGE.
DISPATCHING RESISTANCE.
KRAKKRUNNCH

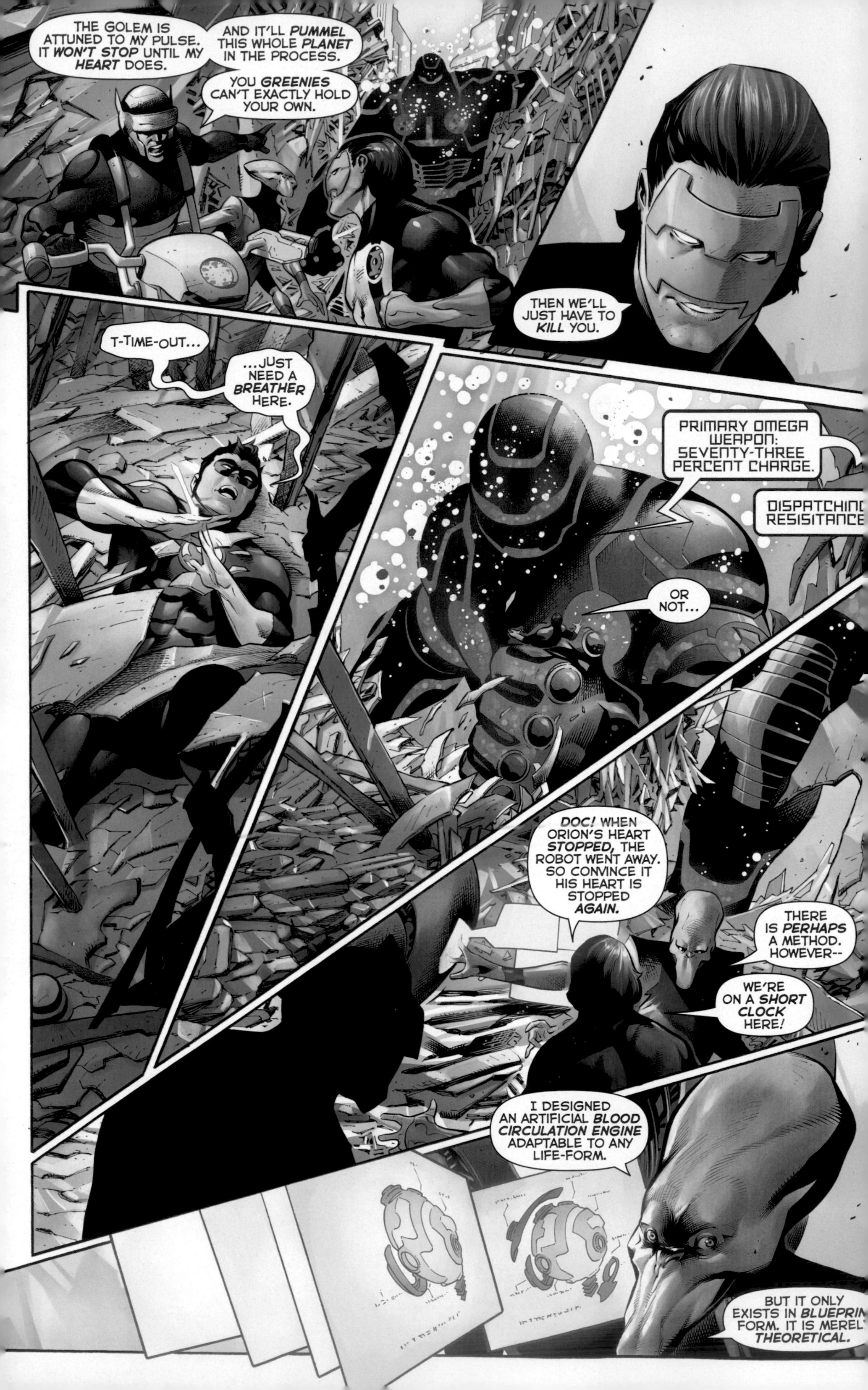
THE GOLEM IS ATTUNED TO MY PULSE. IT WON'T STOP UNTIL MY HEART DOES.
AND IT'LL PUMMEL THIS WHOLE PLANET IN THE PROCESS.
YOU GREENIES CAN'T EXACTLY HOLD YOUR OWN.
THEN WE'LL JUST HAVE TO KILL YOU.
T-TIME-OUT...
...JUST NEED A BREATHER HERE.
PRIMARY OMEGA WEAPON: SEVENTY-THREE PERCENT CHARGE.
DISPATCHING RESISITANCE
OR NOT...
DOC! WHEN ORION'S HEART STOPPED, THE ROBOT WENT AWAY. SO CONVINCE IT HIS HEART IS STOPPED AGAIN.
THERE IS PERHAPS A METHOD. HOWEVER--
WE'RE ON A SHORT CLOCK HERE!
I DESIGNED AN ARTIFICIAL BLOOD CIRCULATION ENGINE ADAPTABLE TO ANY LIFE-FORM.
BUT IT ONLY EXISTS IN BLUEPRIN FORM. IT IS MEREL THEORETICAL.

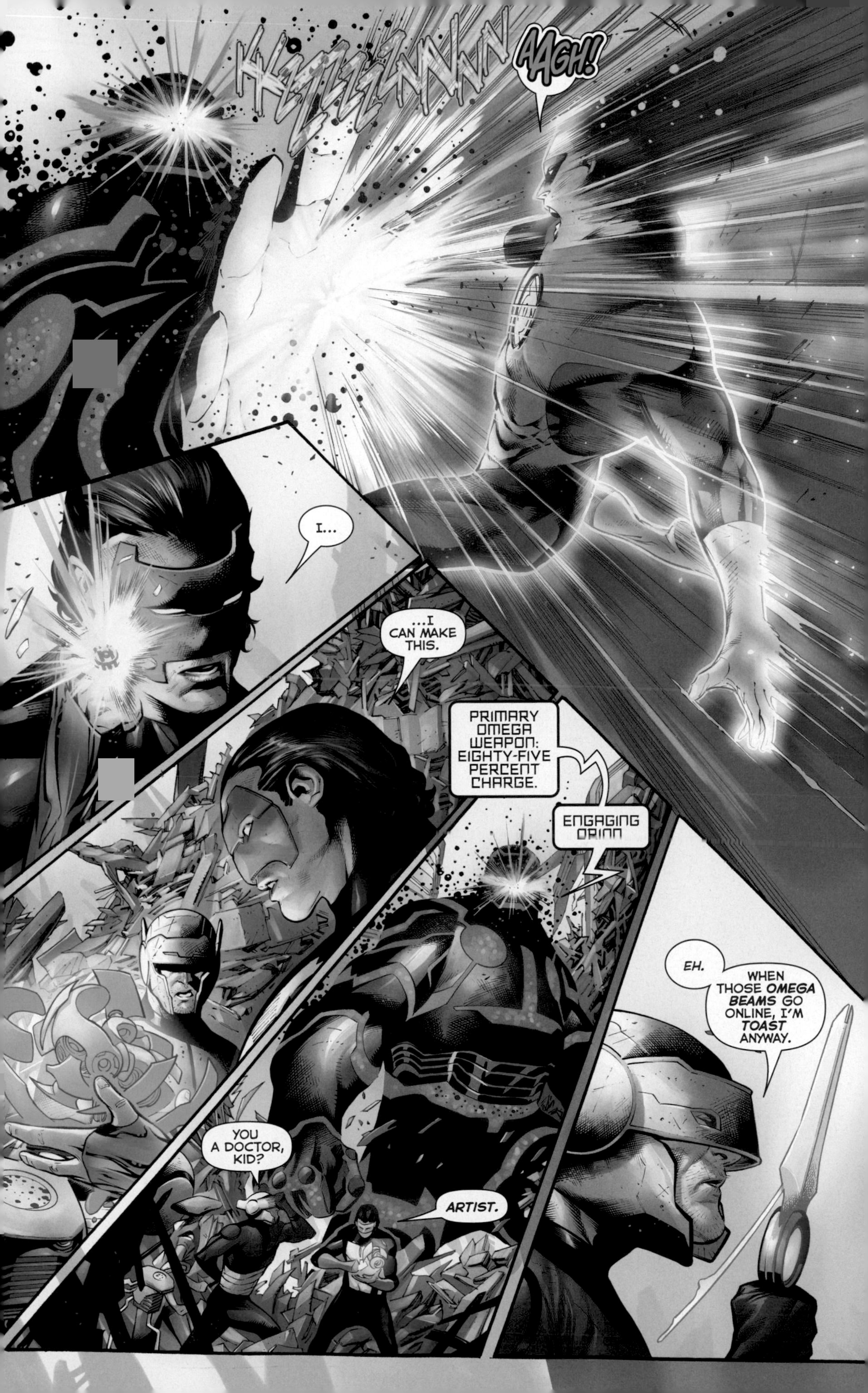
KHZZZZZNNNN
AAGH!
I...
...I CAN MAKE THIS.
PRIMARY OMEGA WEAPON: EIGHTY-FIVE PERCENT CHARGE.
ENGAGING ORION
EH.
WHEN THOSE OMEGA BEAMS GO ONLINE, I'M TOAST ANYWAY.
YOU A DOCTOR, KID?
ARTIST.

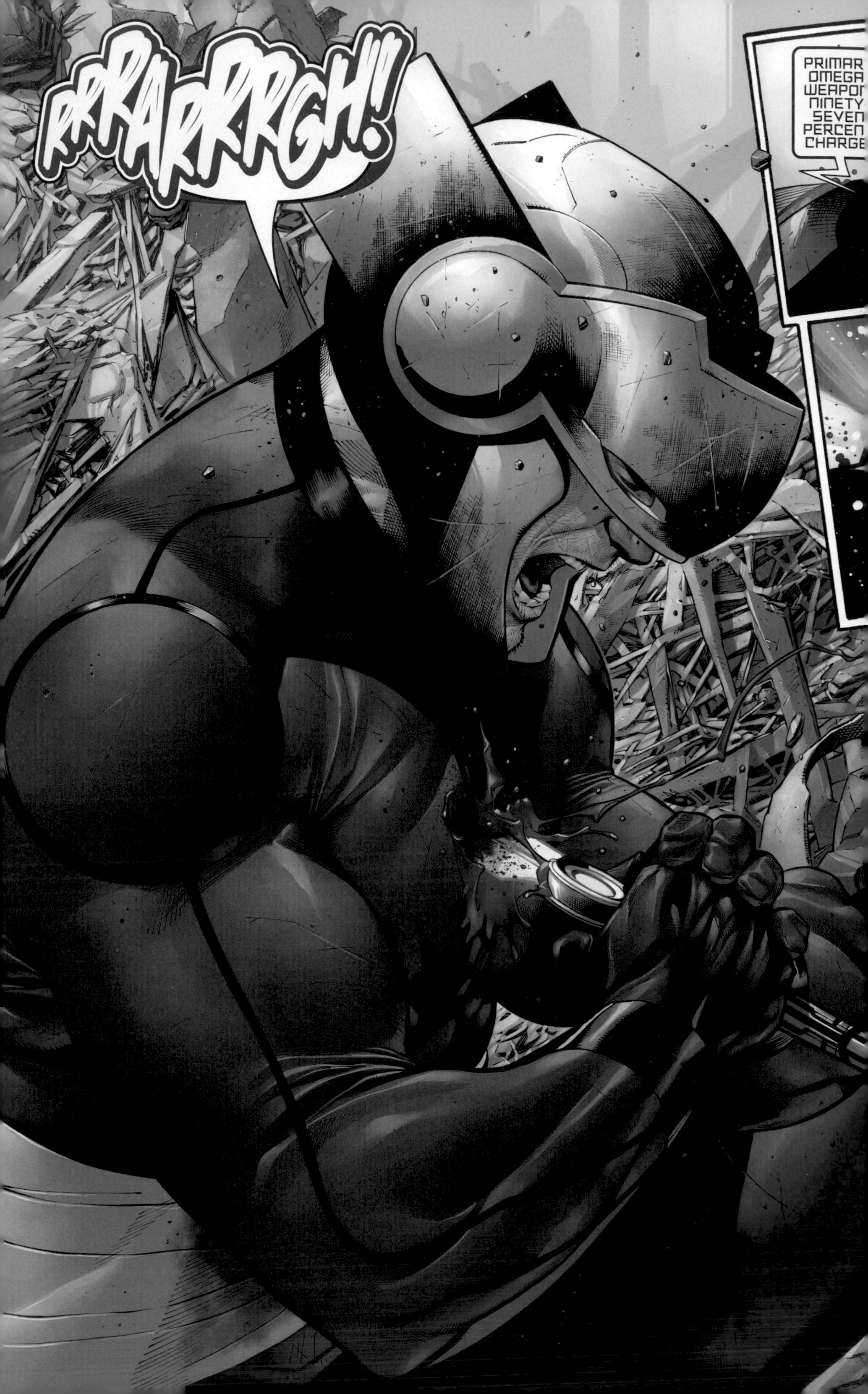
RRRARRRGH!!
PRIMAR OMEGA WEAPON NINETY SEVEN PERCEN CHARGE

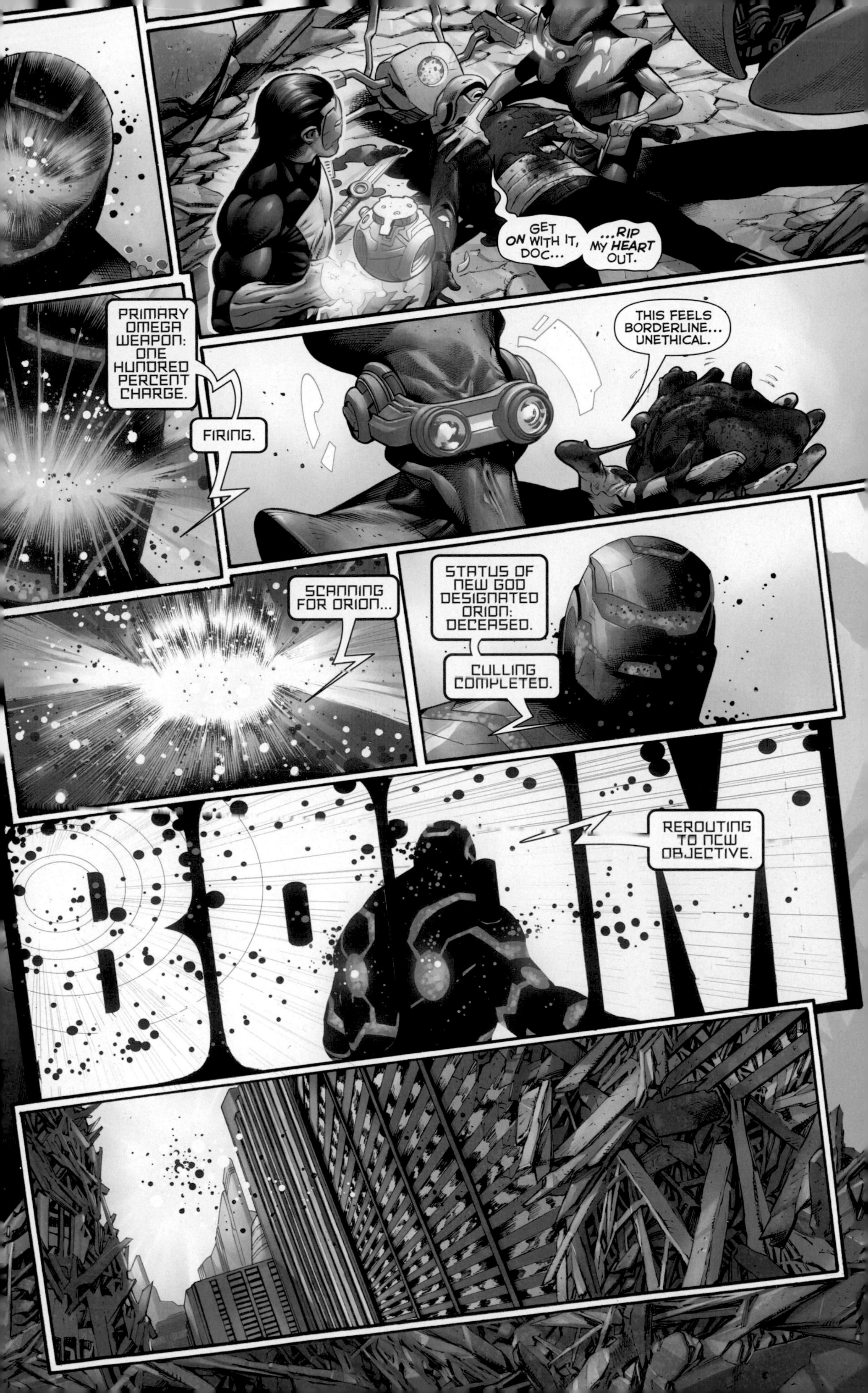
GET ON WITH IT, DOC...
...RIP MY HEART OUT.
PRIMARY OMEGA WEAPON: ONE HUNDRED PERCENT CHARGE.
FIRING.
THIS FEELS BORDERLINE... UNETHICAL.
SCANNING FOR ORION...
STATUS OF NEW GOD DESIGNATED ORION: DECEASED.
CULLING COMPLETED.
BOOM
REROUTING TO NEW OBJECTIVE.

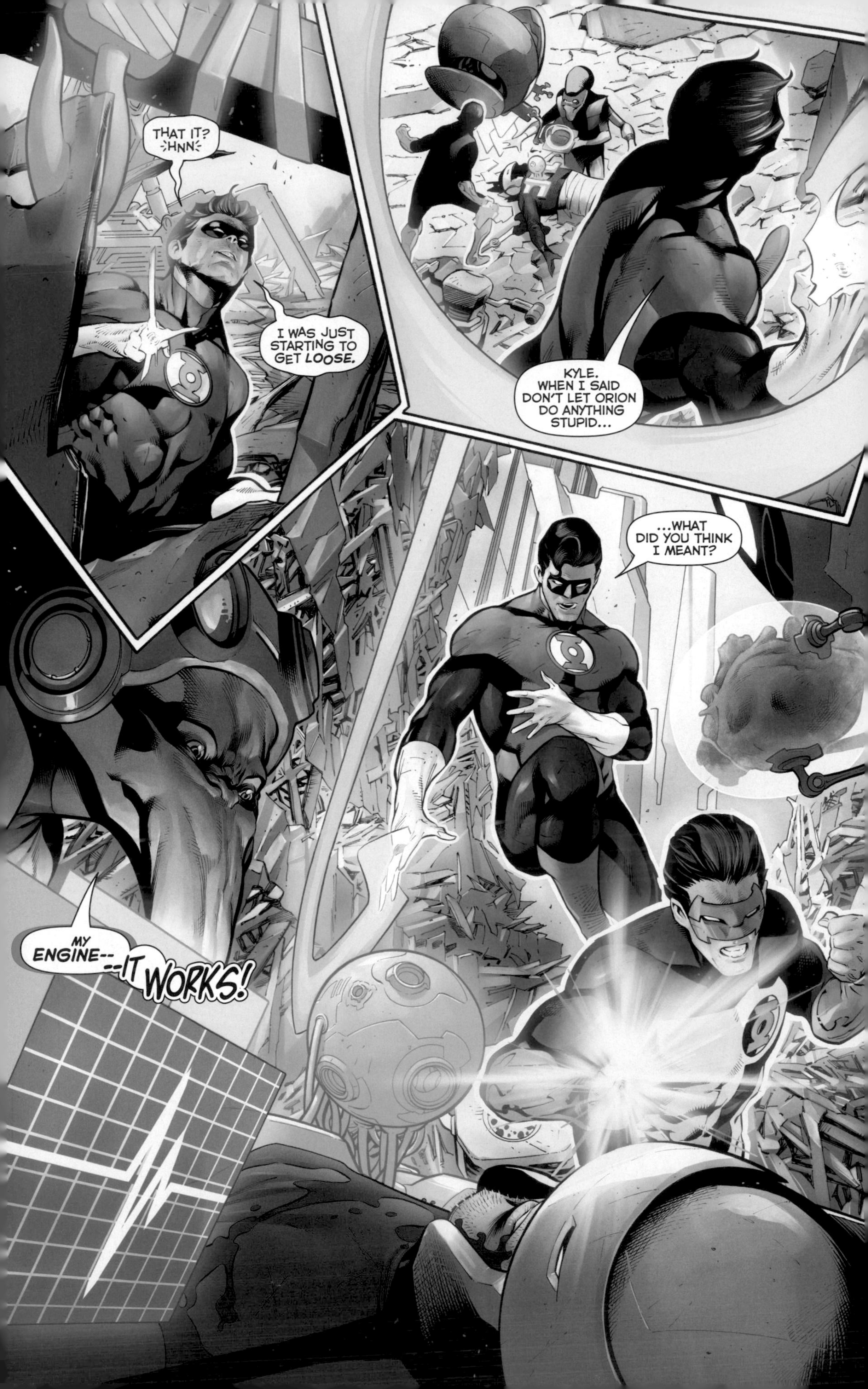
THAT IT? HNN
I WAS JUST STARTING TO GET LOOSE.
KYLE. WHEN I SAID DON'T LET ORION DO ANYTHING STUPID...
...WHAT DID YOU THINK I MEANT?
MY ENGINE-- --IT WORKS!

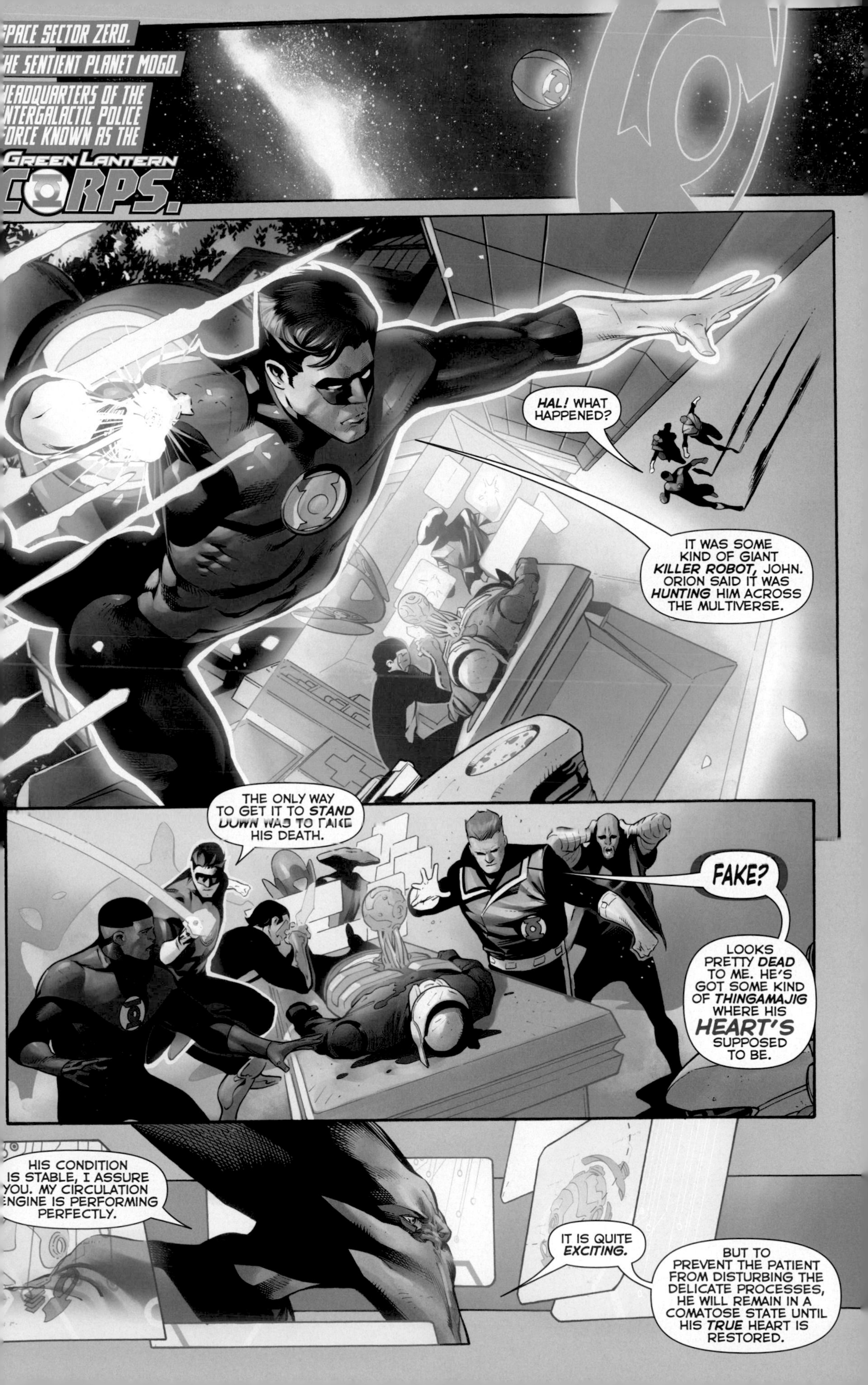
SPACE SECTOR ZERO.
THE SENTIENT PLANET MOGO.
HEADQUARTERS OF THE INTERGALACTIC POLICE FORCE KNOWN AS THE
GREEN LANTERN CORPS.
HAL! WHAT HAPPENED?
IT WAS SOME KIND OF GIANT KILLER ROBOT, JOHN. ORION SAID IT WAS HUNTING HIM ACROSS THE MULTIVERSE.
THE ONLY WAY TO GET IT TO STAND DOWN WAS TO FAKE HIS DEATH.
FAKE?
LOOKS PRETTY DEAD TO ME. HE'S GOT SOME KIND OF THINGAMAJIG WHERE HIS HEART'S SUPPOSED TO BE.
HIS CONDITION IS STABLE, I ASSURE YOU. MY CIRCULATION ENGINE IS PERFORMING PERFECTLY.
IT IS QUITE EXCITING.
BUT TO PREVENT THE PATIENT FROM DISTURBING THE DELICATE PROCESSES, HE WILL REMAIN IN A COMATOSE STATE UNTIL HIS TRUE HEART IS RESTORED.

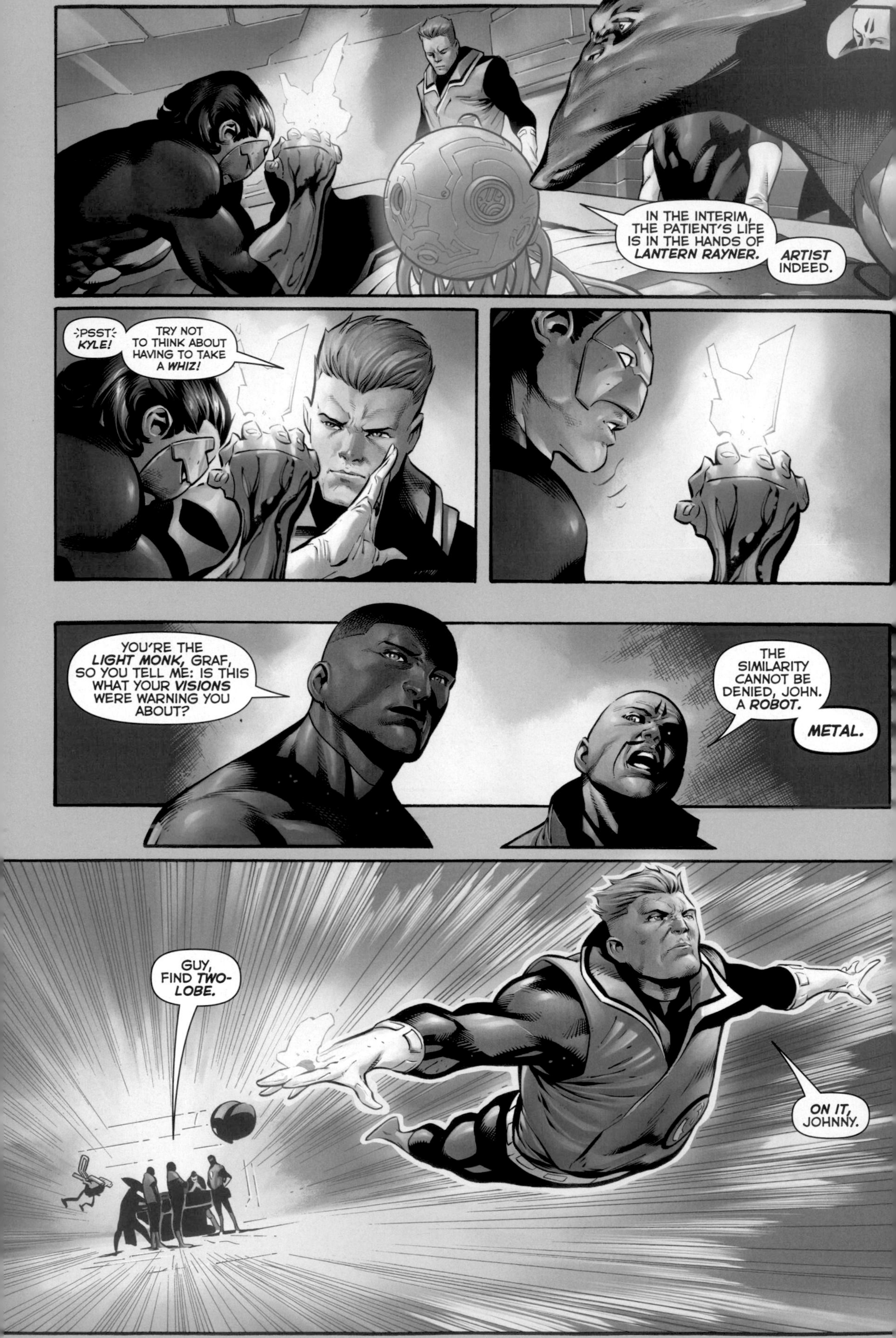
IN THE INTERIM, THE PATIENT'S LIFE IS IN THE HANDS OF LANTERN RAYNER.
ARTIST INDEED.
PSST! KYLE!
TRY NOT TO THINK ABOUT HAVING TO TAKE A WHIZ!
YOU'RE THE LIGHT MONK, GRAF, SO YOU TELL ME: IS THIS WHAT YOUR VISIONS WERE WARNING YOU ABOUT?
THE SIMILARITY CANNOT BE DENIED, JOHN. A ROBOT.
METAL.
GUY, FIND TWO-LOBE.
ON IT, JOHNNY.

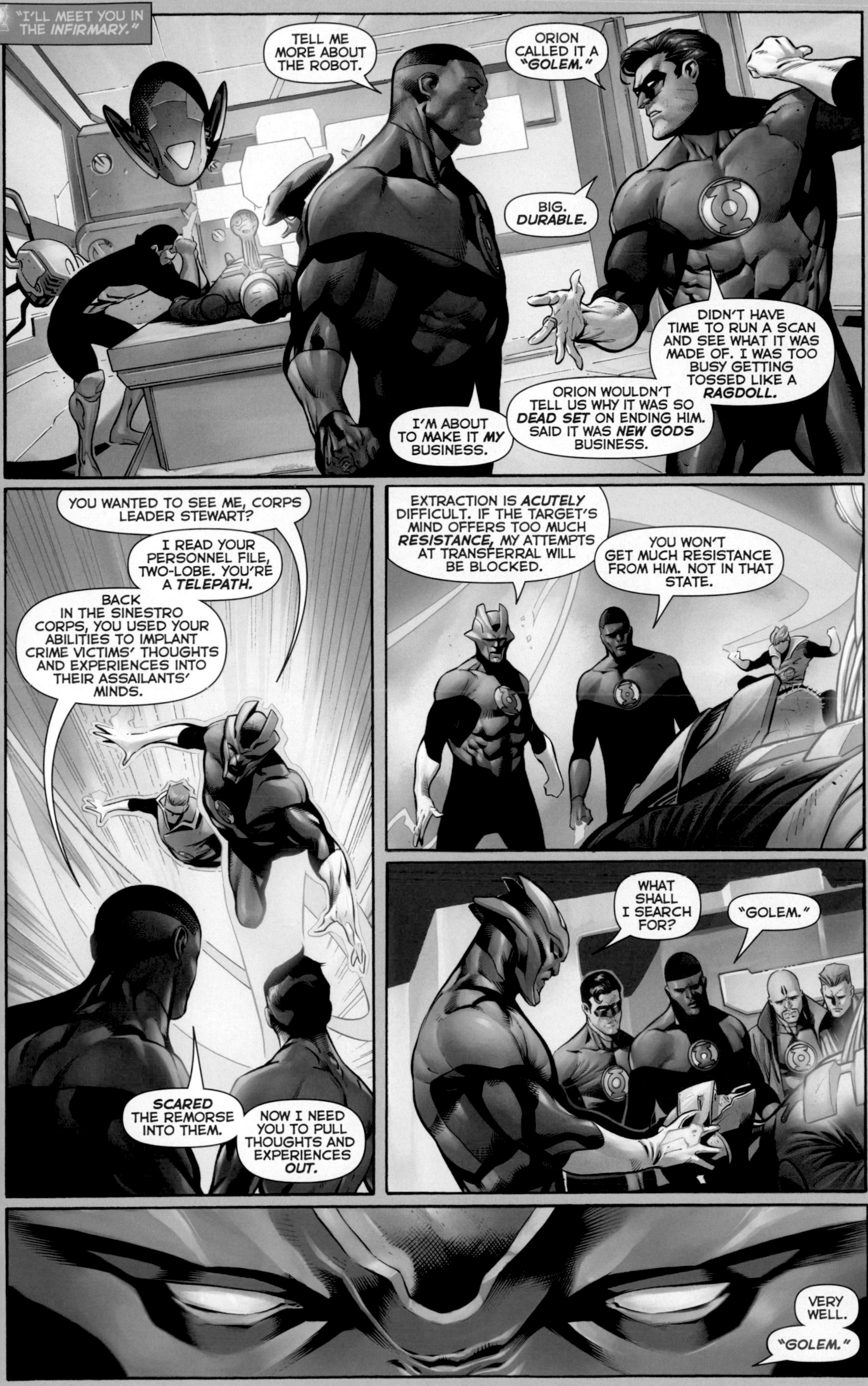

"I'LL MEET YOU IN THE INFIRMARY."
TELL ME MORE ABOUT THE ROBOT.
ORION CALLED IT A "GOLEM."
BIG. DURABLE.
DIDN'T HAVE TIME TO RUN A SCAN AND SEE WHAT IT WAS MADE OF. I WAS TOO BUSY GETTING TOSSED LIKE A RAGDOLL.
ORION WOULDN'T TELL US WHY IT WAS SO DEAD SET ON ENDING HIM. SAID IT WAS NEW GODS BUSINESS.
I'M ABOUT TO MAKE IT MY BUSINESS.
YOU WANTED TO SEE ME, CORPS LEADER STEWART?
I READ YOUR PERSONNEL FILE, TWO-LOBE. YOU'RE A TELEPATH.
BACK IN THE SINESTRO CORPS, YOU USED YOUR ABILITIES TO IMPLANT CRIME VICTIMS' THOUGHTS AND EXPERIENCES INTO THEIR ASSAILANTS' MINDS.
SCARED THE REMORSE INTO THEM.
NOW I NEED YOU TO PULL THOUGHTS AND EXPERIENCES OUT.
EXTRACTION IS ACUTELY DIFFICULT. IF THE TARGET'S MIND OFFERS TOO MUCH RESISTANCE, MY ATTEMPTS AT TRANSFERRAL WILL BE BLOCKED.
YOU WON'T GET MUCH RESISTANCE FROM HIM. NOT IN THAT STATE.
WHAT SHALL I SEARCH FOR?
"GOLEM."
VERY WELL.
"GOLEM."

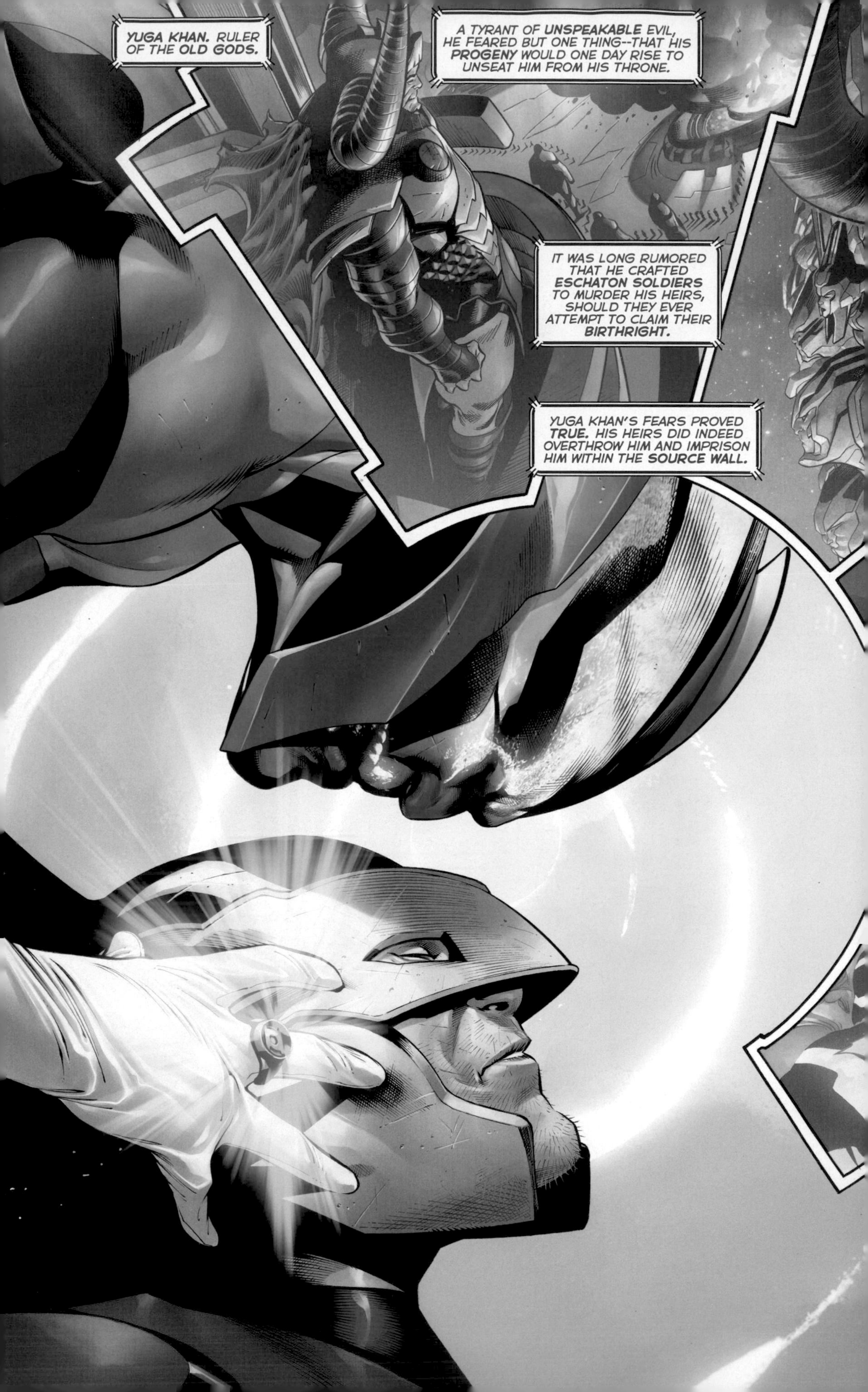
YUGA KHAN. RULER OF THE OLD GODS.
A TYRANT OF UNSPEAKABLE EVIL, HE FEARED BUT ONE THING--THAT HIS PROGENY WOULD ONE DAY RISE TO UNSEAT HIM FROM HIS THRONE.
IT WAS LONG RUMORED THAT HE CRAFTED ESCHATON SOLDIERS TO MURDER HIS HEIRS, SHOULD THEY EVER ATTEMPT TO CLAIM THEIR BIRTHRIGHT.
YUGA KHAN'S FEARS PROVED TRUE. HIS HEIRS DID INDEED OVERTHROW HIM AND IMPRISON HIM WITHIN THE SOURCE WALL.

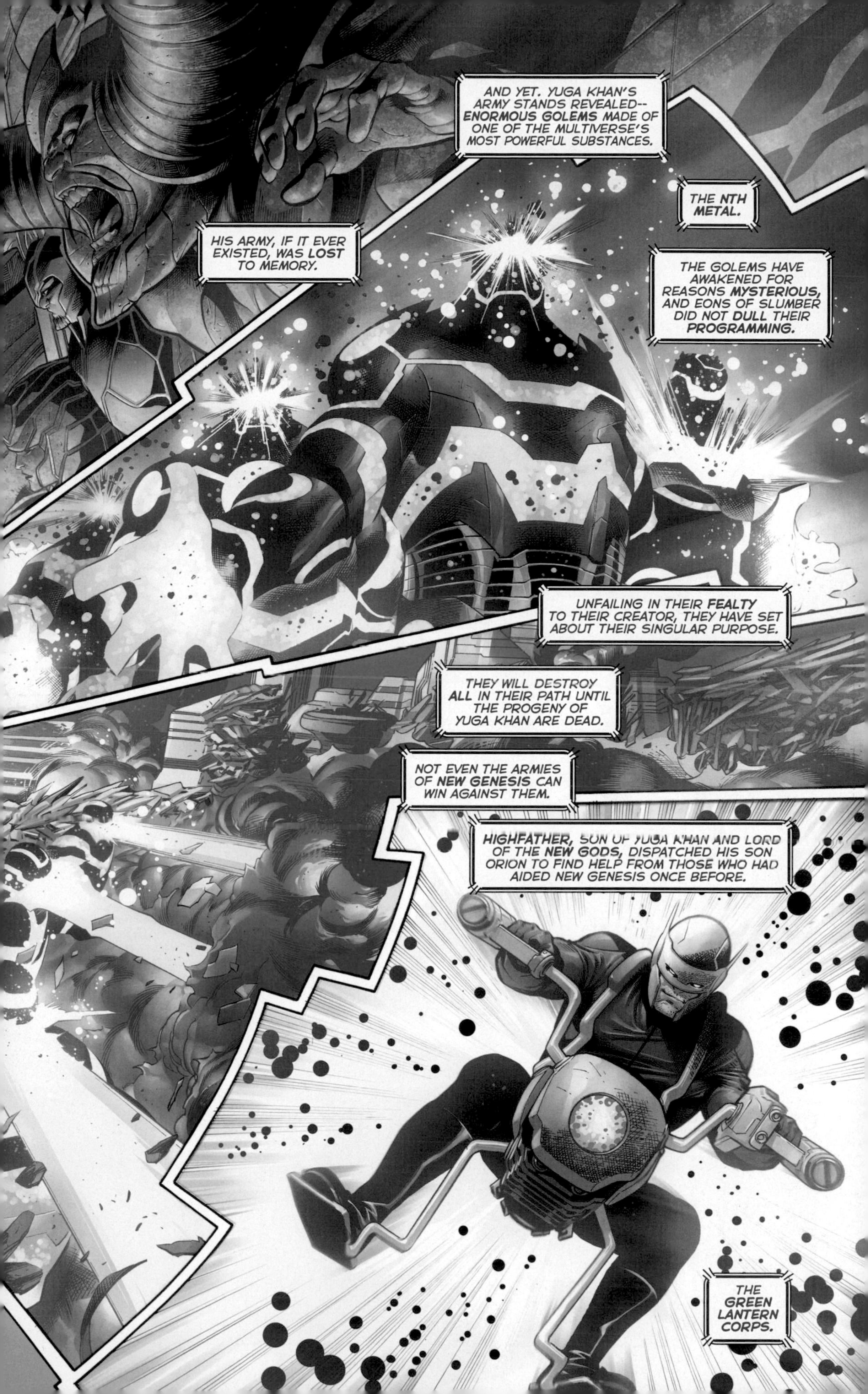
HIS ARMY, IF IT EVER EXISTED, WAS LOST TO MEMORY.
AND YET. YUGA KHAN'S ARMY STANDS REVEALED-- ENORMOUS GOLEMS MADE OF ONE OF THE MULTIVERSE'S MOST POWERFUL SUBSTANCES.
THE NTH METAL.
THE GOLEMS HAVE AWAKENED FOR REASONS MYSTERIOUS, AND EONS OF SLUMBER DID NOT DULL THEIR PROGRAMMING.
UNFAILING IN THEIR FEALTY TO THEIR CREATOR, THEY HAVE SET ABOUT THEIR SINGULAR PURPOSE.
THEY WILL DESTROY ALL IN THEIR PATH UNTIL THE PROGENY OF YUGA KHAN ARE DEAD.
NOT EVEN THE ARMIES OF NEW GENESIS CAN WIN AGAINST THEM.
HIGHFATHER, SON OF YUGA KHAN AND LORD OF THE NEW GODS, DISPATCHED HIS SON ORION TO FIND HELP FROM THOSE WHO HAD AIDED NEW GENESIS ONCE BEFORE.
THE GREEN LANTERN CORPS.

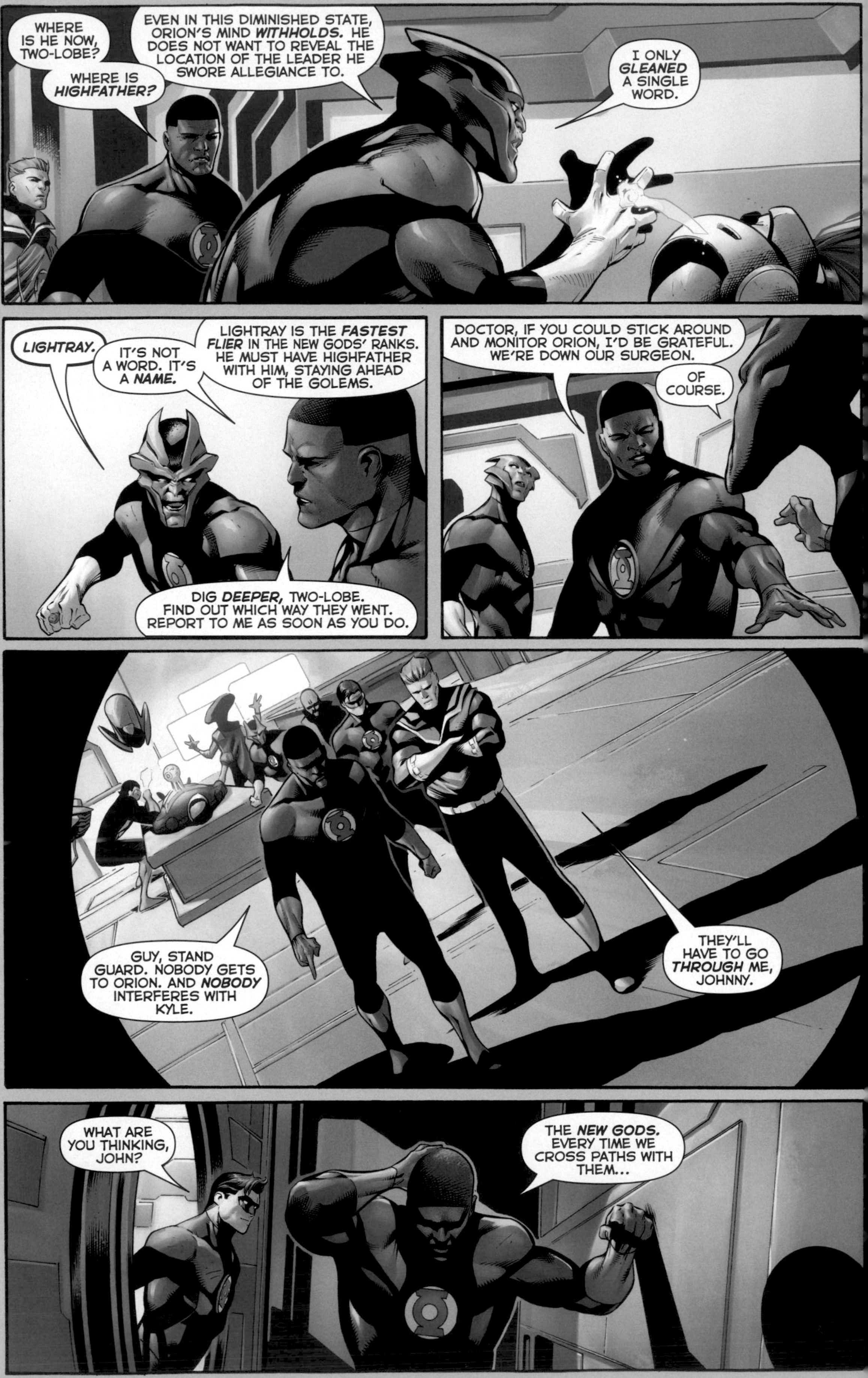
WHERE IS HE NOW, TWO-LOBE?
WHERE IS HIGHFATHER?
EVEN IN THIS DIMINISHED STATE, ORION'S MIND WITHHOLDS. HE DOES NOT WANT TO REVEAL THE LOCATION OF THE LEADER HE SWORE ALLEGIANCE TO.
I ONLY GLEANED A SINGLE WORD.
LIGHTRAY.
IT'S NOT A WORD. IT'S A NAME.
LIGHTRAY IS THE FASTEST FLIER IN THE NEW GODS' RANKS. HE MUST HAVE HIGHFATHER WITH HIM, STAYING AHEAD OF THE GOLEMS.
DIG DEEPER, TWO-LOBE. FIND OUT WHICH WAY THEY WENT. REPORT TO ME AS SOON AS YOU DO.
DOCTOR, IF YOU COULD STICK AROUND AND MONITOR ORION, I'D BE GRATEFUL. WE'RE DOWN OUR SURGEON.
OF COURSE.
GUY, STAND GUARD. NOBODY GETS TO ORION. AND NOBODY INTERFERES WITH KYLE.
THEY'LL HAVE TO GO THROUGH ME, JOHNNY.
WHAT ARE YOU THINKING, JOHN?
THE NEW GODS. EVERY TIME WE CROSS PATHS WITH THEM...

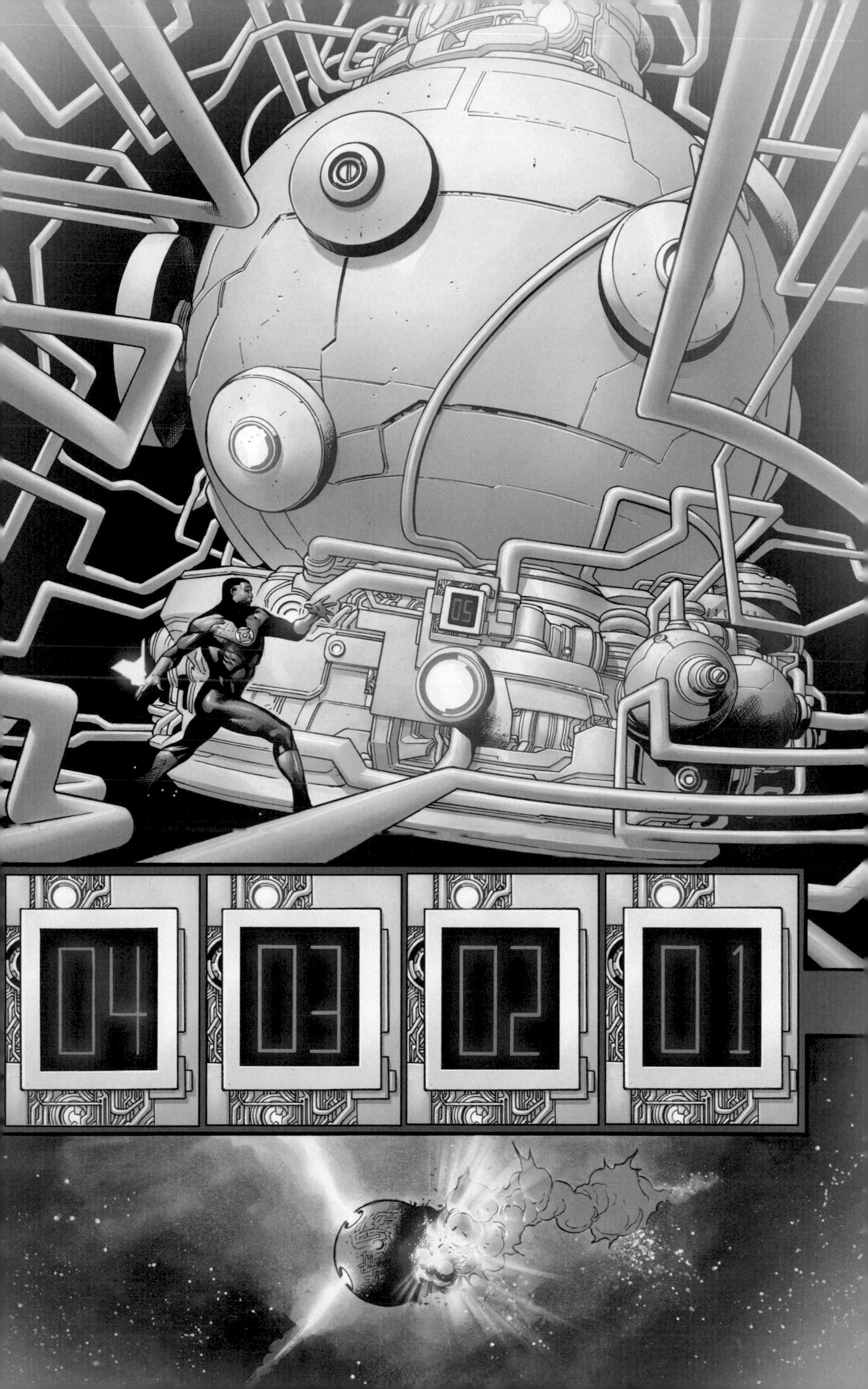
05
04
03
02
01

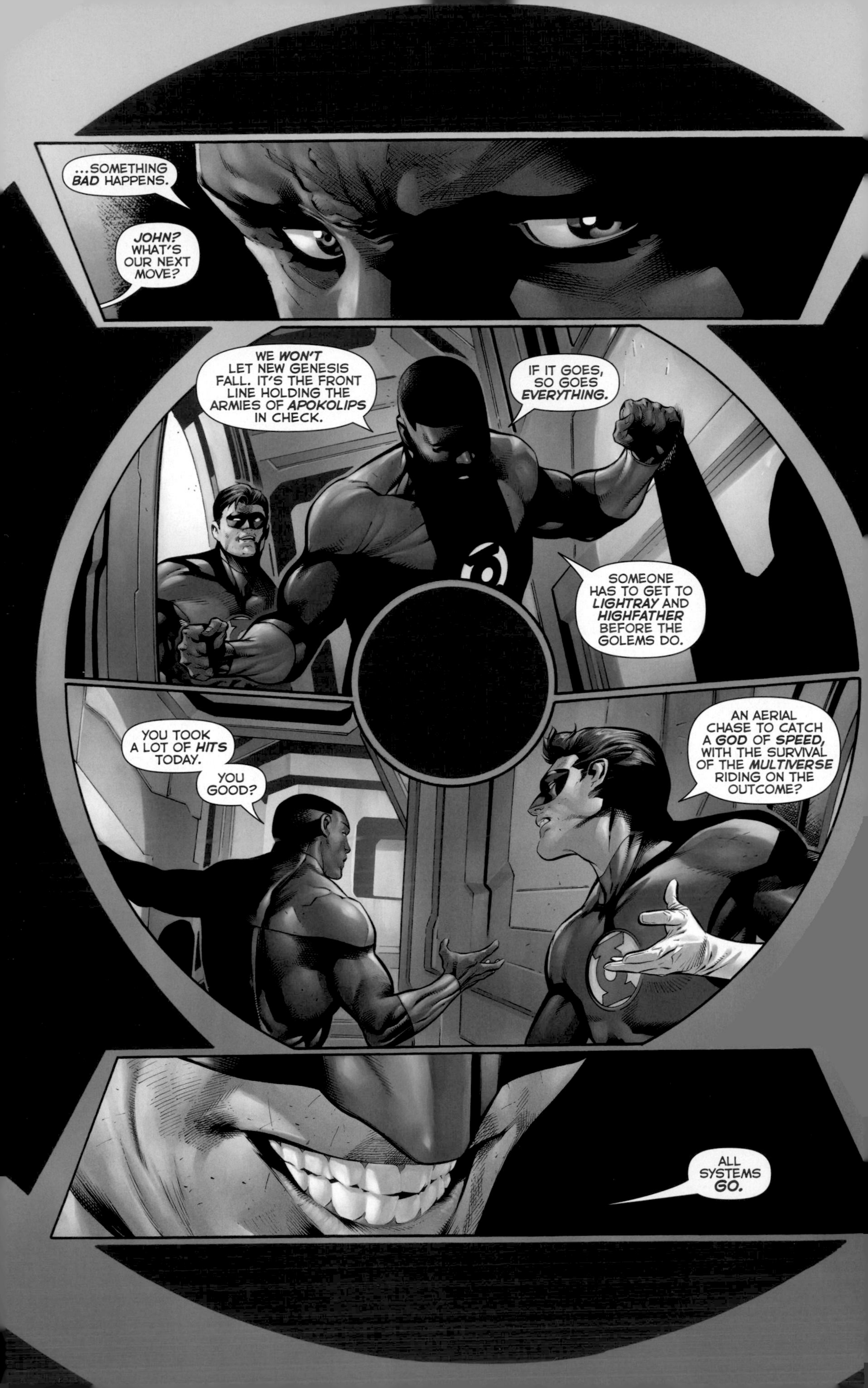
...SOMETHING BAD HAPPENS.
JOHN? WHAT'S OUR NEXT MOVE?
WE WON'T LET NEW GENESIS FALL. IT'S THE FRONT LINE HOLDING THE ARMIES OF APOKOLIPS IN CHECK.
IF IT GOES, SO GOES EVERYTHING.
SOMEONE HAS TO GET TO LIGHTRAY AND HIGHFATHER BEFORE THE GOLEMS DO.
YOU TOOK A LOT OF HITS TODAY.
YOU GOOD?
AN AERIAL CHASE TO CATCH A GOD OF SPEED, WITH THE SURVIVAL OF THE MULTIVERSE RIDING ON THE OUTCOME?
ALL SYSTEMS GO.

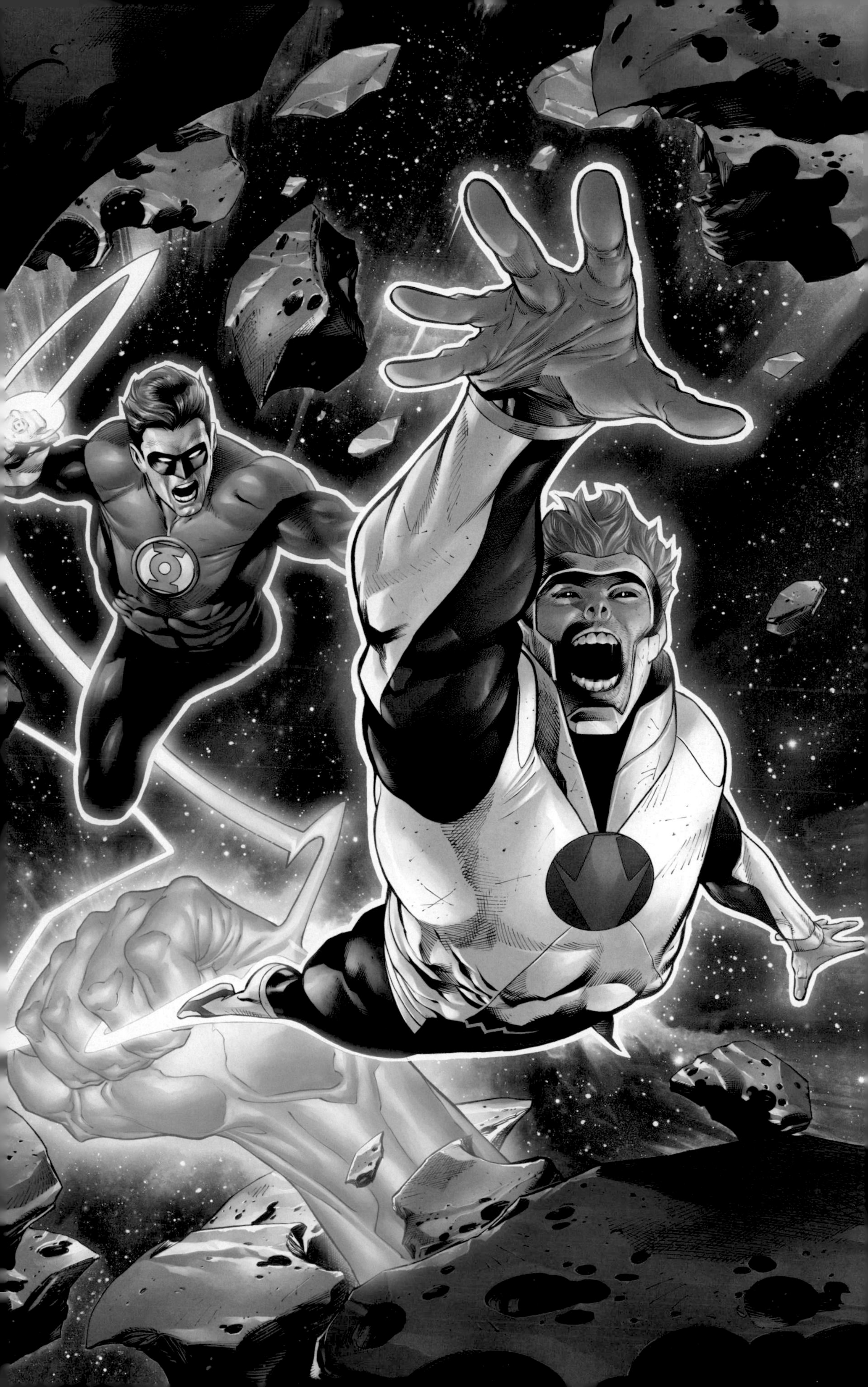

"FALL OF THE GODS PART THREE: GODSPEED"

RAFA SANDOVAL penciller * JORDI TARRAGONA inker * TOMEU MOREY colorist
cover art by RAFA SANDOVAL, JORDI TARRAGONA, and TOMEU MOREY

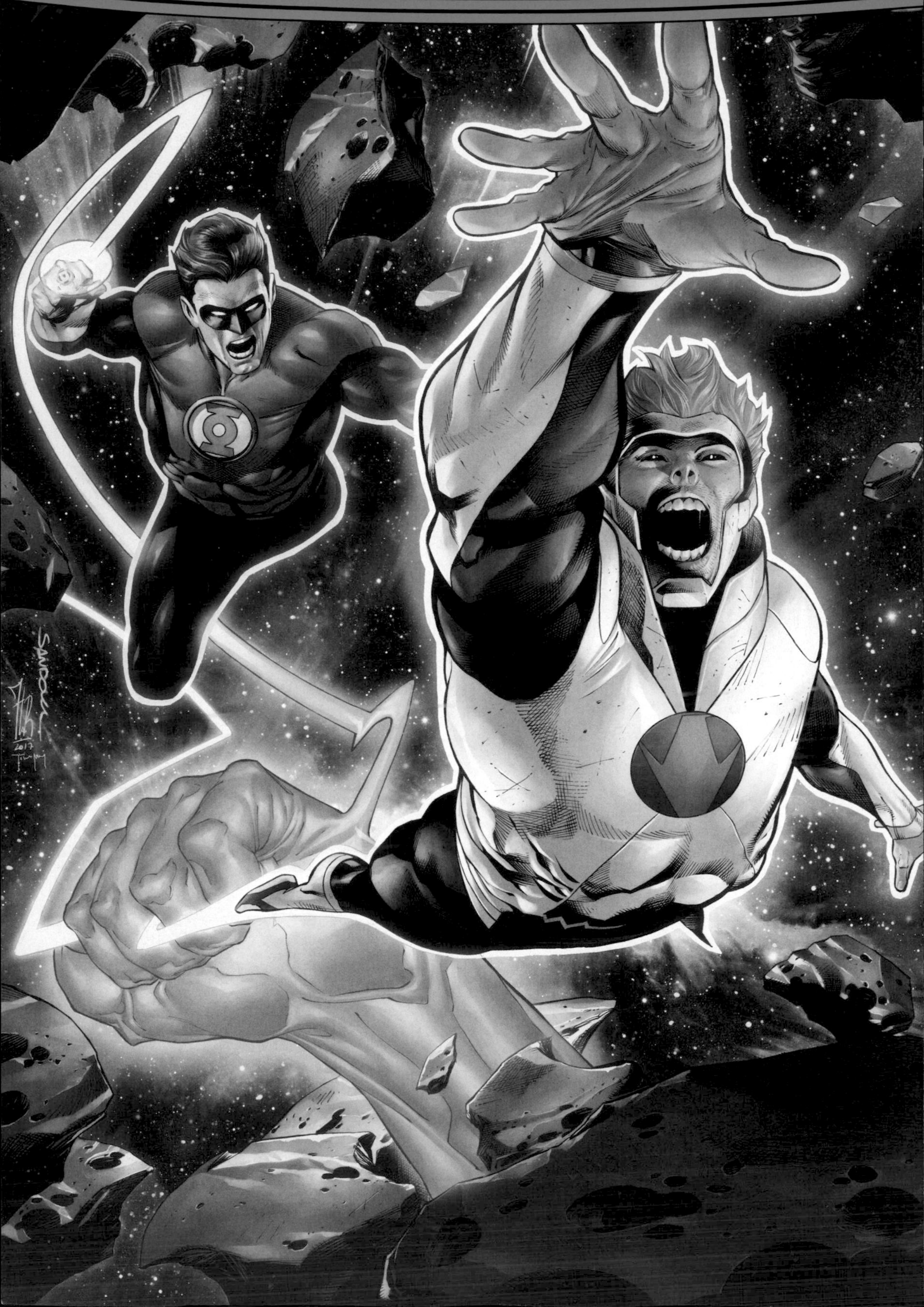

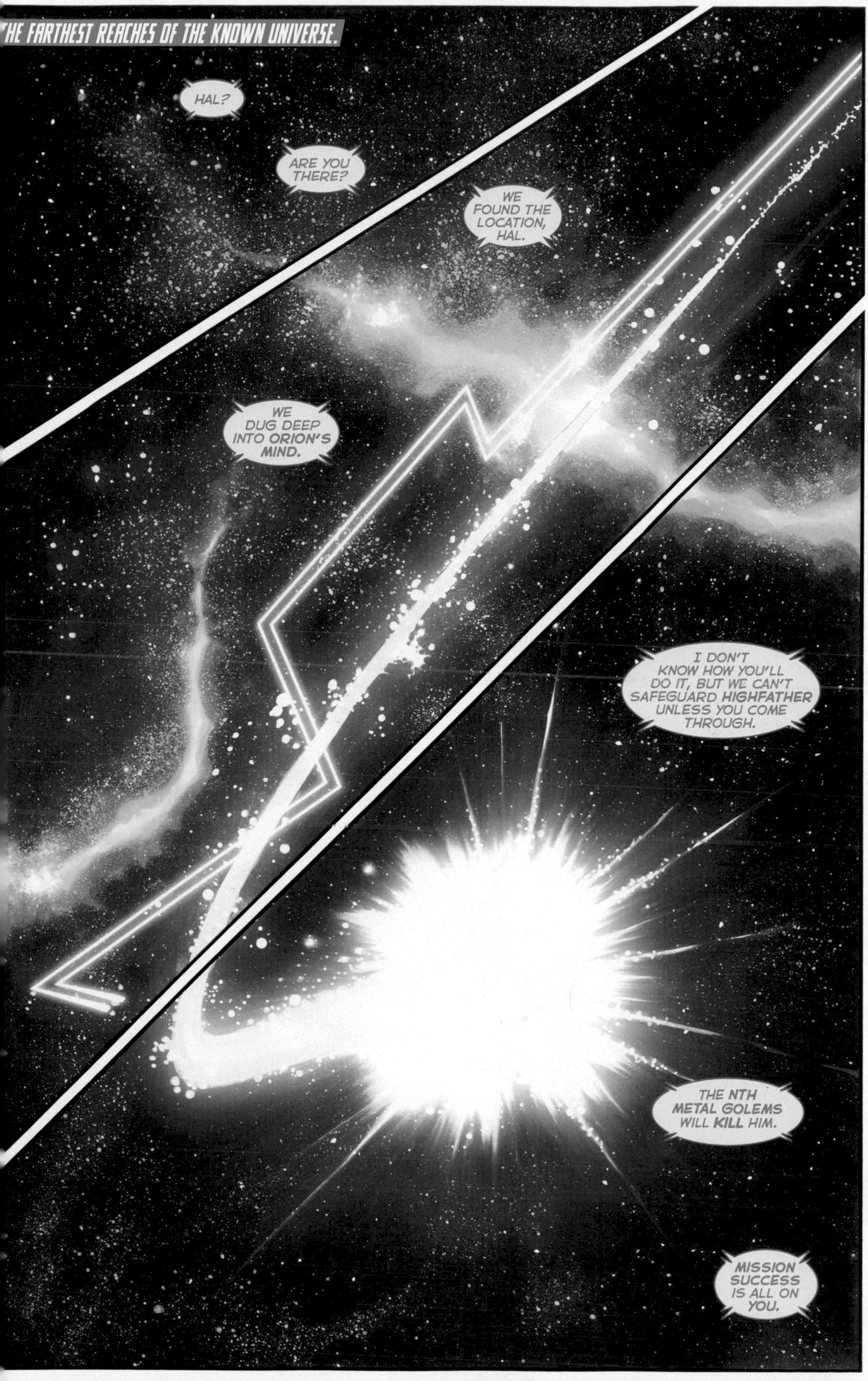
THE FARTHEST REACHES OF THE KNOWN UNIVERSE.
HAL?
ARE YOU THERE?
WE FOUND THE LOCATION, HAL.
WE DUG DEEP INTO ORION'S MIND.
I DON'T KNOW HOW YOU'LL DO IT, BUT WE CAN'T SAFEGUARD HIGHFATHER UNLESS YOU COME THROUGH.
THE NTH METAL GOLEMS WILL KILL HIM.
MISSION SUCCESS IS ALL ON YOU.

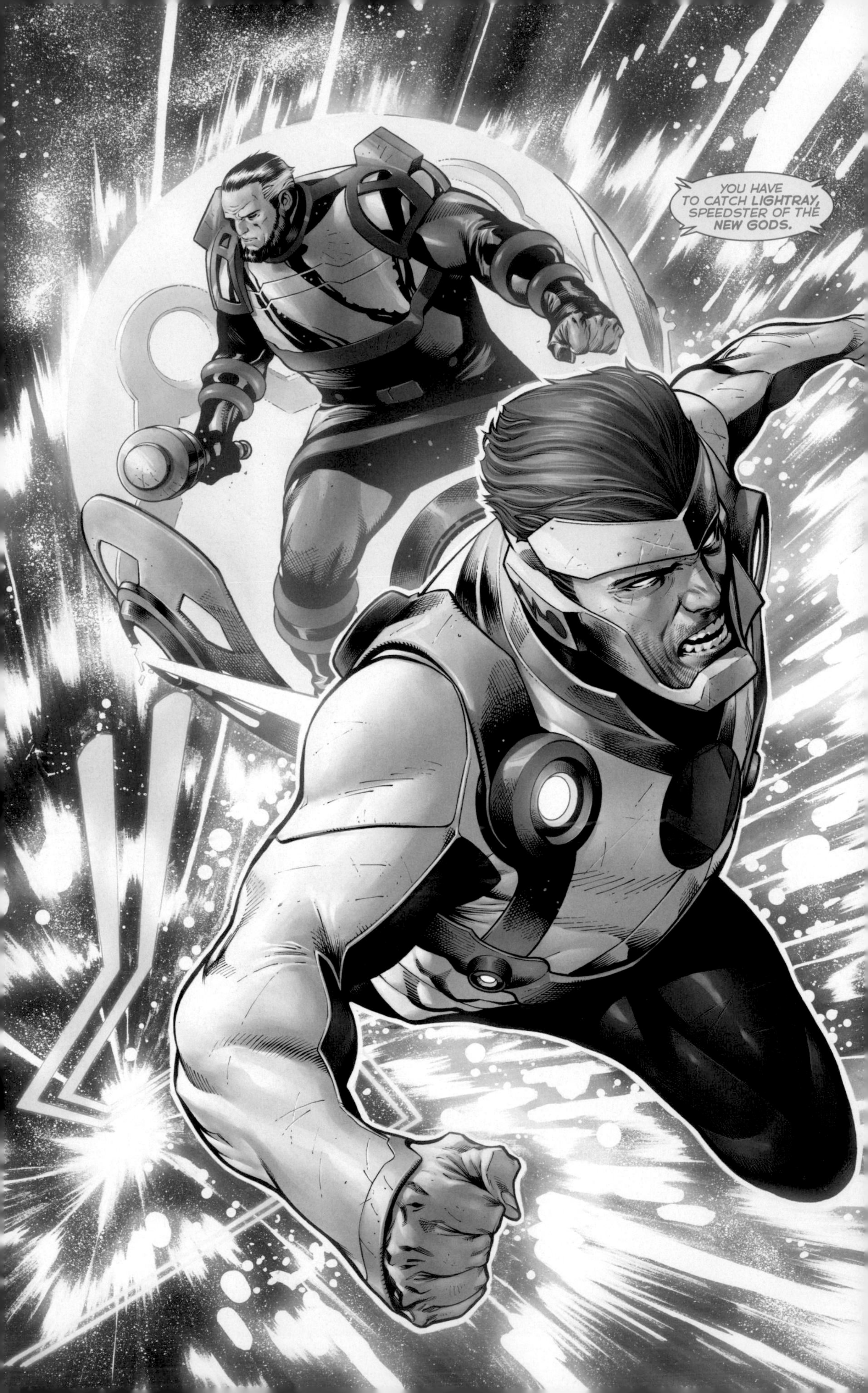
YOU HAVE TO CATCH LIGHTRAY, SPEEDSTER OF THE NEW GODS.

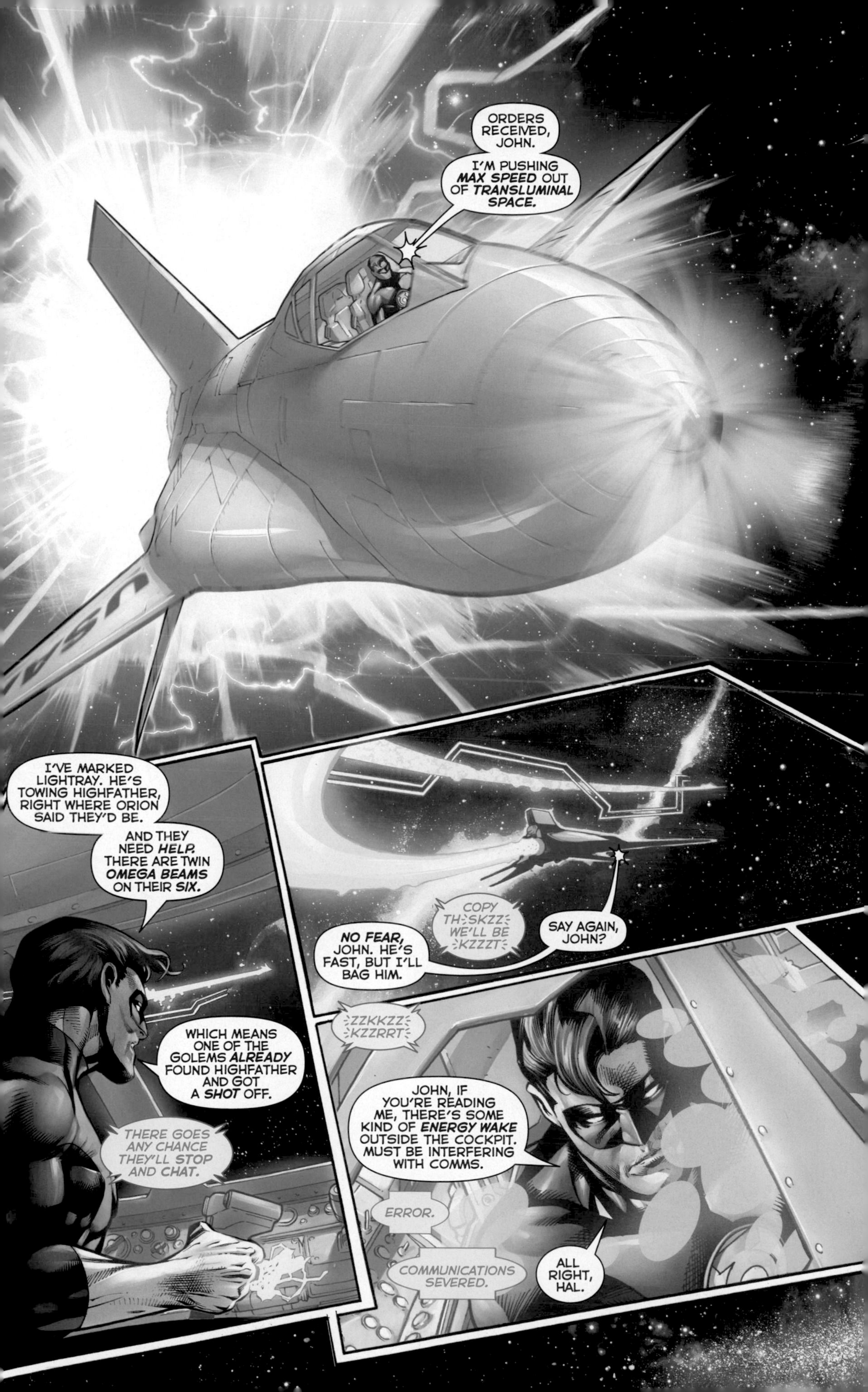
ORDERS RECEIVED, JOHN.
I'M PUSHING MAX SPEED OUT OF TRANSLUMINAL SPACE.
I'VE MARKED LIGHTRAY. HE'S TOWING HIGHFATHER, RIGHT WHERE ORION SAID THEY'D BE.
AND THEY NEED HELP. THERE ARE TWIN OMEGA BEAMS ON THEIR SIX.
WHICH MEANS ONE OF THE GOLEMS ALREADY FOUND HIGHFATHER AND GOT A SHOT OFF.
THERE GOES ANY CHANCE THEY'LL STOP AND CHAT.
NO FEAR, JOHN. HE'S FAST, BUT I'LL BAG HIM.
COPY TH-SKZZ WE'LL BE KZZZT
SAY AGAIN, JOHN?
ZZKKZZ KZZRRT
JOHN, IF YOU'RE READING ME, THERE'S SOME KIND OF ENERGY WAKE OUTSIDE THE COCKPIT. MUST BE INTERFERING WITH COMMS.
ERROR.
COMMUNICATIONS SEVERED.
ALL RIGHT, HAL.

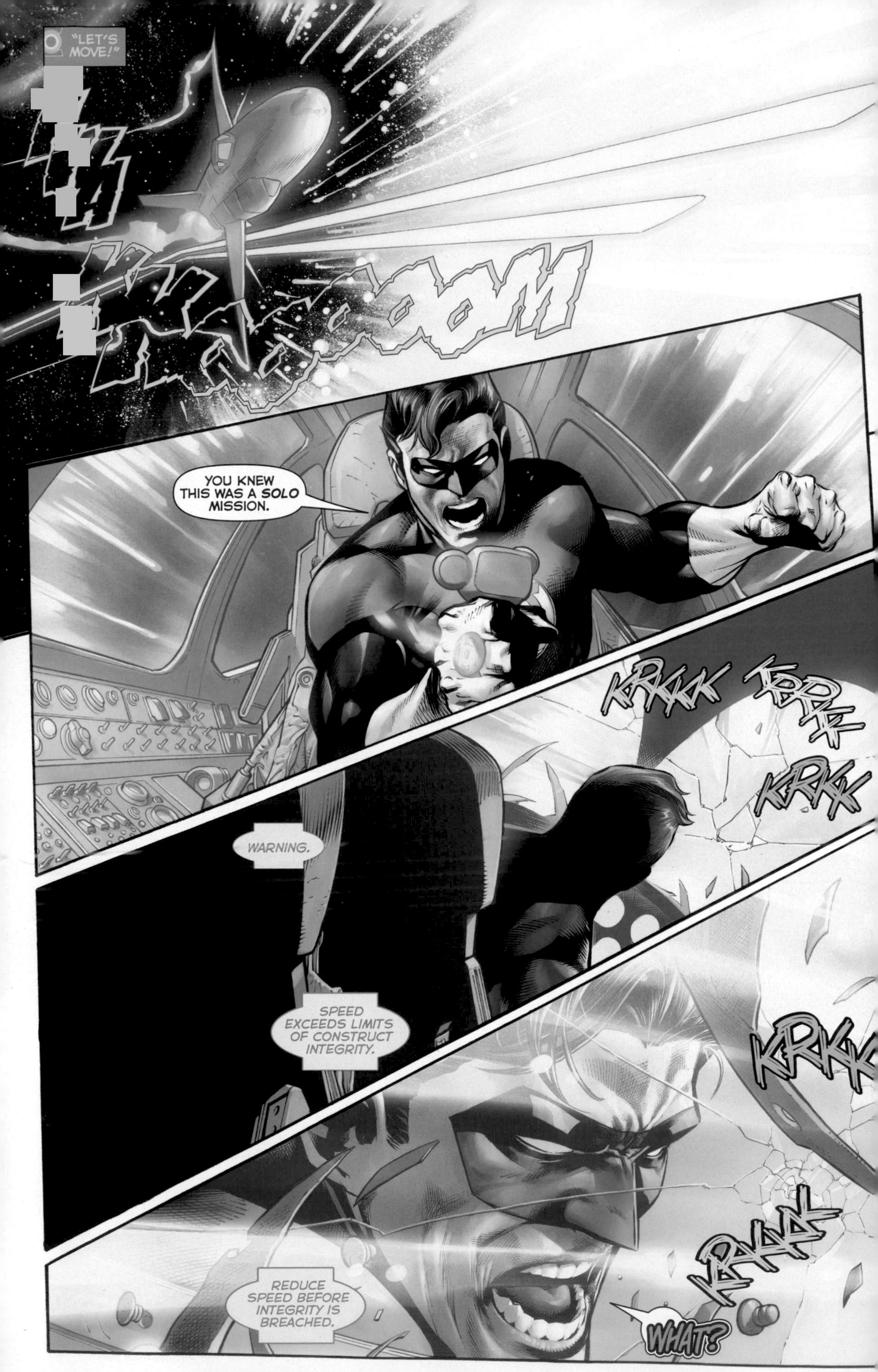
"LET'S MOVE!"
YOU KNEW THIS WAS A SOLO MISSION.
KRKKK
KRKK
WARNING.
SPEED EXCEEDS LIMITS OF CONSTRUCT INTEGRITY.
KRKK
REDUCE SPEED BEFORE INTEGRITY IS BREACHED.
WHAT?

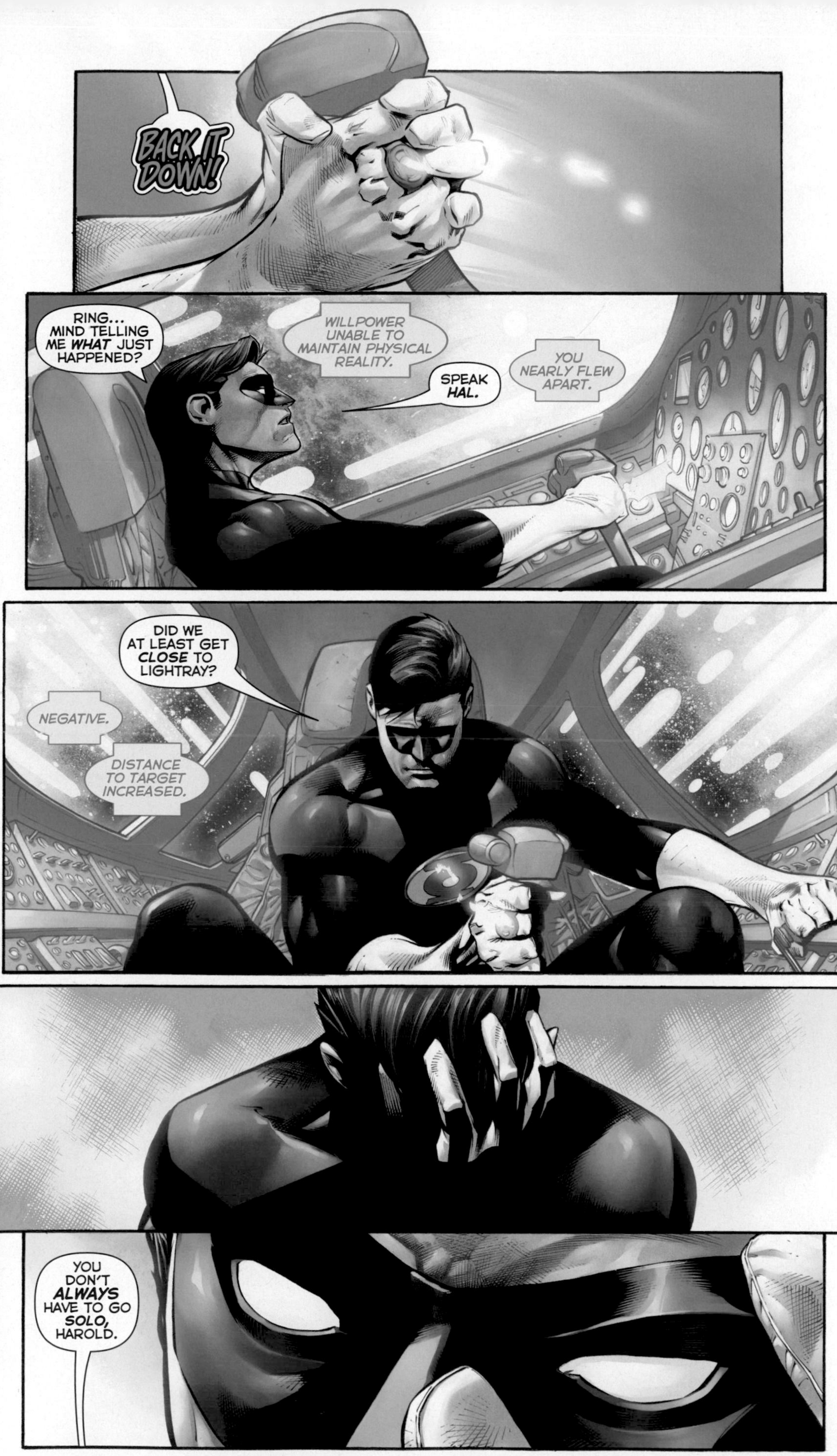
BACK IT DOWN!
RING... MIND TELLING ME WHAT JUST HAPPENED?
WILLPOWER UNABLE TO MAINTAIN PHYSICAL REALITY.
SPEAK HAL.
YOU NEARLY FLEW APART.
DID WE AT LEAST GET CLOSE TO LIGHTRAY?
NEGATIVE.
DISTANCE TO TARGET INCREASED.
YOU DON'T ALWAYS HAVE TO GO SOLO, HAROLD.

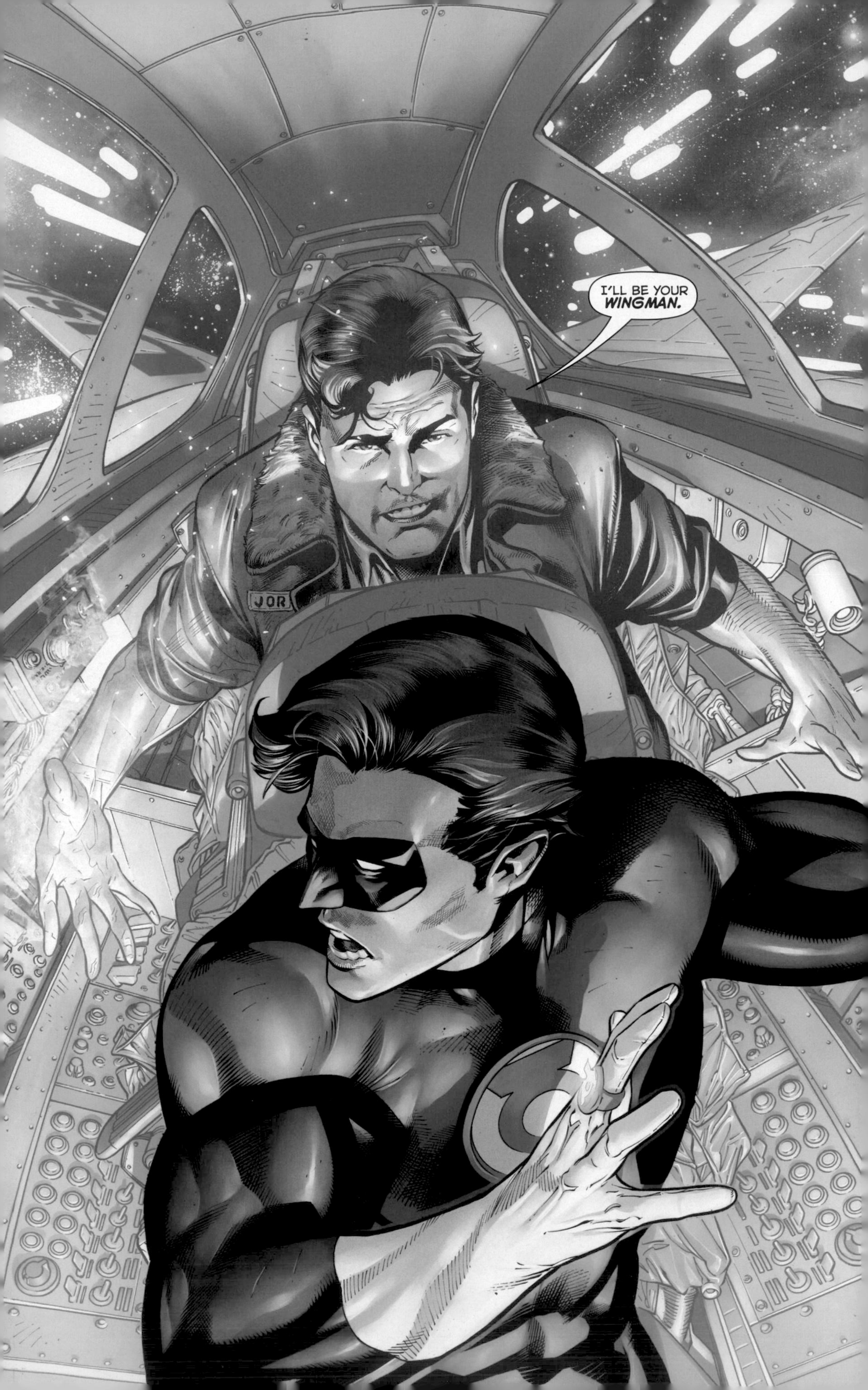
I'LL BE YOUR WINGMAN.
JOR

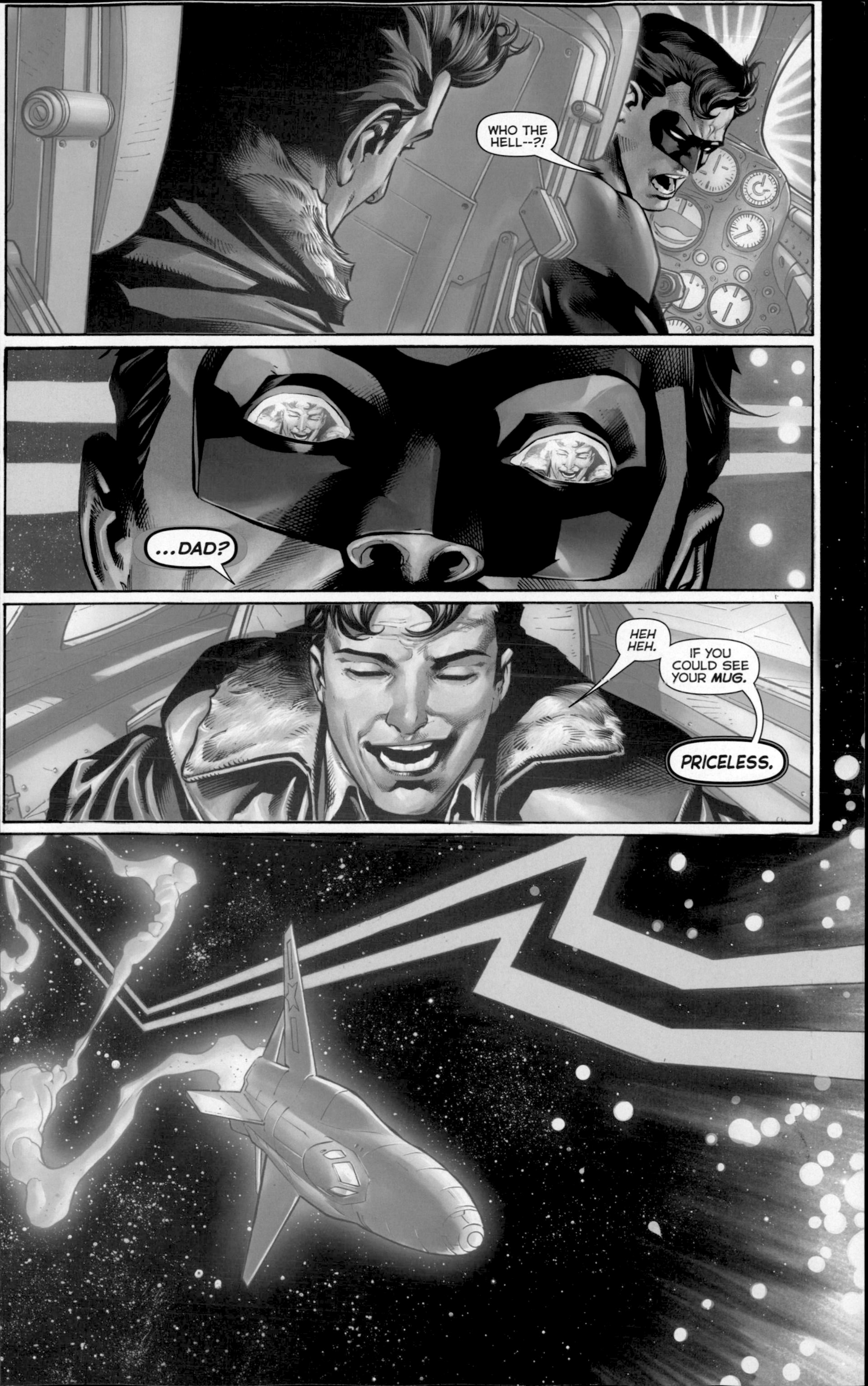
WHO THE HELL--?!
...DAD?
HEH HEH.
IF YOU COULD SEE YOUR MUG.
PRICELESS.

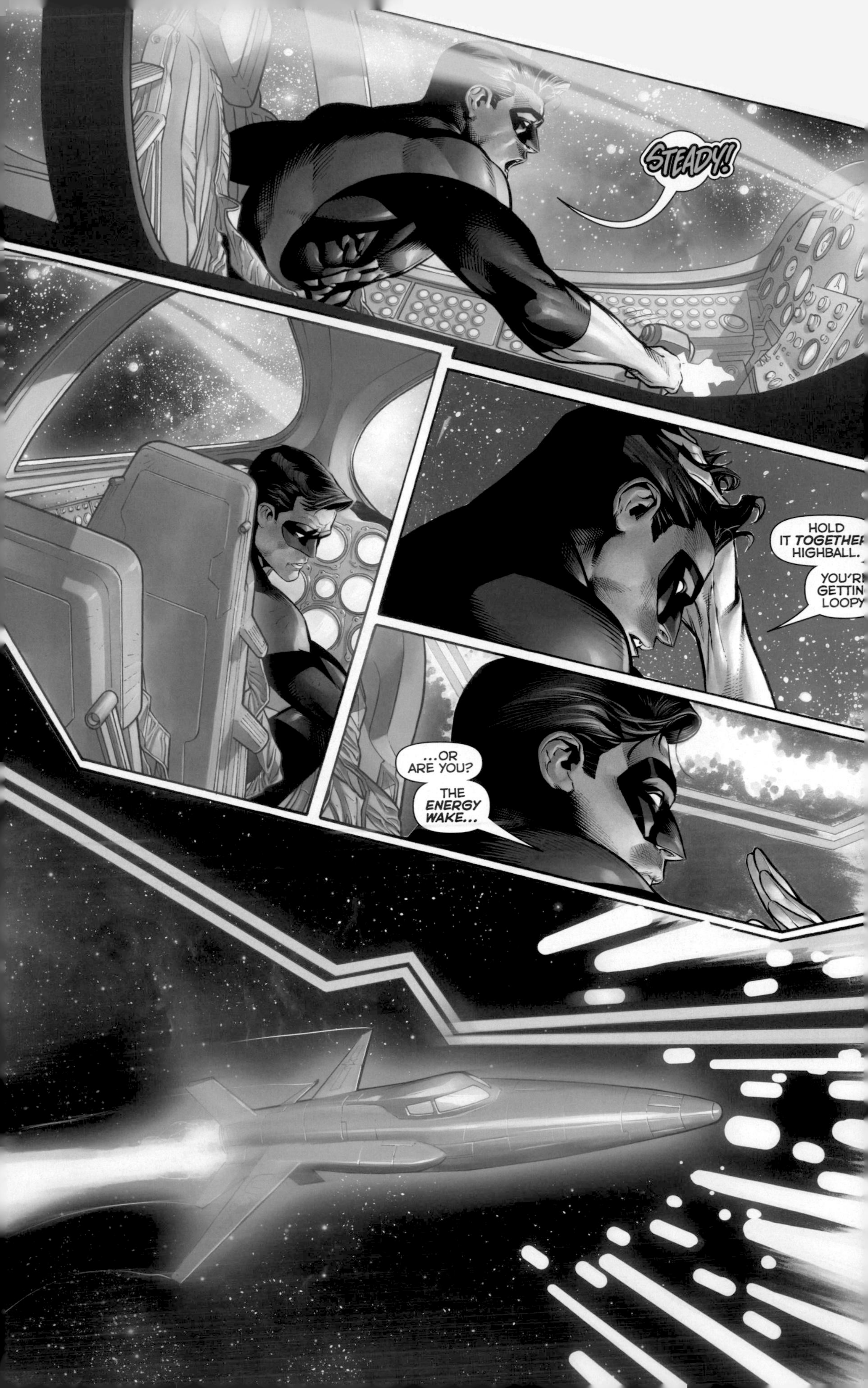
STEADY!
HOLD IT TOGETHER HIGHBALL.
YOU'RE GETTING LOOPY.
...OR ARE YOU?
THE ENERGY WAKE...

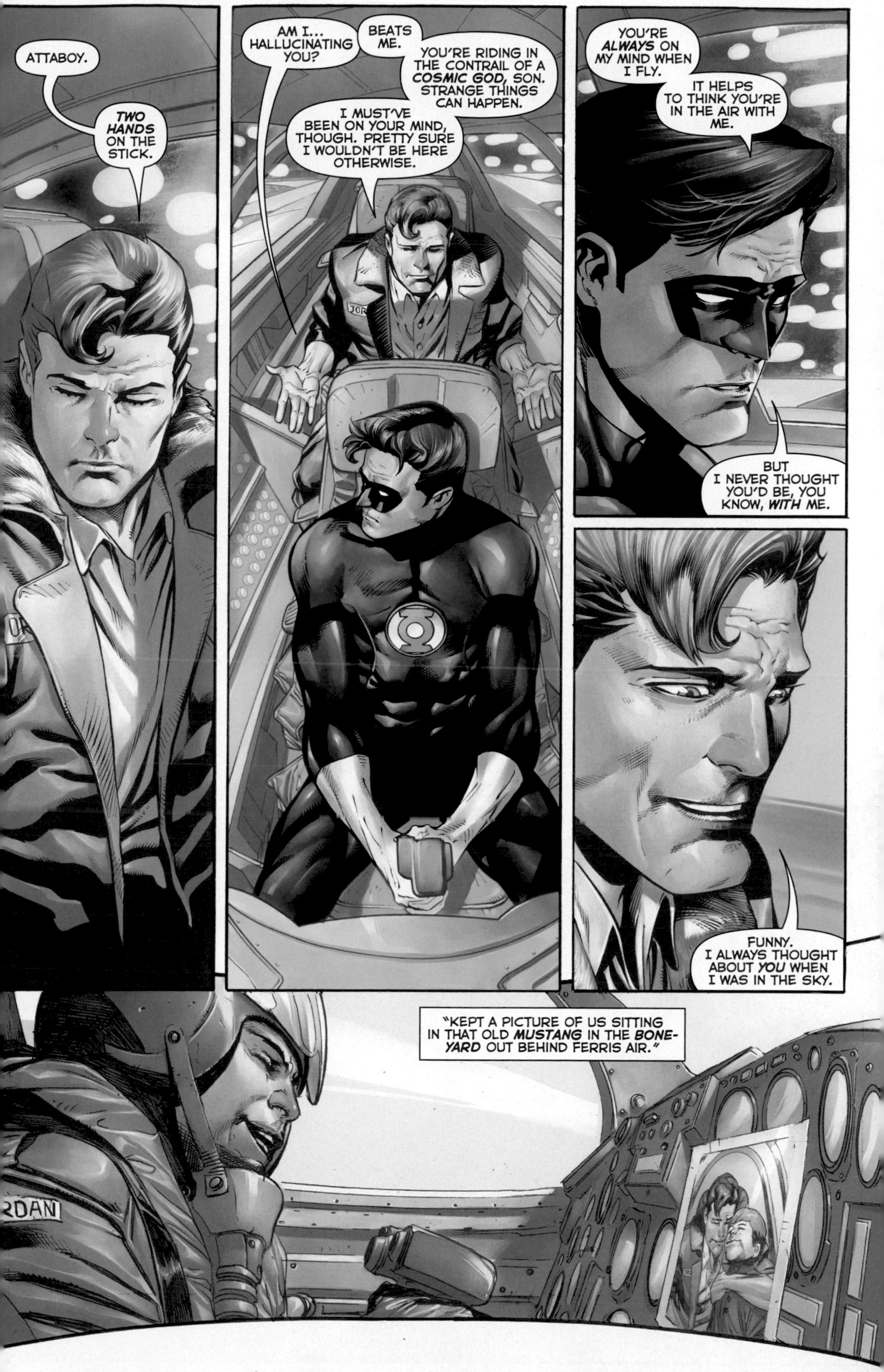

ATTABOY.
TWO HANDS ON THE STICK.
AM I... HALLUCINATING YOU?
BEATS ME.
YOU'RE RIDING IN THE CONTRAIL OF A COSMIC GOD, SON. STRANGE THINGS CAN HAPPEN.
I MUST'VE BEEN ON YOUR MIND, THOUGH. PRETTY SURE I WOULDN'T BE HERE OTHERWISE.
YOU'RE ALWAYS ON MY MIND WHEN I FLY.
IT HELPS TO THINK YOU'RE IN THE AIR WITH ME.
BUT I NEVER THOUGHT YOU'D BE, YOU KNOW, WITH ME.
FUNNY. I ALWAYS THOUGHT ABOUT YOU WHEN I WAS IN THE SKY.
"KEPT A PICTURE OF US SITTING IN THAT OLD MUSTANG IN THE BONEYARD OUT BEHIND FERRIS AIR."
RDAN

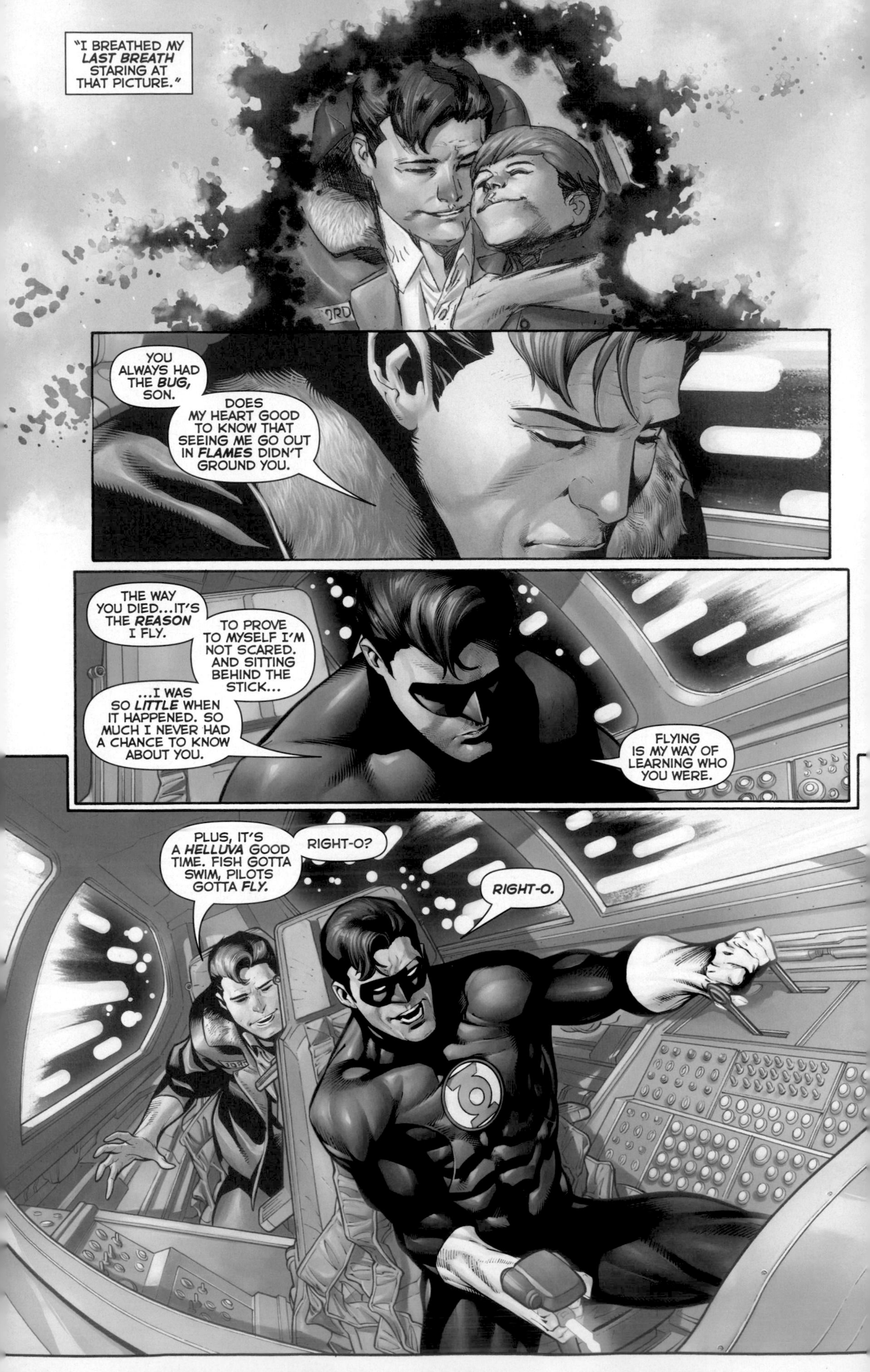
"I BREATHED MY LAST BREATH STARING AT THAT PICTURE."
YOU ALWAYS HAD THE BUG, SON.
DOES MY HEART GOOD TO KNOW THAT SEEING ME GO OUT IN FLAMES DIDN'T GROUND YOU.
THE WAY YOU DIED...IT'S THE REASON I FLY.
TO PROVE TO MYSELF I'M NOT SCARED. AND SITTING BEHIND THE STICK...
...I WAS SO LITTLE WHEN IT HAPPENED. SO MUCH I NEVER HAD A CHANCE TO KNOW ABOUT YOU.
FLYING IS MY WAY OF LEARNING WHO YOU WERE.
PLUS, IT'S A HELLUVA GOOD TIME. FISH GOTTA SWIM, PILOTS GOTTA FLY.
RIGHT-O?
RIGHT-O.

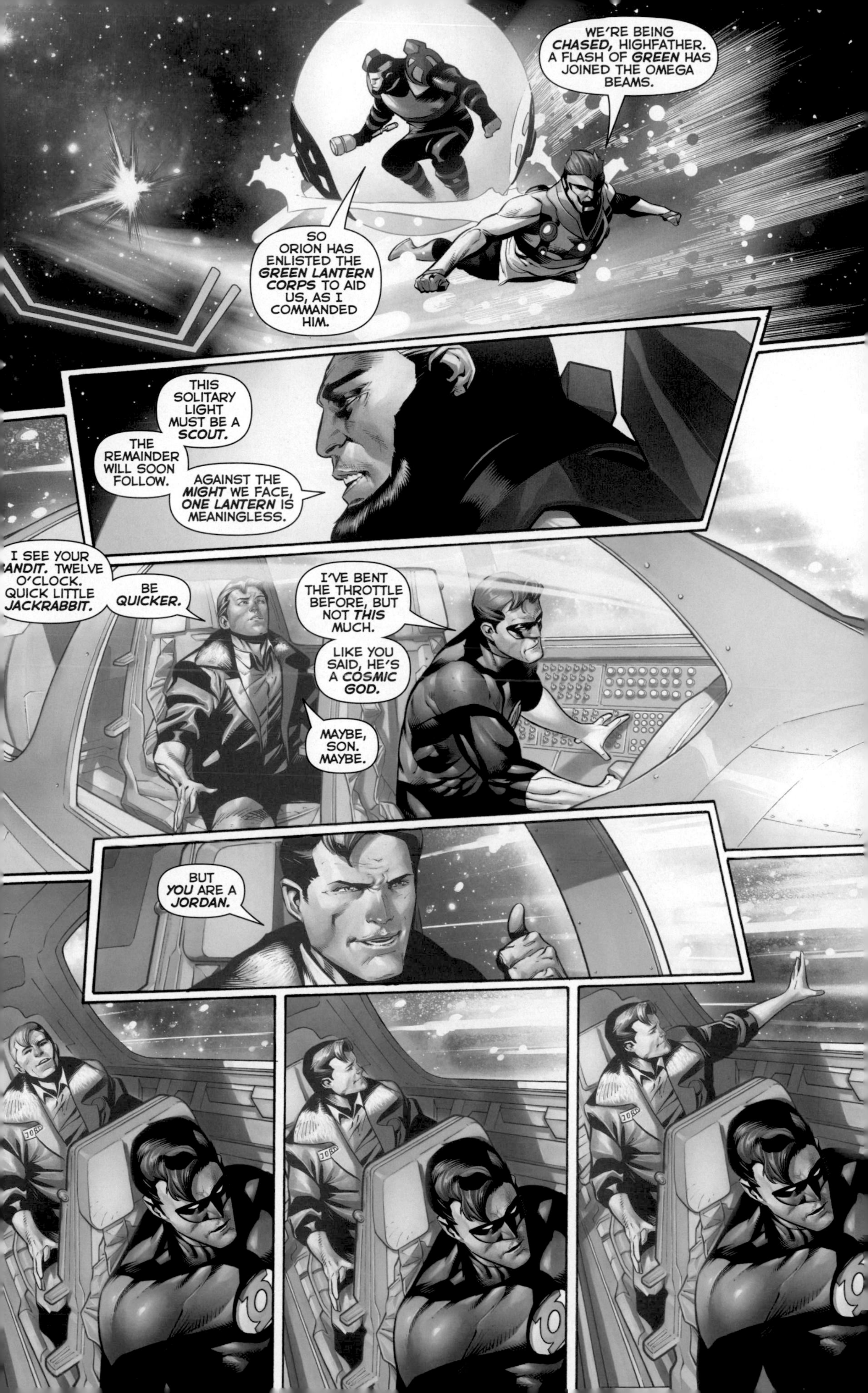
WE'RE BEING CHASED, HIGHFATHER. A FLASH OF GREEN HAS JOINED THE OMEGA BEAMS.
SO ORION HAS ENLISTED THE GREEN LANTERN CORPS TO AID US, AS I COMMANDED HIM.
THIS SOLITARY LIGHT MUST BE A SCOUT.
THE REMAINDER WILL SOON FOLLOW.
AGAINST THE MIGHT WE FACE, ONE LANTERN IS MEANINGLESS.
I SEE YOUR BANDIT. TWELVE O'CLOCK. QUICK LITTLE JACKRABBIT.
BE QUICKER.
I'VE BENT THE THROTTLE BEFORE, BUT NOT THIS MUCH.
LIKE YOU SAID, HE'S A COSMIC GOD.
MAYBE, SON. MAYBE.
BUT YOU ARE A JORDAN.

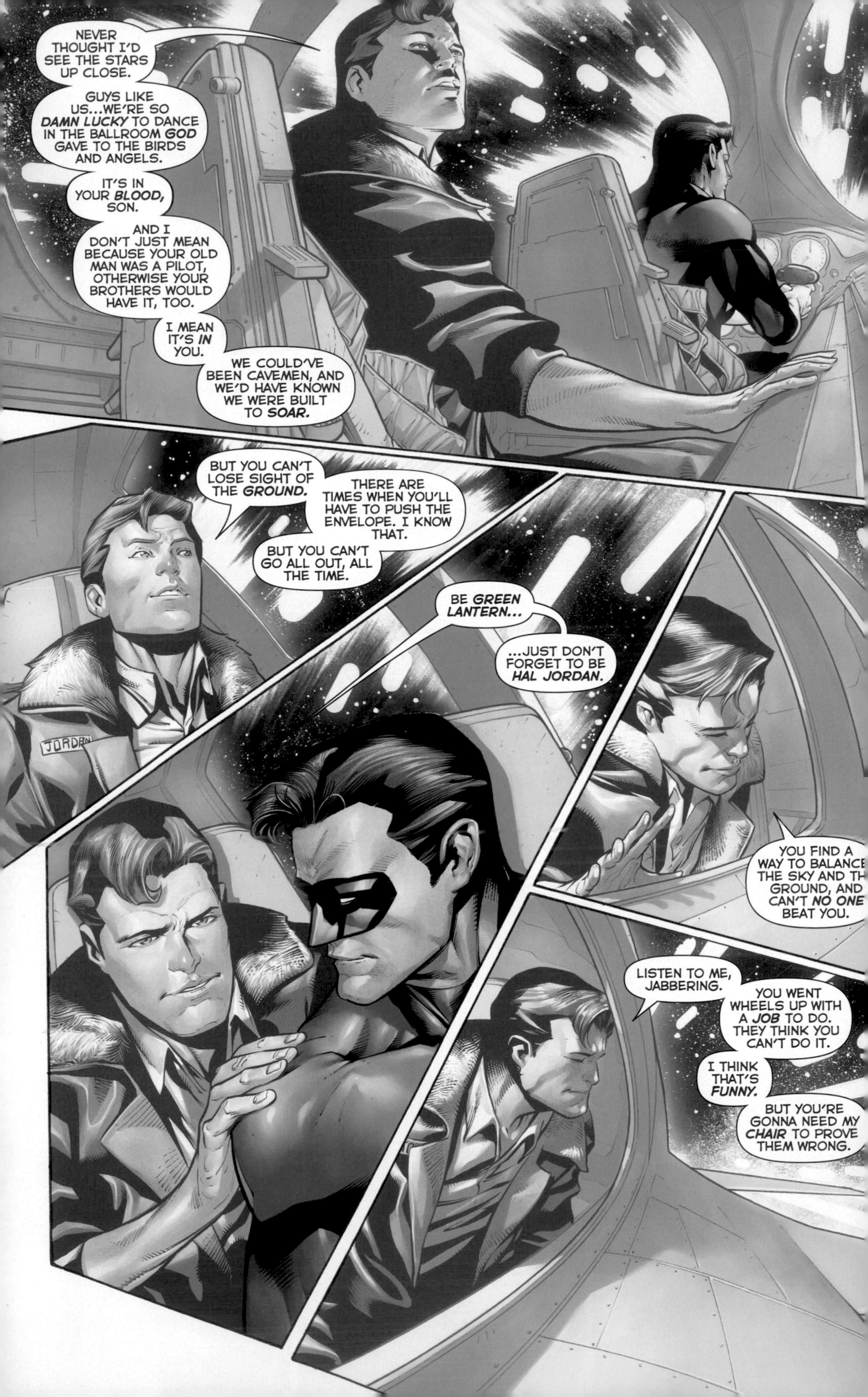
NEVER THOUGHT I'D SEE THE STARS UP CLOSE.
GUYS LIKE US...WE'RE SO DAMN LUCKY TO DANCE IN THE BALLROOM GOD GAVE TO THE BIRDS AND ANGELS.
IT'S IN YOUR BLOOD, SON.
AND I DON'T JUST MEAN BECAUSE YOUR OLD MAN WAS A PILOT, OTHERWISE YOUR BROTHERS WOULD HAVE IT, TOO.
I MEAN IT'S IN YOU.
WE COULD'VE BEEN CAVEMEN, AND WE'D HAVE KNOWN WE WERE BUILT TO SOAR.
BUT YOU CAN'T LOSE SIGHT OF THE GROUND.
THERE ARE TIMES WHEN YOU'LL HAVE TO PUSH THE ENVELOPE. I KNOW THAT.
BUT YOU CAN'T GO ALL OUT, ALL THE TIME.
JORDAN
BE GREEN LANTERN...
...JUST DON'T FORGET TO BE HAL JORDAN.
YOU FIND A WAY TO BALANCE THE SKY AND TH GROUND, AND CAN'T NO ONE BEAT YOU.
LISTEN TO ME, JABBERING.
YOU WENT WHEELS UP WITH A JOB TO DO. THEY THINK YOU CAN'T DO IT.
I THINK THAT'S FUNNY.
BUT YOU'RE GONNA NEED MY CHAIR TO PROVE THEM WRONG.

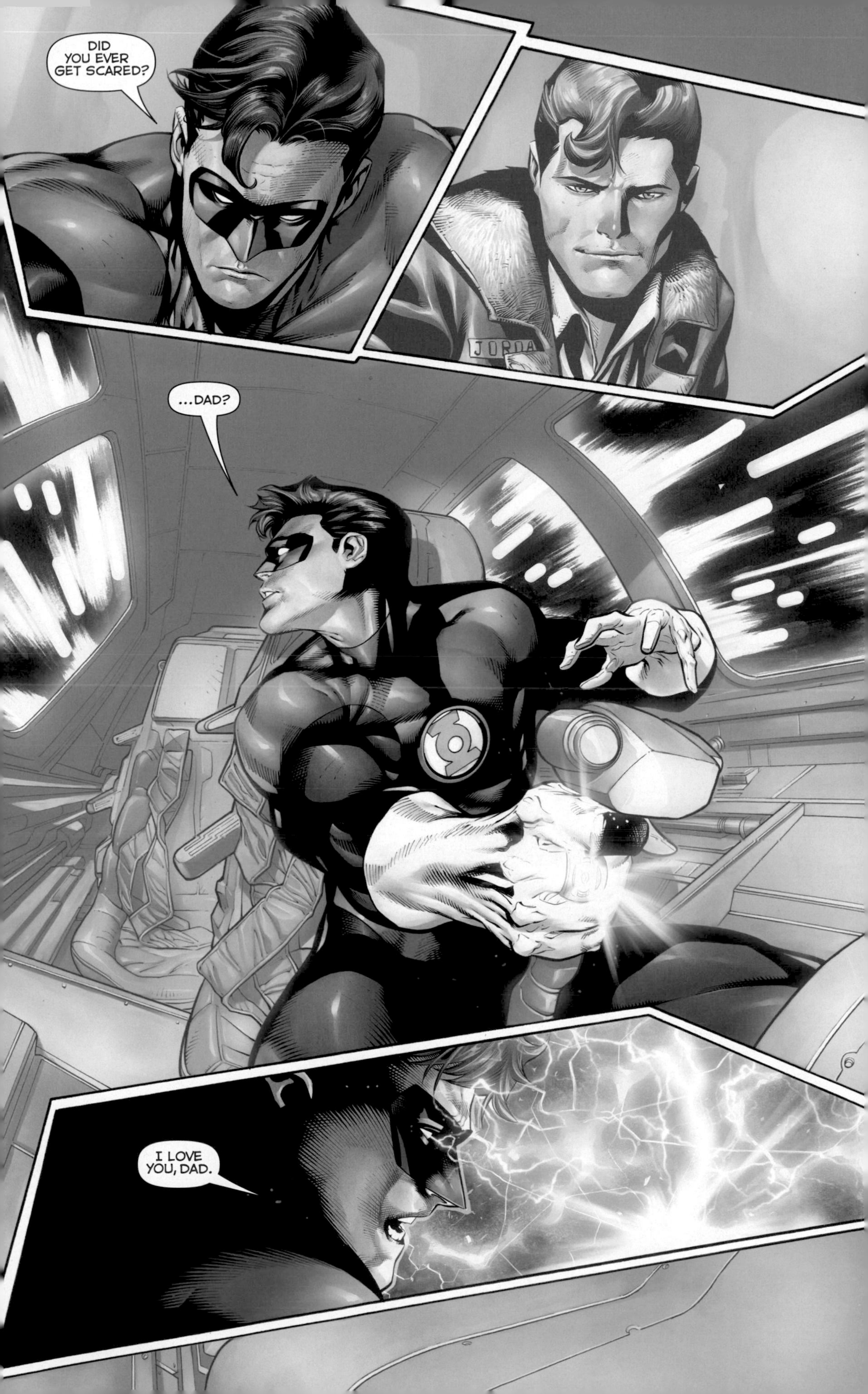
DID YOU EVER GET SCARED?
JORDA
...DAD?
I LOVE YOU, DAD.

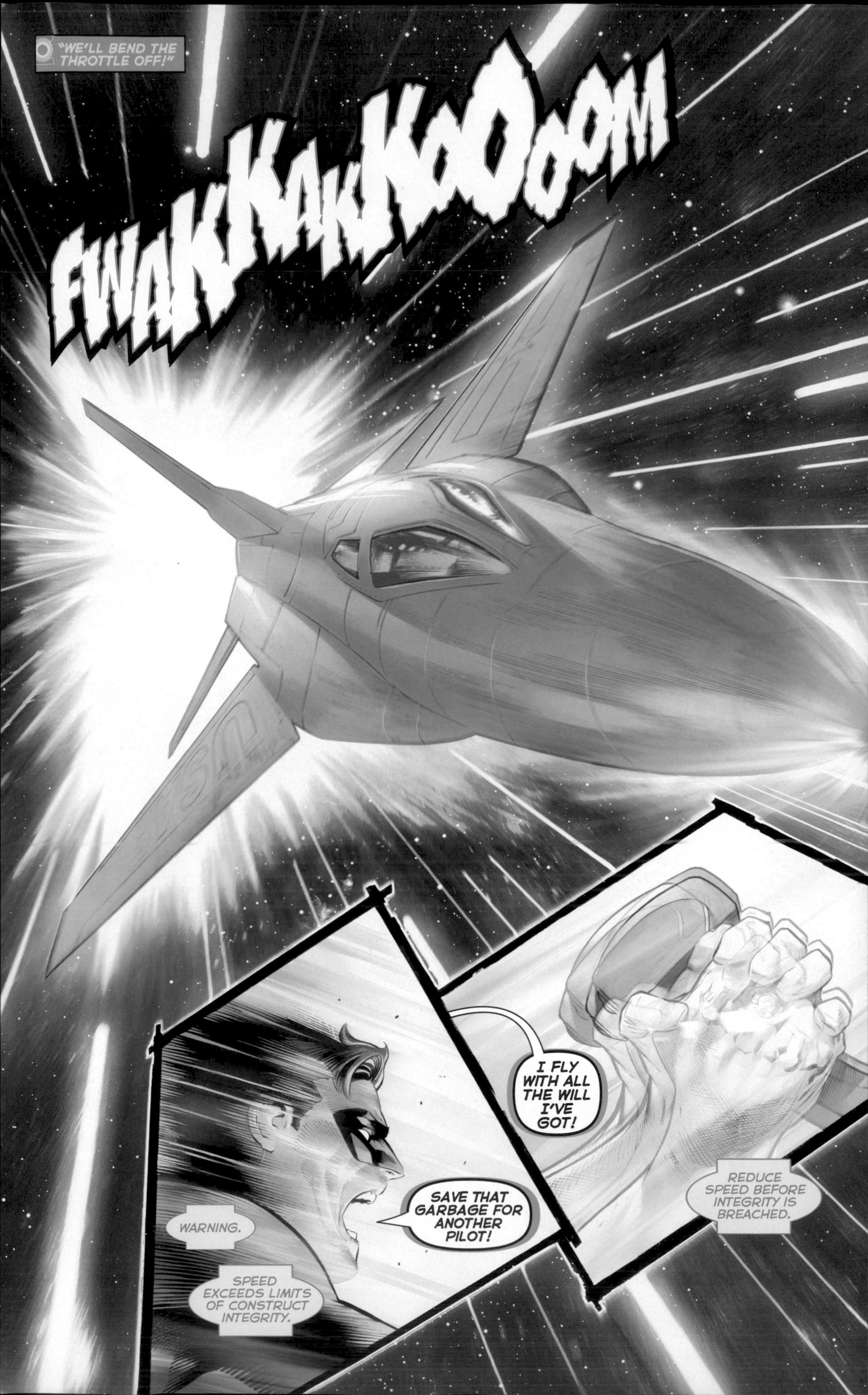
"WE'LL BEND THE THROTTLE OFF!"
FWAKKAKKAKOOOOM
I FLY WITH ALL THE WILL I'VE GOT!
REDUCE SPEED BEFORE INTEGRITY IS BREACHED.
WARNING.
SAVE THAT GARBAGE FOR ANOTHER PILOT!
SPEED EXCEEDS LIMITS OF CONSTRUCT INTEGRITY.

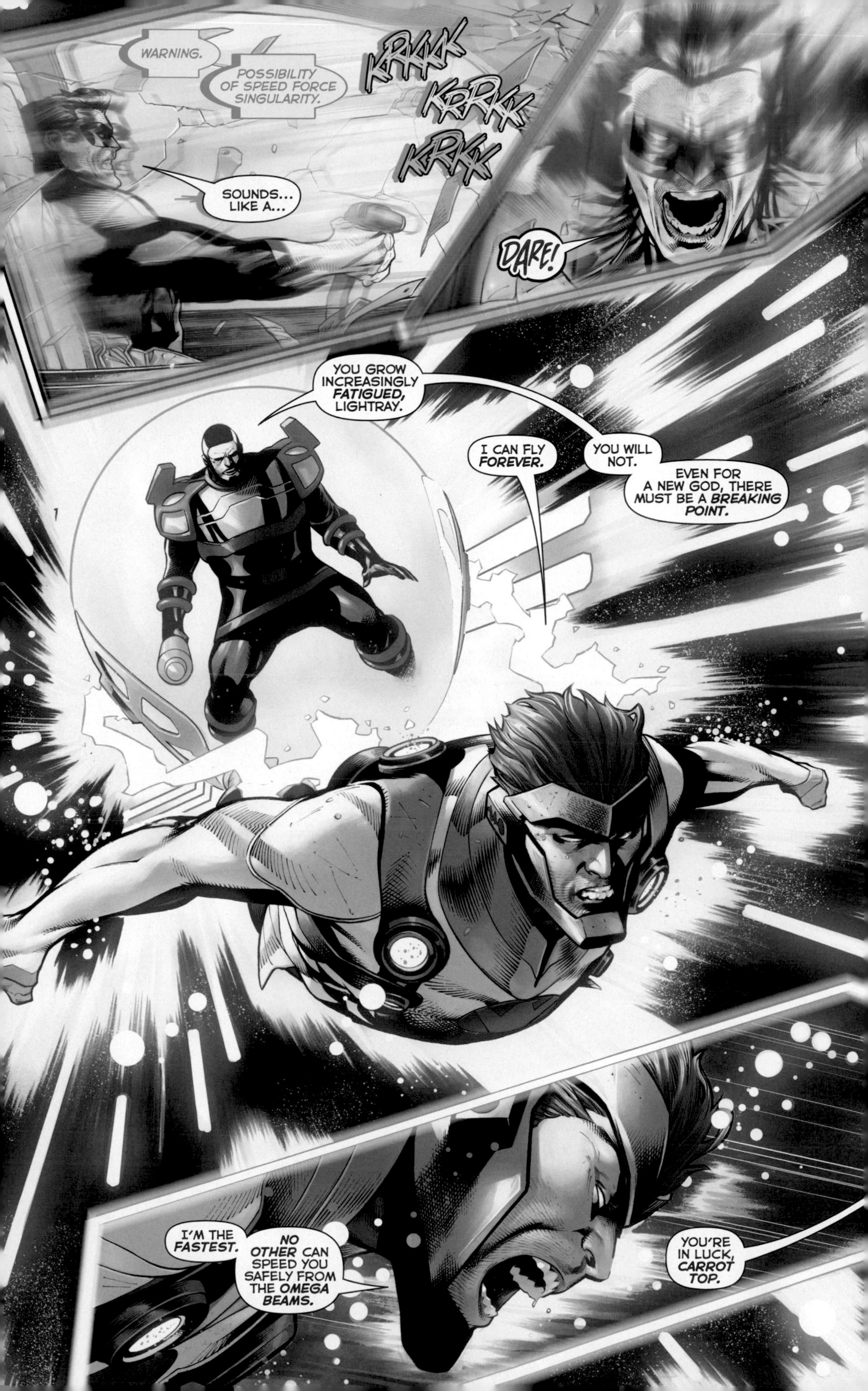
WARNING.
POSSIBILITY OF SPEED FORCE SINGULARITY.
KRAKK KRRKK KRKK
SOUNDS... LIKE A...
DARE!
YOU GROW INCREASINGLY FATIGUED, LIGHTRAY.
I CAN FLY FOREVER.
YOU WILL NOT.
EVEN FOR A NEW GOD, THERE MUST BE A BREAKING POINT.
I'M THE FASTEST.
NO OTHER CAN SPEED YOU SAFELY FROM THE OMEGA BEAMS.
YOU'RE IN LUCK, CARROT TOP.

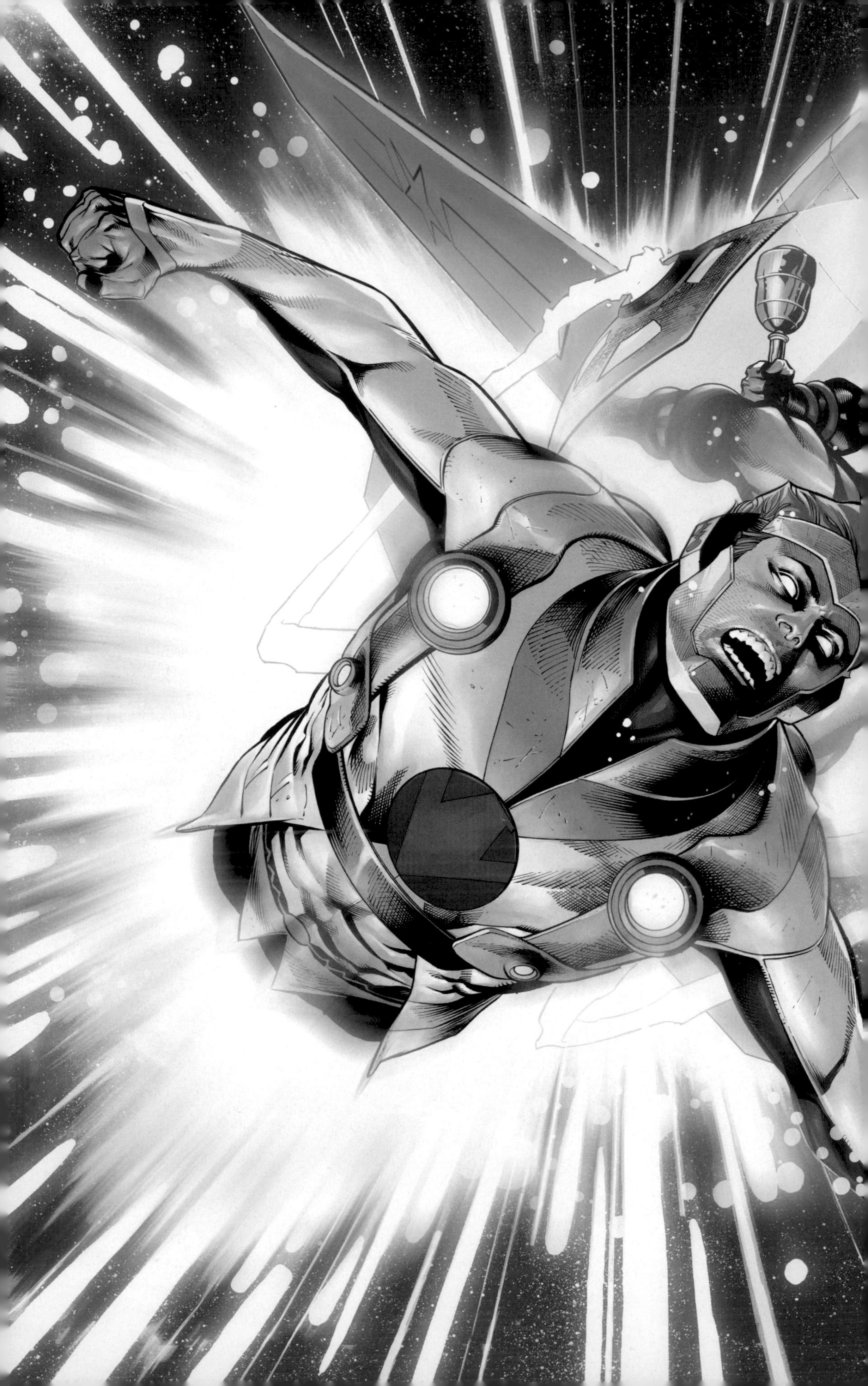

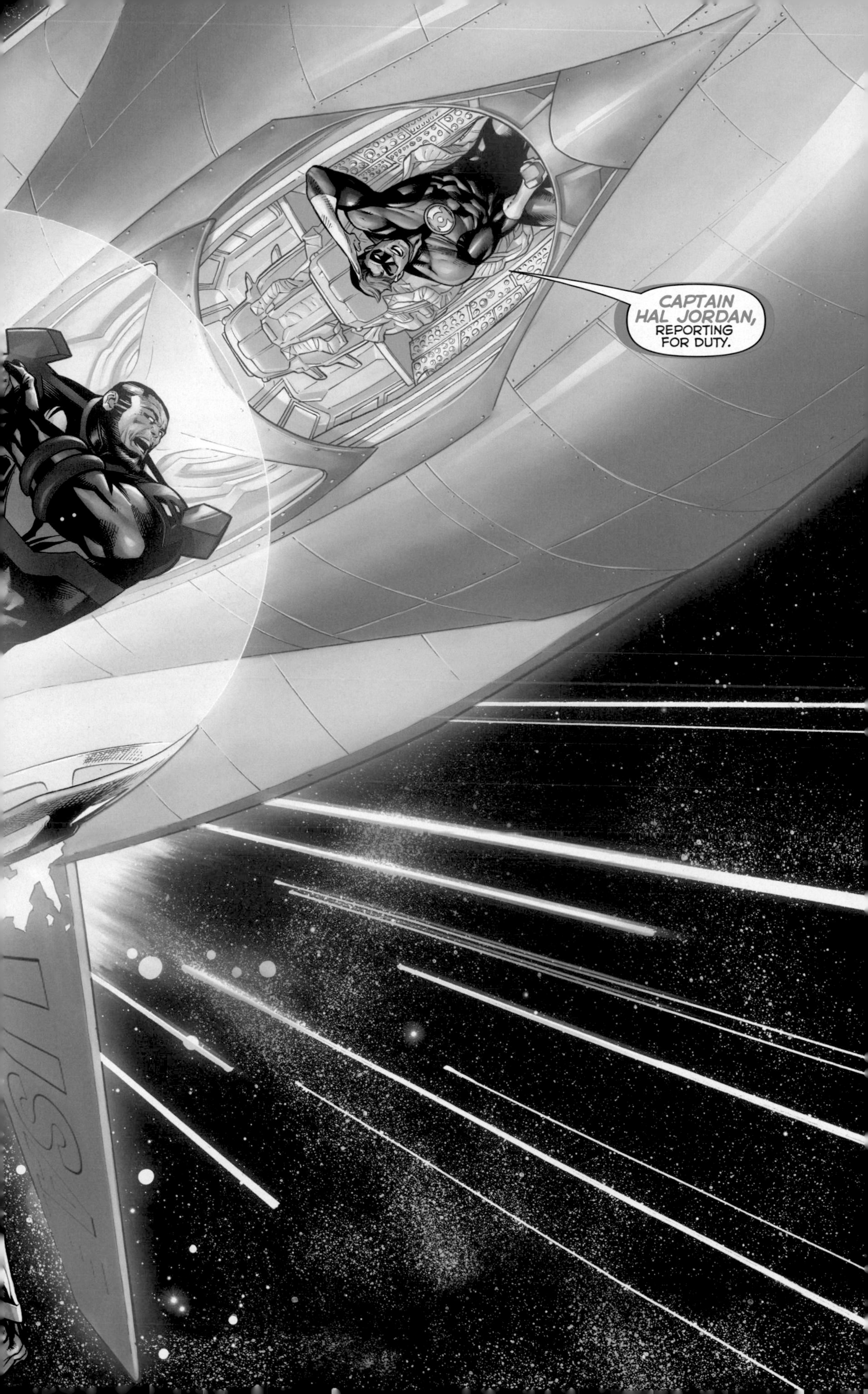
CAPTAIN HAL JORDAN, REPORTING FOR DUTY.

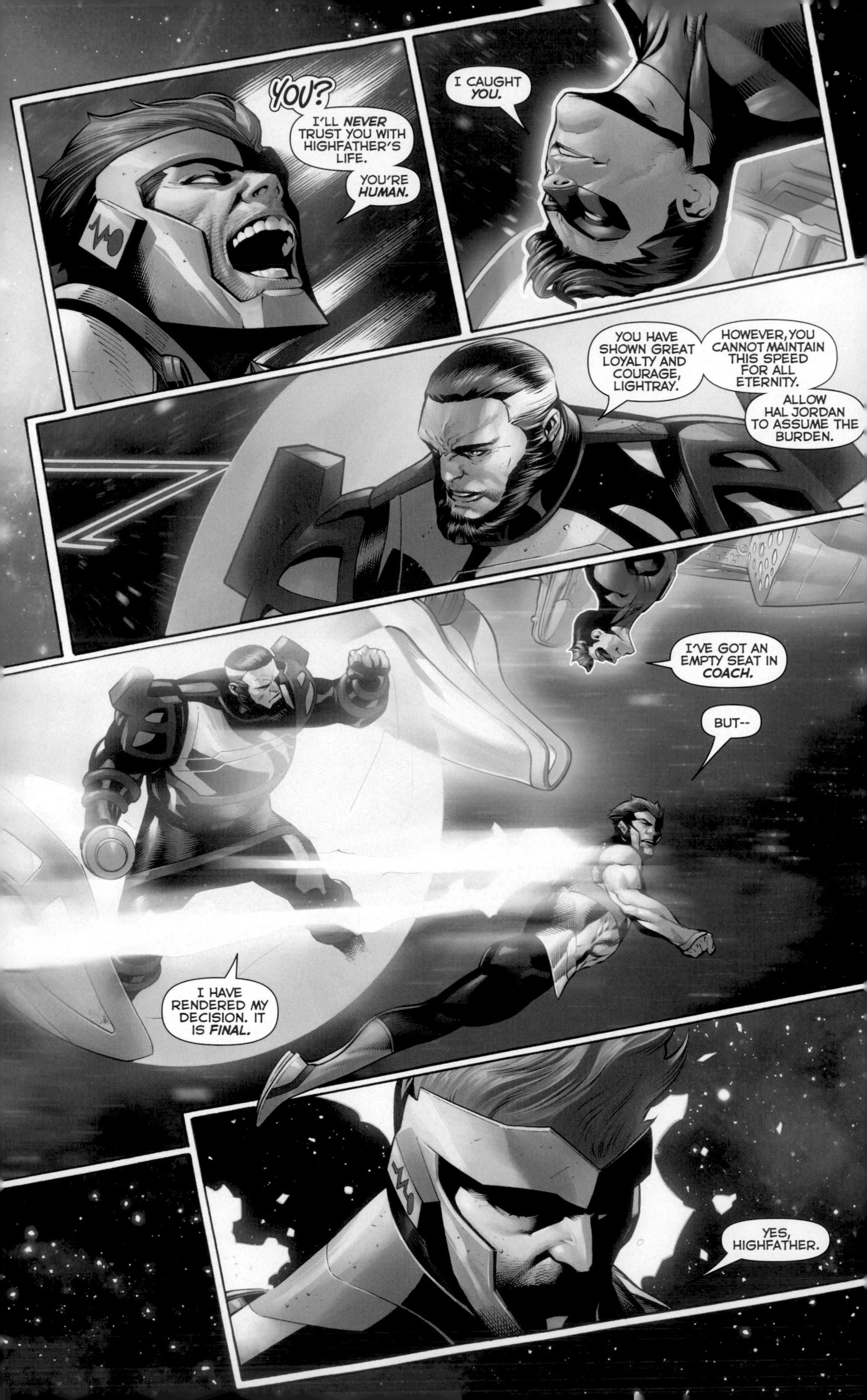
YOU?
I'LL NEVER TRUST YOU WITH HIGHFATHER'S LIFE.
YOU'RE HUMAN.
I CAUGHT YOU.
YOU HAVE SHOWN GREAT LOYALTY AND COURAGE, LIGHTRAY.
HOWEVER, YOU CANNOT MAINTAIN THIS SPEED FOR ALL ETERNITY.
ALLOW HAL JORDAN TO ASSUME THE BURDEN.
I'VE GOT AN EMPTY SEAT IN COACH.
BUT--
I HAVE RENDERED MY DECISION. IT IS FINAL.
YES, HIGHFATHER.

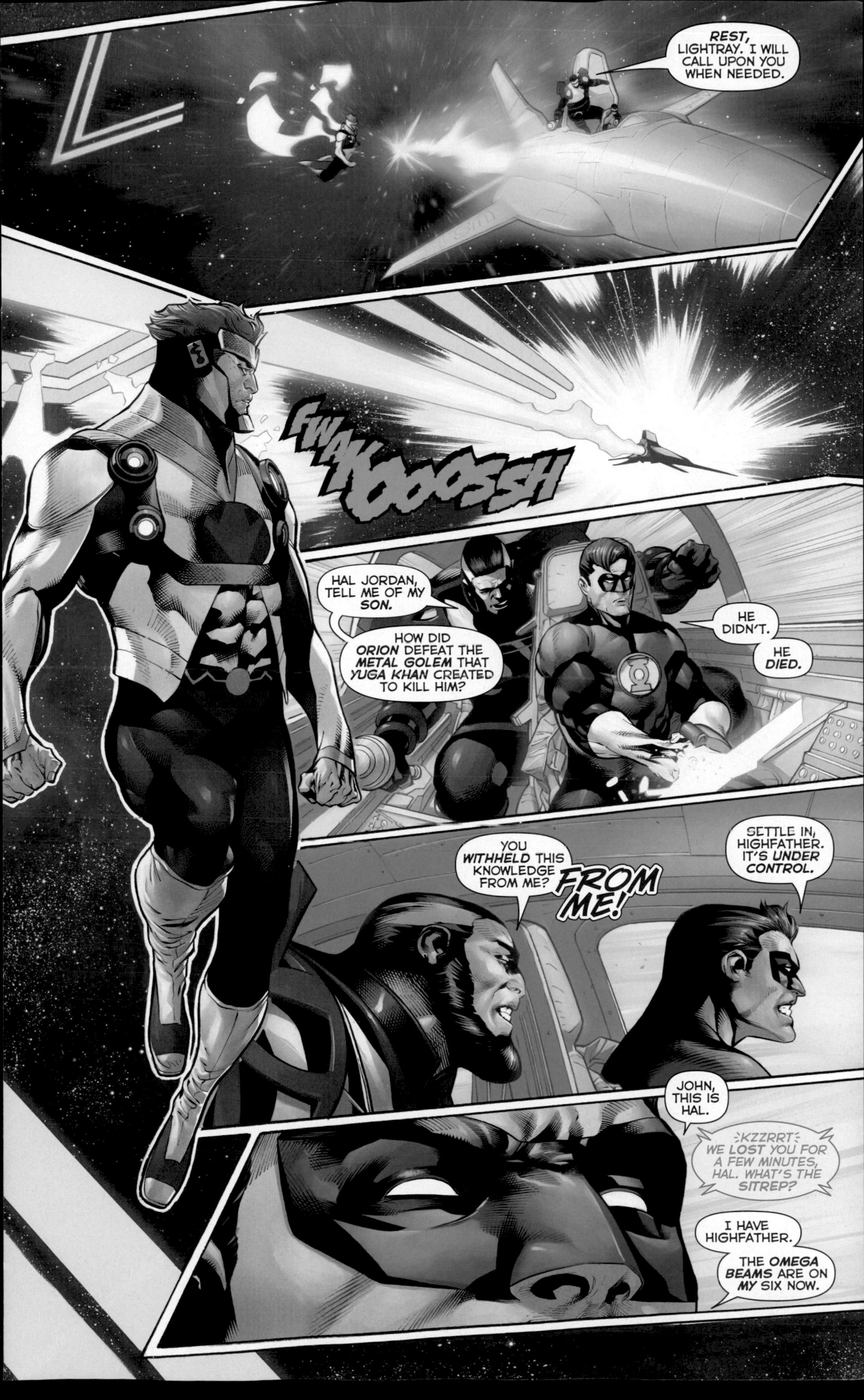
REST, LIGHTRAY. I WILL CALL UPON YOU WHEN NEEDED.
FWAKOOOSSH
HAL JORDAN, TELL ME OF MY SON.
HOW DID ORION DEFEAT THE METAL GOLEM THAT YUGA KHAN CREATED TO KILL HIM?
HE DIDN'T.
HE DIED.
YOU WITHHELD THIS KNOWLEDGE FROM ME? FROM ME!
SETTLE IN, HIGHFATHER. IT'S UNDER CONTROL.
JOHN, THIS IS HAL.
KZZRRT WE LOST YOU FOR A FEW MINUTES, HAL. WHAT'S THE SITREP?
I HAVE HIGHFATHER.
THE OMEGA BEAMS ARE ON MY SIX NOW.

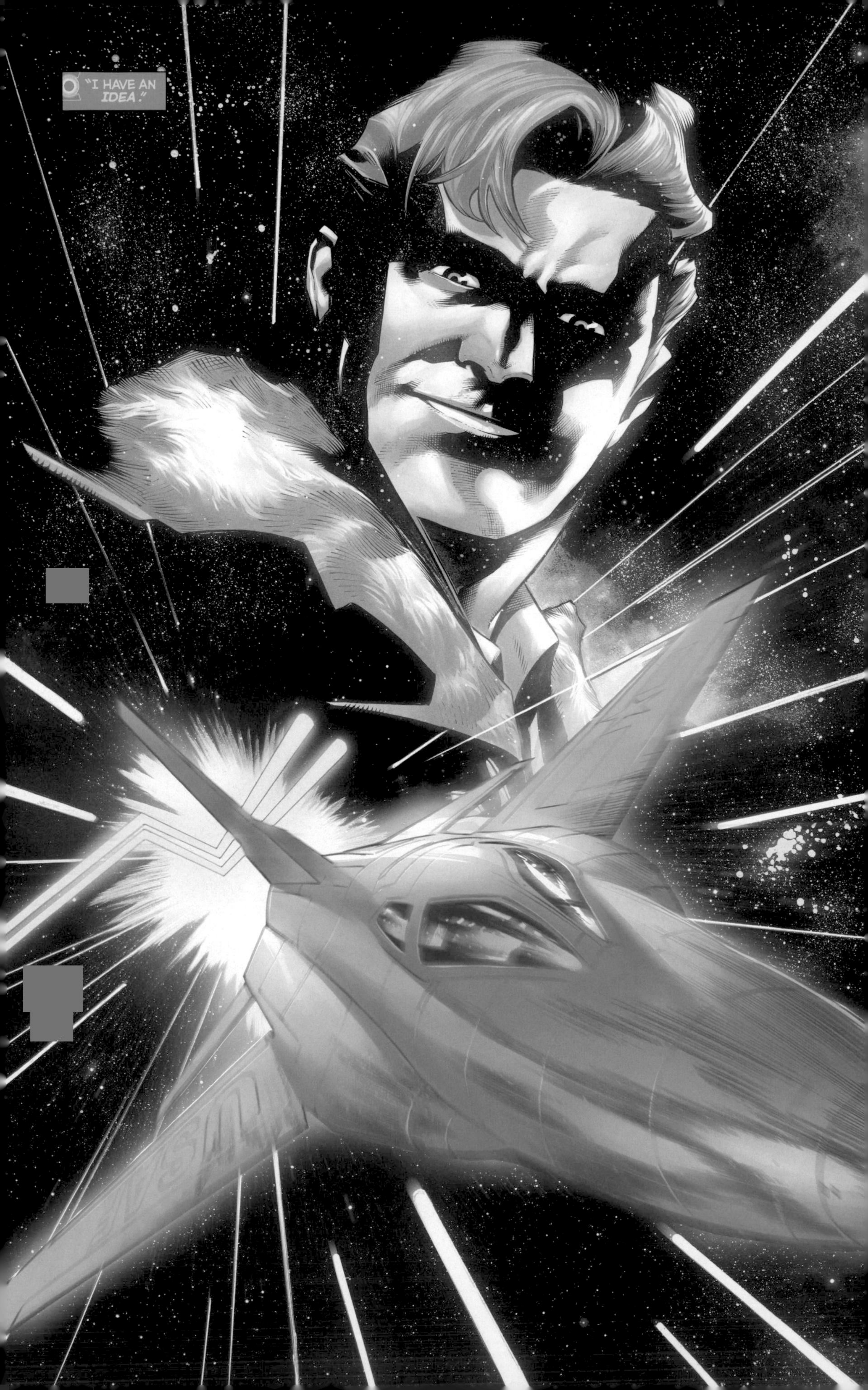
"I HAVE AN IDEA."

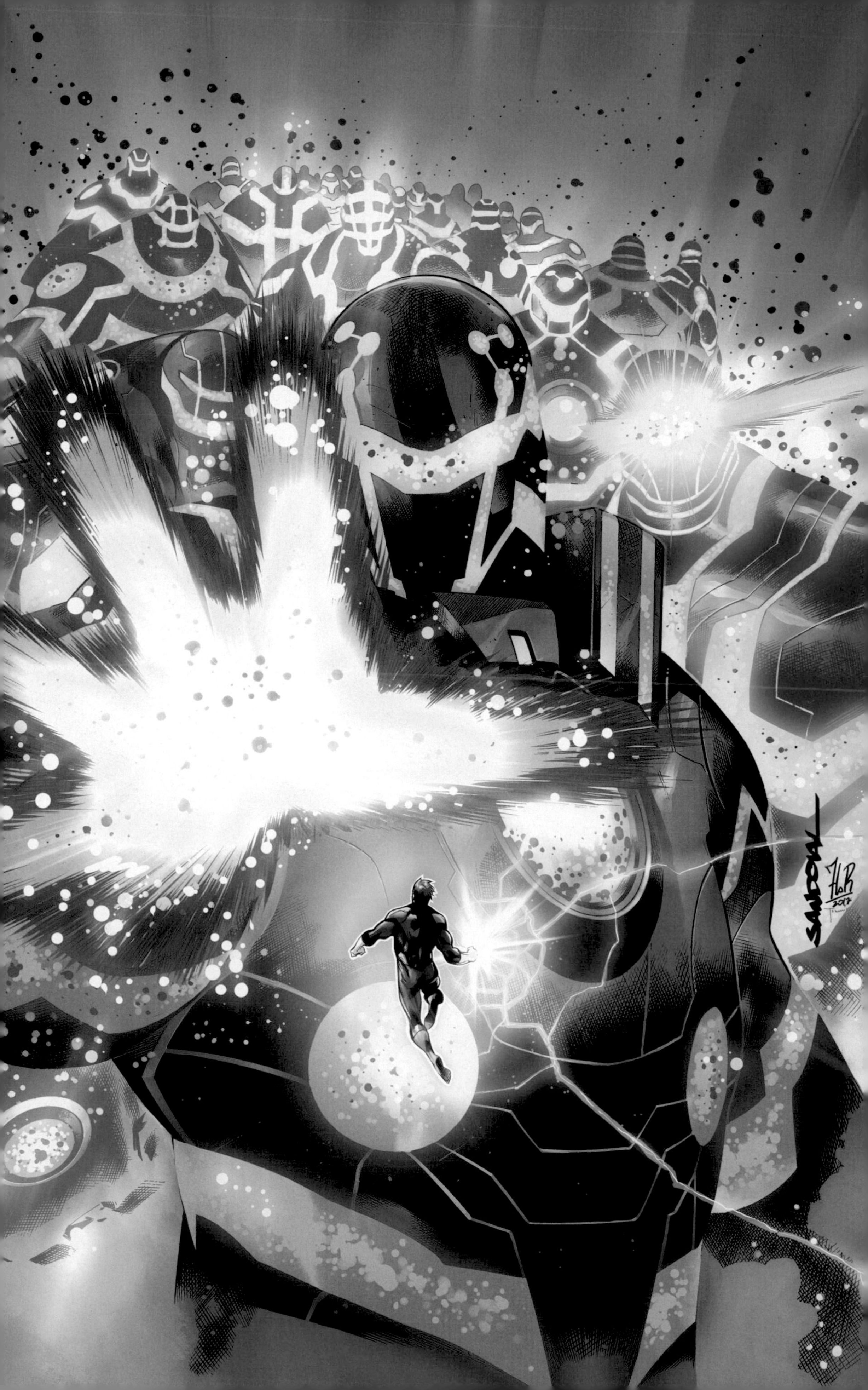

“FALL OF THE GODS PART FOUR: THE DEAD WILL RISE

RAFA SANDOVAL penciller * JORDI TARRAGONA inker * TOMEU MOREY colorist

cover art by RAFA SANDOVAL, JORDI TARRAGONA, and TOMEU MOREY

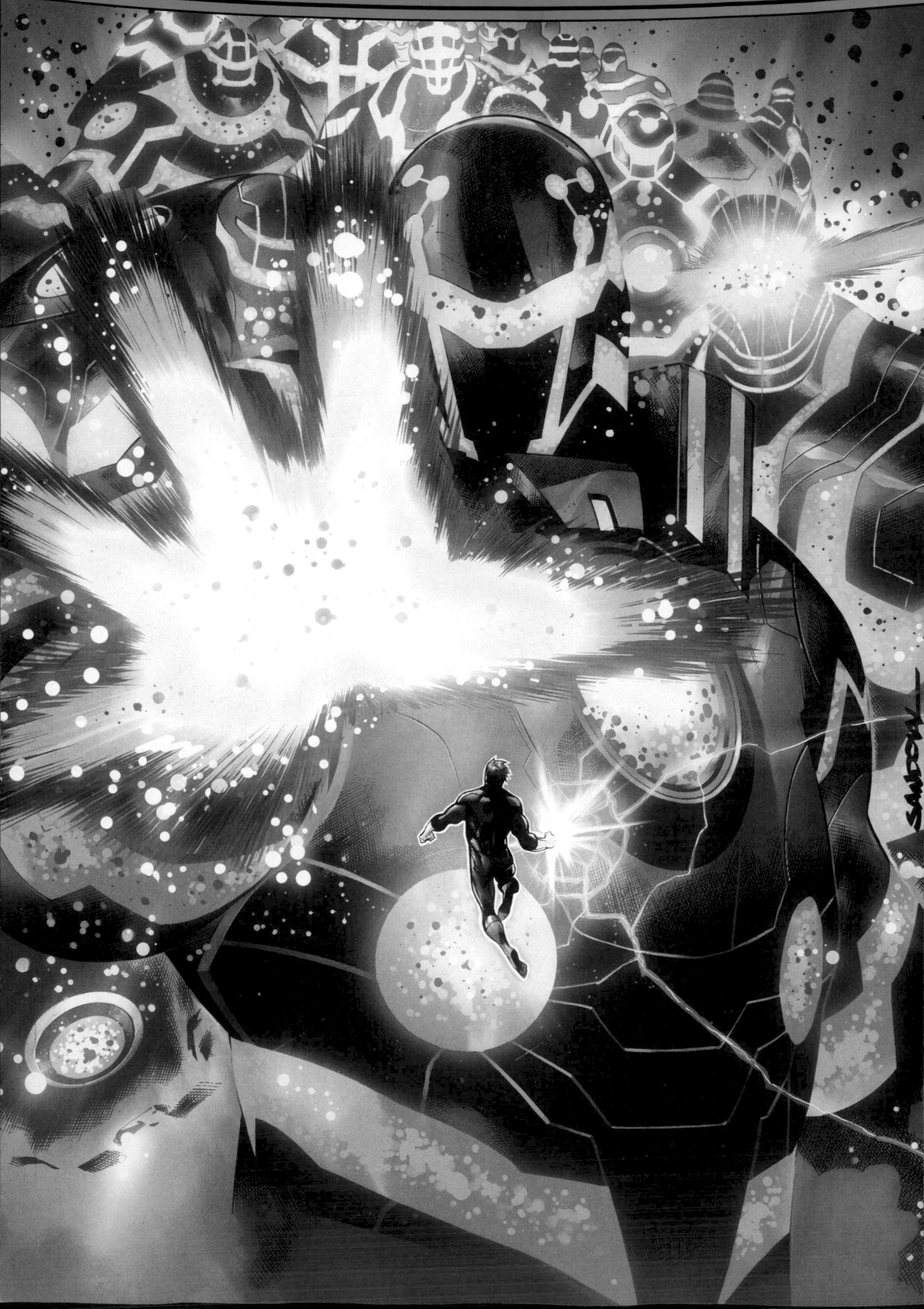

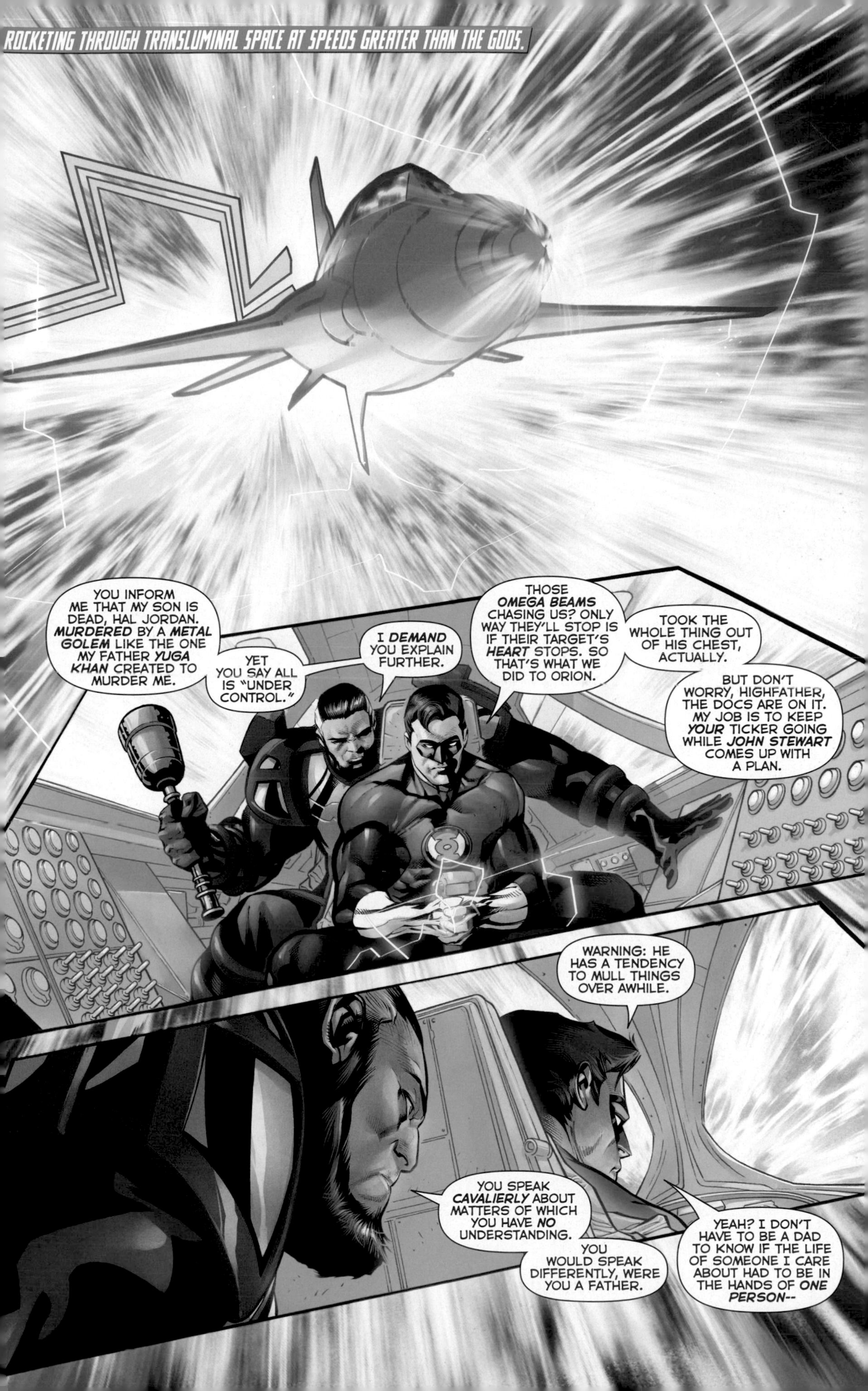
ROCKETING THROUGH TRANSLUMINAL SPACE AT SPEEDS GREATER THAN THE GODS.
YOU INFORM ME THAT MY SON IS DEAD, HAL JORDAN. MURDERED BY A METAL GOLEM LIKE THE ONE MY FATHER YUGA KHAN CREATED TO MURDER ME.
YET YOU SAY ALL IS "UNDER CONTROL."
I DEMAND YOU EXPLAIN FURTHER.
THOSE OMEGA BEAMS CHASING US? ONLY WAY THEY'LL STOP IS IF THEIR TARGET'S HEART STOPS. SO THAT'S WHAT WE DID TO ORION.
TOOK THE WHOLE THING OUT OF HIS CHEST, ACTUALLY.
BUT DON'T WORRY, HIGHFATHER, THE DOCS ARE ON IT. MY JOB IS TO KEEP YOUR TICKER GOING WHILE JOHN STEWART COMES UP WITH A PLAN.
WARNING: HE HAS A TENDENCY TO MULL THINGS OVER AWHILE.
YOU SPEAK CAVALIERLY ABOUT MATTERS OF WHICH YOU HAVE NO UNDERSTANDING.
YOU WOULD SPEAK DIFFERENTLY, WERE YOU A FATHER.
YEAH? I DON'T HAVE TO BE A DAD TO KNOW IF THE LIFE OF SOMEONE I CARE ABOUT HAD TO BE IN THE HANDS OF ONE PERSON--

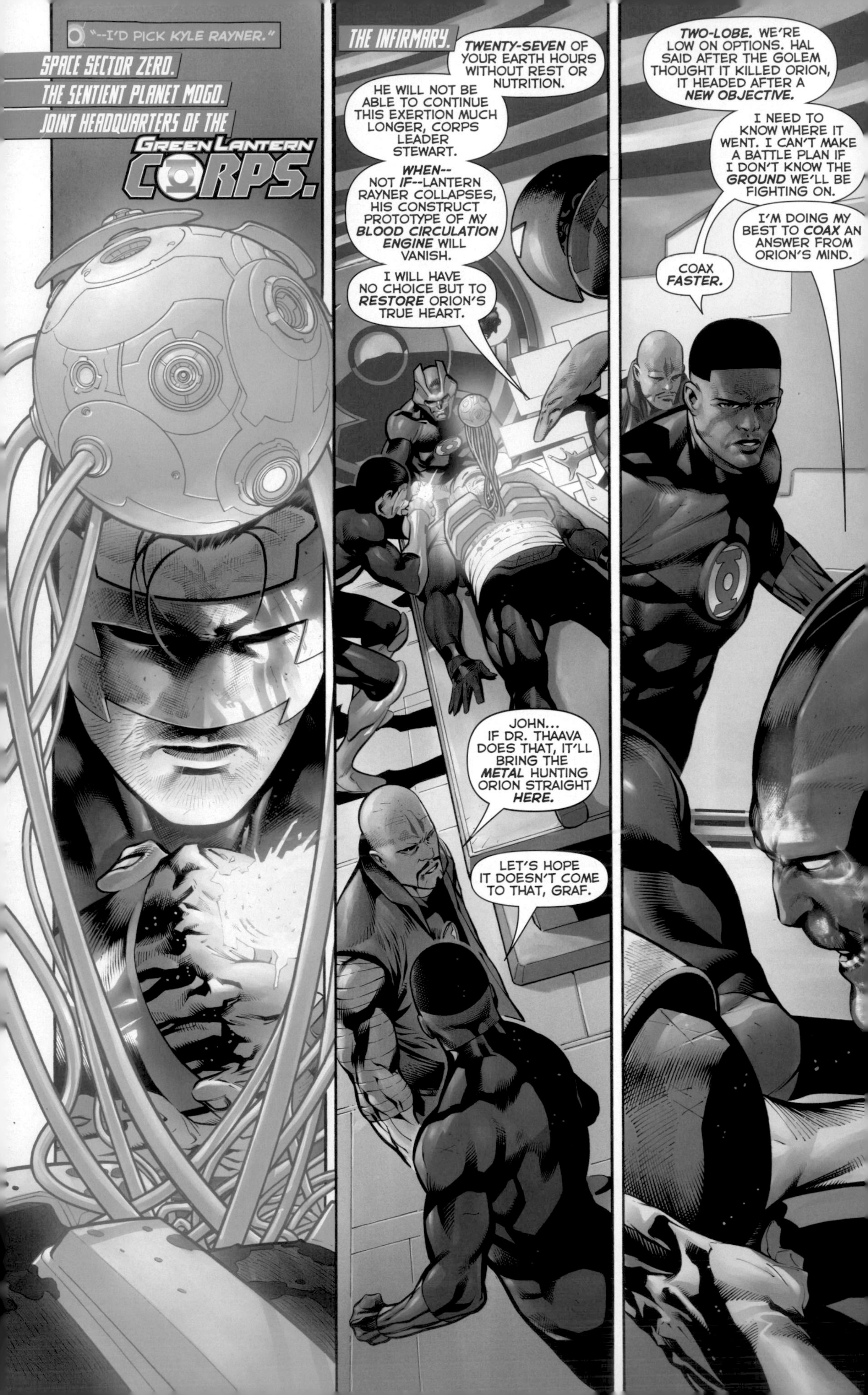
"--I'D PICK KYLE RAYNER."
SPACE SECTOR ZERO.
THE SENTIENT PLANET MOGO.
JOINT HEADQUARTERS OF THE
GREEN LANTERN CORPS.
THE INFIRMARY.
TWENTY-SEVEN OF YOUR EARTH HOURS WITHOUT REST OR NUTRITION.
HE WILL NOT BE ABLE TO CONTINUE THIS EXERTION MUCH LONGER, CORPS LEADER STEWART.
WHEN--NOT IF--LANTERN RAYNER COLLAPSES, HIS CONSTRUCT PROTOTYPE OF MY BLOOD CIRCULATION ENGINE WILL VANISH.
I WILL HAVE NO CHOICE BUT TO RESTORE ORION'S TRUE HEART.
JOHN... IF DR. THAAVA DOES THAT, IT'LL BRING THE METAL HUNTING ORION STRAIGHT HERE.
LET'S HOPE IT DOESN'T COME TO THAT, GRAF.
TWO-LOBE. WE'RE LOW ON OPTIONS. HAL SAID AFTER THE GOLEM THOUGHT IT KILLED ORION, IT HEADED AFTER A NEW OBJECTIVE.
I NEED TO KNOW WHERE IT WENT. I CAN'T MAKE A BATTLE PLAN IF I DON'T KNOW THE GROUND WE'LL BE FIGHTING ON.
I'M DOING MY BEST TO COAX AN ANSWER FROM ORION'S MIND.
COAX FASTER.

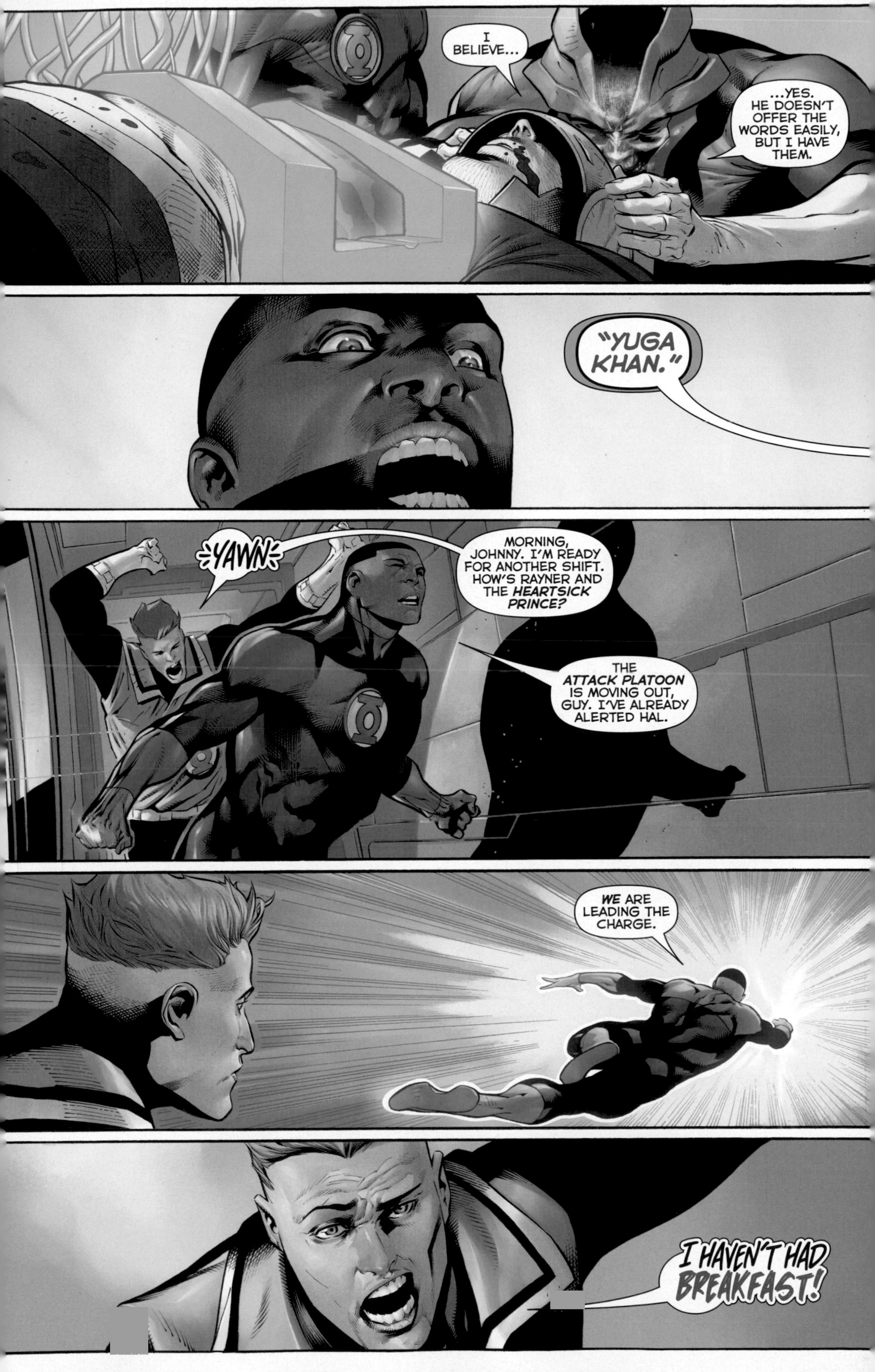
I BELIEVE...
...YES. HE DOESN'T OFFER THE WORDS EASILY, BUT I HAVE THEM.
"YUGA KHAN."
YAWN
MORNING, JOHNNY. I'M READY FOR ANOTHER SHIFT. HOW'S RAYNER AND THE HEARTSICK PRINCE?
THE ATTACK PLATOON IS MOVING OUT, GUY. I'VE ALREADY ALERTED HAL.
WE ARE LEADING THE CHARGE.
I HAVEN'T HAD BREAKFAST!

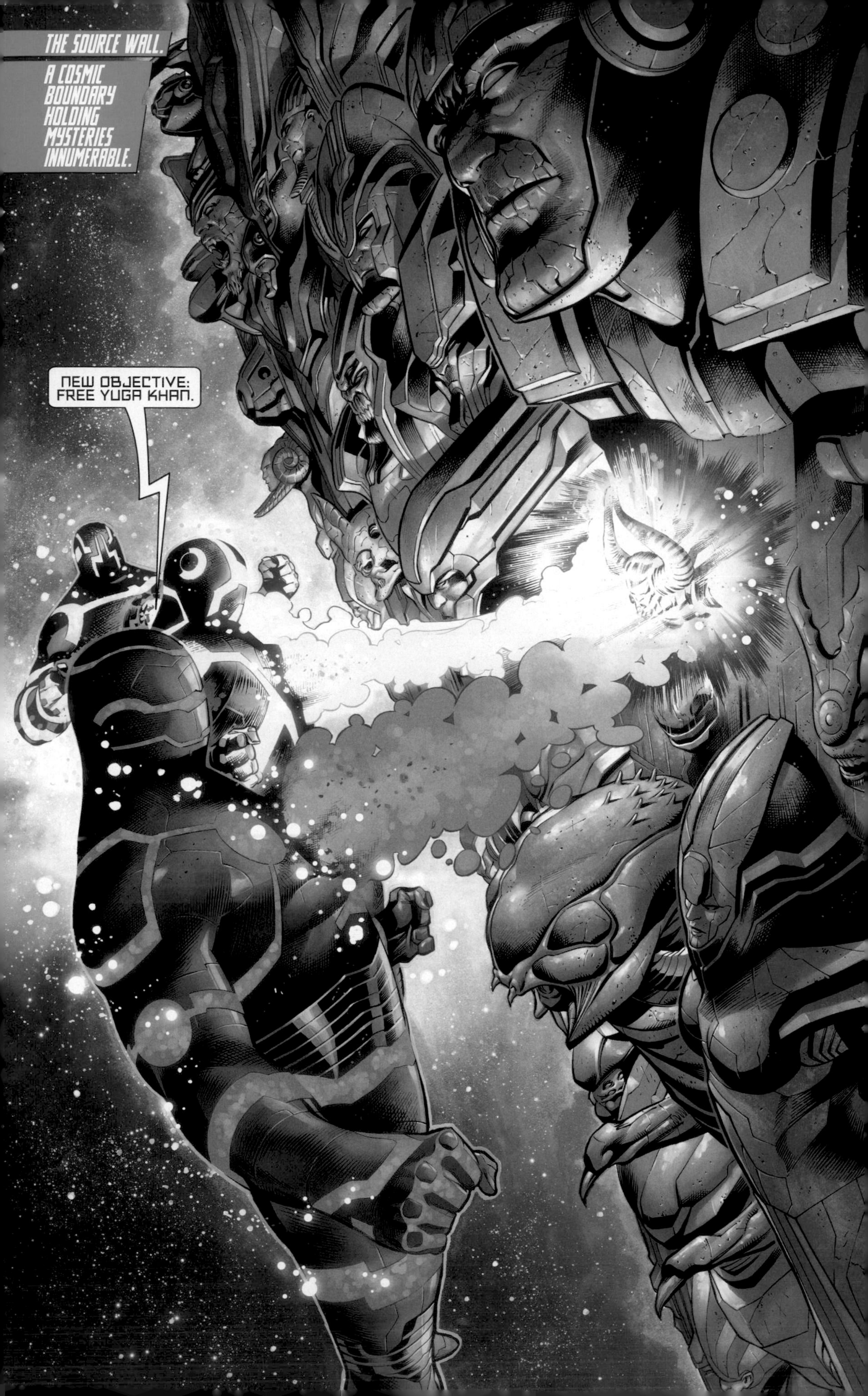
THE SOURCE WALL.
A COSMIC BOUNDARY HOLDING MYSTERIES INNUMERABLE.
NEW OBJECTIVE: FREE YUGA KHAN.

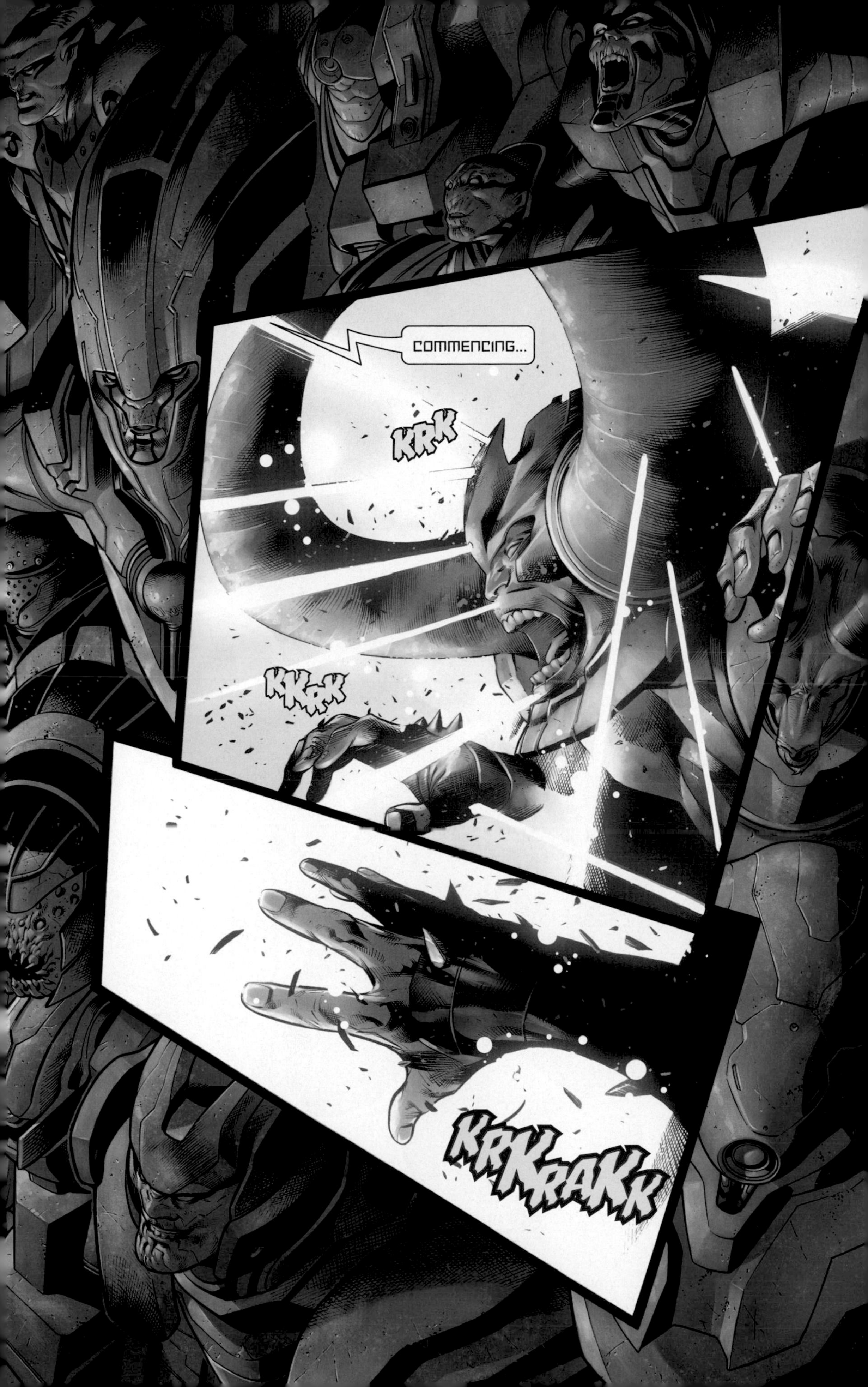
COMMENCING...
KRK
KKRK
KRKRAKK

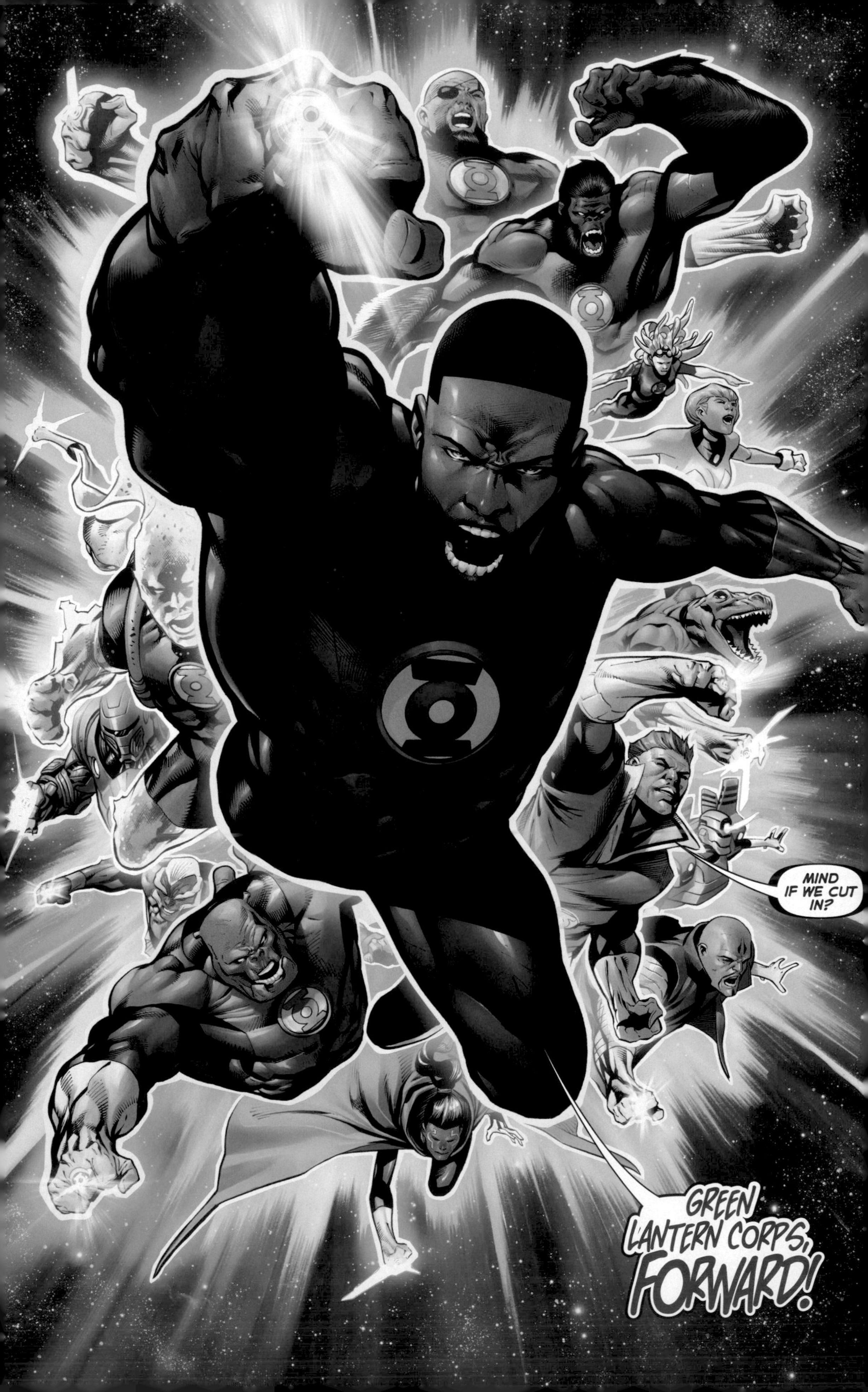
MIND IF WE CUT IN?
GREEN LANTERN CORPS, FORWARD!

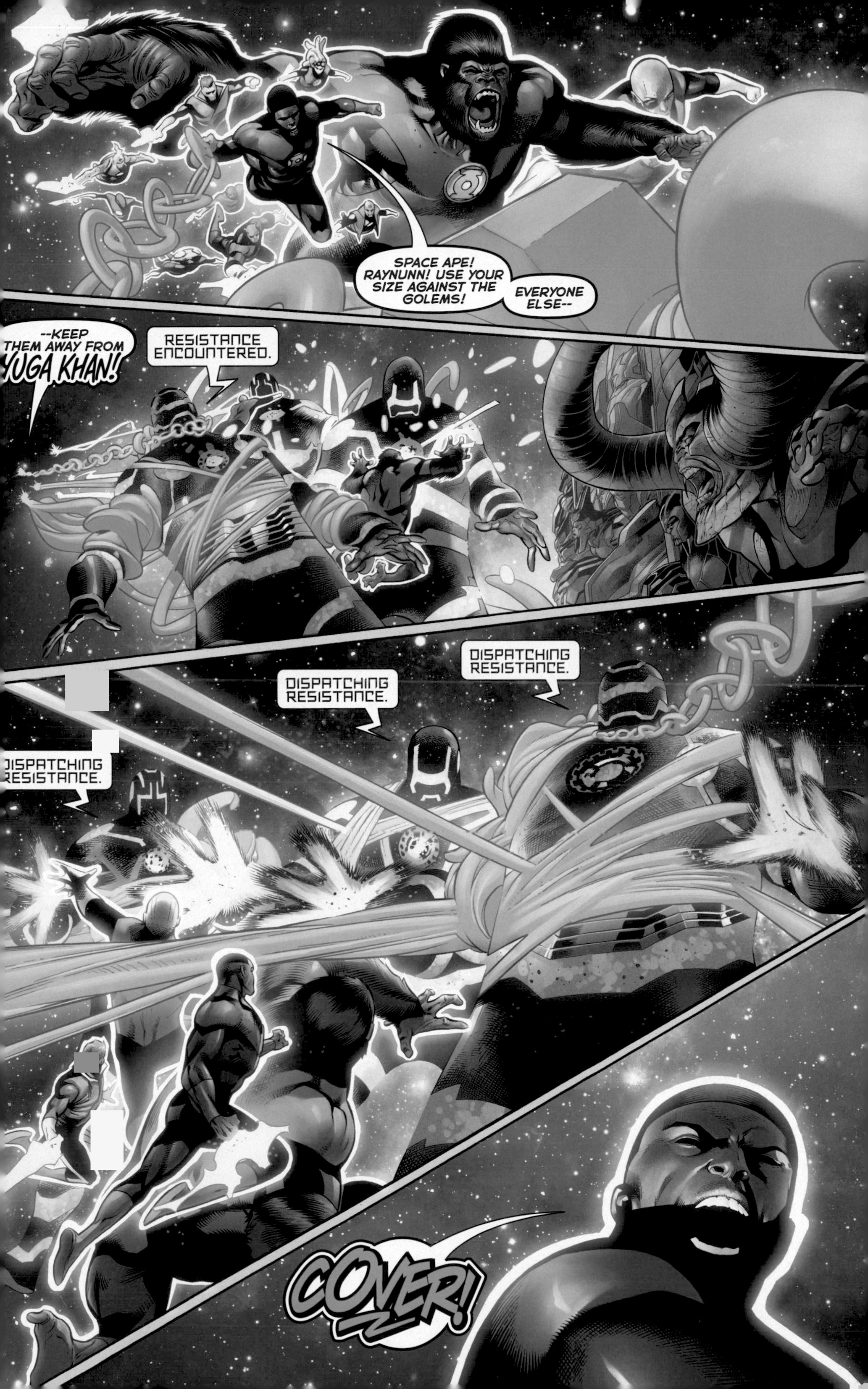
SPACE APE! RAYNUNN! USE YOUR SIZE AGAINST THE GOLEMS!
EVERYONE ELSE--
--KEEP THEM AWAY FROM YUGA KHAN!
RESISTANCE ENCOUNTERED.
DISPATCHING RESISTANCE.
DISPATCHING RESISTANCE.
DISPATCHING RESISTANCE.
COVER!

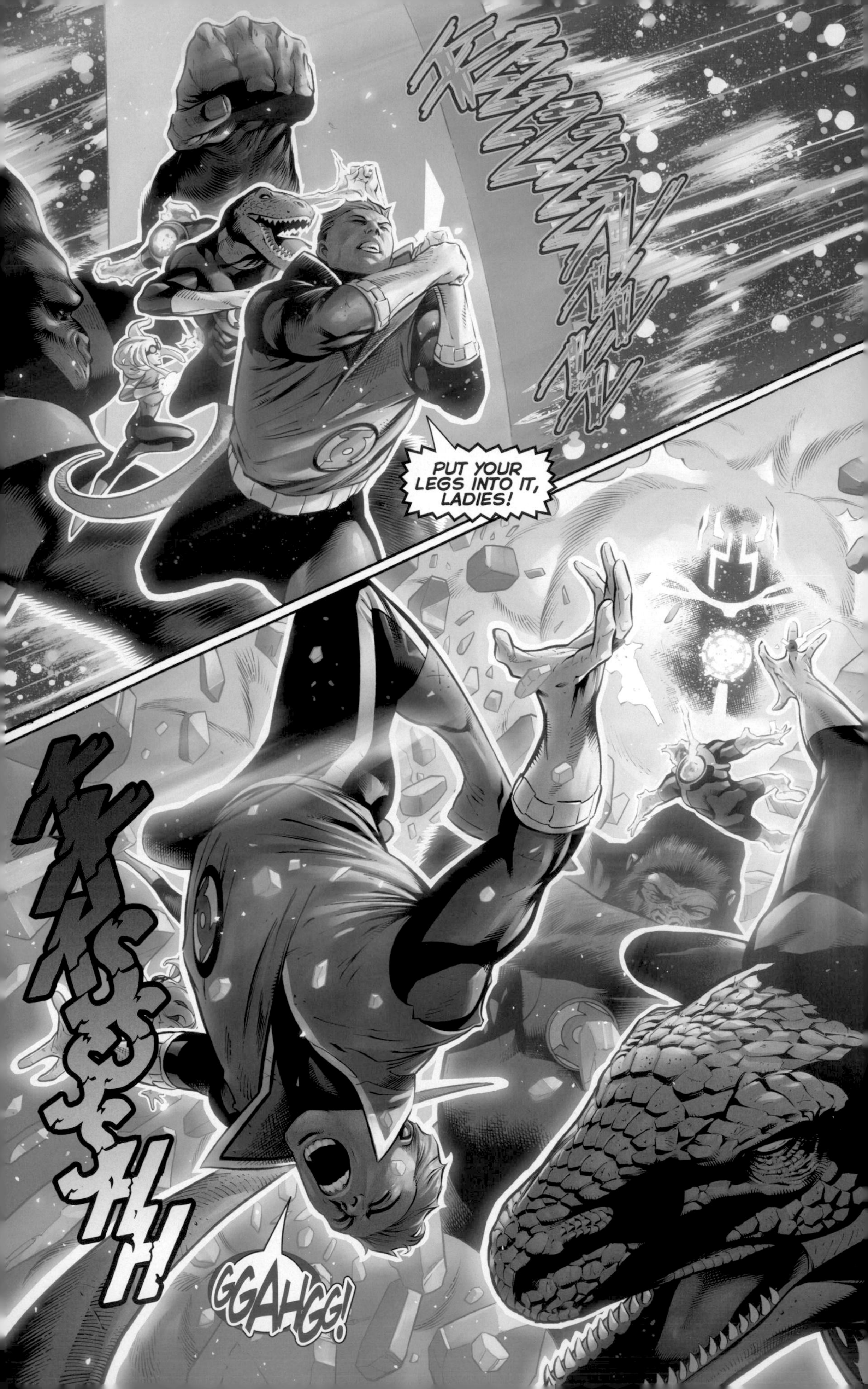
PUT YOUR LEGS INTO IT, LADIES!
GGAHGG!

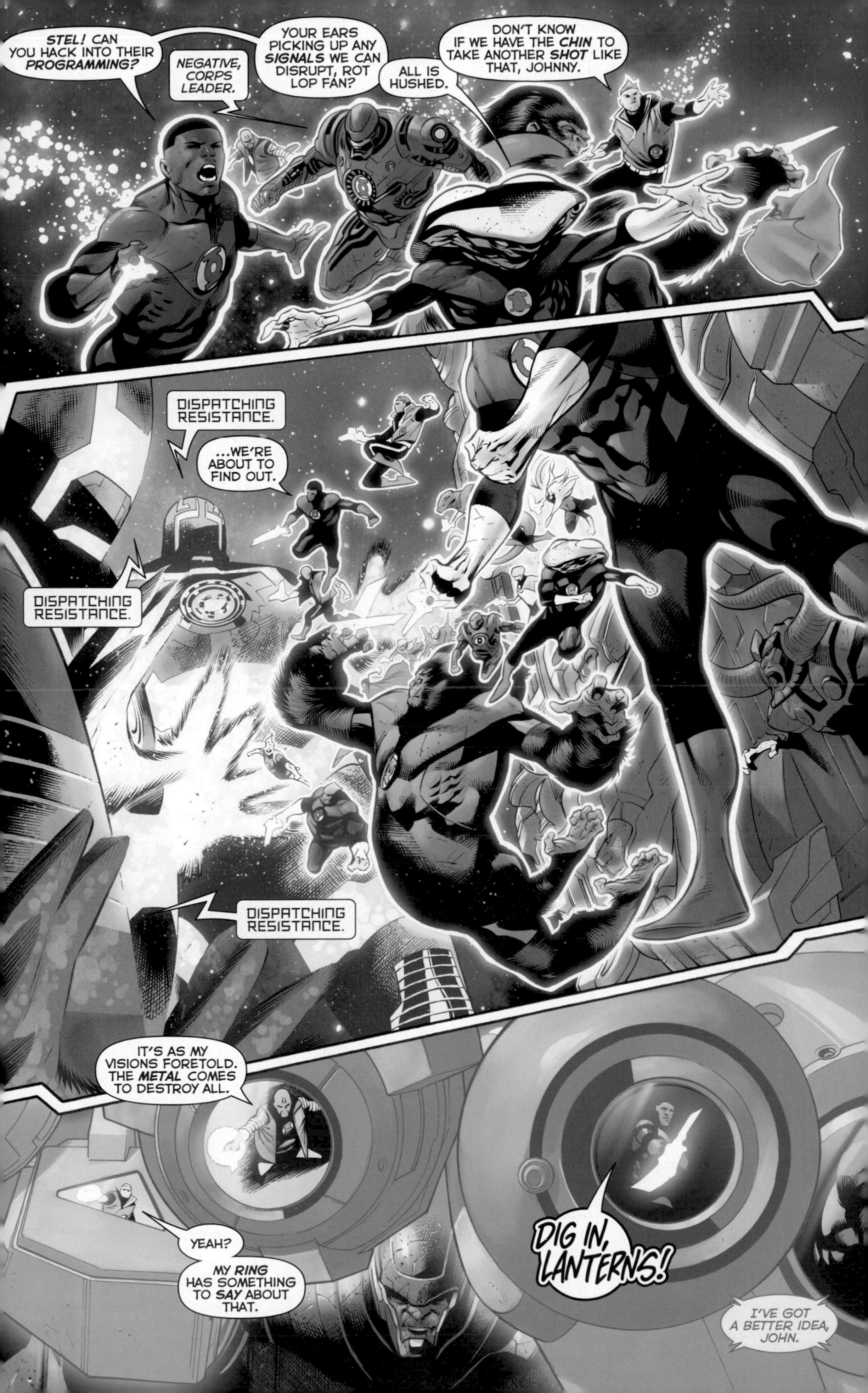
STEL! CAN YOU HACK INTO THEIR PROGRAMMING?
NEGATIVE, CORPS LEADER.
YOUR EARS PICKING UP ANY SIGNALS WE CAN DISRUPT, ROT LOP FAN?
ALL IS HUSHED.
DON'T KNOW IF WE HAVE THE CHIN TO TAKE ANOTHER SHOT LIKE THAT, JOHNNY.
DISPATCHING RESISTANCE.
...WE'RE ABOUT TO FIND OUT.
DISPATCHING RESISTANCE.
DISPATCHING RESISTANCE.
IT'S AS MY VISIONS FORETOLD. THE METAL COMES TO DESTROY ALL.
YEAH?
MY RING HAS SOMETHING TO SAY ABOUT THAT.
DIG IN, LANTERNS!
I'VE GOT A BETTER IDEA, JOHN.

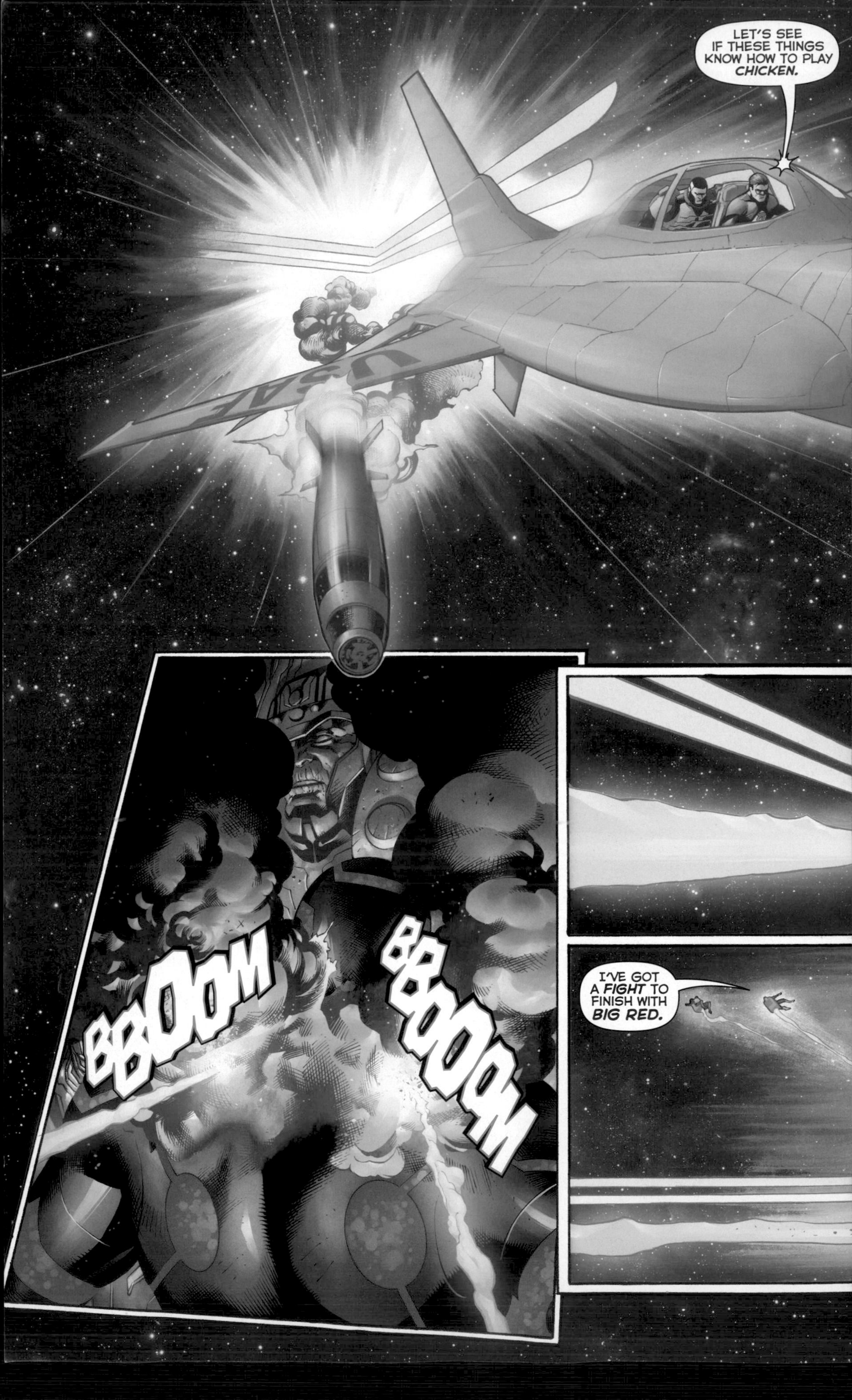
LET'S SEE IF THESE THINGS KNOW HOW TO PLAY CHICKEN.
U.S.A.F.
BBOOM
BBOOOM
I'VE GOT A FIGHT TO FINISH WITH BIG RED.

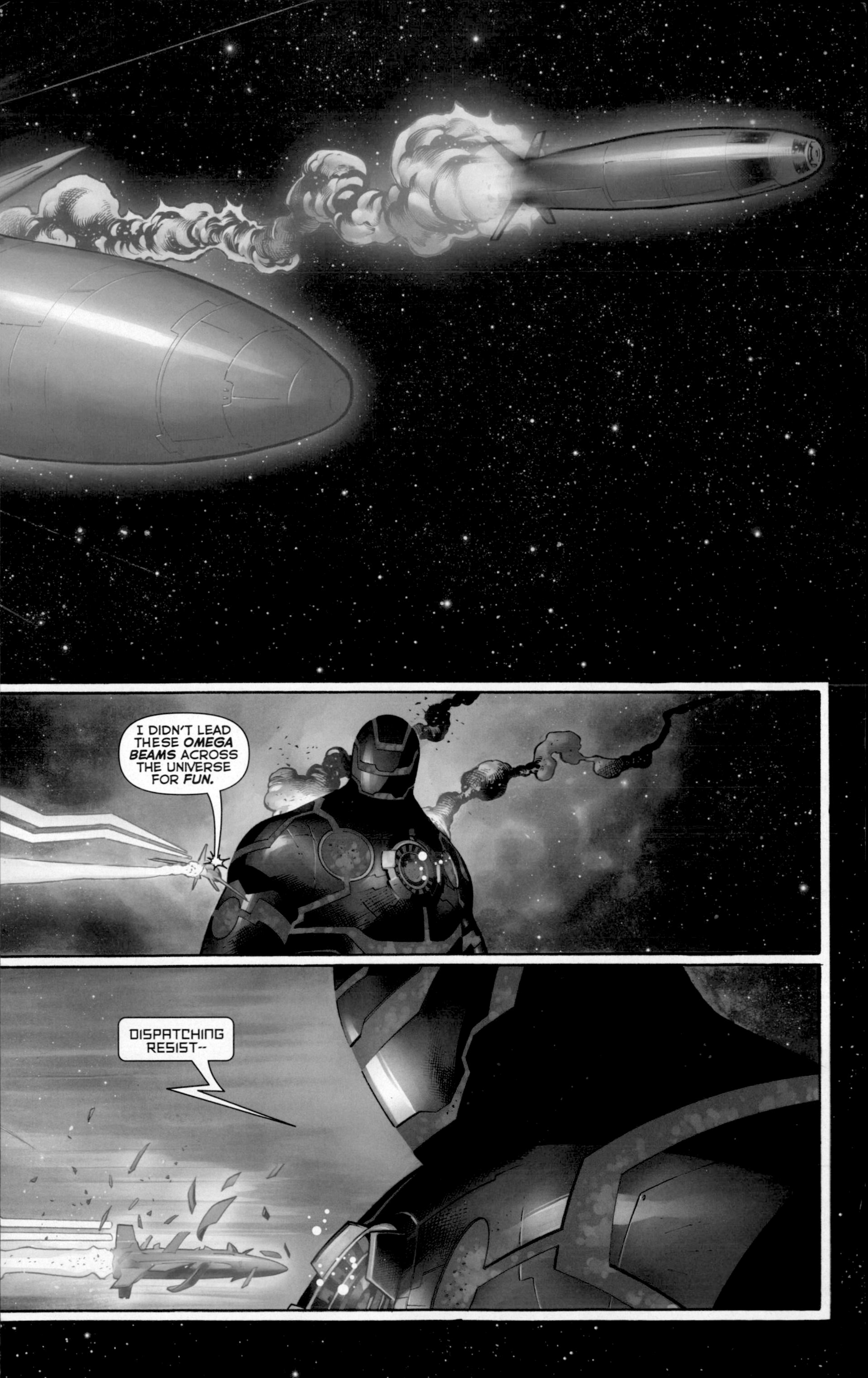
I DIDN'T LEAD THESE *OMEGA BEAMS* ACROSS THE UNIVERSE FOR *FUN.*
DISPATCHING RESIST--

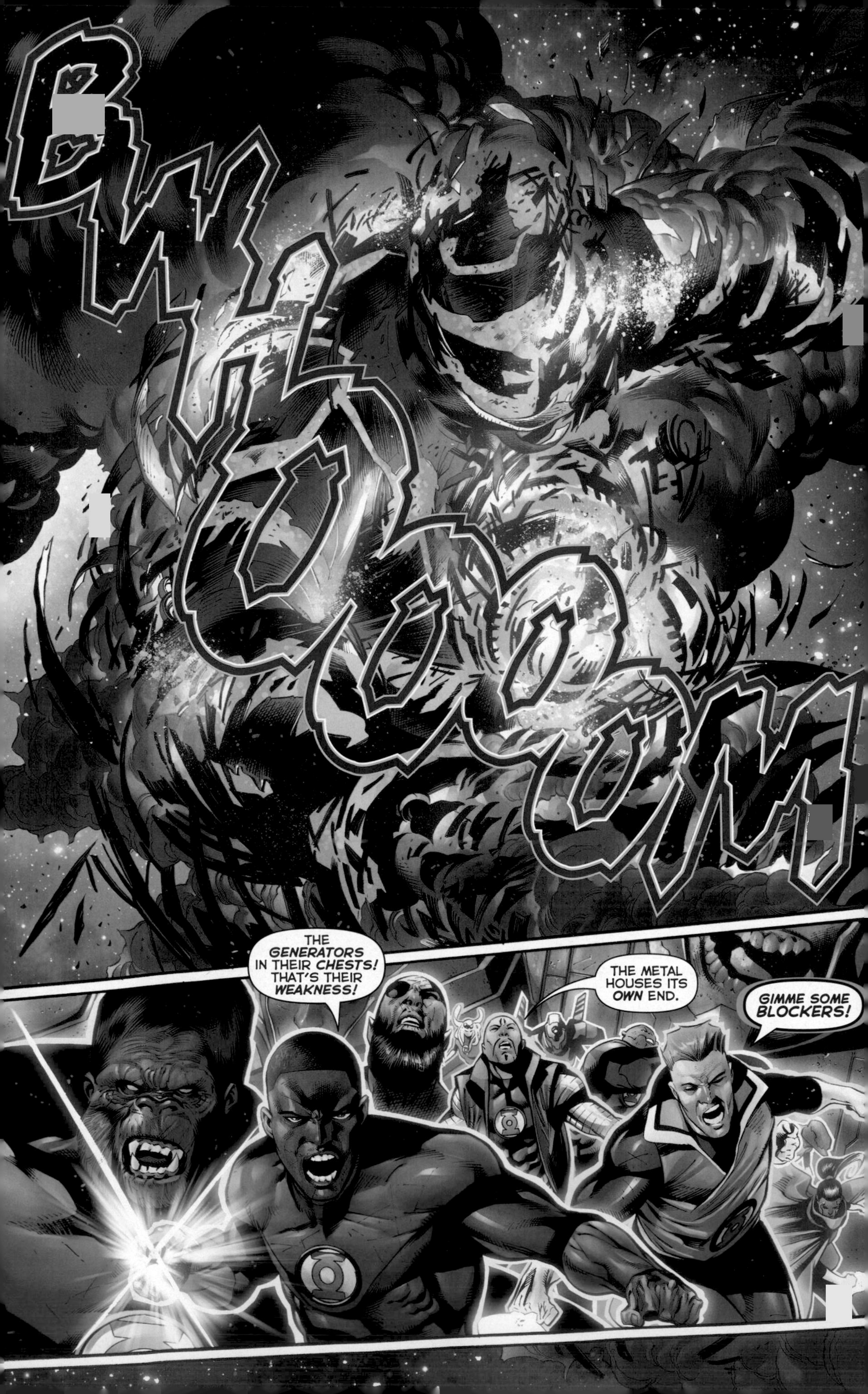
THE GENERATORS IN THEIR CHESTS! THAT'S THEIR WEAKNESS!
THE METAL HOUSES ITS OWN END.
GIMME SOME BLOCKERS!

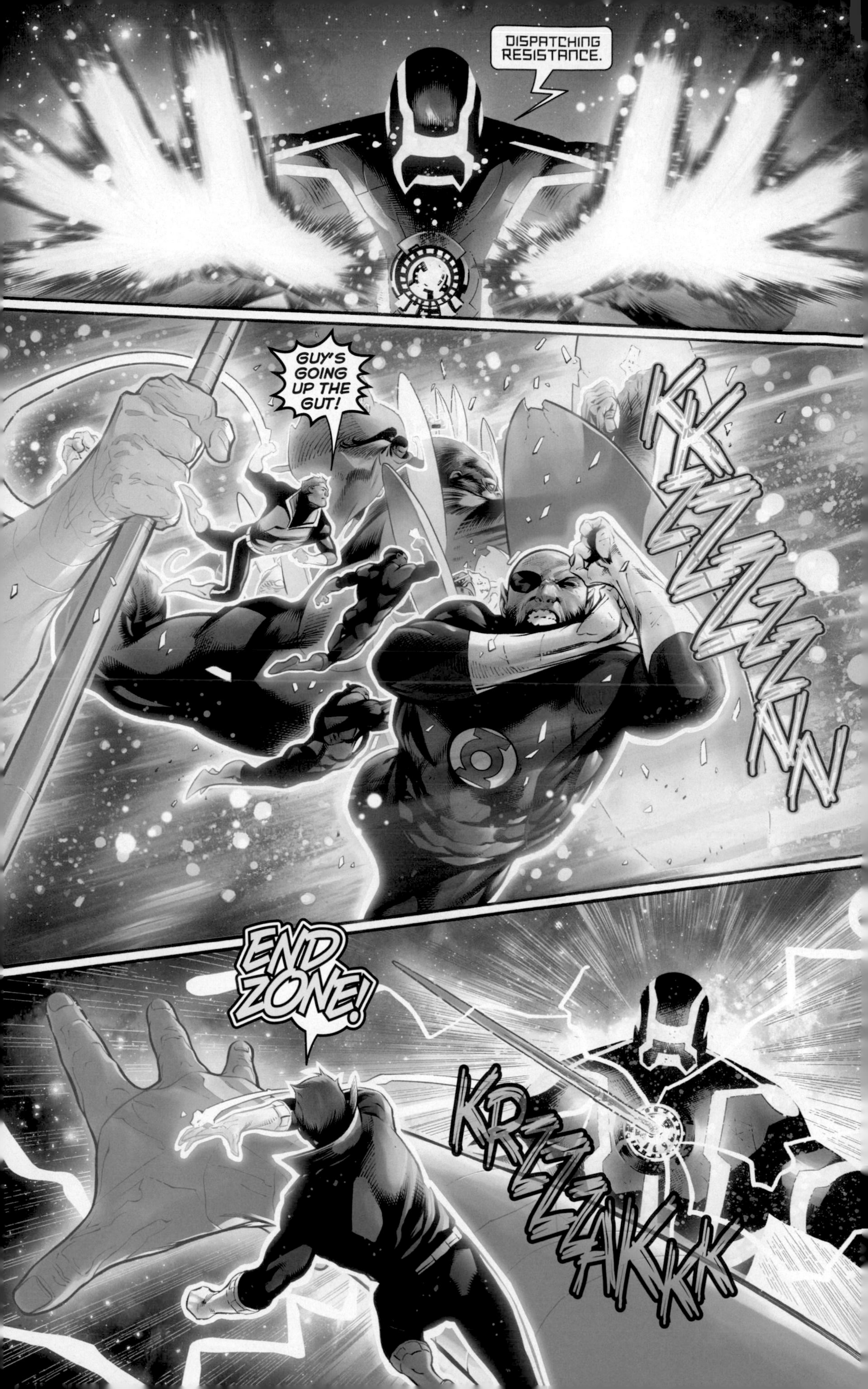
DISPATCHING RESISTANCE.
GUY'S GOING UP THE GUT!
KKZZZZNN
END ZONE!
KRZZZAKKK

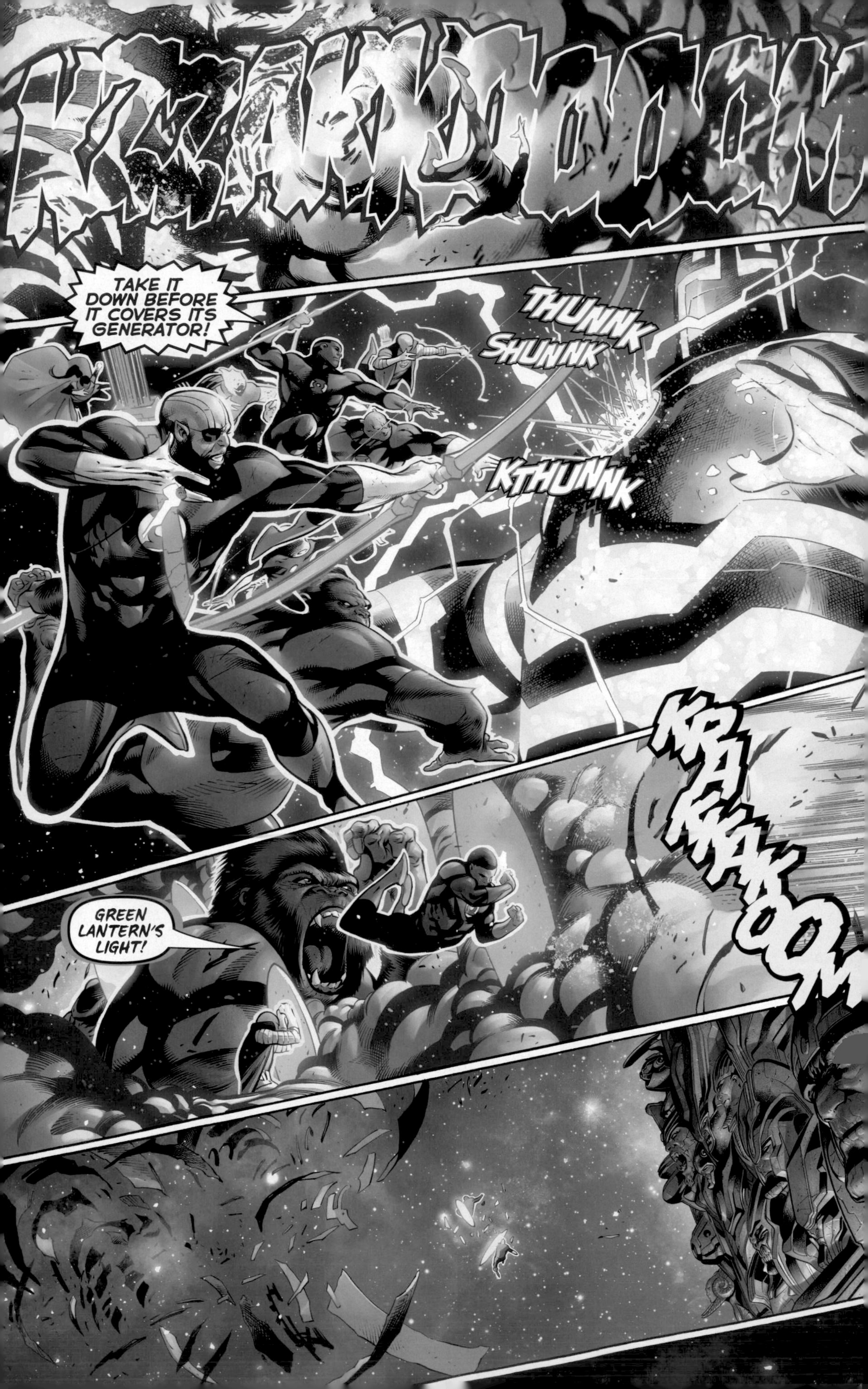
TAKE IT DOWN BEFORE IT COVERS ITS GENERATOR!
THUNNK
SHUNNK
KTHUNNK
GREEN LANTERN'S LIGHT!

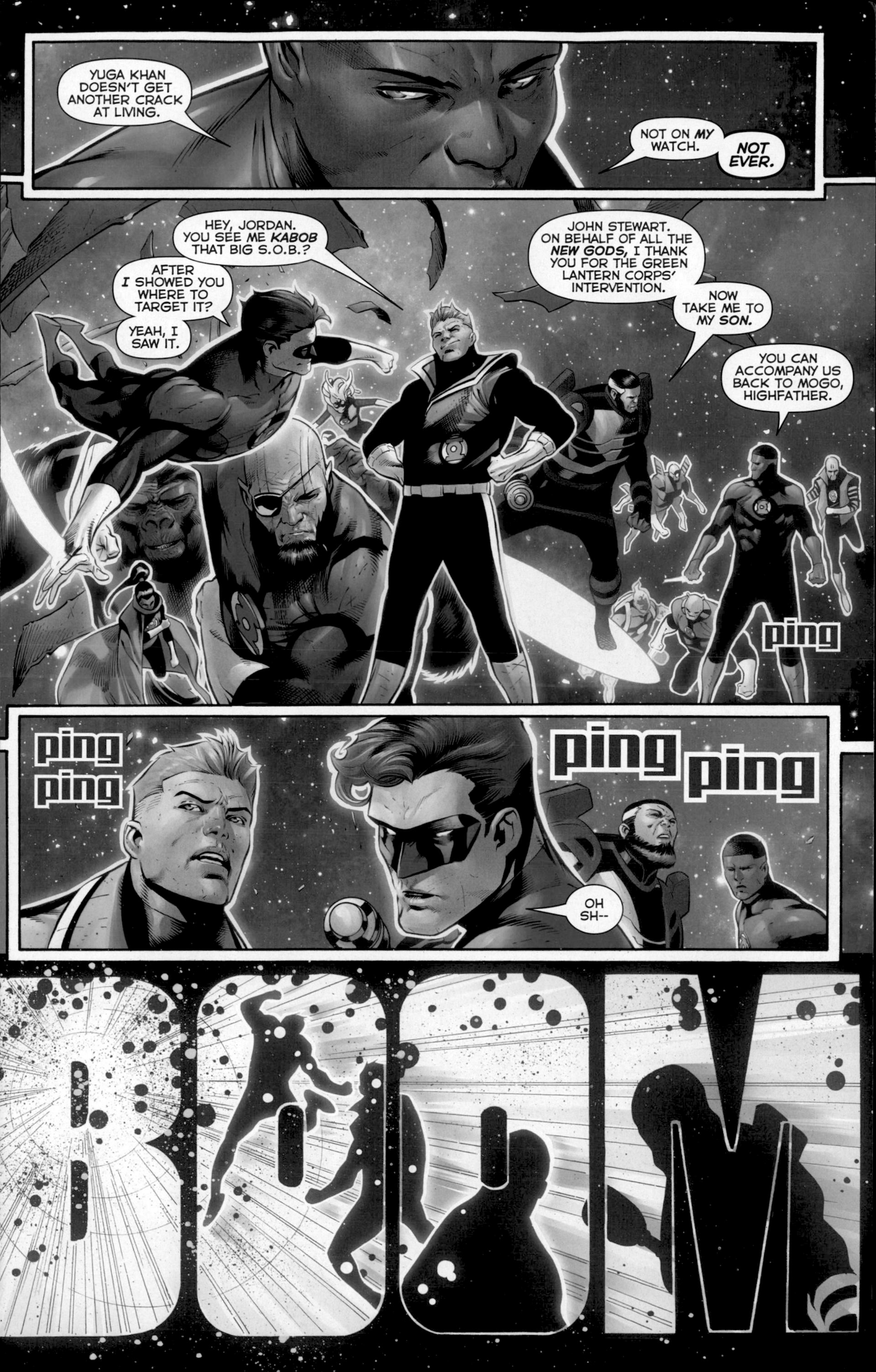
YUGA KHAN DOESN'T GET ANOTHER CRACK AT LIVING.
NOT ON *MY* WATCH.
NOT EVER.
HEY, JORDAN. YOU SEE ME *KABOB* THAT BIG S.O.B.?
AFTER *I* SHOWED YOU WHERE TO TARGET IT?
YEAH, I SAW IT.
JOHN STEWART. ON BEHALF OF ALL THE *NEW GODS,* I THANK YOU FOR THE GREEN LANTERN CORPS' INTERVENTION.
NOW TAKE ME TO MY *SON.*
YOU CAN ACCOMPANY US BACK TO MOGO, HIGHFATHER.
ping
ping
ping
ping ping
OH SH--
BOOM

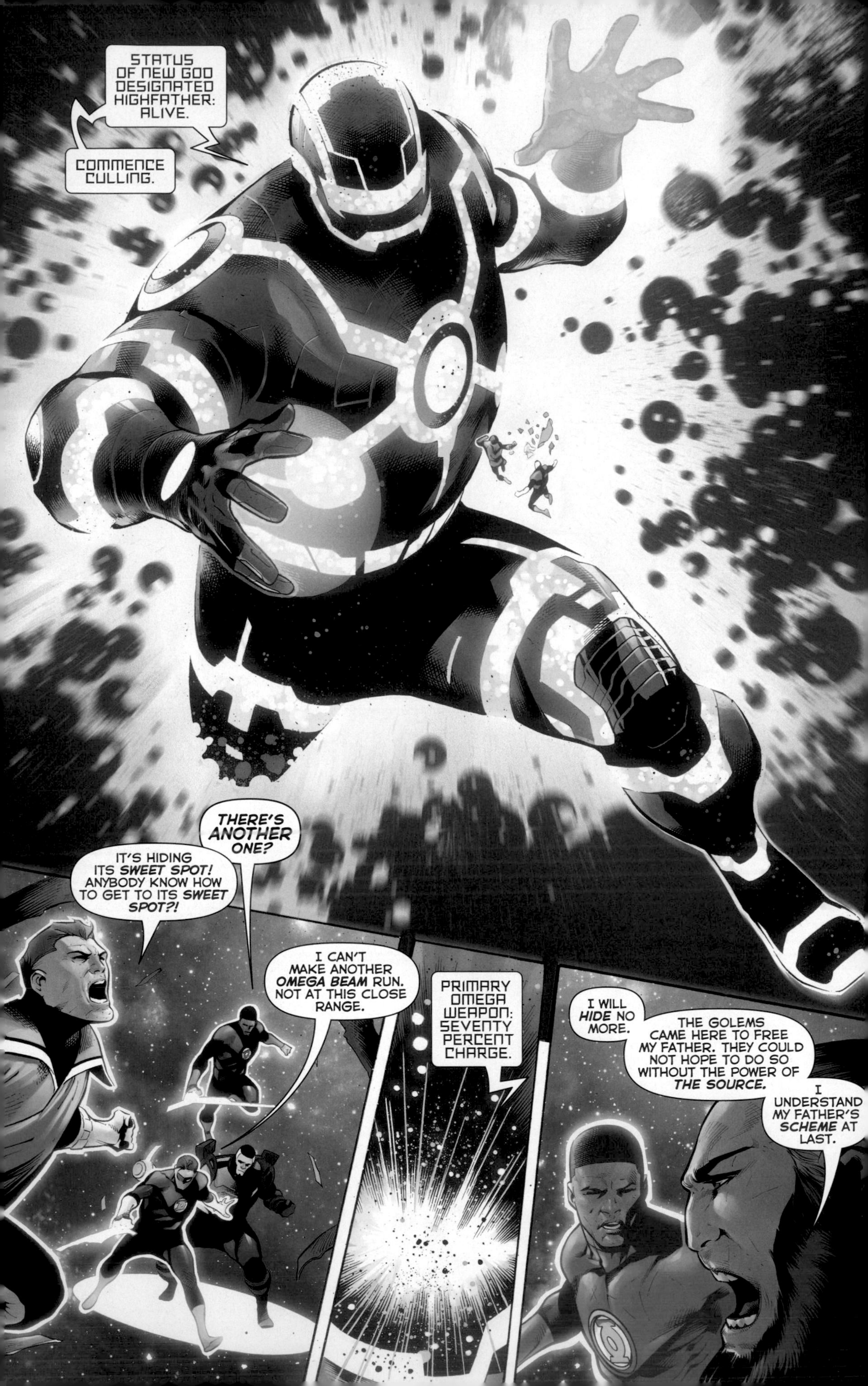
STATUS OF NEW GOD DESIGNATED HIGHFATHER: ALIVE.
COMMENCE CULLING.
IT'S HIDING ITS **SWEET SPOT!** ANYBODY KNOW HOW TO GET TO ITS **SWEET SPOT?!**
THERE'S ANOTHER ONE?
I CAN'T MAKE ANOTHER **OMEGA BEAM** RUN. NOT AT THIS CLOSE RANGE.
PRIMARY OMEGA WEAPON: SEVENTY PERCENT CHARGE.
I WILL **HIDE** NO MORE.
THE GOLEMS CAME HERE TO FREE MY FATHER. THEY COULD NOT HOPE TO DO SO WITHOUT THE POWER OF **THE SOURCE.**
I UNDERSTAND MY FATHER'S **SCHEME** AT LAST.

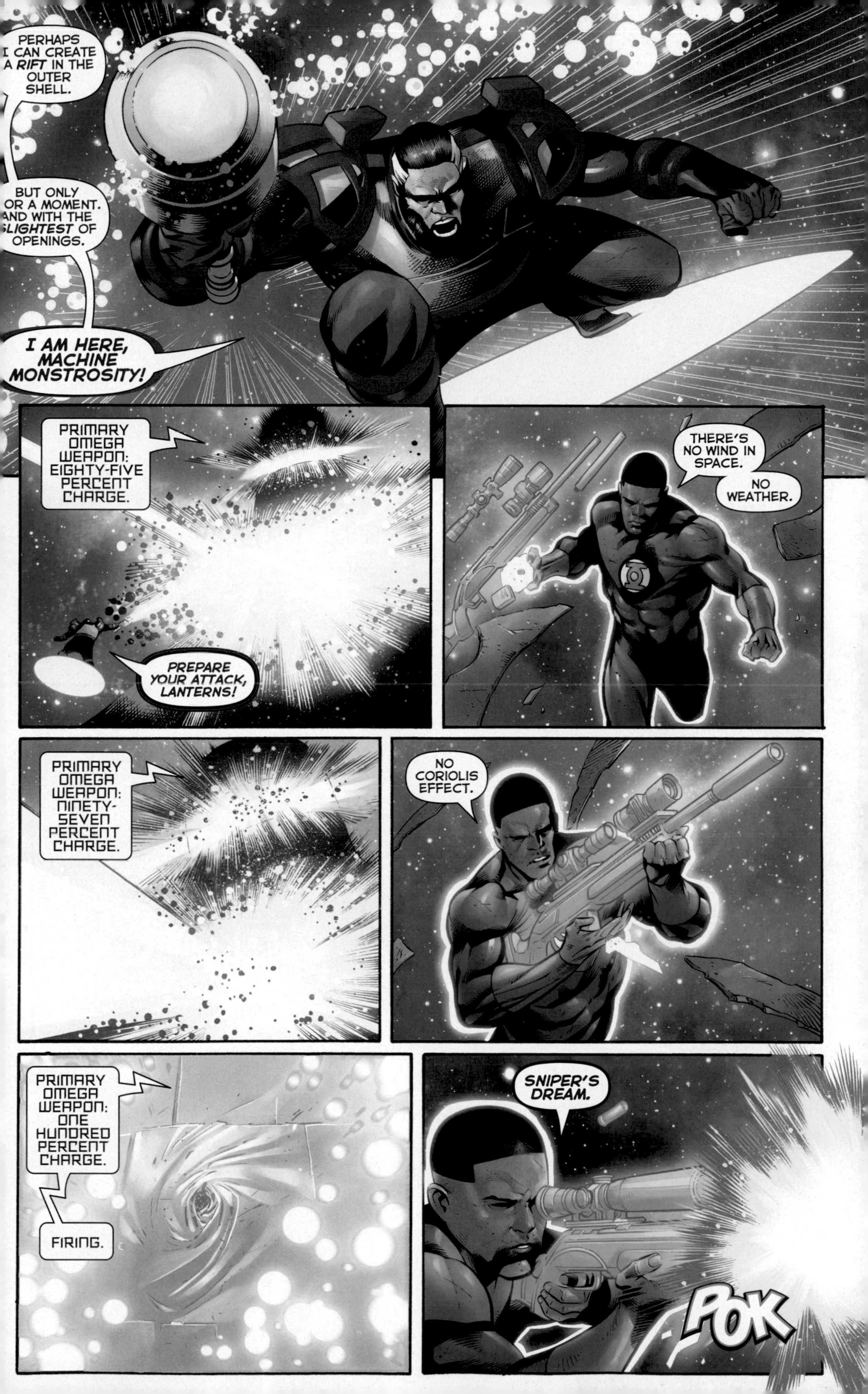
PERHAPS I CAN CREATE A *RIFT* IN THE OUTER SHELL.
BUT ONLY OR A MOMENT. AND WITH THE *SLIGHTEST* OF OPENINGS.
I AM HERE, MACHINE MONSTROSITY!
PRIMARY OMEGA WEAPON: EIGHTY-FIVE PERCENT CHARGE.
PREPARE YOUR ATTACK, LANTERNS!
THERE'S NO WIND IN SPACE.
NO WEATHER.
PRIMARY OMEGA WEAPON: NINETY-SEVEN PERCENT CHARGE.
NO CORIOLIS EFFECT.
PRIMARY OMEGA WEAPON: ONE HUNDRED PERCENT CHARGE.
FIRING.
SNIPER'S DREAM.
POK

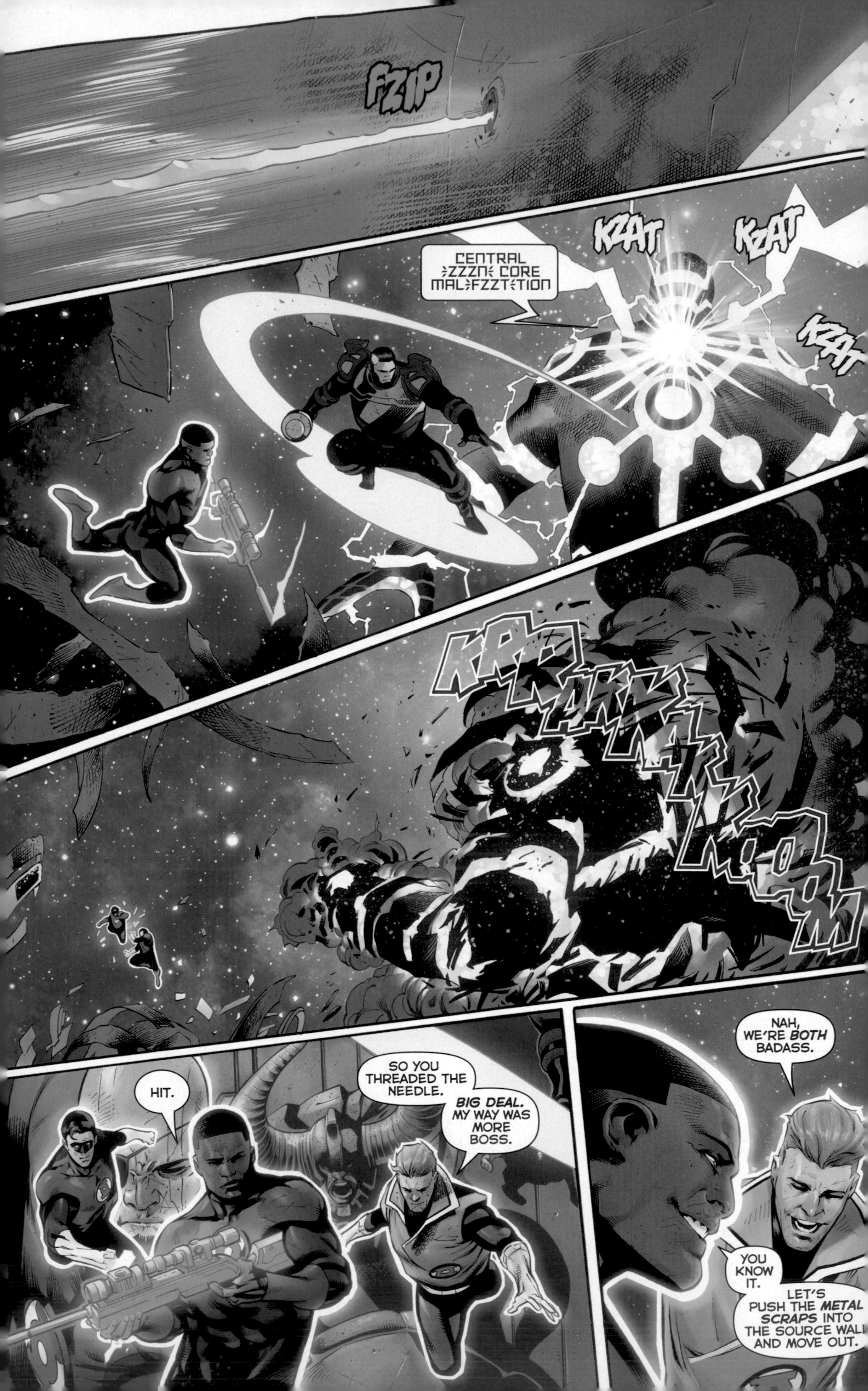
FZIP
KZAT
KZAT
CENTRAL ZZZN CORE MAL FZZT TION
KZAT
HIT.
SO YOU THREADED THE NEEDLE.
BIG DEAL. MY WAY WAS MORE BOSS.
NAH, WE'RE BOTH BADASS.
YOU KNOW IT.
LET'S PUSH THE METAL SCRAPS INTO THE SOURCE WALL AND MOVE OUT.

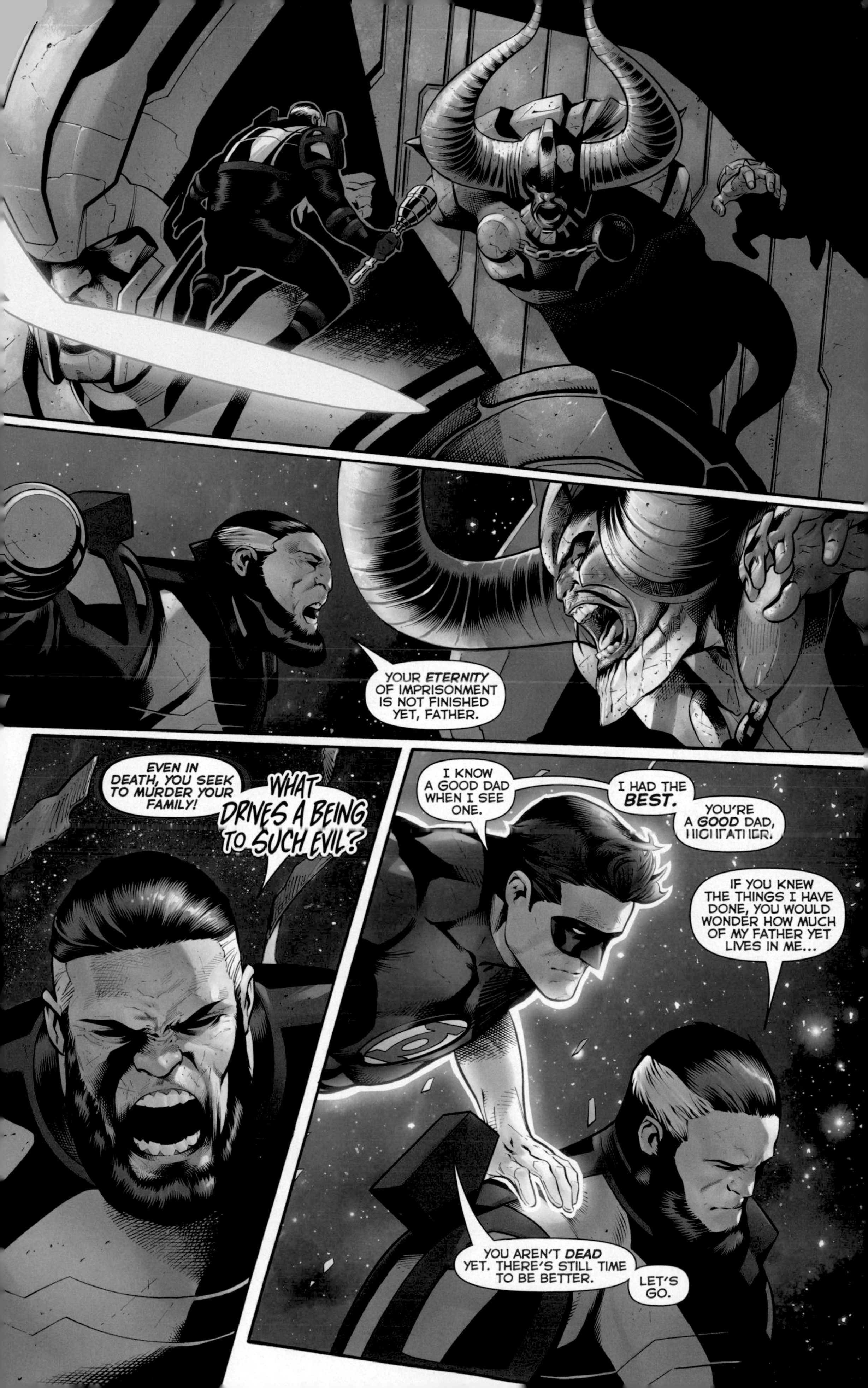
YOUR ETERNITY OF IMPRISONMENT IS NOT FINISHED YET, FATHER.
EVEN IN DEATH, YOU SEEK TO MURDER YOUR FAMILY!
WHAT DRIVES A BEING TO SUCH EVIL?
I KNOW A GOOD DAD WHEN I SEE ONE.
I HAD THE BEST.
YOU'RE A GOOD DAD, HIGHFATHER.
IF YOU KNEW THE THINGS I HAVE DONE, YOU WOULD WONDER HOW MUCH OF MY FATHER YET LIVES IN ME...
YOU AREN'T DEAD YET. THERE'S STILL TIME TO BE BETTER.
LET'S GO.

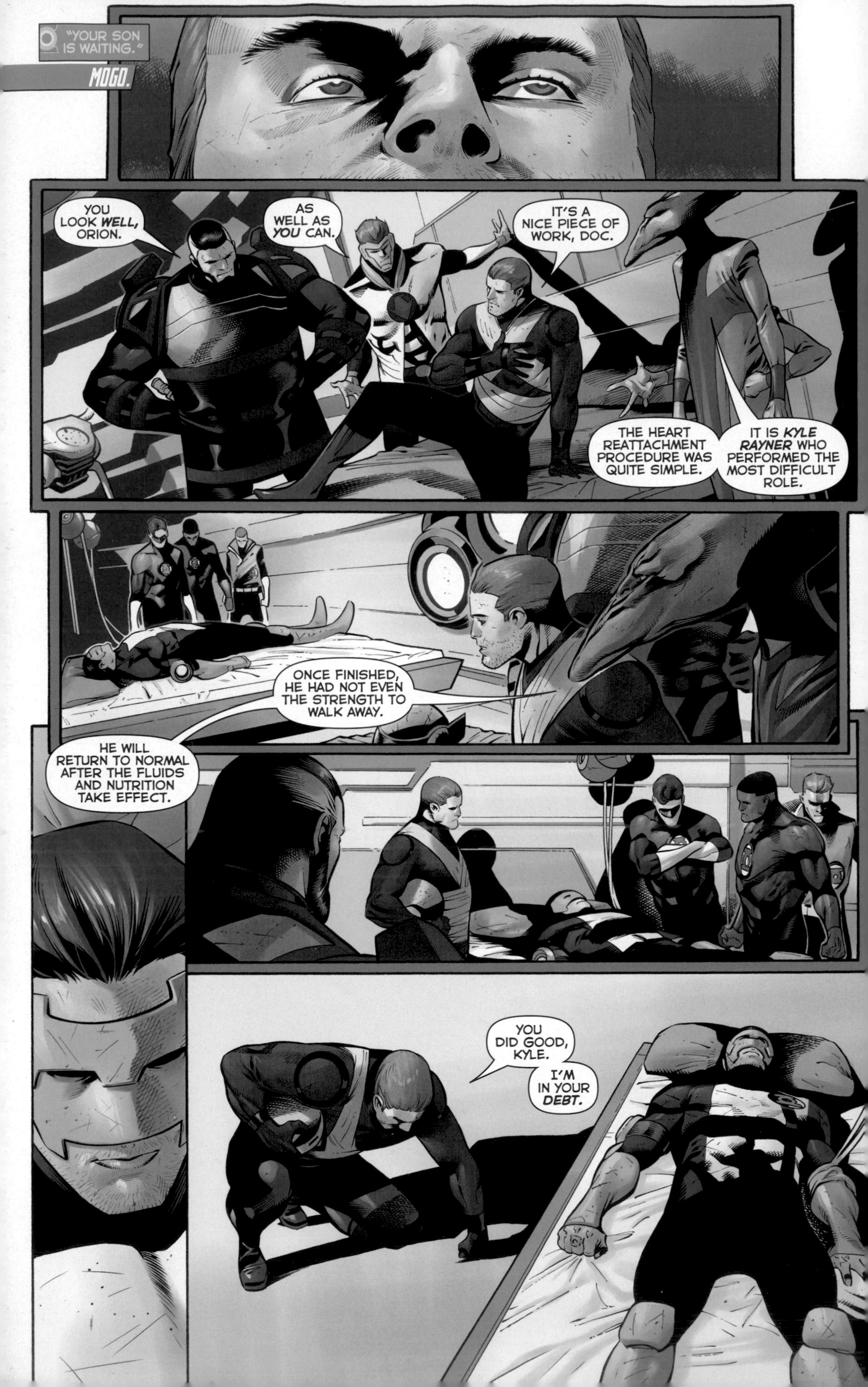

"YOUR SON IS WAITING."
MOGO.
YOU LOOK WELL, ORION.
AS WELL AS YOU CAN.
IT'S A NICE PIECE OF WORK, DOC.
THE HEART REATTACHMENT PROCEDURE WAS QUITE SIMPLE.
IT IS KYLE RAYNER WHO PERFORMED THE MOST DIFFICULT ROLE.
ONCE FINISHED, HE HAD NOT EVEN THE STRENGTH TO WALK AWAY.
HE WILL RETURN TO NORMAL AFTER THE FLUIDS AND NUTRITION TAKE EFFECT.
YOU DID GOOD, KYLE.
I'M IN YOUR DEBT.

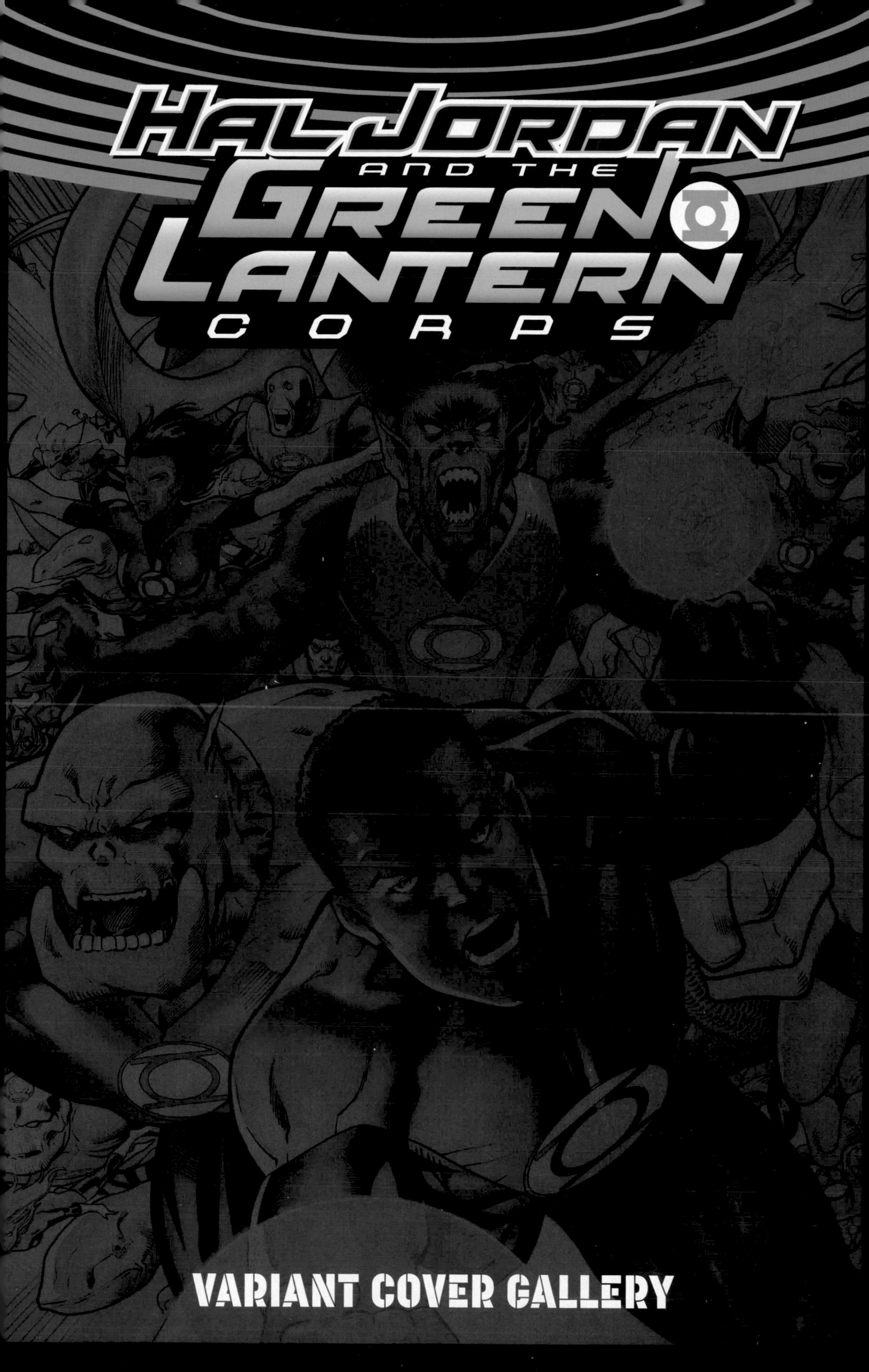
HAL JORDAN AND THE GREEN LANTERN CORPS

VARIANT COVER GALLERY

Variant Cover Art by KEVIN NOWLAN

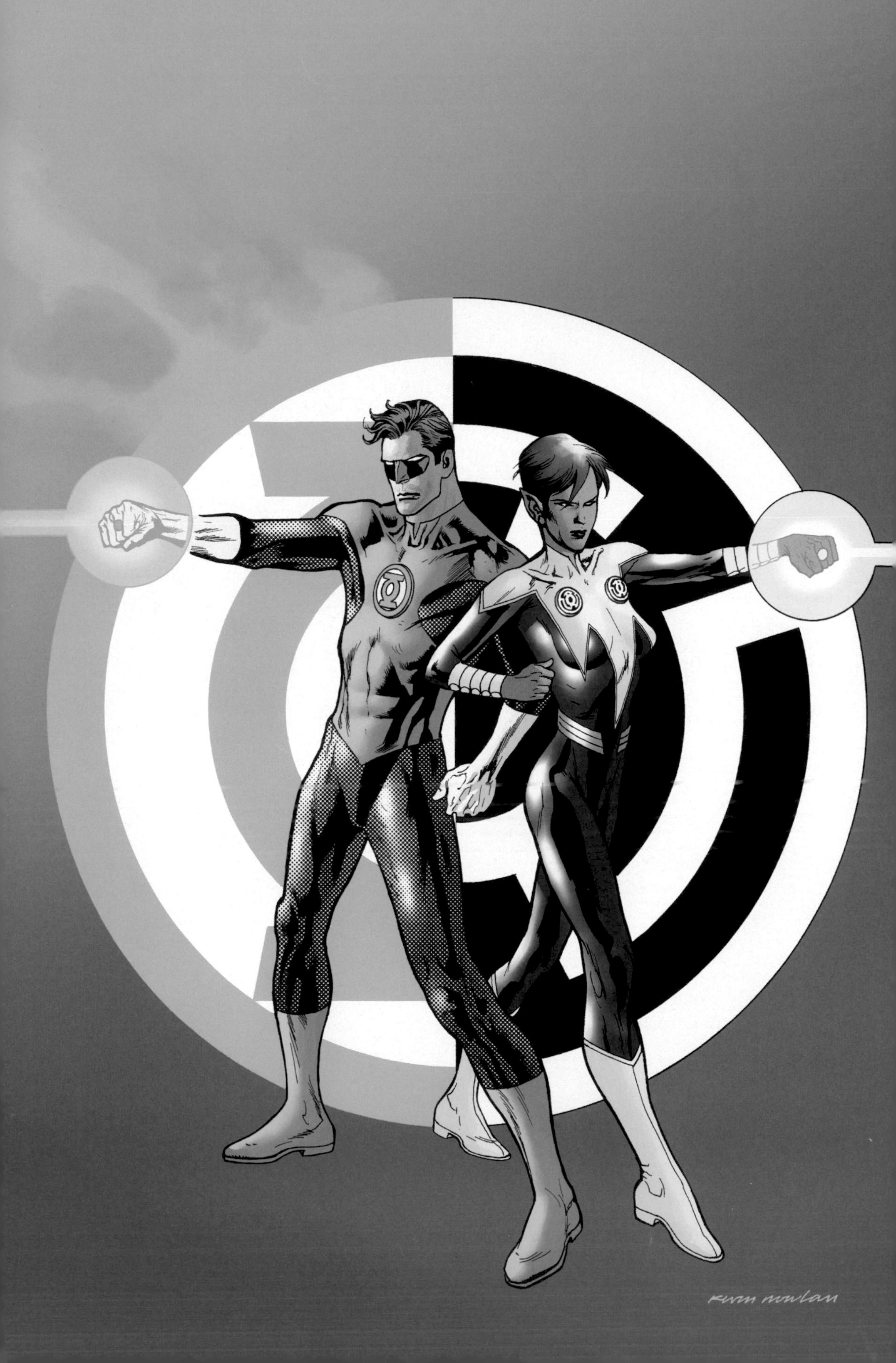
kevin nowlan

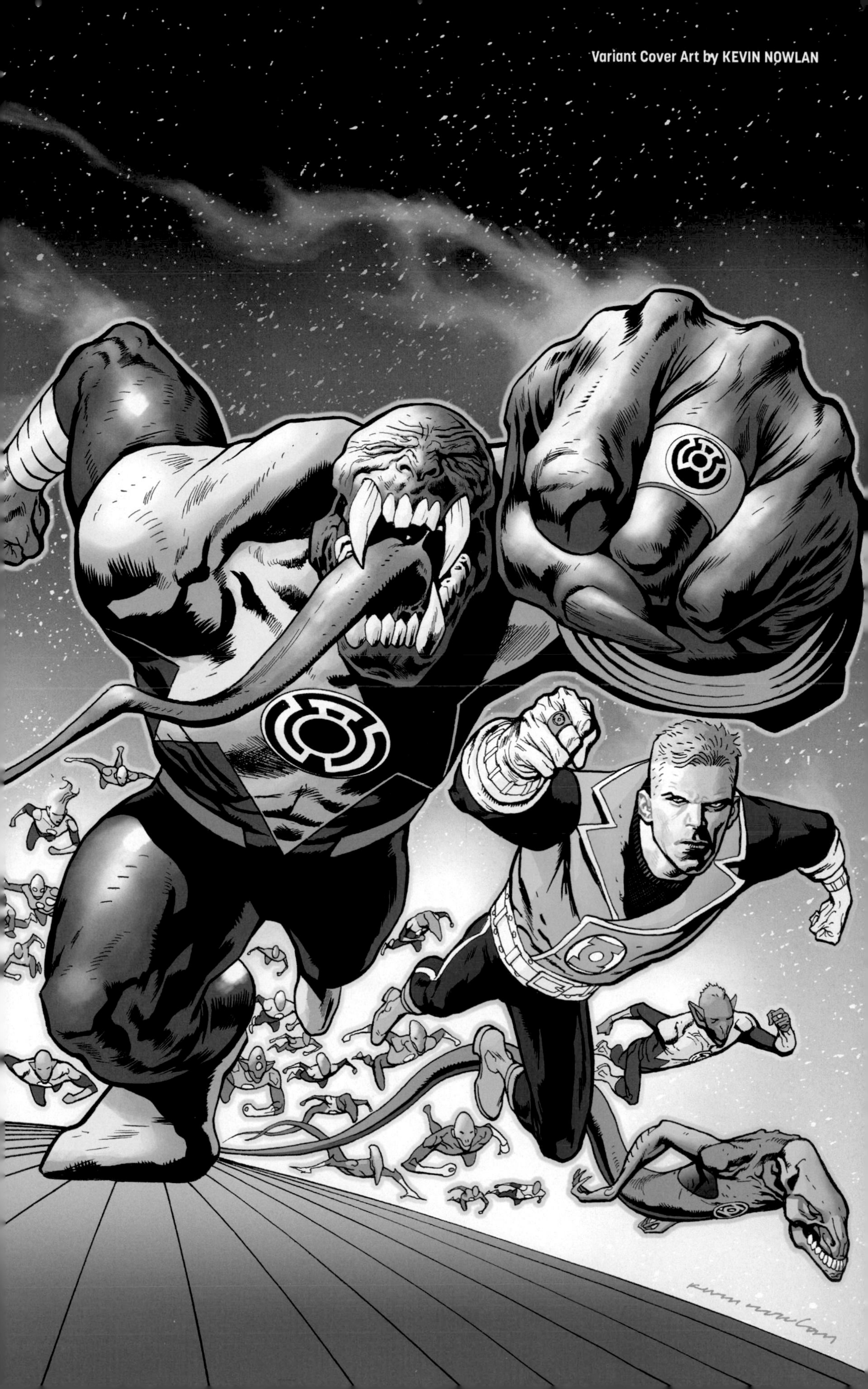

Variant Cover Art by KEVIN NOWLAN

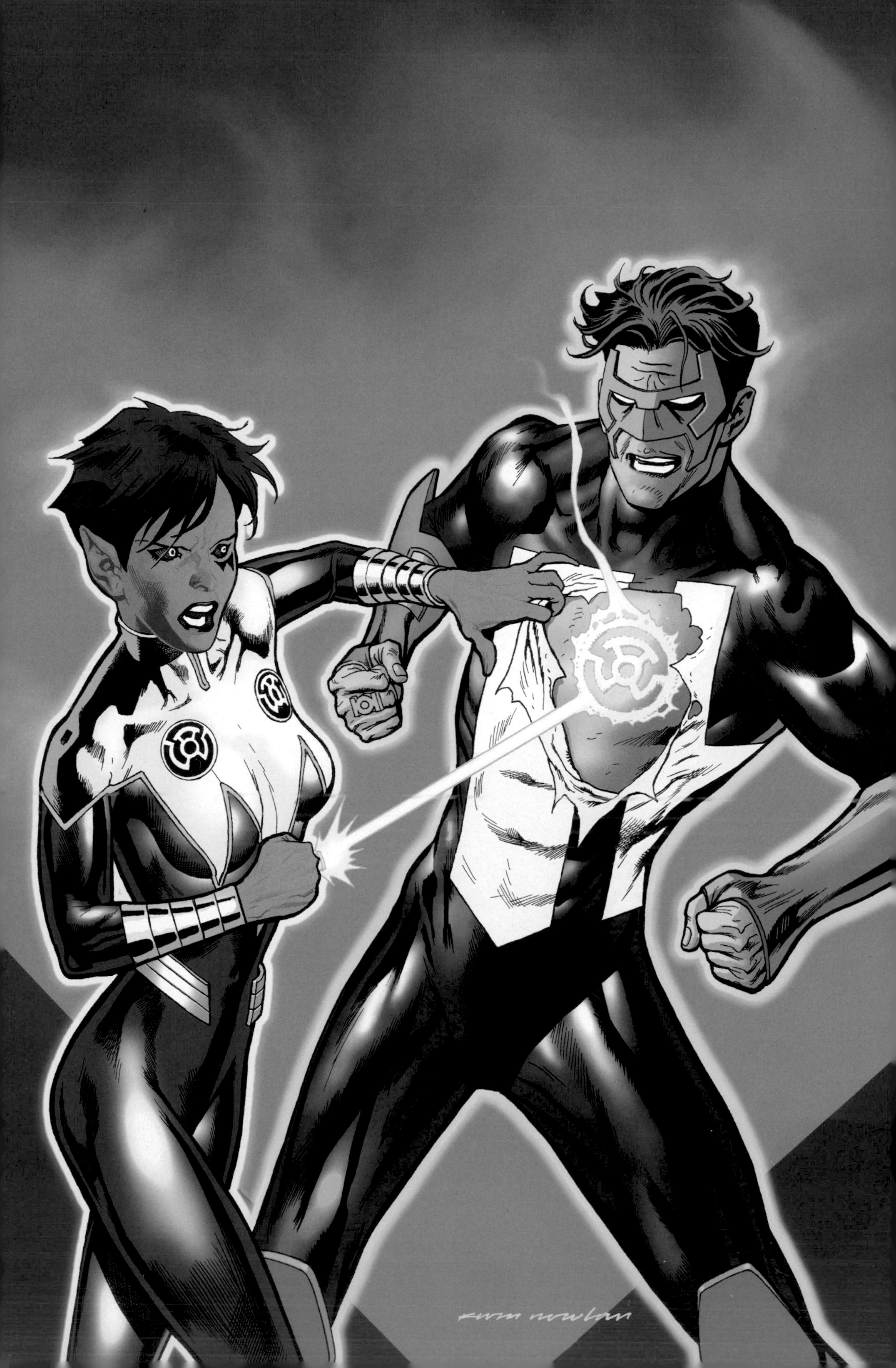
kevin nowlan

Variant Cover Art by KEVIN NOWLAN

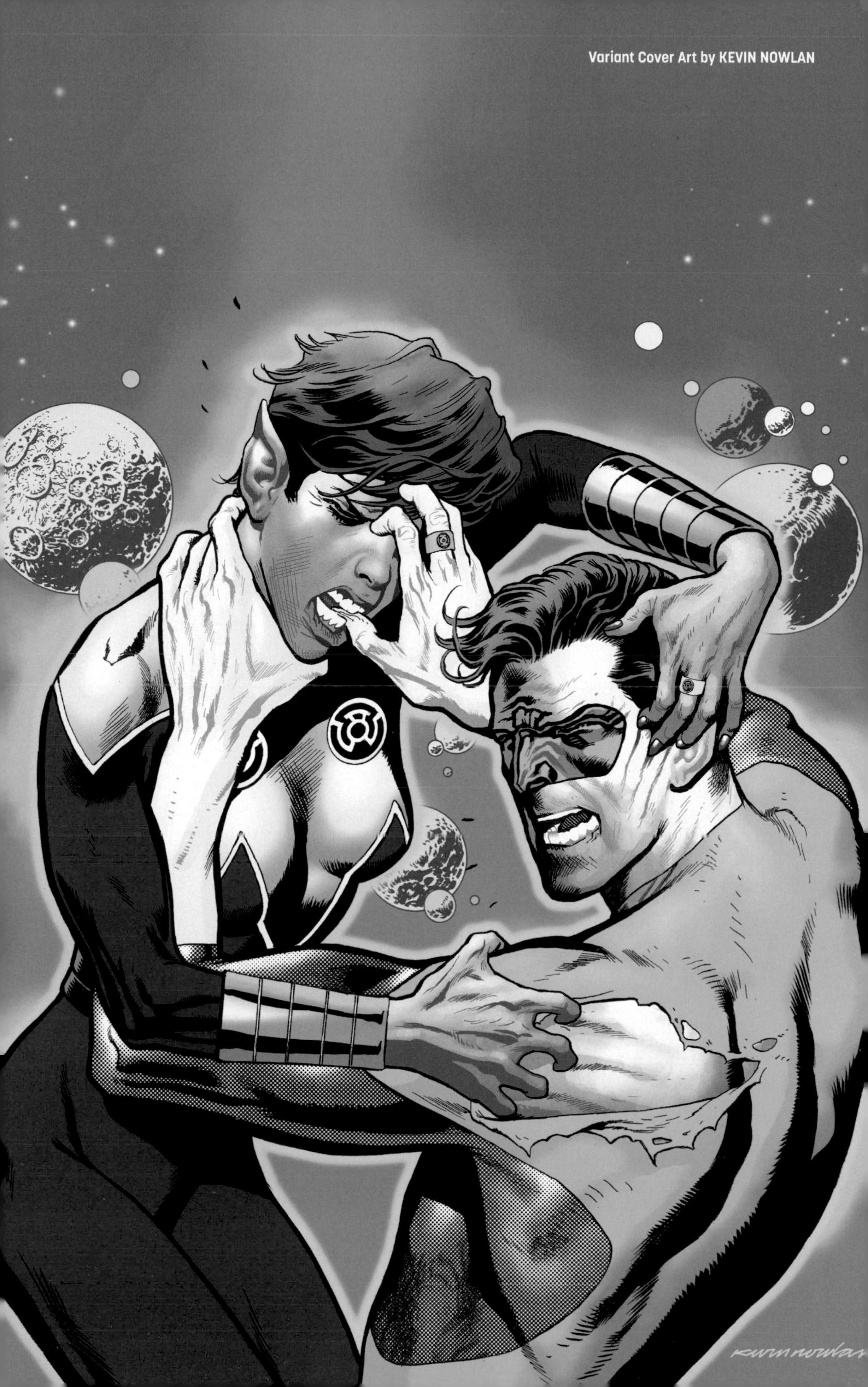

Variant Cover Art by KEVIN NOWLAN

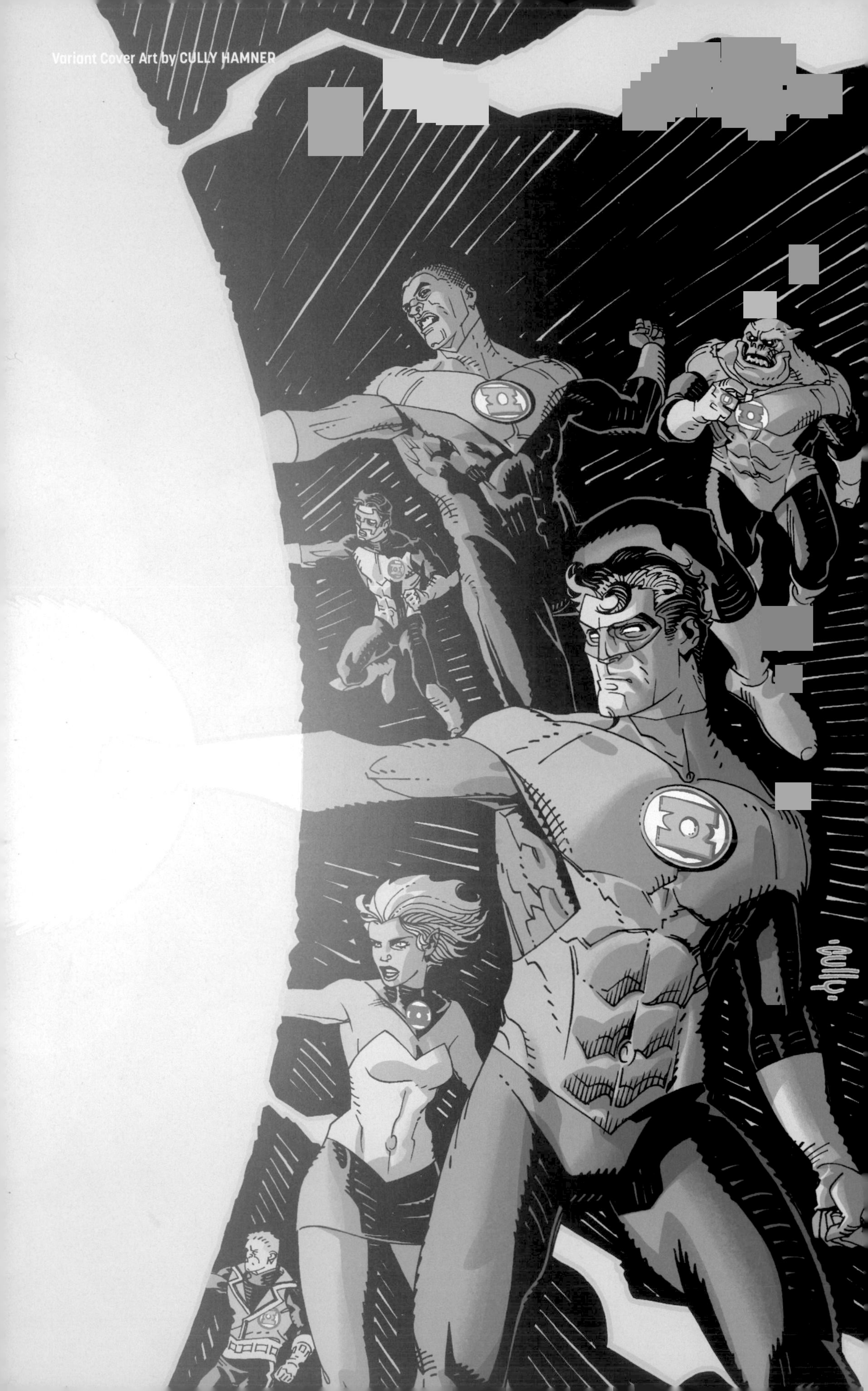

Variant Cover Art by CULLY HAMNER

Variant Cover Art by CULLY HAMNER

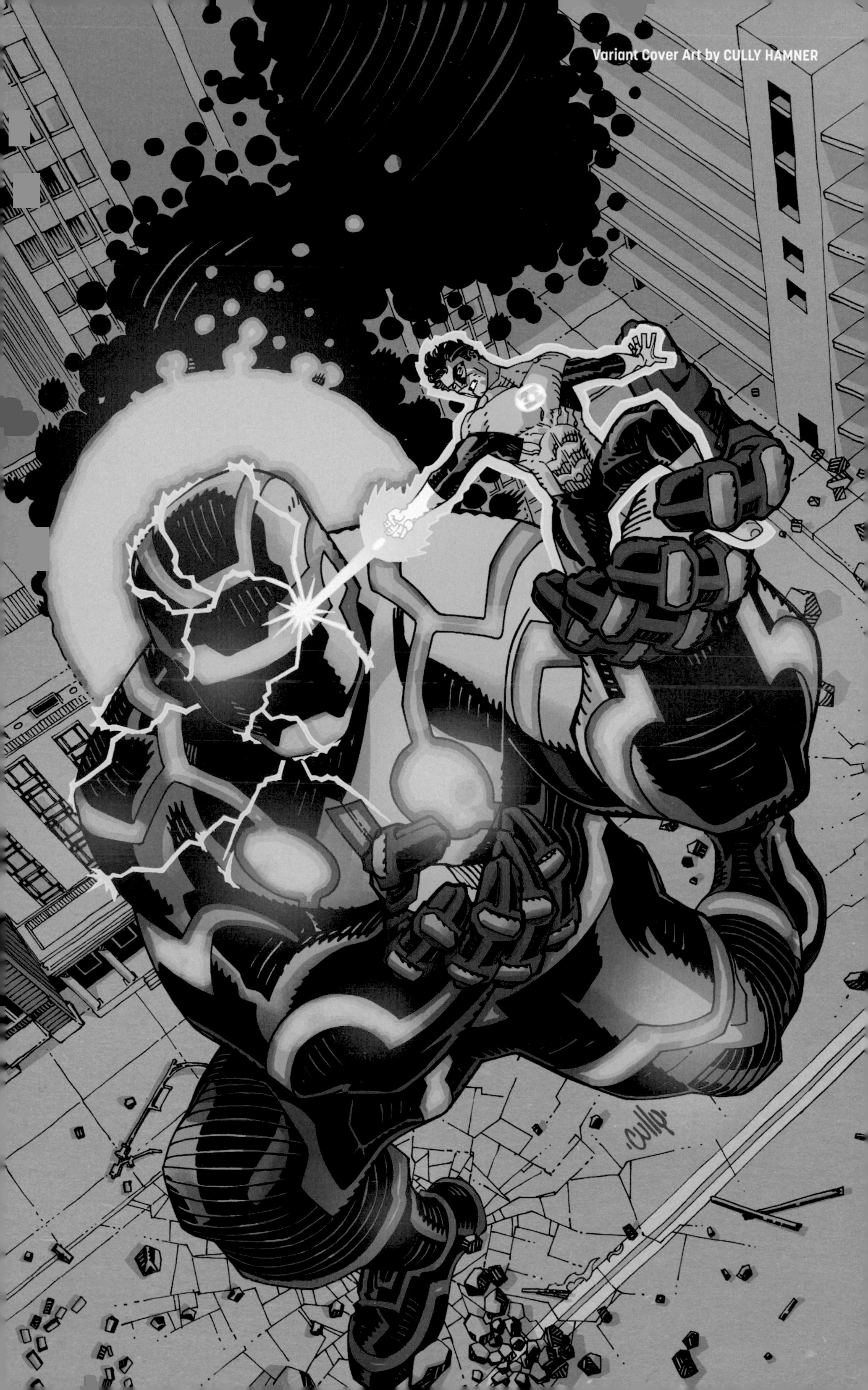
Cully

Variant Cover Art by BARRY KITSON and HI-FI

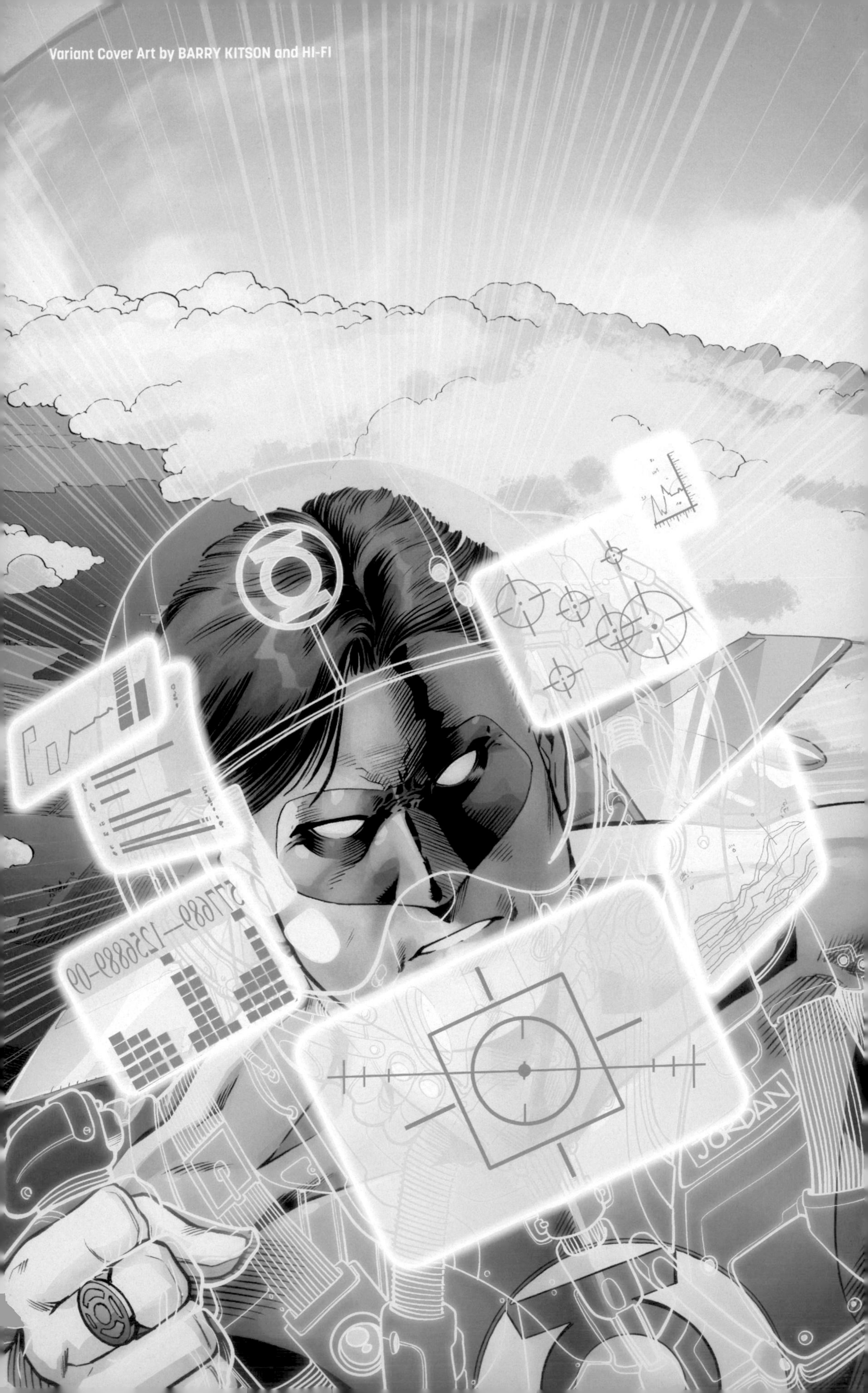
JORDAN

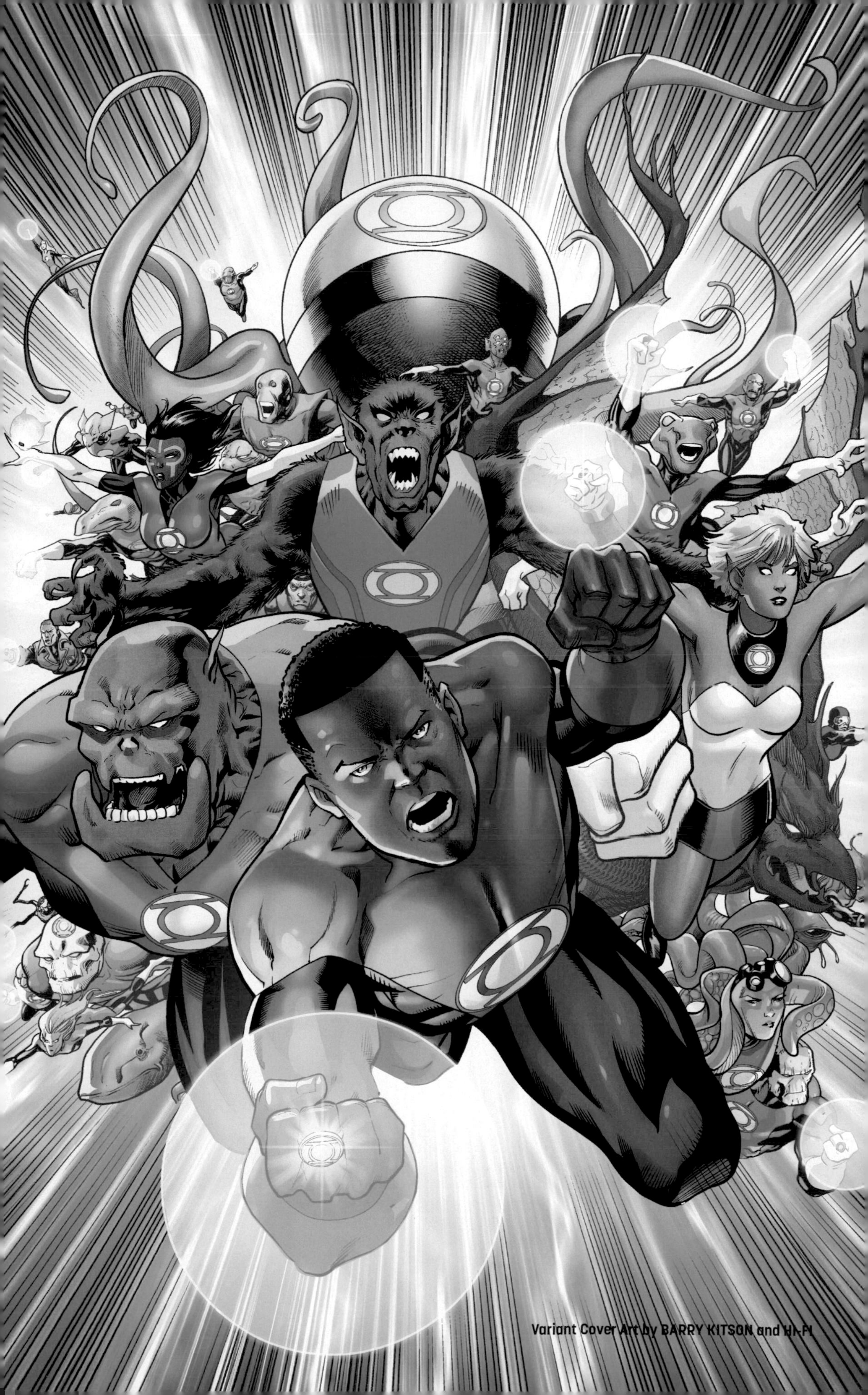

Variant Cover Art by BARRY KITSON and HI-FI

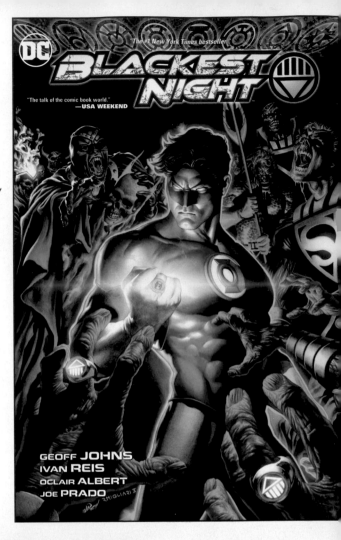
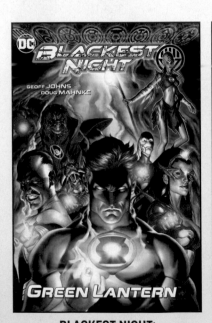

"This is comic book storytelling at its absolute finest."
—IGN

"If you've read a superhero comic book published by DC Comics within the last few years, and were completely blown away by it, there's a good chance that it was something written by Geoff Johns." **—WASHINGTON EXAMINER**

FROM THE WRITER OF
JUSTICE LEAGUE AND *THE FLASH*

GEOFF JOHNS
GREEN LANTERN: REBIRTH

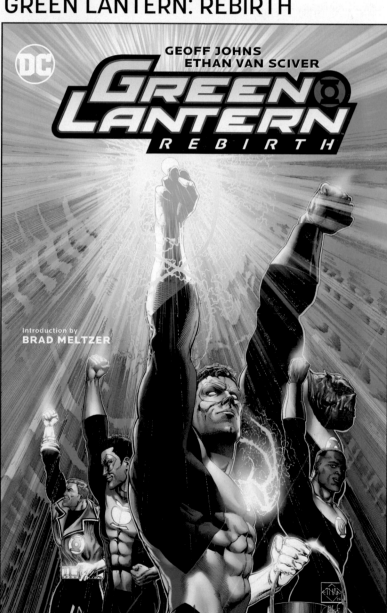

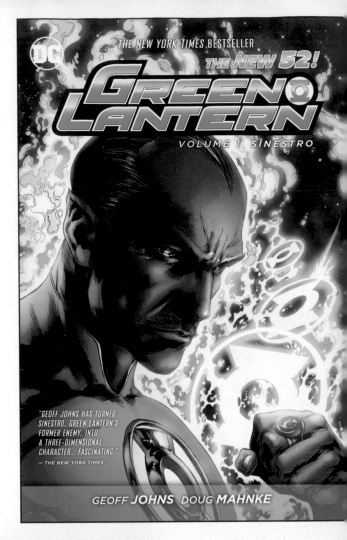
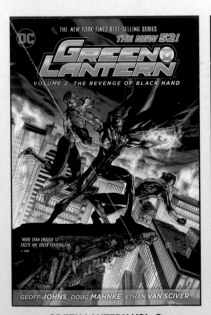